Religions of India

India is a highly diverse country, home to a wide array of languages, religions, and cultural traditions. Analyzing the dynamic religious traditions of the largest democratic nation sheds light on the complex evolution from India's past to today's modern culture. Written by leading experts in the field, *Religions of India* provides students with an introduction to India's vibrant religious faiths. To understand its heritage and core values, the early chapters introduce the indigenous Dhārmic traditions of Hinduism, Jainism, Buddhism, and Sikhism, while the later chapters examine the outside influences of Zoroastrianism, Judaism, Christianity, and Islam. These chapters are designed for cross-religious comparison, with the history, practices, values, and worldviews of each belief system explained. The final chapter helps students relate what they have learned to current scholarly discussions about significant unresolved issues in the study of religion, preparing the way for future study.

This thoroughly revised second edition combines solid scholarship with clear and lively writing to provide students with an accessible and comprehensive introduction to religion in India. This is the ideal textbook for students approaching religion in Asia, South Asia, or India for the first time. Features to aid study include discussion questions at the end of each chapter, images, a glossary, suggestions for further reading, and a companion website with additional links for students to further their study.

Gene Thursby is Emeritus Associate Professor of Religion at the University of Florida in Gainesville, USA.

Sushil Mittal is Professor of Hindu Studies and Gandhi Studies at James Madison University in Harrisonburg, Virginia, USA, and Honorary Professor of Gandhian Studies at GITAM University in Visakhapatnam, Andhra Pradesh, India.

Together the *guru-śiṣya* team has also edited *The Hindu World* and *Studying Hinduism*, both published by Routledge.

Religions of India Companion Website

The companion website for this text can be found at www.routledge.com/cw/Mittal

On the companion website, students and instructors can find additional materials and resources including:

- Coverage on another religion of India, the Bahā'ī faith. A bonus chapter covering this religion from the previous edition is included in full on the website and can be downloaded for free by students and instructors.
- A downloadable PDF of the glossary to help students study new terms.
- Additional discussion questions, suggestions for further reading, and lists of links to helpful external resources to further reinforce the content are available for each chapter in the book.

EDITED BY SUSHIL MITTAL AND GENE THURSBY

Religions of India

An Introduction

SECOND EDITION

Routledge
Taylor & Francis Group
NEW YORK AND LONDON

First published 2018
by Routledge
711 Third Avenue, New York, NY 10017

and by Routledge
2 Park Square, Milton Park, Abingdon, Oxon, OX14 4RN

Routledge is an imprint of the Taylor & Francis Group, an informa business

Library of Congress Cataloging-in-Publication Data
Names: Mittal, Sushil, editor. | Thursby, Gene R., editor.
Title: Religions of India : an introduction / edited by Sushil Mittal and Gene Thursby.
Other titles: Religions of South Asia
Description: Second edition. | New York : Routledge, 2018. | Includes bibliographical references and index.
Identifiers: LCCN 2017028224 (print) | LCCN 2017030528 (ebook) | ISBN 9781315545967 | ISBN 9781134791934 | ISBN 9781134791866 | ISBN 9781134792009 | ISBN 9781138681255 (hardback : alk. paper) | ISBN 9781138681262 (pbk. : alk. paper)
Subjects: LCSH: South Asia—Religion—Textbooks.
Classification: LCC BL1055 (ebook) | LCC BL1055 .R473 2018 (print) | DDC 200.98—dc23
LC record available at https://lccn.loc.gov/2017028224

ISBN: 978-1-138-68125-5 (hbk)
ISBN: 978-1-138-68126-2 (pbk)
ISBN: 978-1-315-54596-7 (ebk)

Typeset in SouthAsia
by Apex CoVantage, LLC

Visit the companion website: www.routledge.com/cw/Mittal

The cover image reproduces a painting titled "Lifegiving" by the Mumbai artist Lalita Davjekar who became inspired by Warli folk art in mid-life. A tree of life motif is central to her painting. It shelters and energizes the living beings around it.

To Our Parents:

Maya Devi and Khyali Ram Mittal
and
Mariella Icenhower and Gene F. Thursby

"This revised and updated edition is one of the best introductory sources on Indian religions being both accessible and authoritative. An excellent feature is the final chapter which raises critical questions about 'religion' as a concept and demonstrating the permeability and interconnections between the traditions discussed in the South Asia context."

Paul Hedges, S. Rajaratnam School of International Studies, Singapore

"This book is a thorough and accessible introduction to the various religious communities of India. It should be the starting point for non-specialists and a point for deeper entry for intermediate students of the region. This book is the answer to teaching the religions of India through multiple perspectives in one semester."

Yogendra Trivedi, Columbia University, USA

CONTENTS

NOTE ON TRANSLITERATION

We have, in general, adhered to the standard transliteration system for each of the Indic languages. Although Indic languages make no distinction between uppercase and lowercase letters, we use capitals to indicate proper names and titles; all other Indic terms, with the exception of those used as adjectives, are italicized and not capitalized. Terms that have been anglicized in form or have come into English usage are nevertheless given in their standard transliterated forms, with diacritics. Modern place-names are given in their current transliterated forms, but without diacritics. If references to such places are made in a literary or historical context, however, they are given in their standard transliterated forms, with diacritics. Modern proper names are given in their current transliterated forms, but without diacritics. All premodern proper names, however, are in their standard transliterated forms, with diacritics.

ACKNOWLEDGMENTS

It is important to acknowledge that any work of cooperative scholarship, at whatever level of specialization, depends on the goodwill, assistance, and advice of a large team of people who are crucial to the outcome but are unlikely to see in print an adequate statement of appreciation for their valuable contributions. We are indebted to Irene Bunnell (Development Editor at Routledge), Adam Guppy (Books Production Editor at Taylor & Francis), and Kerry Boettcher (Project Manager at Apex CoVantage), and their respective staff at Routledge for production management throughout the preparation of this book. We thank our colleagues at James Madison University and the University of Florida who have offered encouragement at times when we most needed it. In addition to our parents, to whom the book is dedicated and who are a continuing inspiration to us, our extended families and close friends inside and outside the academic community have enabled us to appreciate this project as "deep fun"—which is the way that one of them refers to transformative learning experiences.

CONTRIBUTOR BIOGRAPHIES

Peter Gottschalk is Professor of Religion and Director of the Office for Faculty Career Development at Wesleyan University.

John Grimes, retired Professor of Hinduism and Indian Philosophy, now resides in Chennai.

Christina A. Kilby is Assistant Professor of Religion at James Madison University.

T. M. Luhrmann is the Watkins University Professor in the Department of Anthropology at Stanford University.

Sushil Mittal is Professor of Hindu Studies and Gandhi Studies at James Madison University in Harrisonburg, Virginia, and Honorary Professor of Gandhian Studies at GITAM University in Visakhapatnam, Andhra Pradesh, India.

Rakesh Peter Dass is Assistant Professor of Religion at Hope College.

Pashaura Singh is Professor and Jasbir Singh Saini Endowed Chair of Sikh and Punjabi Studies at the University of California, Riverside.

M. Thomas Thangaraj is D.W. and Ruth Brooks Professor Emeritus of World Christianity at Candler School of Theology at Emory University.

Gene Thursby is Emeritus Associate Professor of Religion at the University of Florida in Gainesville.

Anne Vallely is Associate Professor in the Department of Classics and Religious Studies at the University of Ottawa.

Shalva Weil is Senior Researcher at RIFIE (Research Institute for Innovation in Education) at the Hebrew University of Jerusalem, and Research Fellow in the Department of Biblical and Ancient Studies at the University of South Africa.

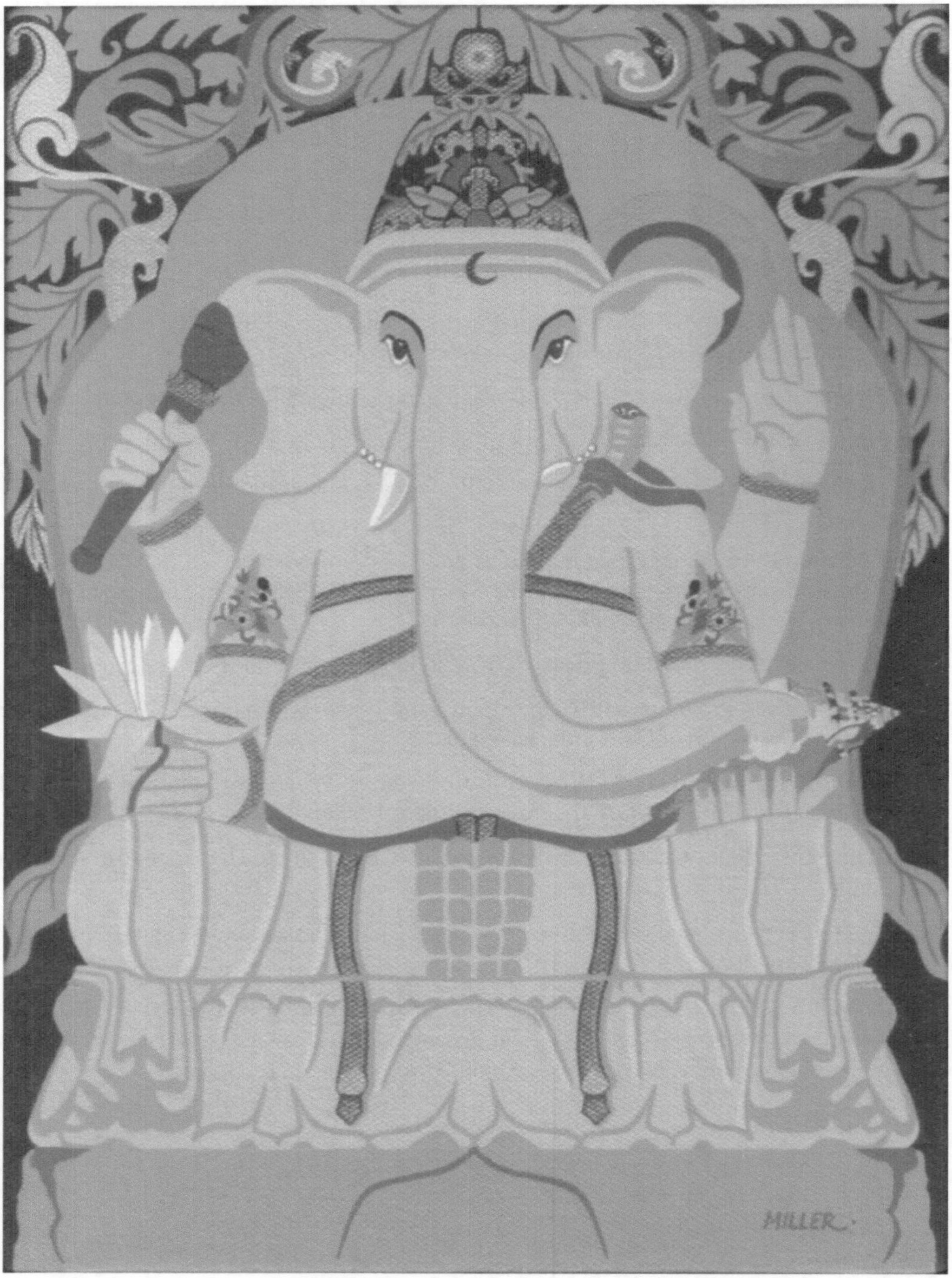

FIGURE 1 Gaṇeśa, divine remover of obstacles.

Courtesy of the artist P. R. VanderMeer (née Miller)

Introduction

SUSHIL MITTAL AND GENE THURSBY

> Our attempts to understand the simplest aspects of the world involve making generalizations that, by simplifying, both make the world intelligible and falsify it to some extent by editing out some of its complexity. How much more difficult it is, then, to describe something as multifaceted as Indian civilization, involving as it does millions of people living in a large portion of the earth's surface over several thousand years, without severely distorting and misrepresenting it. This problem is general and inescapable, and we must always keep in mind the simplifying nature of all our generalizations—that is to say, of everything we say or write. It is equally important to remember that what we are trying to describe is real, even though we can never capture it fully in words because of its intricacy.
>
> (Trautmann 2016: 1–2)

Today's India is an independent nation, a dynamic democracy with a large population of young, active, and highly educated citizens. About one out of five people now alive is either a citizen of India or a person of Indian descent who lives elsewhere. More than twenty different languages are recognized officially, and there are far more Indian languages than those officially designated. Although many languages are spoken throughout Africa or across the European Union, in India the multiple languages contribute to the life and cultural expressions of a single nation. The value of this "composite culture" is explicitly affirmed in Article 51A of the nation's constitution.

Not only does the future of this highly diverse nation look bright, but when we look to the past we see that extraordinary achievements have been part of the story of people on the Indian subcontinent from earliest times. The very name India (and its variant forms in languages other than English) has had a remarkable elasticity through the centuries due to the influence and importance of the subcontinent's people and what they have produced. The so-called "new world," with its West Indies and natives called Indians, was discovered as a fortuitous part of a seafaring search for India and the East Indies, which were widely recognized as sources of wealth and rare spices. The expansion of sea trade from the subcontinent outward in earlier centuries explains the older name Indochina for a large mainland Southeast Asian area and the still current name Indonesia for the world's largest island country. On the subcontinent itself, in classical times all the landmass south of the world's highest mountains was India. In short, what the word India means will depend on when and where

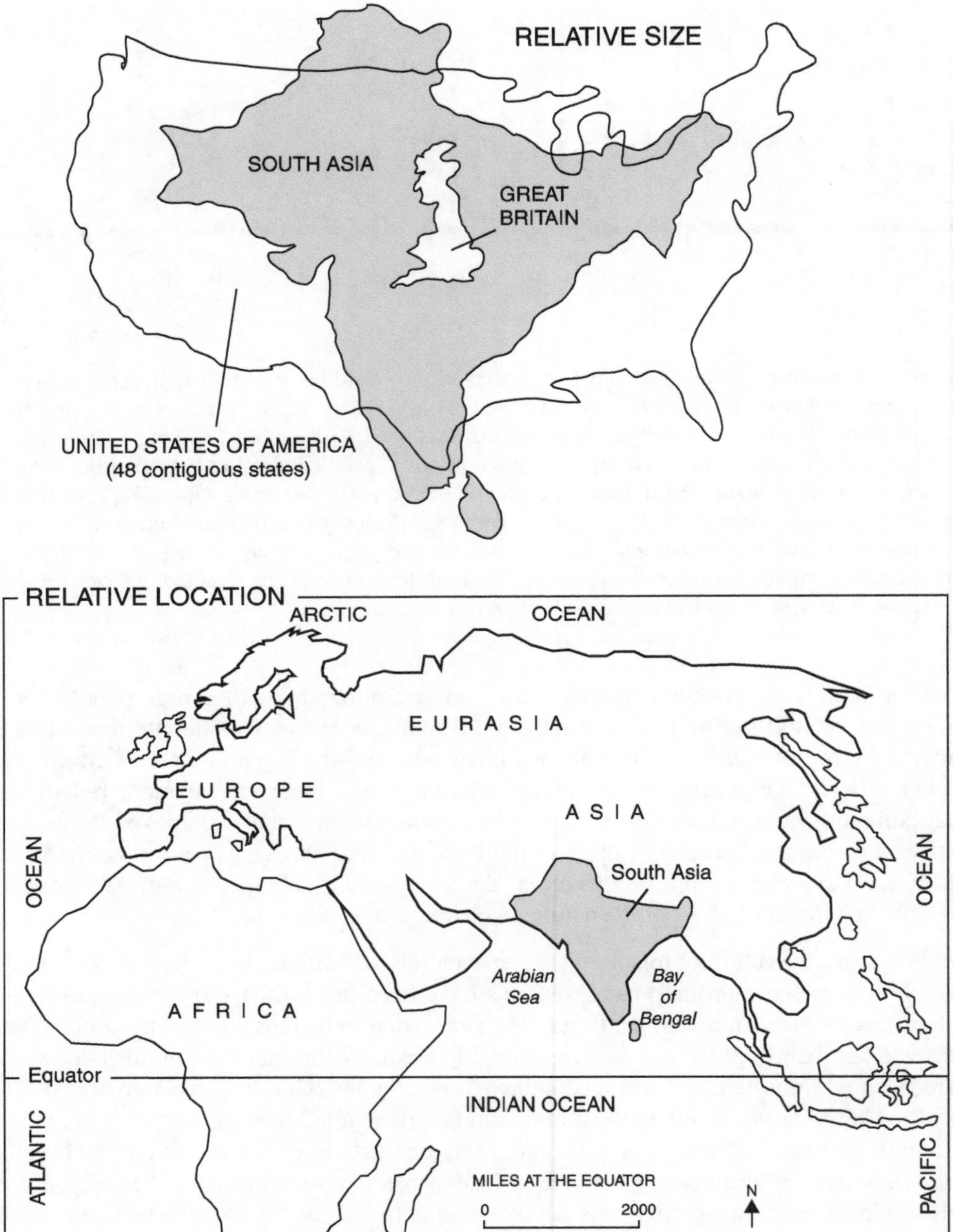

MAP 1 Relative size and location of the Indian subcontinent.

you seek it. In this book on the religions of India, it extends beyond current national boundaries to cover the vital influence of ideas and practices that had their origin, or their formative home, on the subcontinent and from there have spread throughout the world.

• TRADITIONS OF INDIA: FROM INSIDE AND OUTSIDE

To understand the heritage and aspirations of people of the Indian subcontinent, it is necessary to have a basic knowledge of Hindu, Jaina, Buddhist, and Sikh categories of thought and practice. These four traditions originated in India and have deeply informed its core values and the ways in which its people interact with one another. Among present-day Indians, by far the greatest number identify with Hindu ways of living and modes of religious practice. When and where Hindu religion first was practiced is unknown, and many contemporary Hindus prefer to say that it is a timeless wisdom that proceeds from a higher source and becomes evident to human beings again and again through diverse sages and saints, as well as by direct intervention of divine beings who return things to their proper course from time to time and renew the power of the human spirit. The influential minority traditions of the Jainas and Buddhists are at least twenty-five hundred years old, perhaps more, and the practices of the Sikhs have their source in revelations received by Gurū Nānak about five hundred years ago. In this book, these distinctively Indic traditions are referred to, as they refer to themselves, with the term "*dharma*" or its near-equivalents *dharam* or *dhamma*. The meanings of these key terms will become clearer to you while you continue reading this book. For now, let us simply say that *dharma* refers to the deep nature of reality and the kind of action (ranging from a single act right up to a general pattern of behavior and a way of life) that is in accord with it and is appropriate to the circumstances in which a person is involved at a particular time in their life.

During the many centuries that it has taken for the *dharma*-based traditions from India to spread throughout the world, the subcontinent has been receptive to outside influences, too. Zoroastrian religion was brought to India by Parsi or Persian people who were seeking religious freedom. Other religions from West Asia arrived in India in the company of adventure travelers, explorers, traders, missionaries, and invading armies. These have included all three main versions of Abrahamic or Semitic religious traditions—Jewish, Christian, and Muslim or Islamic—and their several subgroups, sects, or denominations. Over the centuries, most Christians and Muslims in India have been local converts, and inevitably their adopted traditions "indigenized" or took on local features and practices to a sufficient extent so that it would make sense to speak and write about them and other religions of foreign origin as hyphenated traditions, whether Indo-Zoroastrian, Indo-Judaic, Indo-Christian, or Indo-Muslim.

• DHARMA IN INDIC RELIGIONS

Dharma, as mentioned above, is a key term in religious traditions from the Indian subcontinent. The word's root in Sanskrit, the language of the Vedic scriptures and of classical

Hindu tradition, has the sense of "that which supports or holds together," while in Pali, the language of early monastic Buddhists, the variant form *dhamma* refers to one of the smallest and most temporary of the many constituent units that together make up the world as it appears to our senses. In Jaina teachings, the term *dharma* refers technically to the noncreated medium within which all movement takes place but generally is used much as it is in Hindu tradition. As Buddhist tradition developed, two meanings of the term *dharma* or *dhamma* coexisted and complemented one another. The first refers to the changing world of appearances that may beguile and mislead us so that we suppose that suffering (*duhkha*) is our life's deepest potential. The second refers to the body of teaching or doctrine of the Buddha that offers an understanding of things that can make it possible to pass beyond suffering and the world of temporary, fluctuating appearances. The teaching (*dhamma*), the teacher (Buddha), and the community of monks (*saṅgha*) are considered the three gems or jewels of the religion. When contemporary Buddhists speak of "the Dhamma," typically they mean the truth as transmitted through the teachings of the Buddha. Similarly, contemporary Sikhs would think of the teachings of Gurū Nānak as the core of the Sikh Dharam that is developed in the *Ādi Granth* and through the continuing tradition. For Hindus, reference to *dharma* typically has the underlying meaning of the structural power that holds things together and arranges them into a meaningful cosmos. *Dharma* in this sense is manifested in the order of nature, in the lawful patterns of traditional society, and in the integrity of a person embodying and enacting their traditionally prescribed roles and responsibilities. As a principle of order, *dharma* is complemented by the dynamic principle of *karma* (from the root *karman*). *Karma* refers to the acts and their consequences that generate discernable patterns in the lives of individuals, families, and societies and in the world at large over time.

In Hindu thinking, *dharma* organizes by differentiating. The *dharma* of various people will differ in correlation with their birth into a specific genetic endowment (gender, family, extended kin group, and caste), their current age, and their marital status. The *Bhagavad Gītā*, a popularly respected Hindu text, repeatedly advises that it is better to live in accordance with your own *dharma*, even if you do that poorly, than to live according to another's *dharma*, even if you could do it well. Any Hindu who speaks to you seriously about their duty is likely to be speaking about *dharma* and about deep promptings of their conscience or inner nature—and perhaps about the pressures they feel from family and society to face up to their solemn responsibilities, too. *Dharma* is so important that a widely held conviction in India has been that a person should not rely upon their own unexamined tendencies and preferences alone, but should instead look to the guidance offered by traditional sources of authority that are transmitted in both oral and written form. In the twentieth century, Mohandas K. Gandhi renewed the power of this idea by bringing out its inherently social and ethical components as resources for nonviolent resolution of conflicts. Running all through the great traditions from India, in significantly varying ways that will be made clear in the chapters to follow, is the theme of *dharma* or deep patterns in the nature of things and inner promptings toward the highest possibilities available to human beings.

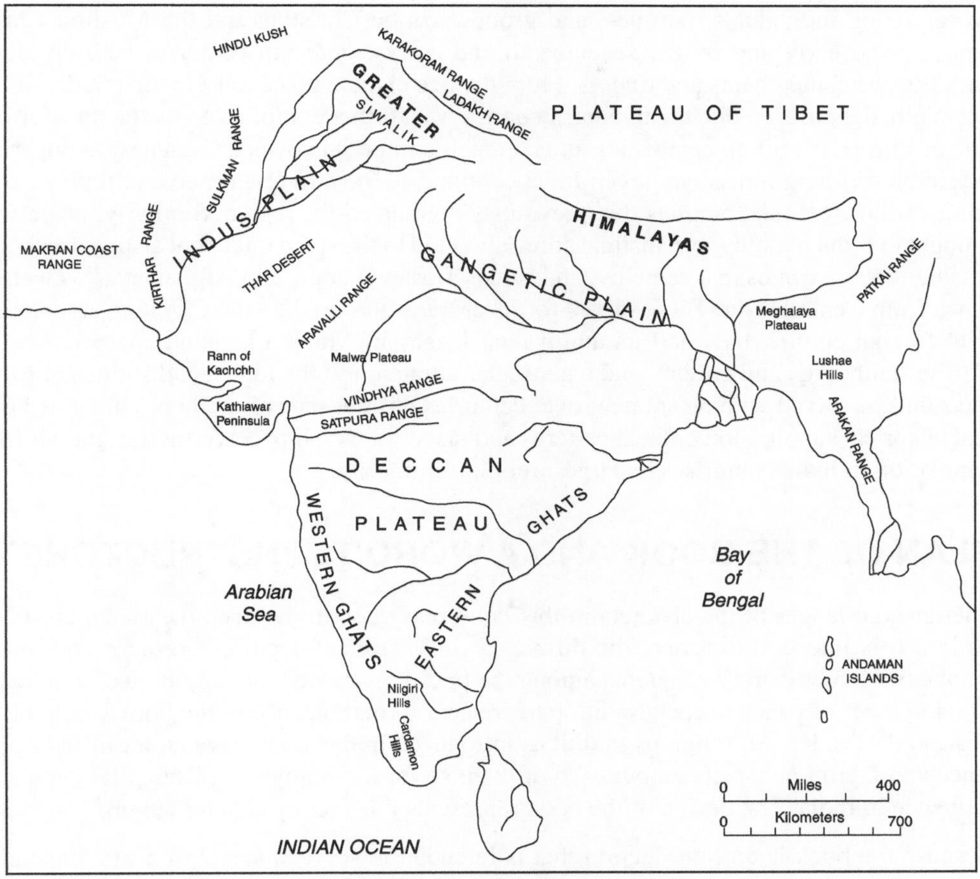

MAP 2 Physical features of the Indian subcontinent.

• TRADITIONS OF OUTSIDERS: THE WORLD'S GIFTS TO INDIA

Among the great traditions that came to India and then developed a lasting presence on the subcontinent, two that are generally nonproselytizing and nonconverting religions are Zoroastrianism and Judaism. By and large, the Parsi people who follow the practices of Zoroastrianism and the Jews who follow the way of Torah each recruit new participants into their faith by means of the birth of a child to a mother and into a family already identified with that genetic inheritance and religious tradition. Converts who are assimilated by means of marriage or who are individually instructed, tested, and initiated into membership are relatively few in number.

Two great traditions from outside the subcontinent that actively recruit by converting or proselytizing individuals, families, and groups are the Christian and the Muslim. Christians arrived early and by the seventeenth and early eighteenth centuries became allied with European merchants and traders. From the late eighteenth century to the middle of the twentieth, the position of Christian missionaries was further complicated by the transformation of European trading companies into colonizing imperial powers. Even now, a lingering suspicion of foreign missionaries in India continues to be a long-term cost of their association with the colonial empires that previously dominated the region. Similarly, Islam was brought to India not only by Muslim sailors attracted to the spice trade, but also by freebooters and foreign armies that came by land across Turkey, Persia, and Afghanistan, as well as down from Central Asia. These mixed forms of transmission, like the Christian association with foreign empire, have left an ambivalent legacy in which a genuine appreciation for Muslim faith, arts, and culture, and a particular attraction to the tombs and shrines of Muslim saints, is mixed with resentment over centuries of imposed rule and both imagined and real historical suppression of local patterns and places of worship. Nevertheless, the Muslim population in India comprises its largest religious minority.

• PLAN OF THE BOOK AND A WORD TO INSTRUCTORS

The unequal length of the chapters in this book may seem to be unconventional but is by design. It is intended to reflect the differences in historical depth of presence and in the number of contemporary adherents among the traditions treated by our authors. To allot an equal number of pages to each tradition to create a formal balance in the book would be to mislead the reader. All religious traditions introduced in this book have an intrinsic importance and merit one's respect, but each of them so far has enjoyed a differential degree of influence in India. The design of the book represents this fact by chapter length.

Because the book is an introduction that is intended to serve students in a first course of study of the religions of India and to be understandable to intelligent general readers, the chapters in Part I and II are free from detailed accounts of currently unresolved arguments among scholar-specialists concerning category formation, prehistory, alternative chronologies of events and epochs, and other heavily theoretical or metatheoretical issues. Those are endemic to academic life and of utmost importance, but we believe that they are best appreciated after students have an opportunity to master the new vocabulary required for meaningful study of religions of India. Each instructor will have his or her own preferences about how and when to share with students a selection of ongoing problems and alternative perspectives that are debated at scholarly conferences and in academic journals. Authors of the chapters in Part I and II each present a "good to think with" prototype or first model of a tradition, which is suitable for an introductory or survey course, although the book may have a place in intermediate and advanced courses, too. The model versions of the traditions that are introduced in this book are not quite Max Weber's heuristic device of the "ideal type" but have a similar purpose. They offer a place to begin one's study and a reasonably clear image of what one is studying.

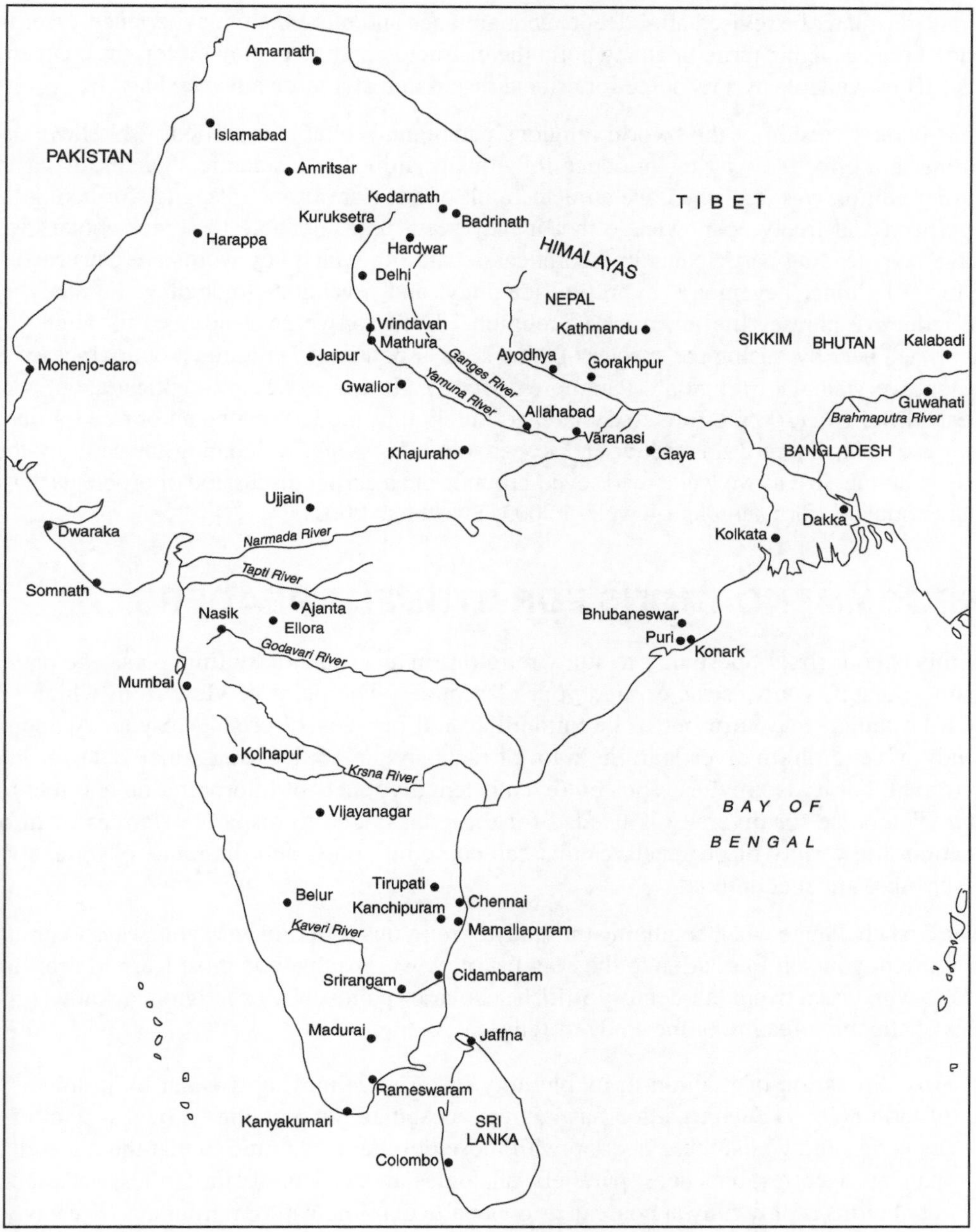

MAP 3 Historical and holy sites in the Indian subcontinent.

Every beginning student and advanced scholar knows, without being told, that first impressions must later be revised after deeper acquaintance and more mature experience. Near the end of the academic term, or at any point the instructor or student may prefer, the chapter in Part III is available as a resource for critical discussion at a more advanced level.

This book's version of the "world religions paradigm," suitably modified, we believe, is a fitting and effective way to introduce religious traditions to academic students. After the earlier edition was published, we attracted a bit of criticism from colleagues for taking this approach and freely acknowledge that it may seem unfashionable to some scholars who have been leading participants in theoretical debates, in which key words are construction, critics, defining, hegemony, hybridity, ideology, and invention—including the analytical or reductive phrase "the invention of religion." Even so, we have no need to defend our approach here by raising the specter of "this kind of politicized culturalist outlook based on pejorative visions of religion" (Paramore 2016: 5). However, we are skeptical about some post-Masuzawa (2005) efforts to declare world religions models redundant or ripe for burial (for example, Owen 2011; Cotter and Robertson 2016) while welcoming the scrutiny they are receiving, just as we welcomed several rounds of an earlier discussion of problems defining Hinduism (for example, Llewellyn 2005; Sweetman 2003).

• RECOMMENDATIONS FOR STUDENT READERS

If this is your first opportunity to study religions in an academic setting, please be patient with yourself, your instructor, and your classmates. The point of view from which you will be taught may turn out to be unfamiliar and perhaps surprising to you. Academic study of religion involves learning a lot of facts and an ability to organize data for later retrieval, but it also invites repeated (even if tentative) acts of interpretation and theorizing. Tolerance for diversity is needed for these tasks due to disparate sources of information, the variety of perspectives that can come into play, and the range of unresolved issues that are encountered.

The first challenge when beginning the study of religions is to find workable ways to ground and orient yourself in relation to the long list of new terms that you must learn to use. John Hick, who was a twentieth-century British scholar of philosophy of religion, acknowledges this challenging feature of the study of religions:

> Any discussion of religion in its plurality of forms is inevitably beset by problems of terminology. Each tradition has its own vocabulary, expressing its own system of concepts; and whilst these overlap with those of other traditions, so that there are all manner of correspondences, parallels, analogies and structural similarities, yet each set of terms is only fully at home in its own particular linguistic environment. We have very little in the way of a tradition-neutral religious vocabulary.
>
> (2004: 9)

A closely related reason for the need to get grounded and stay oriented while you study is that when religious worlds that are new to you begin to come into clear focus, some features of them are likely to seem intriguing and desirable and others disgusting and repulsive. You may begin to see previously unknown ways to understand and inhabit the world that could seem to you amazingly plausible or absurdly impossible. Either could be upsetting. Hick notes: "New knowledge and new ideas do, unfortunately, often cause real mental and emotional distress; but this is not a valid reason for rejecting them" (2004: xl). Nor, we might add, is it a valid reason for accepting them.

Finally, there is another level of challenge when engaging in the academic study of religion. It can be summed up in the question of what to do with one's own faith-based positions and personal ethical commitments. Hick addresses that level of challenge when he writes: "There is no one religion whose adherents stand out as morally and spiritually superior to the rest of the human race. (If anyone claims such a superiority for their own religious community, the onus of proof, or of argument, is clearly upon them)" (2004: xxvi). Whether you can or should "put your own preferences in a box" to be opened only after some time, perhaps near the end of the academic term, is a question you might ask yourself.

One respected approach to the study of religion does ask its practitioners to become neutral about what they study. Sometimes called the phenomenology of religion, it requires the student and scholar to suspend judgment, to put their own commitments in brackets (called, technically, the phenomenological epoché), to be able to engage in unprejudiced study of what may be radically different from their local, familiar, and personally held values. An earlier version of this kind of attitude of respect and acceptance is found, surprisingly, in the work of the nineteenth-century philologist and Christian-influenced scholar of comparative religion Friedrich Max Müller, who wrote: "If people regard their religion as revealed, it is to them a revealed religion, and has to be treated as such by every impartial historian" (1882: 74).

A more recent approach to academic study of religion, and one that proceeds from an assumption that the requirements of the phenomenology of religion are unsuitable and perhaps are unattainable, can be labeled for convenience the critical theory or the postmodernist study of religion. A root assumption of this kind of approach is that each point of view, preference, and practice inevitably carries with it political assumptions and implications. Critical theorists and postmodernists typically express doubt that empathy with the subject under study, which is a second aim of the phenomenology of religion and invited by Max Müller above, is any more attainable than phenomenology's ideal of pure neutrality. Critical theorists claim that every position either openly displays an evident agenda or masks a hidden agenda, and they expect us to ask of ourselves: What is my agenda as I participate in this study? Equally they want us to ask of whatever idea or subject matter is under study: What agenda is at work there? What does it privilege, what does it problematize, and who or what is likely to benefit most from it?

• BIBLIOGRAPHY

Clothey, Fred W. 2006. *Religion in India: A Historical Introduction*. New York: Routledge.

Cotter, Christopher R. and David G. Robertson, eds. 2016. *After World Religions: Reconstructing Religious Studies*. London: Routledge.

Das, Gurcharan. 2009. *The Difficulty of Being Good: On the Subtle Art of Dharma*. New York: Oxford University Press.

Heehs, Peter, ed. 2002. *Indian Religions: A Historical Reader of Spiritual Expression and Experience*. New York: New York University Press.

Hick, John. 2004 [1989]. *An Interpretation of Religion: Human Responses to the Transcendent*. New Haven: Yale University Press.

Hirst, Jacqueline Suthren and John Zavos. 2011. *Religious Traditions in Modern South Asia*. London: Routledge.

Llewellyn, J. E., ed. 2005. *Defining Hinduism: A Reader*. New York: Routledge.

Masuzawa, Tomoko. 2005. *The Invention of World Religions: Or, How European Universalism Was Preserved in the Language of Pluralism*. Chicago: University of Chicago Press.

Max Müller, F. 1882 [1873]. *Introduction to the Science of Religion: Four Lectures Delivered at the Royal Institution, in February and May, 1870*. New Edition. London: Longmans, Green, and Co.

Obeyesekere, Gananath. 2002. *Imagining Karma: Ethical Transformation in Amerindian, Buddhist, and Greek Rebirth*. Berkeley: University of California Press.

Owen, Suzanne. 2011. "The World Religions Paradigm: Time for a Change." *Arts and Humanities in Higher Education* 10, 3: 253–68.

Paramore, Kiri. 2016. "Introduction." *In* Kiri Paramore, ed., *Religion and Orientalism in Asian Studies*, 1–12. London: Bloomsbury Academic.

Schelling, Andrew, ed. 2014. *Love and the Turning Seasons: India's Poetry of Spiritual & Erotic Longing*. Berkeley: Counterpoint.

Sun, Anna. 2013. *Confucianism as a World Religion: Contested Histories and Contemporary Realities*. Princeton: Princeton University Press.

Sweetman, Will. 2003. "'Hinduism' and the History of 'Religion': Protestant Presuppositions in the Critique of the Concept of Hinduism." *Method & Theory in the Study of Religion* 15, 4: 329–53.

Trautmann, Thomas R. 2016 [2011]. *India: Brief History of a Civilization*. New York: Oxford University Press.

Part I

What India Has Given to the World

FIGURE 1.1 Kṛṣṇa and the ten *avatāra*s of Viṣṇu.

Courtesy of the artist Nicola Barsaleau.

1

Hindu Dharma

JOHN GRIMES, SUSHIL MITTAL,
AND GENE THURSBY

THE TRADITIONS DEFINED

To survive and succeed in life, we have to find our way through a world that is made up of diverse authorities, interests, energies, and powers. Many of them, whether they appear to be attractive or repulsive to us or somehow manage to elude our awareness, will influence us and shape the available choices and the eventual outcomes of our lives. How they are named and the extent of their influence is different from one place on this planet to another place—and within the same place over time. The goal of this chapter is to introduce some of the most influential authorities, interests, energies, and powers that have been acknowledged and named in traditional Hindu ways of interpreting, understanding, and living in the world.

Hindus are people who share many assumptions about the nature of the world and acknowledge a wide range of practices that are appropriate responses to living as a human being (whether or not every one of them seems to suit their own specific nature and situation). In this chapter, the term for those generally available assumptions and practices is "Hindu Dharma," although the less well-fitting but more widely adopted label "Hinduism" will be used, too. We begin with a few key categories that have considerable importance in Hindu tradition and perhaps will connect with your own experience.

Kāla (Time)

In every human society, part of becoming an effective adult is learning how to put into practice a maxim that advises that while there may be a time and place for everything, each activity should be done at an appropriate time and in a suitable place. Most of us have learned by now (perhaps in response to pain or embarrassment) that what seems fine at one time and place can cause real problems for oneself and others at another time or in a different place. Hindus have explored this truth for thousands of years and have developed detailed ways to identify auspicious and inauspicious (seemly and unseemly, or helpful and harmful, or supportive and resistant) times and places correlated with various kinds of behavior and activities. Many centuries of astronomical and astrological study, as well as daily observation and deep contemplation, have enabled Hindus to develop sophisticated calendar systems and closely related ideas about types of character and modes of action. Those resources are used by traditional experts to guide people through a lifetime and beyond. Because traditional ideas are their basis, some resources may seem outdated to contemporary academic students (and to some modern Hindus) who have grown up with other notions about how to find their way to a successful or a good life. But because traditional Hindu teachings have directed the aspirations of millions of human beings over countless generations, they merit our consideration. Everyone, after all, can appreciate the value of having methods for time management and character development.

Here is an example of one Hindu traditional idea about time. If you were to go shopping in India on a Saturday morning, whether in a regional town or a large cosmopolitan city, you would be likely to see some small dark iron images in front of a few stores. Probably there would be a bit of incense lit near them and money that had been placed in front of them. If you were to pause near one of the images to observe, it is likely that you would see a few people who join their hands together and bow briefly to acknowledge the image respectfully and perhaps leave a few coins before continuing along their way. What is the significance of this? In India, Śanivāra is a traditional name for the day that we call Saturday, and the iron images are a reminder of the influence of Śani—the distinctive energies, opportunities, and challenges closely associated with this day and different from those of other days of the week. Although this may be your first acquaintance with Śani, perhaps you will agree that not every day is simply the same as the one before. Different days and times have different qualities. For Hindus, then, time has qualitative as well as quantitative dimensions.

Hindus assume and observe that time goes through cycles, and so do people and places. Śanivāra may be distinctive, but it comes around again and again. The characteristics that make days different from one another are embedded in a sequence that is regular and repeated. The moon has its repeating phases, the cycles in which it can be seen to wax, then become "full," and wane until it becomes "new" again. Seasons arrive and depart in a seemingly endless series. These recurring patterns of difference-within-repetition generate a large but limited set of possibilities—unless or until something is able to break through and escape time's ever-repeating cycles.

Veda (Knowledge)

One major breakthrough continues to be highly authoritative today in Hindu tradition. It is associated with extraordinary ancient visionary poets known as *ṛṣis*. Somehow they were able to tune into higher levels of awareness that allowed them to perceive subtle currents of sound that had eluded ordinary human beings. Those sounds, after entering the consciousness of the *ṛṣis* and being recited, became known as Veda and the language Vedic Sanskrit. We still know about Veda now because recitations of the *ṛṣis* were collected together, arranged, and passed down to and through generation after generation of carefully screened and specially prepared pupils. Transmission was directly from mouth to ear—orally rather than in written form—because the chanted Vedic sound was believed to have a power and importance too great to allow it to fall into the possession of just anyone. Collections (*saṃhitā*) of Vedas are known as Śruti because they were first preserved and transmitted orally. That remarkable feat was accomplished with teaching methods similar to ones that would be required to learn how to accurately and reliably perform the metrical patterns and lyrics of a song catalogue at least as complex and extensive as the one by Nobel laureate Bob Dylan. An early part of the *saṃhitā*, for instance, the *Ṛg Veda* has ten major sections with over a thousand hymns in more than ten thousand verses.

This capsule introduction to Veda calls attention to the central place of lineage in Hindu tradition. One form of it comes to be called *guru-śiṣya* lineage, the transmission of knowledge from master to apprentice or from teacher to student. A second form is genetically determined lineage, most typically patriarchal, a line of descent from father to son and more widely through extended kinship groups. When you started reading this chapter, you may have assumed that it is obvious that separate and unique individuals should be central to the study of any religious tradition. An individual within Hindu tradition, even if the chapter may refer here or there to "the individual Hindu," is typically understood to be just a small component part or a link in a more inclusive and more basic genetic and social identity. In Hindu contexts, it is the families, kin groups, and extended lineages—whether created by initiation and training or sustained by genetic connection—that are assumed to be the more basic and fundamental realities.

Veda, in any case, is respected as the key criterion for what is and is not Hindu. Those who reject Vedic authority are called *nāstika* (Cārvākas, Buddhists, and Jainas, for example) and are considered non-Hindu. And yet the notion of what truly is Vedic has been interpreted in Hindu tradition in multiple ways—and not as if the question of what merits the honor of being considered Vedic were merely simple or obvious. Two contrasting ways of thinking about what is Vedic have some similarities with two ways that Americans have viewed their Constitution. The first is strict construction or the Founders' meaning. The second is loose construction or the living document approach. Similar to the first, Veda is understood to refer to the content of the *saṃhitā*s (whether oral or later written). These remain primarily the domain of hereditary lineages of Vedic Brāhmaṇas. Selections from them are chanted in various ritual settings by men who have a hereditary responsibility to act as priests. Similar to the second viewpoint, any teaching or practice that is regarded as derived from or generally consistent with Veda is honored by the adjective Vedic or even the noun "a(nother) Veda." Hindus from across all social classes and hereditary groups have used the second kind of approach to affirm the Vedic status of their texts, teachers, and practices.

Dharma (Order)

Dharma (which can be loosely glossed as "religion") is what the Veda reveals. Literally, *dharma* is "what holds together," and thus it is the basis of all order, whether natural, cosmic, social, or moral. It is the power that makes things what they are. This idea contains the implication that what Hindus do is more important than what they believe. It was by means of ritual (dhārmic) actions that Vedic culture sought to create, reinvigorate, nourish, and maintain cosmic order. Eventually, as classical Hinduism developed from Vedic roots, not just specific rituals but every human action was said to affect the maintenance of social and cosmic order. *Dharma*, when adhered to, was expected to yield a long, robust life full of happiness and blessings.

Although *dharma* is a pivotal concept around which Hindu self-understanding revolves, its range of meanings accounts for much of the tradition's internal diversity, ongoing tensions, and reinterpretations. There is not a single privileged understanding of *dharma*, but a network of interactions between different usages. Each use of the term is indebted to, oriented around, and to some extent reflects traditional Brāhmaṇical usage. This brings us back to the authority of Veda, for Veda ultimately reveals *dharma*.

A major implication of *dharma* is that the ideal human society is composed of separate status groups arranged in a hierarchy from bottom to top, and each group has inherited or inherent functions that complement those of other groups. There are different types of people with distinctive aptitudes, predilections, and abilities. Hereditary classes or castes (*varṇa-dharma*) are responsible for social functions that maintain the vertical and horizontal organization of society. In addition, there are stages of life (*āśrama-dharma*) that support human development toward eventual liberation from *saṃsāra*—the repetitive cycle of births, deaths, and rebirths. This is *varṇāśrama-dharma*. There is also *sanātana-dharma* ("eternal religion"), *sva-dharma* ("one's own duty"), *āpad-dharma* ("law in circumstances of calamity"), *yuga-dharma* ("law in the context of a particular epoch or time-period"), and *sādhāraṇa-dharma* ("general obligations"). These areas of application of *dharma* not only address the fact that humans have different aptitudes, but also acknowledge multiple ways of being and several kinds of spiritual paths, each of which can be a valid way to foster the eventual fulfillment of a particular destiny.

The requirements of responsible worldly life for Hindus involve conforming to social and ritual duties and other rules of conduct for the caste into which one was born, as well as one's kin group and form of labor. Together these constitute one's *dharma*, one's part in ongoing maintenance of the traditional social and cosmic order. Until recently, it was without question that *dharma* could be protected or violated only by Hindus because they are subject to its provisions from birth. Outsiders to the *varṇāśrama-dharma* system, as non-Hindus, had no obligation or any right to uphold it.

Mokṣa (Release)

The requirements of *dharma* to maintain the traditional social and cosmic order are complemented and completed by the ideal of attaining *mokṣa*, liberation from the limitations of temporal existence. They are twin values in the tradition, and many teachings seek to harmonize the two sets of values. Although human beings are physical animals governed by social needs who seek to live in harmony with other beings so far as possible, they are also spiritual souls who are destined at some point to transcend human physical and social limitations. A spiritual orientation is a natural consequence of Hindu worldviews that affirm that life always depends on higher, more powerful, more worthy beings and processes. Because of this, every action, person, place, or thing potentially has religious implications. *Dharma* orders life within time, while *mokṣa* (release from the otherwise endless cycle of births, deaths, and rebirths) brings ultimate resolution beyond time's cycles. And yet what the best way is to describe the characteristics of *mokṣa*—whether as an embodied or disembodied state, as personal or transpersonal—is a matter of continuing debate among various Hindu philosophies, theologies, and scriptures.

Karma and Saṃsāra (Action and Repetition)

Karma and *saṃsāra* are two concepts that provide a context for appreciating the competing yet complementary value orientations of *dharma* and *mokṣa*. *Karma* literally means "actions" and involves the idea that all actions have effects. In a general sense, the idea of *karma* teaches that each actor is ultimately responsible for every action they perform. Every cause produces effects, and every action produces results. From this perspective, the present circumstances and character of every place and person are results from past deeds. Although this is an understanding of the world in which there are no mere coincidences or accidents, *karma* is not a doctrine of despair. Each action when performed creates a residue, a trace, and a dispositional tendency. Past actions made their contributions to forming one's character and make it vitally important to summon one's energies and direct one's efforts toward creating a more honorable and better future.

Saṃsāra is the idea that one's present life is only the most recent in a long chain of lives extending far into the past. *Saṃsāra* is "the cycle of births, deaths, and rebirths" and implies that individual identities are temporal and temporary. All who live have passed through countless lifetimes already, in myriad forms other than their current one, and all of those had some bearing on their present life. Each lifetime is a small part in an enduring drama that includes thousands if not millions of lives, nonhuman and human—even if it is incomprehensible to the one now living that one's birth was actually a rebirth.

Karma binds individuals to the world, it results in a series of redeaths and rebirths, and it is integral to traditional Hindu views of society and cosmos. All social interaction involves exchanges of auspicious and inauspicious *karma*. These serve to justify and ultimately explain the many apparent inequalities in life, and so the world of *karma* is at an opposite pole from the world of European existentialists who see life as merely accidental, literally absurd, and devoid of higher meaning.

Although *karma* and *saṃsāra* do provide an explanation for apparently undeserved sufferings and unmerited blessings, when viewed from the standpoint of *mokṣa*, they are regarded as insufficient. That is because worldly action tends to bind all living beings to an ever-repeating cycle of births and deaths, lasting pains, and short-lived pleasures. Only complete freedom, transcendence, and liberation (*mokṣa*) is sufficient to fully resolve the limitations and sufferings of temporal life.

Mokṣa-Mārga (Paths to Liberation)

Worldly life is not final, nor a cause for regret or resignation. If lived while guided by *dharma*, it is a preparation for liberation. Although exclusive dedication to a search for *mokṣa* has never been the practice of more than a small minority of Hindus, ultimate liberation is a religious ideal that affects all lives. *Dharma* and *mokṣa* determine not only the hierarchical values of traditional social institutions and the range of religious teachings and practices, but more specifically what must be done to obtain release from *saṃsāra* and reach spiritual freedom.

Hindus differ in their aptitudes and preferences concerning a suitable path to *mokṣa*, but three paths (*trimārga*) to liberation have been particularly influential traditional models. They are *karma-mārga* ("path of right action"), the selfless performance of social and ritual obligations; *jñāna-mārga* ("path of knowledge"), the use of meditative wisdom to attain experiential insight into one's higher identity; and *bhakti-mārga* ("path of devotion"), dedication to a personal form of the divine in which the divinity and the devotee remain distinct and yet intimately connected and mutually involved. These paths have been regarded as suited to different types of people, and what is appropriate for one may not be fitting for another type. In addition to these three general ways to liberation, there are also other traditional methods that include yogic, tāntric, māntric, and ascetic disciplines. Among them, *bhakti-mārga*, or devotion, has been the most popular approach to liberation.

Deva and Devī (Divine Beings)

Vedic hymns and classical Hindu tradition acknowledge a huge number of higher beings, but the tradition does not require that everyone exclusively honor any single divine form. According to some ancient teachings and many contemporary Hindus, a basic idea is that a supreme being may suitably be worshiped by means of a variety of rituals and with the aid of many kinds of images. Early sources for this are found in the *Ṛg Veda*, "The one Being the sages contemplate in many ways" (10.114.5) and "The one Being the wise call by many names" (1.164.46). These Vedic affirmations seem to recognize diversity in human capacities, as well as different levels of spiritual development.

Most contemporary Hindus worship the divine as Viṣṇu or Śiva, or some form of the Devī. If a devotee consciously chooses to worship a particular form of the divine, the chosen deity is known as their "favorite or personal god" (*iṣṭadevatā*). The *iṣṭadevatā* becomes the focus of the devotee's love and adoration, effectively directing and satisfying a spiritual longing. Before the development of classical Hinduism, honoring the divine typically involved a sacred fire and temporary altar. That mode of worship was Vedic and continues today. However, the most popular modes of worship from the Classical period through the present have been directed to and through consecrated images (*mūrti*) made by traditional sculptors and metalworkers in conventionally recognizable forms of iconography. Particular sects or subtraditions dedicated to one or another form of the divine have developed their own chants, worship practices, and sacred times and places.

Brahman-Ātman (Ultimate Reality and Self) and Māyā (Enchantment)

In the *Bṛhadāraṇyaka Upaniṣad* (3.9.1–2), the sage Yājñavalkya is asked, "How many gods are there?" His answer: "Three hundred and three, and three thousand and three [= 3,306]." Again and again, he was asked, "Yes, but just how many gods are there?," and each succeeding time his reply narrowed—thirty-three, six, three, two, one and a half, one. "They are all the manifestations of the one."

The concept of the divine in specific personal forms (*īśvara, deva, devī*) is a pervasive and almost defining feature of Hindu tradition. However, a relatively small number of Hindus who follow *jñāna-mārga* ("path of knowledge") would say that the ancient Upaniṣads, at the end of the Veda, revealed a more subtle understanding of the divine as Brahman, or the formless absolute, which is beyond all qualities and so surpasses every particular description. Brahman can only be indirectly evoked by metaphors and analogies and yet is said to be no different from the inmost self (*ātman*) within each human and in all that lives. This teaching is encapsulated in the "great sayings" (*mahāvākya*) of the Upaniṣads: "That thou art" (*tat tvam asi*) and "I am the absolute" (*aham brahmāsmi*). Although only humans can put those affirmations into speech, they attest that every living being is a carrier of inherent and indestructible divinity. Although one may have wandered in *saṃsāra* for millions of incarnations, one's eventual destiny is to experience the supreme goal of life. Therefore, all life forms embody the sacred, and this kind of assumption influences a wide range of Hindu values and practices, including preference for vegetarian diet.

But if those who have been inspired by the Upaniṣads really have discerned a higher truth, then why is it not equally evident to all of us? Their answer is that ignorance (*avidyā*) afflicts us and is the root cause of suffering and bondage. In our ordinary condition, we suffer delusion (*māyā*) rather than enjoy insightful illumination. We attach ourselves to and identify ourselves with all sorts of people, places, and things. The cost is that we overlook and forget what we are essentially.

The Upaniṣads actually teach two significantly different views regarding *māyā*. In the first, it is a mysterious, wondrous, bedazzling, deceptive but divine power—in which case, the world and its phenomena are real as a field of divine play. In the second, it is an energy that produces an illusory manifestation of a universe. The second way of interpreting *māyā* refers to something like the way that exclusive identification with externals, including our body and its brain, obstructs our higher awareness and generates misidentification with artificial worlds that we imagine we inhabit. This is something like becoming addicted to computer games or getting entranced within a virtual reality, so that we end up "beside ourselves" and in need of rehabilitation and recovery. The dreamlike states that *māyā* generates are not ultimately real, but they do appear and so cannot be said to be entirely nonreal. This is one of those conundrums that philosophers love but may only perplex the rest of us. However, it does raise basic religious questions about the source and nature of our spiritual problems and what it would take for them to be resolved. Although not widely popular within Hindu tradition, these ideas from the Upaniṣads have attracted international interest from academic philosophers and self-help teachers, particularly those associated with the so-called New Age movement. In summary, while the subtle teachings of the Upaniṣads profoundly influence philosophy and world literature, far more popular forms of Hindu tradition continue to be focused on the divine with a particular name and form such as Viṣṇu, Śiva, or the Devī.

• HISTORY AND COSMOS

Scholars of ancient history are continuing to make discoveries that will help us to understand the early formation of Hindu tradition, but at present we have access only to relatively sparse and scattered data sources. That is due to the changing ecology and climate in early India and limited availability of well-preserved enduring materials that carry cultural records. An outline history that is divided into five overlapping periods, however, is sufficiently useful for the purposes of this chapter.

The Formative period includes the Harappā culture (named by archaeologists after a modern village near a major ancient site), which was part of a civilization extending from cities and hinterlands in and around the Indus River Valley. It lasted from about 2500 BCE to around 1500 BCE and seems to have overlapped with the era of the Vedic Āryans, which may date from about 2000 to 800 BCE.

The second is the Upaniṣadic period (about 800 to 400 BCE). The Upaniṣads are generally described as marking a transition from an emphasis on ritualism (*karmakāṇḍa*) to philosophic thought (*jñānakāṇḍa*). Another interpretation is that they represent an attempt to recover lost wisdom of the Vedic *ṛṣis* by means of meditation and spiritual experience. Although not systematic treatises, the Upaniṣads provide the theoretical foundations for later Vedānta philosophies.

The third is the Classical period (about 400 BCE to 600 CE), which includes the two great epics (*Rāmāyaṇa* and *Mahābhārata*), most of the Purāṇas, the law books (Dharmaśāstras and Dharmasūtras); the early development of the great devotional traditions of Vaiṣṇavism, Śaivism, and Śāktism; and the condensation of the various philosophical systems (*darśana*) into aphorisms (*sūtra*). Non-Vedic movements, the most successful of them Jainism and Buddhism, arose during this period. Within Hindu tradition, three approaches to the supreme goal of life that characterize the period continue to be central to contemporary discussions and differences among Hindus: world-affirmation (Vedic), world-negation (Upaniṣadic), and being in the world but not of it (*Bhagavad Gītā*).

The Medieval period (about 600 CE to 1600 CE) saw three major developments. The most popular was the flowering of devotion (*bhakti*) to personal deities (Viṣṇu, Śiva, and the Devī), construction of temples dedicated to them, and the composition of devotional literature in Sanskrit and regional languages. Second, Hindu philosophy was systematized into six schools (*saddarśana*), each with commentaries and treatises that explain and expand upon the teachings derived from Veda. Third, this period saw the flourishing of Tāntric tradition, which differs from Veda and has its own rites and practices.

Lastly, the Modern period (since 1600), includes the rise and fall of two conquering empires, the Muslim Mughal and the Christian British, as well as the establishment of the nation of India as an independent republic. Hindu tradition experienced a renaissance in the nineteenth century, and in the twentieth century saw the spread of Hinduism around the globe as a major world religion.

Origins

Scholars generally agree that Hindu tradition grew from two ancient cultural complexes, the Harappā or Indus Valley civilization (about 2500–1500 BCE) and Vedic-Āryan culture (from perhaps 2000 BCE onward). There continues to be controversy concerning the relationship between them. An older theory that is still supported by many scholars maintains that the Āryan culture arrived on the subcontinent from Central Asia as the indigenous Indus Valley civilization declined. An alternative theory is that the Āryan culture continues the Harappā culture or was otherwise indigenous itself and not introduced by migrants from outside the subcontinent.

Questions about Hindu origins continue to generate intense discussion among cultural historians, contemporary politicians, and modern Hindus in general. Regardless of the origins of Indo-Āryan language and culture, which may remain a matter for conjecture for some time, scholars tend to agree that classical and later Hindu tradition incorporates beliefs and practices from many different social groups on the subcontinent as they interacted and formed what is now generally called Hinduism.

Harappā Culture or Indus Valley Civilization

The earliest known technologically advanced culture on the subcontinent is the Harappā or Indus Valley civilization, which was urban-centered and flourished from about 2500 BCE to 1500 BCE (although its roots could reach back as far as the Neolithic period, 7000–6000 BCE). Mohenjodāro and Harappā are the two best known of its cities and are among the several sites unearthed by archaeologists. In 1921 John Marshall supervised excavations in the Indus River Valley (now in Pakistan) and uncovered planned cities that had sophisticated systems for water delivery and waste removal, residential areas with parallel streets, large grain storehouses, community baths, fire-altar pits, stone sculptures, seals, and amulets. The script impressed on the seals is yet to be deciphered. In a recently excavated citadel mound in Kalibagan (in Rajasthan), there has been uncovered a series of raised brick platforms, fire-altars, and a bathing platform situated next to a well. The entire complex seems to indicate that some sort of religious ritual, complete with purificatory water rites and sacrificial offerings, was performed there.

Excavations of the settlements have uncovered large numbers of terracotta figurines and steatite seals. Scholars have surmised, due to the large number of them found, that some of the figurines were used in ritual worship. Many of the statuettes appear to be of a mother goddess, and a small number represent a bull, which also appears frequently on the many seals. A small number of seals picture a seated male figure in what may be called a *yoga*-like posture. One interpretation is that this figure may have been a prototype of Śiva, the great *yogin* and lord of animals. Several stones that appear to be *liṅga*s (an emblem or "mark" of Lord Śiva) have also been unearthed in the excavations. In the absence of texts that can be translated, however, the intended meaning of these material remains continues to be ambiguous.

Many seals seem to illustrate religious themes even if these cannot be interpreted conclusively. Numerous seals appear to depict the theme of a spirit emerging from a Pīpala tree, with worshipers standing in front of it with small plants. We cannot be certain that this is a forerunner of what will develop in later Hinduism; it is noteworthy that the Pīpala tree continues to play an important role in Hinduism down to the present day. Further, some seals depict a horned person emerging from the Pīpala tree with a row of seven figures standing in front of it. Again, later Hinduism identifies seven such figures with both the seven Vedic seers (*ṛṣi*) and the seven mothers (*mātṛ*). Still other seals depict a *svastika* (an auspicious sign long before twentieth-century Europeans debased its meaning) and geometrical designs that resemble the rice-powder (*kōlam*, *raṅgolī*) drawings that continue to be widely used by Hindus.

It is tempting to imagine an unbroken line of connection between the ancient civilization and contemporary Hinduism, but material evidence in the absence of a translated language is open to multiple interpretations. Fire-altars and female figurines, horned deities, Pīpala trees, and *liṅga*s are significant in later Hinduism, but ritual purity, fertility, and female goddesses are common elements throughout the ancient world, while a steatite seal image of a figure wrestling with a lion, which has been the object of competing interpretations, could be viewed as the Hindu *avatāra* Narasiṃha, or the Hindu goddess Durgā battling with the buffalo-demon, or an image from the Mesopotamian epic of Gilgamesh.

The remarkable urban civilization collapsed rather quickly around 1500 BCE. There is no consensus on why this happened. Some speculate that it was due primarily to ecological crises such as flooding, silting, or salting in the river system. Others suppose that a pandemic wiped out a large proportion of the population or that invading Āryans destroyed it, perhaps after it had been otherwise weakened.

Āryans

Sometime between about 2000 BCE and 1500 BCE, according to an older theory based largely on linguistic factors, Āryans began migrating into the northern plains of India (although some scholars think the migration began as early as 6000 BCE and continued in successive waves). Whether it was peaceful or hostile is the subject of controversy. Along their route, some of the migrating tribes stopped in Iran (where they gave their name to the region; "Iran" etymologically means "homeland of the Āryans"), while others continued into India where they destroyed (or were a factor in the destruction of) the Indus Valley civilization and became a dominant power. In India the name "Āryan" took on a social connotation and meant "noble ones" as distinct from the indigenous people they subjugated.

The Āryans spoke an Indo-European language that developed into Vedic Sanskrit and eventually classical Sanskrit, the primary Hindu sacred language. They spread across the northern plains of India until they reached the Gaṅgā, region, which became known as the "Āryan homeland," or *āryāvarta*, and eventually expanded to South India. This is the account offered by the older received theory. In short, it is seldom disputed that Indo-Āryan culture has been a dominant influence in India for thousands of years. The disagreement is about where the Āryans originated.

Vedism and Brāhmaṇism

There are few material remains from Āryans of the early Vedic period. Their great surviving legacy is the Veda or Vedas. Like the imprecise term "Hinduism," the practices and ideas preserved by the Vedas are imprecisely known as "Vedism" and "Brāhmaṇism." The defining features of this period (from about 1500 BCE to 400 BCE) are the Vedic canon and the religious and social theories derived from ideas about duty (*dharma*) and order (*ṛta*). Vedic society seems to have been structured on the basis of an emerging version of castes and stages of life (*varṇāśrama-dharma*). Caste, a label devised by the Portuguese, refers to relatively stable, genetically determined or vocationally based status groups that may be reinforced or challenged through ritual practices. The authority of the Veda lent these components of the social system legitimacy, persuasiveness, and longevity.

The terms "Vedism" and "Brāhmaṇism" are used to distinguish culturally dominant religious and social practices from tāntric and sectarian forms that are based on a variety of non-Vedic texts. Religious life as reflected in Vedic tradition suggests the image of a journey involving progress on the path to truth (*satyam* or *ṛtam*). Life requires action, and this is based on inner and outer sacrifice. The Vedic worldview assumes that the natural order, human society, ritual practice, and the divine are inextricably connected. Each sphere influences the others. By means of ritual offerings, humans directly contribute to the maintenance of universal order and can influence it, too.

Vedic texts do not refer to material images of the divine or permanent buildings designed as temples. Vedic religious life and world maintenance were determined primarily by interaction between two groups: a priestly group, organized around sacerdotal training maintained through family and clan lineages, and a warrior group led by kings. Priests served as sources of sacred lore and ritual techniques; the governing warriors served as patrons of the rites performed by priests. These two groups, ideally complementary but sometimes rivals, stratified into fixed hereditary classes: Brāhmaṇas (priests) and Kṣatriyas (warriors).

Brāhmaṇism developed from Vedism by incorporating religious and social practices from non-Vedic sources. It is called Brāhmaṇism because of the ritual and legal importance of the Brāhmaṇa (priestly) class. It takes as sacred truth, in addition to the Veda, various law books (Dharmaśāstras and Dharmasūtras), the two epics (*Rāmāyaṇa* and *Mahābhārata*), and the major Purāṇas. While both Vedism and Brāhmaṇism acknowledge the Veda as sacred, Brāhmaṇism also includes doctrines not specifically derived from the Vedas, and so it is more inclusive than Vedism. Some of these ideas find expression in various ritual practices and devotional activities such as worship (*pūjā*) in home shrines and in temples, support for vegetarianism, and other non-Vedic themes that come to play an important part in later Hindu religious life. In short, the combination of Vedic and Brāhmaṇical traditions established the "master narrative" for orthodox (or orthoprax) and heterodox in subsequent Hindu tradition.

Theistic Hinduism

Medieval or Theistic Hinduism flourished from 600 CE through 1600 CE. It is characterized by devotional movements to locally known deities as well as the great Hindu deities (Viṣṇu, Śiva, and the Devī), with a corresponding construction of temple structures. This period also saw the composition of enduring poetic devotional literature in Sanskrit, Tamil, and other regional languages. It also was the period in which Hindu philosophy was systematized into six main schools, or *darśana*s, each with their own commentaries and treatises that explain, elucidate, and expand upon their source teachings. Finally, Tāntric traditions flourished too.

Devotion (*bhakti*) to a Deva or Devī in personal form has ancient roots and is a central theme in the *Bhagavad Gītā*, a popular text whose written version may date to 200 BCE. However, it was not until about 600 CE that a devotional revolution gained extraordinary power with the appearance of several South Indian saints who traveled on foot from temple to temple singing the praise of Viṣṇu or Śiva. The Nāyaṉmārs, the sixty-three Śaiva saints, and the Āḻvārs, the twelve Vaiṣṇava saints, inspired a many-sided shift in Hindu religion and culture by expressing their devotion in the South Indian language of Tamil. These poet-saints were on fire with an intense divine love that they expressed in mystical poetry and song.

In the *Bhāgavata Purāṇa*, it was predicted that the devotees of Lord Viṣṇu would appear in South India on the banks of rivers. The twelve Āḻvārs ("one who has taken a deep plunge into the ocean of divinity") lived during the seventh to ninth centuries. These eleven men and one woman (Āṇṭāḷ), from high as well as low castes, spread Viṣṇu's glory through their songs and popularized the path of devotion. They addressed their lord in multiple novel ways: as lover, as king, as friend, as brother, as servant, as mother, as immanent or easily accessible, and as remote and inaccessible. Their compositions are collected in the *Nālāyira Tivyaprapantam* (The Sacred Collection of Four Thousand Verses), and their ecstatic devotion attracted a following throughout India.

As part of the legacy of the Āḻvārs, five Vaiṣṇava (devoted to Viṣṇu) theological traditions (*sampradāya*) emerged that were based on the teachings of five *guru*s: Rāmānuja, Madhva, Vallabha, Nimbārka, and Caitanya. Vaiṣṇava traditions include the Śrīvaiṣṇavas of Tamil Nadu, whose center is the Śrīraṅgam temple; the Gauḍīya Vaiṣṇavas of Bengal, Orissa, and Vrndavana; the Viṭhobā devotees in Maharashtra (whose teachings are derived from Maharashtra's great saints, Jñāneśvar, Nāmdev, Tukārām, Samarth Rāmdās, Eknāth, Muktābāī, Janābāī, and so on); the Rāma tradition of Ayodhyā and Janakpur, along with the Rāmānandī Order; and spilling over and beyond the boundaries of Vaiṣṇava devotion is the northern Sant tradition, a loose amalgam of devotional poets who include Mīrābāī, Sūrdās, Kabīr, Nānak, and Tulsīdās. Comparable Śaiva traditions include the Pāśupata, Lākula, Kāpālika, Kaśmīra Śaiva, Kaula, Śaiva Siddhānta, and Liṅgāyata.

Many of the Vaiṣṇava and Śaiva saints traveled on foot throughout South India and to some extent in the North, visiting temples and singing to glorify their lord. This contributed to popularizing temple worship, and pilgrimage became an important feature of Hindu tradition. Devotion to Rāma and to Kṛṣṇa (as the precocious cowherd boy as well as the *pūrṇa*, or full, *avatāra*) was growing. Open expression of devotional experiences, including uncontrollable joy, frenzy, trance, tears, chanting in roadways, and ecstatic dancing, became more common. This challenged the hierarchical system correlated with distinctions based on caste status and gender identity. The underlying conviction of this *bhakti* movement was that men and women may have differing inherited and prescribed duties and social positions, but all human beings share an inherent duty to love and serve the divine.

The other movement that contributed to the rise of the theistic traditions was Tantra. In a broad sense, Tantra refers to a collection of symbols and practices of a ritualistic, sometimes magical, character that may be used to achieve mundane goals or for spiritual liberation. More narrowly, Tantra relies on symbolic systems of rituals that are predominantly but not exclusively Śākta and are taught to initiates by lineages of spiritual *guru*s. They teach *sādhanā* by means of Kuṇḍalinī Yoga that is intended to lead toward guided awakening of intense, sometimes extreme, inner experiences on the way to spiritual liberation.

Tantra is said to be suited to the current downward stage in the great cosmic cycle, in which seekers are trapped within increasingly demeaning conditions of the Dark Age (Kali Yuga), and so are less able to perform complex rituals from an earlier epoch. Advocates have claimed that tāntric *sādhanā* can lead directly to liberation through initiation by a *guru* and instruction in a variety of techniques that employ *mantra*s ("sacred mystic sounds"), *yantra*s ("sacred geometric diagrams"), *mudrā*s ("hand gestures"), and yogic disciplines.

As a major sectarian phenomenon, Hindu Tantra disappeared or went underground some five hundred years ago except for the Śrīvidyā tradition, which was maintained by Brāhmaṇas and structured to parallel the teachings of the Veda. Other forms of Tantra were a victim to excess. Their teachings flouted traditional *dharma*; their practitioners seemed to think of themselves as if they were a secret spiritual elite free to engage in antinomian behavior; and their spiritual methods became too esoteric for the ordinary person to comprehend.

However, Tantra is an aspect of Hindu tradition that often is misrepresented and disparaged as if it were no more than a medley of magic, superstition, and revolting rituals. Tāntric teachings themselves distinguish between a right-handed path (*dakṣiṇācāra*) and a left-handed path (*vāmācāra*). The right-handed path is a discipline open to everyone, regardless of caste, gender, or age, and consists primarily in the use of *mantra*s, *yantra*s, and rituals based upon maps of energies of the subtle body. The left-handed path, by contrast, tends to enlist borderline antisocial or heroic individuals. Its most infamous ritual requires the initiate to partake of five forbidden substances (alcohol, meat, illicit sexual union, parched grain, and fish), thereby transcending dividing lines between the sacred and the profane, the prescribed and the forbidden, the pure and the impure, with the intent to become free from the bonds of conventional society and be spiritually liberated.

Deities

Vedic texts do not delineate a single fixed pantheon, and the frequently used Vedic term "*deva*" is not a direct and exclusive reference to god as a single ultimate reality, but to some divine being or divine power in general. Etymologically, the term implies "shining, exalted" and refers to everything supernatural: all forms, powers, emotions, poetic meters, melodies, and books—everything that requires a supernatural explanation. The gods (*deva*) typically are associated with one or more of the three levels, realms, or worlds. These are variously termed, depending upon which of the three is their primary location and sphere of activity: celestial/heavenly/causal-vastness-spiritual; atmospheric/mid-region/sky/subtle-mental-cosmogonical; terrestrial/earthly/material-physical-external. The *deva*s are simultaneously physical and psychological forces of nature, personifications of abstract ideas, living realities, and embodiments of a cosmic struggle between forces of order and of chaos that plays out in the universe at large and within humans. For instance, the Vedic Agni, the general term for "fire," is not merely the chemical process of oxidation and carbonization of organic matter but simultaneously a *deva*, the manifestation of a transcendent power. Where a mind with an exclusively modern scientific bent may apprehend no more than physical fire, a Vedic seer was able to sense a divine reality.

Among the most often mentioned of the Vedic gods is Indra. He is cosmic power, god of the mid-region, powerful, and warlike, whose thunderbolt slays the serpent Vṛta, thereby liberating the obstructed waters and the sky. About a quarter of the hymns in the *Ṛg Veda* are addressed to him. Agni is the second most frequently mentioned and indispensable for the Vedic fire sacrifice as the *deva* of fire. He is priest of the sacrifice, the outer fire on the sacrificial altar as well as the inner fire of human aspiration, and the mediator between human and divine. Varuṇa is the guardian of cosmic order (*ṛta*), king and ruler of heaven and earth, lord of the consciousness, and protector of the truth that resides in the oceans. Soma is the subject matter of the entire ninth book of the *Ṛg Veda* and is integral to ritual as the drink of deathlessness and the juice of a plant (no longer known). Its extraction and drinking formed the center and context for much Vedic ritual. Among other deities mentioned are (in alphabetical order): Aditi (mother goddess), Aśvins (twins associated with healing), Dyaus (heaven), Maruts (storm gods), Pṛthvī (earth), Rudra (death and destruction), Sarasvatī (divine word), Sūrya (sun), Uṣas (dawn), Vāyu (wind), and Viṣṇu (preserver).

Knowledge and appreciation of the functions of the Vedic *deva*s seems to have declined as the sacrificial fire rituals decreased in cultural dominance. Because modern culture largely lost the ability to enter into the heart of the ancient mystic doctrine, the Vedic *deva*s tend to be unappreciated and misunderstood. When the Vedic gods declined in importance, in their place remained a more abstract ultimate reality (Brahman) and the increasing importance of popular theistic deities (Viṣṇu, Śiva, and the Devī).

Great theistic deities of classical Hinduism connect back to the Veda but are newly understood as independent of the old sacrificial ritual system. Nārāyaṇa (Viṣṇu) and Śiva appear in some late Upaniṣads, such as the *Śvetāśvatara* and the *Mahānārāyaṇa*. Key ideas of theism—that there is a personal, supreme, distinct god or goddess who creates the universe, sustains it, and eventually dissolves it and has the power to bestow grace—grew with the epics and finally became dominant in the Purāṇas. Many of the Vedic deities like Agni, Indra, and Varuṇa received little later attention, except in the context of rarely performed Vedic rituals by Brāhmaṇa priests when supported by powerful and wealthy patrons.

Viṣṇu

Viṣṇu (literally, "all-pervading") is worshiped by his devotees (Vaiṣṇavas) as the supreme Brahman, free from any trace of evil, possessing countless auspicious qualities of matchless excellence together with an omnipotent power to accomplish his will. He is regarded to be the supreme ruler and controller, personal and loving, the material and efficient cause of the world, and the preserver of the universe. Viṣṇu takes five forms: supreme (*parā*), cosmic (*vyūha*), divine incarnations (*vihava* or *avatāra*), inner controller (*antaryāmi*), and in images (*arca*). Viṣṇu is named in the *Ṛg Veda*, though it contains few references to him. However, just because a deity appears in only few hymns does not necessarily reflect on its qualitative importance. In the Brāhmaṇa section of the Vedas, in any case, Viṣṇu was called "the highest of the gods" and was identified with the sacrifice itself. There is also a well-known Vedic tradition of his three strides across the universe that later formed the basis of the tradition of his *avatāra* as Vāmana, the dwarf.

> Thrice Viṣṇu paced and set his step uplifted out of the primal dust; three steps he has paced, the guardian, the invincible, and from beyond he upholds their laws. Scan the workings of Viṣṇu and see from whence he has manifested their laws. That is his highest pace which is seen ever by the seers like an eye extended in heaven; that the illumined, the awakened kindle into a blaze, even Viṣṇu's step supreme.
>
> (*Ṛg Veda* 1.22.17–21)

In Vaiṣṇavism, Viṣṇu is irrevocably connected with the *avatāra* doctrine. Viṣṇu descends into the local universe to preserve order whenever unrighteousness threatens its existence. Widely accepted, this is the idea of a periodic divine descent to earth in order to vanquish evil and restore righteousness. These divine incarnations are the most popular, and thus important part of Viṣṇu's tradition. He has a foremost place in popular devotion. Among his most widely known *avatāra* forms are Matsya the fish; Kūrma the tortoise; Varāha the boar; Vāmana the dwarf; Narasiṃha the man-lion; Paraśurāma, or Rāma with his axe; Rāma in the *Rāmāyaṇa*; Kṛṣṇa in the *Mahābhārata*; Balarāma (elder brother of Kṛṣṇa) or Buddha (of Buddhism fame); and Kalki. Rāma and Kṛṣṇa have become universal figures in art and popular culture even beyond religious settings, and an immense body of devotional literature has been created in response to them.

Material images of Viṣṇu in temples depict him sitting, usually in the company of his consort Lakṣmī and/or Śrī, or standing, holding various weapons in his four hands (*śaṅkha*, conch; *cakra*, discus; *gadā*, club; *padma*, lotus), blue in color, and dressed in royal yellow garments. He may be represented alternatively as reclining on the coils of the serpent Ādi Śeṣa, asleep on the cosmic ocean during the period between the periodic annihilation and renewal of the cosmos. Viṣṇu's vehicle (*vāhana*) is the eagle Garuḍa. His heavenly abode is known as Vaikuṇṭha. His *mantra* is "*oṃ namo nārāyaṇāya*." His most common devotional name is Hari, and he is also invoked as Nārāyaṇa, Keśava, or Puruṣottama.

Śiva

Śiva (literally, the "auspicious one") is worshiped by his devotees (Śaivites) as the great god (Mahādeva), the cosmic dancer (Naṭarāja), the perfect *yogī* (Śaṅkara), and the primeval *guru* (Dakṣiṇāmūrti). He is variously depicted in his iconography as an ash-besmeared naked ascetic; as a mendicant beggar; as a *yogin*; with a blue neck (from holding in his throat the toxic byproduct from the churning of the cosmic ocean, which otherwise would have threatened to destroy humanity); his hair arranged in a coil of matted locks and adorned with the crescent moon and the Gaṅgā River (according to tradition he brought the goddess Gaṅgā safely to earth by allowing her to trickle through his hair, thus breaking her fall and saving the planet from destruction); with three eyes, the third eye bestowing inward spiritual vision but also capable of destruction when focused outwardly; wearing a garland of skulls and a serpent around his neck and carrying in his hands a deerskin, a trident, a small hand drum, or a club; and as the androgynous half-male and half-female, Ardhanārīśvara. He is one of the most complex or "inclusivist" *deva*s in Hindu religion. He is both the cosmic destroyer and the creative lord of the dance, the great ascetic and the symbol of sensuality, a wrathful avenger and the compassionate lord of souls. He is an embodiment of the polarity that exists within the depths of the divine because he reconciles in his person seemingly opposite qualities: terror and compassion, destruction and creation, ceaseless activity and eternal rest. These seeming contradictions make him a paradoxical figure: mysterious, powerful, aloof, stern, and transcending humanity; and yet, at the same time, erotic, husband, benevolent, and loving lord of all creatures from the highest to the lowest.

Śiva's female consort is known in various manifestations as Umā, Satī, Pārvatī, Durgā, and Kālī. The divine couple, together with their sons, the elephant-headed Gaṇeśa and the six-headed Subramaṇiyaṉ (also known as Kārttikēya, Skanda, Murukaṉ), are said to dwell on Mount Kailāsa in the Himālayas. Śiva's vehicle is the bull Nandi. His *mantra* is "*oṃ namaḥ śivāya*." In temples and shrines, Śiva is worshiped in the form of the *liṅga*, a pillar or an oval-shaped emblem made of stone, metal, or clay.

The Devī

Not only does the goddess appear as the consort of Viṣṇu or Śiva; she alone is the ultimate divine power for her devotees (Śāktas) who consider other deities to be her instruments or servants. The divine motherhood is considered by Hindus to be the most constant and sweetest of relationships, because the connection between mother and child is unparalleled. As a mother's love is constant, so worship of Devī is easy. The love and protective power from the cosmic mother is unbounded.

Female forms of the divine are known and worshiped by various names in the Veda, but none of the Vedic manifestations is considered to be all-powerful. As Vāc, she is word; as Uṣas, dawn; as Pṛthvī, earth; as Aditi, mother; and as Sarasvatī, flowing inspiration. However, no all-inclusive great goddess was acknowledged in early Vedic tradition.

From sometime around the first millennium CE, there is evidence of full-fledged worship of the great goddess. Since then, there has been a tendency to subsume the many manifestations of the goddess under one great female identity. This goddess is most commonly designated as Devī or Mahādevī (great goddess). Some manifestations of the goddess are known individually as benevolent (Ambā, Pārvatī, Sarasvatī, and Lakṣmī), and others as terror (Kālī), and still others as warlike (Durgā).

From the Medieval period onward, there has been a tendency to think of all of the many forms as closely related beings or as various manifestations of a single multidimensional highest being—the goddess. The special character of the goddess is that she is seen as the cosmic mother, the ultimate power (*śakti*), the creatrix of the universe. She is compassionate and saves human beings, is identified with earth (*prakṛti*), is identified with mysterious power and/or illusion (*māyā*), and is queen of the universe. Like some male deities, especially Śiva, she embodies ambiguity and paradox, making it impossible to define "the Hindu goddess" adequately in a few words because of the range of her manifestations and representations. She can be erotic yet detached; gentle yet heroic; beautiful yet terror provoking; a wife and a lover; benevolent and protective; as well as independent, aggressive, malevolent, and destructive.

As Lakṣmī or Śrī, she is the power of abundance, riches, prosperity, health, and beauty. She is perhaps the most popular manifestation of the goddess in the Hindu pantheon. She is the wife or consort of Viṣṇu, and in this role, she plays the part of the model Hindu wife, obediently serving her husband as lord. Also with these qualities, she appears as Sītā, Draupadī, and Rādhā.

As Sarasvatī, she inspires and supports learning and the arts. She is dressed in white and rides her vehicle, a swan, she plays a stringed instrument known as the *vīṇā*, and she carries a manuscript and a rosary in her hands. On a day devoted to her, students in schools honor her as the divine patroness and energy of learning.

As Pārvatī, she is Śiva's consort and *śakti*. By herself, Pārvatī has almost no independent history apart from her connection with Śiva. Since epic times, when Pārvatī first appeared as a significant deity, she has been identified as a reincarnation of the goddess Satī, Śiva's first wife, who committed suicide because of an insult that dishonored her husband. It seems as if the purpose of Pārvatī's birth was to attract Śiva into marriage, and thus bring the world-denying ascetic back into the worldly realm of a householder, complete with a family, because the cosmos would more rapidly disintegrate in the absence of his active energy engaged in the world. The marriage was generative, and Pārvatī as the spouse of Śiva became the mother of Gaṇeśa and Subramaṇiyaṉ. What basic characteristic of Hindu tradition is central here? The importance of sharing responsibility for maintaining the world—whether through formal ritual, through behavior that is guided by *dharma*, or by gracious divine activity in general or in crisis-intervention by an *avatāra*—this is a central Hindu value.

Durgā, the warrior goddess, is one of the most formidable and popular female forms of the divine. She is usually depicted as calm and detached, a battle queen seated on a tiger or a lion who may smile even as she wields a weapon in each of her ten hands. Her primary function is to kill the buffalo-demon Mahiṣāsura. She is born in a time of cosmic crisis, called forth with the destiny to kill the terrible demon that the male gods are not able to destroy. Her appeal stems from her world-sustaining strength, and an autumn festival in her honor is a major feature of the annual Hindu calendar.

As Kālī, the Devī is a ferocious, destructive aspect of the divine. Her iconography presents her with a terrible, frightening appearance. She is jet black, naked, with long disheveled hair. A girdle of severed arms is around her waist, a garland of skulls around her neck, children's corpses are her earrings and serpents her bracelets. Her large bright red tongue protrudes far beyond her blood-besmeared lips. She holds aloft a freshly severed head and a sword in two of her hands while the other two bestow boons and signal "have no fear." Kālī often is depicted on a battlefield or in a cremation ground, but devotees call her mother and those who love her understand her to be compassionate and loving.

Devī also manifests as a group of seven ferocious female deities known as the "seven mothers" (*saptamātṛkā*); as local or regional goddesses in village and family shrines; as aniconic images, such as stones, poles, weapons, and mystical geometric diagrams (*yantra*); as stylized female genitals (*yoni*); and as natural phenomena, such as rivers (Gaṅgā, Sarasvatī, Yamunā, Kāvēri), trees, and mountains.

Other Deities

In addition to the "great" Hindu deities, there are a number of others who have attracted devotees. Perhaps the most popular is the elephant-headed Gaṇeśa. He is known as the lord of beginnings and remover of obstacles and is the son of Pārvatī and Śiva. His image is found throughout India: in temples, autorickshaws, humble wayside shrines, and homes. He made a rather late but dramatic appearance in the Hindu pantheon, and today no new project or venture begins without honoring him. His younger brother, Subramaṇiyaṉ, plays a more limited role in northern India where he is known as Kārttikēya, but in the Tamil region of South India he is Murukaṉ, the supreme lord of wisdom (*jñāna*).

Hanumān, the devoted servant of Rāma in the *Rāmāyaṇa*, is very popular in the North as well as in South India. He is often depicted in a massive orange-hued iconic form, similar to a laṅgūr monkey. He is understood as an embodiment of strength and a model of complete devotion. Poems and songs that honor him are among the most popular in North India.

Deities are known primarily or exclusively by local names in many Indian towns and villages, and a few of them gain a national or international following. For instance, the presiding deity of Tirupati temple is known as Veṅkaṭeśvara (lord of the Veṅkaṭa Hill); the presiding deity of Srirangam temple is Raṅganātha (lord of the stage), and the presiding deity of Madurai temple is Mīnākṣī (fish-eyed goddess). Each of the three temples has become a major center for pilgrimage, and yet each deity has a unique history, tradition, and personality that identify them with the particular place. Their stories are told in books known as Sthalapurānas, and similar local deities, whether as widely honored as these three, play an incredibly important role in Hindu religion. The ones who come to be revered beyond their immediate region eventually tend to be acknowledged as an aspect of one or another of the great Hindu or all-India deities, but continue to have their specific local base and name.

Cosmology

Most Hindu sources agree about the way in which the traditional cosmos is arranged, but there are several different perspectives on how it came to be. Among them are that it is the outcome of a cosmic battle, it is an unintended result of action by a god or gods, it was born from a golden womb, it arose from waters of chaos, it emanated from a word, or it was intentionally created by Viṣṇu or Śiva or the Devī. There is an often told traditional story in which Nārāyaṇa (Viṣṇu) floated on the serpent Ananta ("infinite") in the primeval waters. From his navel grew a lotus from which Brahmā emerged reciting the four Vedas with his four mouths and creating the "egg of Brahmā" that contains all the worlds within the entire cosmos.

An influential Vedic model is the hymn—the Puruṣasūkta—depicting the formation of the universe from the dismembered parts of the body of a single cosmic being at a primordial sacrifice:

> The cosmic person has a thousand heads, a thousand eyes, and a thousand feet. It pervades the universe on all sides. . . . When they divided the cosmic person, into how many parts did they apportion him? . . . His mouth became the priests; his arms were made into the warrior; his thighs the merchants; and from his feet the workers were born.
>
> (*Ṛg Veda* 10.90)

For nondualist or monist philosophies, another Vedic model is the Nāsadīyasūkta hymn that refers to the divine as "that one," *tad ekam*:

> There was neither nonexistence nor existence then; there was neither the realm of space nor the sky which is beyond. What stirred? Where? . . . Who really knows? . . . The one who looks down on it, in the highest heaven, only he knows, or perhaps he does not know.
>
> (*Ṛg Veda* 10.129)

Another cosmological model popularized in the Purāṇas maps the cosmos with a sacred mountain in its center and seven ever-expanding concentric oceans and continents surrounding it. Similar images are found in Buddhist and Jaina texts. An odd feature is that the islands double in size as one moves from the center outwards, and the seven islands are separated by a series of seven oceans, each of which has the width of the island it encircles. In the center of the innermost island, which is Jambudvīpa (earth), stands a great golden mountain, Mount Meru. Jambudvīpa itself is divided into nine regions, and India (Bhārata) lies in the southern area. Bhārata's unique attribute is its designation as a realm (*karma-bhūmi*) where actions are subject to the law of *karma*. Because of this, it is the place where liberation from the cycles of existence (*saṃsāra*) can be realized.

Above and below the earth, within the great cosmic egg, are further layers or realms. This popular Hindu image from the Purāṇas divides reality (as well as the individual person) into seven realms (*loka*): physical (*bhūrloka*), vital breath (*bhuvarloka*), mental (*svarloka*), intellectual (*maharloka*), bliss (*janarloka*), consciousness (*taparloka*), and existence (*satya-loka*). There also are seven netherworlds (*tala*): *pātāla* (the serpent kingdom of the *nāga*s), *atala* (the kingdom of the *yakṣa*s), *rasātala* (the abode of the *asura*s, *daitya*s, and *dānavas*), *talātala* (the kingdom of the *rākṣasa*s), *vitala* (the kingdom of Śiva's demons), *sutala* (ruled by Bali), and *mahātala* (the kingdom of *preta*s and demons). Mount Meru represents the highest realm or true world (*satyaloka*). The entire cosmos is populated by human beings, animals, plants, gods, snakelike beings (*nāga*), celestial nymphs (*apsarās*), heavenly musicians (*gandharva*), and many more types of beings, each of which can be (re)born into any of the realms depending upon the cumulative outcome of their actions (*karma*).

Mahāyuga (Cycles of Four Ages)

According to the tradition, time endlessly repeats itself in cycles of billions of years. The Purāṇas take for granted this endless repetition of cycles of creation, decline, and destruction. There are four ages (*yuga*) in the cycle: Golden (Kṛta or Satya Yuga), which lasts for 1,728,000 human years; Silver (Tretā Yuga), which lasts for 1,296,000 human years; Bronze (Dvāpara Yuga), which lasts for 864,000 human years; and Dark (Kali Yuga), which lasts for 432,000 human years. The current age is a Dark Age that began at the end of the Mahābhārata War, traditionally dated 3102 BCE. A complete cycle of the four ages is a *mahāyuga*, or Great Yuga, lasting 4.32 million years, during which time the universe moves from a state of perfection through ever more degenerate states in which the ability to maintain *dharma* gradually declines. According to the Vaiṣṇavas, the deeply disintegrating cosmos awaits the arrival of the tenth *avatāra*, Kalki, whose presence will bring to an end the age of darkness and usher in a new Golden Age. The cycles cannot continue forever, you may be thinking, and you are correct. After a thousand repetitions of the great cycles, or 4.32 billion years, which comprise one day of Brahmā, it is time for an equally long night of Brahmā. Night implies rest. The entire cosmos is destroyed (*pralaya*) and remains asleep through the long universal night, until the process arises again to play itself out in further stages of movement and rest in cycles small and great that continue without end.

• SACRED LIFE AND LITERATURES

Hindu scriptures comprise some of the world's oldest and most extensive religious literature. In general, it is divided into Śruti and Smṛti. Śruti (literally, "that which is heard") is a class of Sanskrit texts that are regarded as revealed, eternal, authorless (*apauruṣeya*). At first "seen" or sensed by primeval seers (*ṛṣi*) and then transmitted from mouth to ear through subsequent generations to the present, Śruti is primary revelation as Veda (derived from the Sanskrit root *vid*, "to know," meaning "knowledge *par excellence*" or divine wisdom). Tradition affirms that the Veda, the sole extant record of India's earliest ancestors, was eventually collected and arranged by an ancient seer, the compiler Kṛṣṇa Dvaipāyana, better known as Vedavyāsa, into the four different collections (*saṃhitā*) of the *Ṛg*, *Sāma*, *Yajur*, and *Atharva*. Each collection was governed by different considerations about its nature and purpose.

Smṛti (literally, "recollection") is a class of texts that are based on human recollection, and therefore tradition. Its role has been to interpret, elaborate upon, and clarify the primary revelation. This body of texts includes the two epics (*itihāsa*), the *Rāmāyaṇa* and the *Mahābhārata*. The latter includes within it one of the most influential of all Hindu texts, the *Bhagavad Gītā*. Among others in this category of texts are the eighteen major and eighteen minor Purāṇas (compilations of ancient history and tradition); the Dharmaśāstras and Dharmasūtras (texts relating to law and social conduct); and the Tantras. In practice, Hindus acquire their knowledge of religion almost exclusively through Smṛti texts.

Primary Sacred Texts: Śruti

Veda or Vedas

The term "Veda" extends through a range of overlapping but different referents. First, an ancient meaning was a "direct, inner experience of the truth." Second, the term is used to designate a body of oral teachings or written texts to mean "the entire body of Vedic revelation." This second use refers not only to the subject matter or content of the verses (*mantra*), but also to their form of expression. Third, Veda refers to the revealed knowledge as divided into four collections (*saṃhitā*): *Ṛg*, *Sāma*, *Yajur*, and *Atharva* (along with their respective numerous recensions, or *śākhā*) that constitute collections of verses (*ṛc*), chants (*sāman*), sacrificial formulae (*yajus*), and incantations (*atharvan*). Fourth, Veda subsequently was extended to mean not only the four *saṃhitā*s, but also the sacrificial manuals attached to the *saṃhitās* (the Brāhmaṇas), the forest books that reflect on the inner meaning of the sacrificial rituals (the Āraṇyakas), and the wisdom portions of the Vedas (the Upaniṣads). Fifth, in post-Vedic times, Veda has been further expanded to include the two epics (*itihāsa*), the *Rāmāyaṇa* and the *Mahābhārata*, which have been designated as the "fifth Veda." Lastly, for many contemporary Hindus the terms "Veda" and "Vedic" have become an encompassing symbol within which can be subsumed a potentially unlimited set of texts, teachings, and spiritual practices.

Modern scholars typically say that the Vedic texts (as defined in the third instance above) date from approximately 1500 BCE. However, debates over the origins of the Veda are ongoing and so polarized as to be difficult to resolve. A few scholars propose an initial date for the formation of the earliest of the Vedas could be as early as 4500 BCE. Vedic texts do include references to a remote past, and oral transmission may have passed through a long period before the collected texts assumed their present classification, which is based on families involved in their transmission. The word "*saṃhitā*," or "collection," also presupposes that there was a time before the various *mantras* were "collected together." Whether the collection was made to preserve the Veda, to propagate the Veda, to support ritual performance, for remembering and honoring the *ṛṣis* who fashioned the *mantras*, or for systematic arrangement according to subject matter is not the point. Each of these concerns also points to the fact that transmission from master to apprentice across the generations was taking place over a relatively long period of time.

Vedic texts contain multiple themes. A large number of hymns honor divine powers and energies; many provide directions for correct performance of sacrificial rites with accompanying music and chants, while others offer origin traditions, teaching parables, and ethical instructions. Some hymns pose speculative philosophical questions. For instance: Was there being or nonbeing at the beginning? How did the one being become many? What does the empirical person consist of? Key concepts that continue to shape later tradition are introduced in the Vedas. Among them are *ṛta* and *dharma*, *karma* and *saṃsāra*, *ātman* and Brahman, *prakṛti* and *māyā*.

Precisely what the Vedic hymns and their attendant themes mean, however, is complicated and controversial. The Vedas themselves attest to a simultaneous triple meaning to be found in every hymn: *ādhibhautika*, or reference to external ritual worship; *ādhidaivika*, or cosmogonic meaning that includes knowledge of divine powers; and *ādhyātmika*, or spiritual significance that yields knowledge of the enduring self.

Historically, there have been three influential efforts to settle the question of the meaning of the Vedas: in the ancient Brāhmaṇas; by the medieval sage Sāyaṇa; and widely diverging attempts by modern Indian and Western scholars. The twentieth-century scholar-statesman Sarvepalli Radhakrishnan, like the medieval Sāyaṇa, interpreted Vedic hymns as primitive prayers to various gods who were embodiments of natural powers. That naturalistic perspective sees the Vedic hymns as simple, naive attempts to interpret the world. Maurice Bloomfield, a Western scholar influenced by ideas of natural and cultural evolution, offered a ritual-based interpretation that saw the Vedic hymns as primitive descriptions of various methods of sacrifice. Abel Bergaigne attempted to synthesize natural- and ritual-oriented viewpoints by seeing Vedic hymns as allegories and the gods and goddesses as symbols of ancient social customs and conventions. Georges Dumezil's mythological-sociological approach stressed that the three functions of sovereignty, physical force, and productivity mirrored the tripartite organization of Vedic society. Ārya Samāj founder Svāmī Dayānanda Sarasvatī (1824–83) proposed a monotheistic interpretation of Veda. Brāhmo Samāj founder Rammohun Roy (1772–1883) preferred a monistic interpretation in which Vedic gods were allegorical representations of one absolute or supreme reality. Early twentieth-century activist Balgangadhar Tilak (1856–1920) presented an arctic theory of the Veda by tracing the original home of the Āryans to the polar regions. Aurobindo Ghose (1872–1950) claimed that Vedic hymns expressed India's ancient psychological and spiritual wisdom but in a symbolic language long lost. Recently, Subhash Kak claimed to decode the *Ṛg Veda*. According to him, it is in an astronomical code. Deciphering it reveals a complete map of space and sky as a symbolic altar. He believes that this astronomical paradigm was lost about three thousand years ago, and with it the key to correct understanding of the *Ṛg Veda*.

The Four Vedas

The *Ṛg Veda* usually is said to be the oldest collection (*saṃhitā*) of verses (*ṛc*). It is divided into ten books (*maṇḍala*) containing 1,028 hymns addressed primarily to various deities and recited by priests during rituals. The priests of the *Ṛg Veda* are known as *hotṛ* ("invoker"). Books Two through Seven form the core of the collection, and the others appear to be later additions. The verses were composed in a variety of meters and by a number of sages and bardic families. Since they differ in meter, language, and style, it is often thought that they had been intermittently revealed or composed over a long period. The ten books were organized into separate collections, each identified with an ancient family. The first seven books resemble each other in character and arrangement. They open with hymns addressed to Agni, and (with the exception of the tenth *maṇḍala*) they are followed by hymns addressed to Indra. Book Nine is entirely devoted to hymns to Soma. According to the *Muktikā Upaniṣad*, there were originally twenty-one *śākhā*s, or versions, belonging to different schools. All but one of them are now lost.

The *Sāma Veda* is a collection of songs (*sāman*) set to fixed melodies. It contains 1,810 verses, all but seventy-five of which are found in the *Ṛg Veda*. They are to be sung by priests known as *udgātṛ* during the fire sacrifice. According to the *Muktikā Upaniṣad*, there were originally one thousand *śākhā*s of the *sāman* verses, belonging to different schools, all but three of which are now lost.

The *Yajur Veda* is a collection of sacrificial formulae (*yajus*) set to fixed melodies. Unlike the *Sāma*, which is concerned with just one feature of the *soma* sacrifice, the *Yajur* treats the entire system of Vedic sacrifice. It is concerned with correct ritual performance and the duties of the *adhvaryu* priest. Eventually the *adhvaryu* became the Brāhmaṇa priest, who was entrusted to supervise the entire sacrificial ritual in order to counteract with expiatory formulae (*prāyaścitta*) any mistakes other priests might make in the course of completing the ritual. Two main recensions of the *Yajur Veda* are called *Kṛṣṇa* ("Black") and *Śukla* ("White"). Among the Vedas, the contents of the *Yajur* are the most fully preserved.

The *Atharva Veda* is the wisdom of the fire priests (*atharvan*) and a collection of auspicious "white" magic incantations and terrible "black" magic curses. It is also known as the *Brahma Veda* perhaps because it consists of the Brāhmaṇas (magical formulas), or because it is the special concern of the Brāhmaṇa priest in Vedic ritual, or possibly as a reaction against being excluded from the other three Vedas (*trayī*), and thus declaring its own greatness by stating that it alone of the Vedas deals fully with the absolute reality (Brahman).

Brāhmaṇas and Āraṇyakas

The Brāhmaṇa portion of the Veda contains teachings about "that fundamental principle or power known as Brahman," which involves *mantras* (empowering sacred words) and priests (Brāhmaṇa) who are the repositories of this "expansive sacred sacrificial power." Written mostly in prose rather than verse, they are concerned with practical, everyday duties and rules of conduct. They explain the meaning of a given *mantra*, in what ritual it is to be used, how to use it, and what the result of the ritual will be. The Brāhmaṇa texts trace the origins and importance of individual ritual acts, and this is where we find many enduring ancient cosmogonic traditions and linguistic and etymological explanations that continue to be influential in Hindu tradition. The prose Brāhmaṇas, together with the collected metrical, or *mantra*, portions, are Śruti and are concerned mainly with the solemn, or *śrauta*, ritual. Over time the Brāhmaṇas developed into a separate textual genre characterized by a standardized expository style and a fixed set of Vedic ritual forms. Perhaps this was an impetus for a shift away from actual ritual performances toward internalizing ritual symbols for contemplation and meditation as found in the Āraṇyakas and the Upaniṣads.

The Āraṇyakas (forest books) seem originally to have existed to give mystical, esoteric explanations of secret or dangerous information concerning the fire sacrifices that transformed it into material for meditation. They are a loosely defined class of texts that vary in their contents and serve as a transitional link between the Brāhmaṇas and the Upaniṣads.

Upaniṣads

The Upaniṣads reformulate the earlier Vedic worldview by redirecting the emphasis from the external to the internal, from extrovert to introvert, from object to subject, from ritual to meditation. The term "Upaniṣad" suggests this. Etymologically it means "(steadfastly) sitting (*sad*) nearby (*upa*)," suggesting that pupils are sitting around a teacher or an individual who is opening to awareness of the inner self (*ātman*).

Upaniṣads no longer focused centrally on sacrificial rites, but rather on a direct and life-transforming knowledge of self (*ātman*) and absolute reality (Brahman). The Upaniṣads answer the question, "Who is that one being?" with the equation, Brahman is *ātman*. Brahman—that which is greater than the greatest as well as that which bursts forth as the manifest universe, that one being—is no other than *ātman*, the innermost self in all beings. The Upaniṣads mark a major turning point in the development of Vedic Hindu thought by placing meditation and mystical experience at the center of the religious quest. The quest guided by these sages is deeply experiential. The Upaniṣads, with their focus on experience based in meditation, became used as a sourcebook and reference point not only by subsequent orthodox Hindu thinkers, but also by heterodox dissidents.

The Upaniṣads are not the work of a single author, nor are they systematic treatises on philosophy. A great deal of their immediate appeal consists in their approach to questions about what is real and who is the self, as well as in the fact that they contain riddles, debates, and dialogues. They form the concluding portion of the Veda, and so are called "Vedānta" (*veda* and *anta*; end of Veda). The term "Vedānta" also suggests that the Upaniṣads represent the essence or the goal of the Vedas. The Sanskrit word "*anta*" like the English word "end" can mean both the terminus and the realization or fulfillment.

It is difficult to determine the original date and the total number of the Upaniṣads. They are not a uniform set of texts and seem to have attained the relatively fixed form in which we have received them over several hundreds of years, from about 800 to 300 BCE. Although it is generally said that there are one hundred Upaniṣads, as listed in the *Muktikā Upaniṣad*, more than two hundred ancient texts that bear the name "Upaniṣad" are now known. Orthodox *paṇḍitas* regard ten to fourteen of the ancient texts to be original and important. They include the *Bṛhadāraṇyaka, Chāndogya, Taittirīya, Aitareya, Kauṣītaki, Kena, Kaṭha, Īśā, Śvetāśvatara, Muṇḍaka, Mahānārāyaṇa, Praśna, Māṇḍūkya*, and *Maitrāyaṇīya* (*Maitri*).

One of the great Upaniṣadic seers is Yājñavalkya. In the *Bṛhadāraṇyaka Upaniṣad*, he introduces a number of concepts that remain basic in later Hindu tradition. He speaks about transmigration, which holds that upon death a person is neither annihilated nor transported to some other world, but rather returns to worldly life, to be born and die in some mortal form again. This continuing cycle of births, deaths, and rebirths is called *saṃsāra* ("to wander; to circle") in the Upaniṣads. Yājñavalkya goes on to say that *karma* determines the form of rebirth. In the earlier portions of the Veda, *karma* typically refers to ritual acts, but Yājñavalkya extended the concept to the moral dimension. Thus, character is determined by action and as one sows so one reaps—if not within this lifetime then in some future one. Yājñavalkya foresees an end to the cycle of births and deaths in *mokṣa* as liberation from the suffering one experiences while in the ocean of existence.

Uddālaka Āruṇi, another great sage like Yājñavalkya and also a family man rather than an ascetic, followed ancient tradition by sending his son Śvetaketu away for twelve years of Vedic training. When his son returned, he asked him some questions to see what he had learned about the nature of reality. Concerned by his son's answers, Uddālaka engaged him in an extended conversation to help awaken his appreciation for the nature of things and the deep mystery of Brahman and *ātman*. Two basic learning experiments from their longer dialogue have become famous:

> "Bring a fig," says the father. The son brings it. "Divide it. What do you see there?" "Tiny seeds." "Divide one of the seeds. What do you see?" "Nothing." Then the father told the son: "That subtle essence which you do not perceive, that is the source of this mighty fig tree. That which is so tiny is the self (*ātman*) of this whole world. That is the truth; that is the self. And that's how you are, Śvetaketu."
>
> "Put a handful of salt into a vessel filled with water." The son did as he was told, and the father asked him: "Bring me the salt that you put in the water last evening." "I can't; I can't find it." "Sip from this side of the vessel. What do you taste?" "Salty." "Sip from the other side." "Salty." "Sip from the center." "Salty." "Throw out the water and come back later." Śvetaketu throws it out and when he returns later, the salt is lying there on the ground. The father told him: "You did not see the salt, but it was

always right there. That finest essence is the self (*ātman*) of this whole world. That is the truth; that is the self. And that's how you are, Śvetaketu."

(*Chāndogya Upaniṣad* 6.12–13)

According to these sages, every living being is on the journey of life. At some stage, a human being is likely to become aware that someone or something seems to be missing. The thought arises that "there must be more to life than this." What or where it is one does not know. This begins a search to discover someone or something that can bring fulfillment and complete one's sense of incompleteness. Some people give up, discontinue the search, and settle for coping with immediate pains and seeking passing pleasures. Others become committed to the search, and a wise person eventually may offer them a key insight into the mystery. That wise person may even enable them to directly discern a higher truth as if it were their own discovery. That insight could dissolve their deep sense of frustration, fear, and loss. At the same time, it could awaken the profound bliss of the enduring innermost self. This assessment of the human plight and resolution is Upaniṣadic.

Secondary Sacred Texts: Smṛti

Vedāṅgas

Toward the end of the Vedic period (at about the same time as the production of the principal Upaniṣads) and due to the importance of reciting the Vedic hymns in correct sequence with precisely the right pronunciation when performing the rituals, six Vedāṅgas (Vedic Supplements, or literally, "limbs of the Veda") were composed (between about 800 and 400 BCE). They provided concise technical guidance about subjects that were crucial for proper performance of the Vedic sacrificial rituals. This intense preoccupation with the liturgy gave rise to scholarly disciplines that were part of Vedic learning. These six "limbs" of the Veda are *śikṣā* (instruction) that teaches proper pronunciation; *chandas* that specializes in the explanation and practice of verse meters; *vyākaraṇa*, or the study of grammar; *nirukta* that provides meanings and etymology for rare, difficult, and unusual words (represented by the *Nirukta* of Yāska, about 600 BCE); *kalpa* that discusses correct ways to perform the rituals; and *jyotiṣa*, which is a system of astronomy and astrology used to determine the right times for rituals. The Vedāṅgas themselves are not part of the Śruti, but they are indispensable for those who perform Vedic rituals.

Between the Śruti and the Smṛti texts fall a number of texts of special importance known as the Kalpasūtras. They are a collection of aphorisms dealing with ritual performance. The composition of these texts began around 600 BCE by Brāhmaṇas belonging to the ritual schools (*śākhā*), each of which was attached to a particular recension of one of the four Vedas. A complete Kalpasūtra contains four principal components: Śrautasūtra, which establishes the rules for performing the more complex rituals of public Vedic sacrifices; Śulbasūtra, which shows how to make the geometric calculations necessary for the proper construction of the ritual arena; Gṛhyasūtra, which explains the rules for performing domestic rites, including the lifecycle rituals called *saṃskāra*s; and a Dharmasūtra, which contains rules for the conduct of life. By the time these were produced, society probably was becoming ritually stratified into the four main hereditary classes, each of which had its own duties (*dharma*). The ideal life was constructed through sacramental rituals, performed for the upper classes. These guided the development of a person from conception to cremation through a series of lifecycle rites.

Dharmasūtra and Dharmaśāstra

The Dharmasūtras and Dharmaśāstras are manuals on *dharma*, which contain rules of conduct as they were practiced in the traditional Vedic schools. They address the duties of people at various stages of life, or *āśrama*s, dietary regulations, offenses and expiations, and the rights and duties of kings. They also discuss purification rites, funeral ceremonies, forms of hospitality, and daily oblations and mention juridical matters. The more important of these texts are the Gautamasūtras, Baudhāyanasūtras, and Āpastambasūtras. Their contents were further developed in the more systematic Dharmaśāstra, which in turn became the basis of Hindu law. The most famous of these texts is the *Mānavadharmaśāstra* (Dharma Text of Manu) or the *Manusmṛti* (Laws of Manu) (about 200 CE). It is a work of encyclopedic scope and creates a model of how life is and should be lived, in public and in private, by priests and kings and their subjects, by women as well as by men. It is about *dharma* and *karma*. The influence of Manu is enormous. It guided Hindu society in practical morality and law, and later served as a lens through which Western Orientalists during the colonial era sought to reconstruct an adequate picture of classical Hinduism.

Itihāsa

The two Hindu epics (*itihāsa*) about 400 BCE to 600 CE—the *Rāmāyaṇa* (third–sixth centuries BCE) and the *Mahābhārata*—though not Śruti, are still considered inspired and authoritative. In fact, they have a far more influential role in the everyday lives of most Hindus than the Vedas. Children grow up hearing these stories from their parents and grandparents. Heroes from the epics are depicted on television and in the movies. For most Hindus, the term "sacred book" connotes these two epics in particular. They depict the wanderings of prince Rāma in the *Rāmāyaṇa* and the Great War of the Bharata clan in the *Mahābhārata*.

Rāmāyaṇa (The Deeds of Rāma)

The story of the life and adventures of Rāma is narrated in the *Rāmāyaṇa* by Sage Vālmiki, who is the traditional author of the epic. The epic has been memorized, publicly recited, and enjoyed by Hindus for centuries as a source of inspiration and spiritual uplift. It serves as a sourcebook for *dharma* as depicted through its main characters. Vaiṣṇavas call it the key scripture for teaching absolute self-surrender to god (*śaraṇāgati śāstra*).

In the introduction, the sage Vālmiki goes into the forest in search of firewood and *dūrvā*-grass for his daily sacrificial ritual. He looks up into a tree where he sees a pair of lovebirds sitting on a branch. Suddenly, the male bird is shot dead by the arrow of a hunter. The female bird lets out a cry of anguish and terror. A spontaneous utterance wells up in the soon-to-be poet's heart, and he utters the now-famous line condemning the terrible crime, "Since, O hunter, you killed one of this pair of birds, distracted at the height of passion, you shall not live for very long" (*Rāmāyaṇa* 1.2.14). He reflects on this utterance. By observing life, especially the tragic and painful side of life, something higher emerges. The tragic cry of the bird when it was separated from its mate by the cruel blow of destiny stirs the poet's heart, and the *Rāmāyaṇa* itself becomes a text of parting and separation. The main characters Daśaratha (Rāma's father), Kausalyā (mother), Bharata (younger brother), and Sītā (wife) are all separated from Rāma.

The main story focuses on the young prince Rāma, who is born by a boon given to his father Daśaratha. He has three half-brothers, Lakṣmaṇa, Bharata, and Śatrughna, also born due to the same boon. On the eve of his coronation, Daśaratha exiles Rāma due to a promise he had made to his youngest wife, Kaikeyī, with the result that Rāma is deprived of the kingdom to which he is heir and is sent into the forest with his wife Sītā and his brother Lakṣmaṇa. His father dies of a broken heart, and his brother Bharata serves as the kingdom's caretaker while Rāma is in exile. Sītā is abducted from the forest by Rāvaṇa, the demon-king of Laṅkā. While they search for Sītā, the brothers ally themselves with a monkey-king, Sugrīva, whose general, Hanumān, is sent to Sītā in Laṅkā to let her know that her rescue is being arranged. Rāma and his allies then defeat Rāvaṇa, rescue Sītā, and return to the kingdom. When they return, their subjects express doubt that Sītā was able to protect her chastity while abducted. To placate them, Rāma banishes Sītā to a hermitage, where she bears him two sons, Lava and Kuśa, and eventually dies by reentering the earth from which she had been born.

Both Rāma and Sītā have become idealized figures in Hindu tradition. Rāma is depicted as the perfect male human being and a model of the ideal son, brother, husband, warrior, and ruler. Rāma's reign becomes the prototype of a harmonious and just kingdom. Rāma and Sītā model the ideal of conjugal love; Rāma's relationship to his father is the ideal of filial love; and Rāma and Lakṣmaṇa represent perfect fraternal love. The *Rāmāyaṇa* also identifies Rāma with Viṣṇu (as Viṣṇu's seventh *avatāra*), and so makes him divine as well as human.

There are many vernacular versions of the *Rāmāyaṇa*. The most famous of them include Tulsīdās' (about 1570 CE) Hindi *Rāmcaritmānas* (The Lake of Rāma's Deeds); Kampaṉ's (about 1100 CE) Tamil *Irāmāvatāram* (The Descent of Lord Rāma); *Adhyātma Rāmāyaṇa*, in which Rāma is no longer merely an *avatāra*, but the supreme *parabrahman*; *Yoga Vāsiṣtha Rāmāyaṇa*, a nondualistic philosophical allegory; and *Adbhūta Rāmāyaṇa*, a devotional text that presents Sītā as the *śakti* and more powerful than Rāma. Though details of the story differ in the alternative versions, the story of Rāma and Sītā and their supreme devotee Hanumān have endured. Temples to them are found throughout India, and, according to tradition, as long as the rivers flow on earth and human beings live, so will the story of Rāma and Sītā endure. Most versions of the *Rāmāyaṇa* end with the declaration, "Whoever hears, sings, recites, or meditates on this story, attains the highest state" (4.30.15).

Mahābhārata (The Great War of the Bharata Tribe)

The *Mahābhārata* is an encyclopedic work, the longest poem in the world, and a veritable treasure house of secular and religious Hindu lore. It contains stories of seers, sages, and divine incarnations; family feuds; beautiful women and dutiful wives; valiant warriors and righteous kings; heinous villains and evil demons; law, morality, and justice; and the way to ultimate happiness and liberation.

The *Mahābhārata*, a text of some one hundred thousand verses attributed to the sage Vyāsa, is the story of a great struggle among the descendants of a king called Bhārata (the modern name of India). The central plot concerns a war between the five sons of Pāṇḍu, known as the Pāṇḍavas (Yudhiṣṭhira, Bhīma, Arjuna, and the twins Nakula and Sahadeva), and the sons of Pāṇḍu's blind brother Dhṛtarāṣṭra, known as the Kauravas. They are cousins, but the Kauravas try to cheat the Pāṇḍavas out of their share of the kingdom, and thus war becomes inevitable, a war that eventually leads to the destruction of the entire race, except for one survivor who continues the dynasty. Each of the Pāṇḍavas is the son of a god (Dharma, Vāyu, Indra, and the Aśvins, respectively), and the epic is deeply infused with religious implications.

By the time of the *Mahābhārata*, Vedic *dharma* and the way of life that was centered in sacrificial rituals had fallen into neglect and become virtually forgotten. In the *Rāmāyaṇa*, everyone knows what should be done and how to do it. The only issue is whether they will. But in the *Mahābhārata*, doubt and uncertainty pervade the text. This is most evident when Arjuna, facing his cousins and other relatives on the battlefield as the war is about to begin, becomes filled with doubt and refuses to fight. Kṛṣṇa, the eighth *avatāra* of Viṣṇu, is on the side of the Pāṇḍavas. He is Arjuna's brother-in-law and friend, and having refused to wield arms in the battle, he nevertheless serves as Arjuna's charioteer, a role with allegorical significance. Kṛṣṇa tells Arjuna that he must fight; it is the duty of a warrior to do battle in a righteous cause. One must fight for *dharma* after exhausting all peaceful means. The conversation that Arjuna and Kṛṣṇa have on the battlefield before the start of the war is known as the *Bhagavad Gītā*.

The Great War lasts for eighteen days. The Pāṇḍavas, employing both fair and foul means, emerge victorious. However, very few who had entered the war on either side are alive when it ends. After they win the war and after the demise of Kṛṣṇa, the Pāṇḍavas leave the kingdom in the hands of Arjuna's grandson Parikṣit and depart towards the Himālayas on their way to Indra's heaven. This war, according to Hindu tradition, marks the beginning of the current Kali Yuga, the darkening age of unrighteousness, dissention, and strife.

The Kṛṣṇa of the *Mahābhārata* is primarily a hero, a king, a friend, and an ally of the Pāṇḍavas. Although the epic furnishes some information about Kṛṣṇa, the primary religious sourcebook for him is the *Bhāgavata Purāṇa*. In the *Mahābhārata* not everyone considers Kṛṣṇa to be a divine incarnation of Viṣṇu. Kṛṣṇa helps the Pāṇḍava brothers to obtain their kingdom and when the kingdom is taken from them, helps them to regain it. In the process, he emerges as a great teacher who reveals the *Bhagavad Gītā* to Arjuna and subsequently achieves heroic feats.

Apart from their influence as Sanskrit texts, the *Rāmāyaṇa* and the *Mahābhārata* have made an impact throughout India and Southeast Asia, where their stories are repeatedly retold. When these two epics were made into television series and broadcast throughout India (during 1987–88 and 1988–90, respectively), they attracted the largest audience in the history of Indian television.

Bhagavad Gītā (The Song of the Lord)

The *Bhagavad Gītā* became a highly influential Hindu religious text from the early modern period to the present even though it is not Śruti. It is a brief text in the form of a reported dialogue, with seven hundred verses divided into eighteen short chapters. A well-known analogy declares that "The Upaniṣads are the cow; Arjuna is the calf; Kṛṣṇa is the milkman; and the *Bhagavad Gītā* is the milk." Another analogy is that "The Vedas are the cow; the Upaniṣads are the milk; the *Bhagavad Gītā* is the butter."

The *Bhagavad Gītā* is esteemed for many reasons. It is part of the *Mahābhārata*; it features two charismatic characters, Arjuna and Kṛṣṇa; the dialogue structure gives it dramatic interest; the setting is extremely serious with the future of the country and the fate of righteousness at stake; it has a simple style and a spirit of inclusive toleration; at its center is a dilemma for which a solution is provided; and Kṛṣṇa makes several avatāric statements about himself, including the promise that he will incarnate from age to age to protect *dharma* whenever righteousness diminishes and evil arises.

While the opposing armies in the Mahābhārata War are prepared to begin battle, Arjuna, the most famous warrior of his day, despairs at the thought of having to kill his kinsmen. He puts down his weapons. Kṛṣṇa, his charioteer, cousin, friend, and adviser, chides Arjuna for his failure to do his duty as a warrior and tells him not to grieve for what is about to happen. The dilemma is that if he fights he will kill his kinsmen and if he does not fight he will disregard his *dharma*, be guilty of cowardice, and allow injustice and unrighteousness to triumph.

Kṛṣṇa advises Arjuna by describing the soul (*ātman*): it is immortal and cannot be killed when the body is killed. The soul neither is born nor dies. It is indestructible and periodically discards worn out bodies and takes on new ones just as a person will discard old clothes and acquire new ones.

> The truly wise mourn neither for the living nor for the dead. . . . Material bodies are known to come to an end, but the embodied soul is eternal, indestructible, and immeasurable; therefore, Arjuna, fight the battle. He who thinks this soul a slayer and he who thinks it slain, both fail to understand it neither slays nor is slain.
>
> (*Bhagavad Gītā* 2.11, 2.18–19)

Arjuna's concerns seem to have merit, but Kṛṣṇa soon reveals that the attraction to "renunciation" is escapist and motivated by the wish to avoid worldly responsibilities. Arjuna distinguishes between his own people and others, but for a true renunciant all people are the same. His sadness and despondency reveal that he is attached to things of this world, and not his duty (*dharma*) as a warrior. Finally, Arjuna fails to understand for what he should fight. A warrior serves his king and country, but he fights in a just cause for the sake of *dharma* itself, regardless of the outcome. The cause is just, and so Kṛṣṇa admonishes him to go into battle.

Kṛṣṇa teaches Arjuna that even if he does not comprehend the nature of the soul or the indestructible inner self, he should perform his duty for its own sake. In contrast to the world-affirming orientation of Vedic ritualists and in contrast to the world-renouncing ideal of the sages in the Upaniṣads, Kṛṣṇa in the *Bhagavad Gītā* harmonizes the two paths by teaching that in the world action is necessary and unavoidable, but that the right relationship to action requires the sacrifice of selfish desire and the renunciation of attachment to the outcome while continuing to act responsibly as determined by one's *dharma*.

> Be intent on action, not on the fruits of action; avoid attraction to the fruits and attachment to inaction. Perform actions, firm in discipline, relinquishing attachment; be impartial to failure and success, this equanimity is called Yoga. . . . Wise men disciplined by understanding relinquish the fruits born of action; freed from these bonds of rebirth, they reach a place beyond sorrow.
>
> (*Bhagavad Gītā* 2.47–48, 2.51)

Kṛṣṇa presents three different ways to release the inner self from the bondage of rebirths and to release Arjuna from his moral dilemma. These ways are the path of selfless action (*karma-yoga*), the path of devotion (*bhakti-yoga*), and the path of divine wisdom (*jñāna-yoga*). As he does this, Kṛṣṇa also makes statements about himself that are unique and open a new dimension in Hindu theology. The Upaniṣads were reluctant to describe Brahman, but in the *Bhagavad Gītā*, Kṛṣṇa reveals himself as the highest spirit or supreme lord and grants Arjuna a vision of his multiple (and overwhelmingly powerful and awe-inspiring) forms.

> Though myself unborn, undying, the lord of creatures, I fashion nature, which is mine, and I come into being through my own mysterious power (*māyā*). . . . I am the universal father, mother, granter of all, grandfather, object of knowledge, purifier, holy syllable *oṃ*, and the *Ṛg*, *Sāma*, and *Yajur Vedas*. I am the goal, sustainer, lord, witness, shelter, refuge, friend, creation and annihilation, basis of everything, resting place, and eternal seed.
>
> (*Bhagavad Gītā* 4.6, 9.17–18)

Kṛṣṇa also makes an avatāric promise to humanity, that "Whenever and wherever there is decline of righteousness and rise of unrighteousness, at that time I descend myself. To preserve good, destroy evil, and set the standard for sacred duty, I come into being, age after age" (*Bhagavad Gītā* 4.7–8). And he promises, "Whoever worships me, thinking solely of me, always disciplined, will reach me" (*Bhagavad Gītā* 8.8).

The *Bhagavad Gītā* is a classic of spiritual literature, and its worldwide influence is enormous. Although brief and accessible, it has inspired many interpretations and commentaries, the earliest known being Bhāskara and Śaṅkara in the seventh–eighth centuries. Among its several contributions to Hindu tradition are a strong emphasis on devotion to a personal god inclusive of the Upaniṣadic Brahman, integration of renunciation with action (living in the world without being of it), three main paths to liberation (the basis for a *dharma*-based Brāhmaṇism, an enlightenment-based asceticism, and a devotion-based theism), and an *avatāra* doctrine.

By requiring that devotees fulfill their *dharma*-based duties ("better one's own duty ill-performed than another's well-performed" [18.47a]), the *Bhagavad Gītā* integrates liberation-oriented ascetic disciplines into the demands of daily and family life. For those who support a family and work in this world, the *Bhagavad Gītā* gives a promise of final liberation. Kṛṣṇa's teaching of divine presence in all beings means that the wise see no differences of value between their fellow creatures and will love the divine in all of them. Yet, by emphasizing that different types of people prefer one path to liberation rather than another and have specific responsibilities based on birth into a particular caste, the *Bhagavad Gītā* provides support for the caste system's genetic determinism. In short, it is progressive and universalistic, and yet at the same time, conservative and particularistic.

Purāṇas

The Purāṇas (literally, "ancient") are an extensive body of literature concerned with the creation of the cosmos; traditions and genealogies of deities, kings, and sages; rituals and rules for living; and descriptions of pilgrimages, hells, heavens, and the end of the world. In short, they are a compendium of histories of India and repositories of popular religious lore. Traditionally they are supposed to deal with five topics (*pañcalakṣaṇa*): creation (*sarga*), dissolution (*pratisarga*), lineage (*vaṃśa*), epochs (*manvantara*), and predictions of future lineage (*vaṃśānucarita*), though not all of them actually do so. There are eighteen major Purāṇas, characterized into three categories: (1) *sāttvika* that honor Viṣṇu: the *Bhāgavata*, *Garuḍa*, *Nārada*, *Padma*, *Varāha*, and *Viṣṇu Purāṇa*s; (2) *rājasika* that honor Brahmā: the *Brahmā*, *Brahmāṇḍa*, *Brahmavaivarta*, *Bhaviṣya*, *Mārkaṇḍeya*, and *Vāmana Purāṇa*s; and (3) *tāmasika* that honor Śiva: the *Agni*, *Kūrma*, *Liṅga*, *Matsya*, *Śiva* (*Vāyu*), and *Skanda Purāṇa*s. This system of classification is mentioned often but reveals little about the contents of these texts. Most do not deal exclusively with only one deity, even though each has a sectarian affiliation.

The Purāṇas preserve a wealth of material for understanding the traditions associated with what are now known as the great Purānic deities, Viṣṇu, Śiva, the Devī, Gaṇeśa, Agni, Skanda, and others. Each text presents a version of the world and a representation of Hindu beliefs and practices from that perspective. The Purāṇas, along with the epics, became the *de facto* scriptures of most Hindus. Unlike Vedic knowledge, which was limited to initiated males from the three highest status groups by birth, the Purāṇas were available to all men, women, and children. How have most people learned the contents of these texts? Performances by musicians, poets, storytellers, dancers, and dramatic actors, as well as paintings and sculptures at small shrines and great temples, communicated their contents selectively but memorably. Through all of these media, the Purāṇas influenced the arts of societies all across South, Southeast, and East Asia. Much of their contents may have been originally non-Brāhmaṇaic, but they were accepted and adapted by the Brāhmaṇas, which extended the range of traditional practices and beliefs.

The Purāṇas are said to have been composed starting around 300 BCE and continuing until around 1000 CE. Tradition ascribes authorship of the eighteen major Purāṇas to Vyāsa.

There are also eighteen subordinate texts known as Upapurānas, though there are variations as to which texts are reckoned part of each set of eighteen. There is also a different class of Purāṇas known as Sthalapurānas, which deal with cultural histories associated with a particular holy place or temple.

Vernacular Literature

For a long time, it was considered a sacrilege to write a religious or philosophical work in a language other than Sanskrit, but to be read or heard and understood by most people, scriptural texts had to be written in a language everyone would understand. In the Tamil country of the south, the *Tēvāram* (The Garland for the God) and the *Tiruvācakam* (The Sacred Utterance) appeared among the Śaiva saints; and the *Nālāyira Tivyaprapantam*, a collection of four thousand hymns of the Āḷvārs, appeared among the Vaiṣṇava saints. Another important Tamil text is Kampaṉ's *Rāmāyaṇam*. In Maharashtra in the west, singer-saints composed hymns and *abhaṅgas*, devotional songs in the Marathi language that express longing for the divine. These include the works of Jñāneśvar (about 1275–96), Nāmdev (about 1270–1350), Tukārām (about 1598–1649), Eknāth (about 1548–1609), and Samārth Rāmdās (about 1608–81). In Karnataka in the upper southwest, the *vacanas* by Basava (about 1106–68) are simple prose poems set to music. There are also twelfth-century compositions by Allamaprabhu and by Mahādēviyakka. In the northern region, a number of religious works were produced in an evolving Hindi language: the nonsectarian song-poems of Kabīr (about 1440–1518); the *Rāmcaritmānas* of Tulsīdās (about 1543–1623); Sūrdās' (about 1483–1563) *Sūrsāgar*, or "Ocean of the Poems of Sūr," which is a collection of poems on the theme of the childhood of Kṛṣṇa; and Mirābāi's (about 1503–73) passionate love songs (*bhajan*) to Kṛṣṇa. In northeast India, there is a rich tradition of devotional works in Bengali, Maithili, and other regional languages that are inspired by the love of Rādhā for Kṛṣṇa (Caṇḍidās, about 1339–99; Vidyāpati, about 1360–1448; and Caitanya, about 1458–1533), as well as works in honor of Kālī (Rāmprasād, about 1718–75).

Philosophical Systems

The term "*darśana*" is the nearest analogue to "philosophy" in Hindu tradition and refers to traditional systems of argument, commentary, and analysis. The *darśanas*, or six classical philosophical systems, are Nyāya, Vaiśeṣika, Sāṃkhya, Yoga, Mīmāṃsā, and Vedānta. They developed in parallel to one another over the course of ongoing debates for the past two thousand years. These systems include a diversity of theories and subschools, so it is difficult to single out characteristics common to all of them. However, these *darśanas* accept Vedic revelation even when highly critical of it, begin with spiritual dissatisfaction and culminate in a spiritual orientation, are exegetical, and assume there is a higher reality beyond the physical, whether or not it is theistic.

The various philosophical systems were based on presystematic Vedic and Upaniṣadic teachings and at first were systematized in the form of condensed aphorisms (*sūtra*) or brief threads of thought that expressed the gist of the system by using language in a concise, telegraphic style. Each *sūtra* was easy to memorize and enabled their founders to express precisely the content of the system. However, because the aphorisms are pithy, abstruse, and difficult to understand without additional explanation, they are open to different interpretations. Therefore, commentary (*bhāṣya*) literature became the way to teach or communicate a system. Beyond them, subcommentaries (*vārttika*) and glosses (*ṭīkā*) were composed to interpret both *sūtra* texts and commentaries. A third category of philosophical works consists of manuals, independent treatises, dialectical classics, and critiques. They instruct students belonging to a school and offer resources to combat criticism from opponents. Even though no new *darśana*s were subsequently founded, independent thinking, new innovations, and original insights have continued to develop within the context created by the classical ones.

Little is known about the founders (*sūtrakāra*) and central commentators (*bhāṣyakāra*) who helped to shape the main philosophical systems. Nothing can be said with any precision about their dates and places of birth, identity, or life's activities. But, traditionally, the classical philosophers disclaim any originality for themselves or for the doctrines they expound. They understand themselves to be only faithful transmitters of an ancient tradition that preserves a timeless truth that is great enough to merit repeated refinement and exposition without needing or allowing any originality or innovation. An underlying assumption in Hindu tradition is that no individual can claim to be the first to see the truth. The most one can do is (re)state, explicate, and defend unchanging truth. The result is respect for the tasks of preserving and expounding what came before and commands priority of place and position.

It was in traditional Sanskrit doxographies, literature that summarizes and classifies the main schools or systems, that the term "*darśana*" gained currency. We will follow the doxographical approach, which classifies Hindu philosophy into six orthodox or "affirmative" (*āstika*) schools that are linked together in three pairs or allied systems: Nyāya-Vaiśeṣika, Sāṃkhya-Yoga, and Mīmāṃsā-Vedānta.

Nyāya School

Nyāya is famous for acute analysis of discursive thought. It consists of three main parts: a methodology for investigating the nature of things through valid means of knowledge (*pramāṇa*), the art of debate through syllogistic reasoning (logic), and specific knowledge about the meaning of words, nature, the soul, and the divine. The term "Nyāya" means "logical reasoning," and this school is best known for developing the rules of logic and epistemology, for providing a framework and set of concepts to practice philosophy. Gautama (about 400–100 BCE) is said to be the founder of the Nyāya school and author of the *Nyāyasūtra*. Gautama's ideas were later explained, amplified, systematized, and fashioned into a coherent system by Vātsyāyana (about 300–400 CE) in his *Nyāyasūtrabhāṣya*.

Vaiśeṣika School

Vaiśeṣika emphasizes ontology and cooperates closely with Nyāya on matters of epistemology. Kaṇāda (about 500–300 BCE) is the founder of the Vaiśeṣika school. He is the author of the *Vaiśeṣikasūtra*. Vaiśeṣika's name is derived from "*viśeṣa*," which means "the characteristics that distinguish a particular thing from all other things." Thus, the Vaiśeṣika, like Nyāya, is a school of pluralistic realism, which implies that the world exists independent of a thinking mind and consists of a plurality of reals that are externally related. The distinguishing doctrine of the Vaiśeṣika school is that nature is atomic. Atoms are eternal and indivisible, and thus creation or recreation consists in the combination of separate atoms into the elements. Prasastapāda (about 400 CE) wrote the earliest extant commentary on the *Vaiśeṣikasūtra* known as the *Padārthadharmasaṃgraha*.

Sāṃkhya School

The Sāṃkhya school is said by its expositors to be one of the oldest (if not the oldest) among the schools of systematic Hindu philosophy. They claim that many of its ideas can be found in the *Ṛg Veda* and scattered throughout the Upaniṣads. The supreme sage Kapila, who is said to be the founder of Sāṃkhya, is the author of the *Sāṃkhyasūtra* (about 500 BCE, now lost). The earliest extant authoritative text of the classical Sāṃkhya is the *Sāṃkhyakārikā* of Īśvarakṛṣṇa (about 300–400 CE). It enumerates the patterns and processes of the material elements as they evolve and dissolve in the material reality. It teaches liberation through discrimination between spirit (*puruṣa*) and nature (*prakṛti*). Sāṃkhya had a significant influence on the development of the other philosophical schools and on many aspects of Hindu culture. Some of its teachings, such as the three qualities or constituents (*guṇa*), the dualism of consciousness and material nature (*puruṣa, prakṛti*), and the evolutionary theory of the twenty-four principles (*tattva*) have become an integral part of Hindu tradition at large.

The key teaching of Sāṃkhya is that reality is twofold. Spirit (*puruṣa*) is of the nature of noninteractive consciousness. It is untouched by matter, unchanging, and multiple. Its observing presence is the reason that matter evolves and changes. Matter (*prakṛti*) is nonconscious, single, ever changing, subtle, and invisible, and therefore must be inferred from its creations. *Prakṛti* is composed of the three qualities (*guṇa*) and is the ultimate cause of the universe, though without cause itself. Nothing exists apart from the two principles: selves or spirits that never are an object and matter that always is an (inferred) object. Selves can discriminate, matter cannot. Spirits neither are born nor die, are nonactive, and are patient observers. Matter is active, ever changing, and undergoes cycles of evolution and absorption. The supreme goal of life is for selves to know by discrimination that they have nothing to do with matter and always are inherently free from it. Liberation, then, is a phenomenal appearance because truly spirit always is free. Bondage is misidentification, the mere seeming activity of nature toward one who does not discriminate and fails to observe the difference of *puruṣa* from *prakṛti*.

Material nature, according to Sāṃkhya, undergoes continuous transformations. It is the primary matrix out of which all differentiations arise and to which they return. Of nature's three qualities, *sattva* is luminosity and intelligence; *rajas* is energy and the activity of discontinuity and change; and *tamas* is inertia, heavy, coarse, and the principle of continuity. When the equilibrium of the three qualities is disturbed, matter evolves in the following order: *prakṛti* → *mahat* or *buddhi* (intelligence) → *ahaṃkāra* (egoism) → *manas* (mind) →

jñānendriya (sense organs): hearing (*śrota*), touch (*tvak*), sight (*cakṣus*), taste (*rasana*), and smell (*ghrāṇa*) → *karmendriya* (action organs): speech (*vāk*), prehension (*pāṇi*), movement (*pāda*), excretion (*pāyu*), and generation (*upastha*) → *tanmātra* (subtle elements): sound (*śabda*), touch (*sparśa*), sight (*rūpa*), taste (*rasa*), and smell (*gandha*) → *mahābhūta* (gross elements): ether (*ākāśa*), air (*vāyu*), fire (*tejas*), water (*ap*), and earth (*pṛthivī*). This emanation scheme may be seen as both an account of cosmic evolution and an analysis of the factors involved in experience.

Yoga School

Various yogic spiritual practices are mentioned in several of the major Upaniṣads. Etymologically, the word "*yoga*" derives from the Sanskrit root *yuj*, meaning "to bind together, to unite." What is joined? Some say it is the individual self with the transcendental self; others say it is union with one's chosen deity (*Yogasūtra* 2.44); still others say it is the process of joining the breath, the syllable *oṃ*, and this world in its manifoldness. *Yoga* has been defined by Vyāsa as "enstasis" and by Patañjali as the "cessation of the mind's fluctuations." In its broadest sense, *yoga* is a method for unifying consciousness as well as the resulting state of union with the object of contemplation, and it can refer to nearly all of the spiritual techniques, values, attitudes, and systems of traditional India.

The basic principles of the Yoga *darśana* were first summarized systematically in the *Yogasūtra* of Patañjali (third century BCE). The Yoga system stands in close relation to Sāṃkhya, adopting its metaphysics, though it adds a twenty-sixth principle (the supreme lord, Īśvara) to the Sāṃkhya list of twenty-five. While Sāṃkhya is primarily intellectualistic and emphasizes metaphysical knowledge and discrimination as the means to liberation, Yoga is voluntaristic and emphasizes self-control as the primary means to liberation.

The *Yogasūtra* is a short work of 196 aphorisms divided into four chapters. The first chapter defines *yoga* as "the cessation of the mind's fluctuations." Modulations of thought disturb pure consciousness, and practice of detachment stills them. A general goal is to experience the isolation of spirit (*puruṣa*) from nature (*prakṛti*) by mental discipline. The second chapter begins by delineating afflictions of the disturbed mind and describing the "limbs" of practice. External practices of the eightfold yogic path (*aṣṭānga-mārga*) include the five abstentions (*yama*) of nonviolence, truthfulness, nonstealing, continence, and nonpossession, as well as the five observances (*niyama*) of purity, contentment, austerity, study, and surrender. These are supported by physical postures (*āsana*); breathing techniques (*prāṇāyāma*); and withdrawal of attention from sensory objects (*pratyāhāra*). The third chapter introduces the last three limbs: concentration (*dhāraṇā*), meditation (*dhyāna*), and absorption (*samādhi*). The fourth chapter is a general exposition of yogic study and practice leading to liberation.

Mīmāṃsā School

The first four orthodox schools of Nyāya, Vaiśeṣika, Sāṃkhya, and Yoga are orthodox in name only. They are not directly dependent upon the Veda, do not explicitly interpret the

Veda, and do not look to the Veda for justification of their doctrines. But Mīmāṃsā is a genuinely Vedic tradition. Its basic assumption is that the scriptural texts are authoritative and faultless and have to be interpreted in order to explain away any apparent contradictions. It is a system centered on investigating the nature of Vedic injunctions; its investigation led to the development of principles of scriptural interpretation and to theories of meaning. The Pūrva Mīmāṃsā (First Investigation), also known as Karma Mīmāṃsā (Study of [Ritual] Action), of Jaimini (about 300–200 BCE) concerns the proper interpretation of Vedic texts. Jaimini, who composed the *Pūrvamīmāṃsāsūtra*, proposed that Vedic injunctions prescribe actions and that those actions are the means to the attainment of desirable goals including heaven. The earliest extant commentary upon Jaimini's work is the *Pūrvamīmāṃsāsūtra-bhāṣya* of Śabara (about 200 CE). Prabhākara (about 700 CE) and Kumārila Bhaṭṭa (about 700 CE) interpreted his commentary, which gave rise to two main schools of interpretation: Prabhākara's and Kumārila Bhaṭṭa's.

Mīmāṃsā's central concern is "duty" (*dharma*), which it defines as the desired object (*artha*) whose desirability is testified only by the injunctive statements of the Vedas. The *Pūrvamīmāṃsāsūtra* commences with the aim of ascertaining the nature of religious *dharma*. Religious duty is not a physical entity, so it cannot be known through perception or any other means of valid knowledge that presuppose the effort of perception. Thus, Mīmāṃsā concludes that religious duty is knowable only through scripture, and the essence of the scripture is injunctions and commandments which tell what ought to be done (*vidhi*) and what ought not to be done (*niṣedha*).

Vedānta School

Historically, the concluding portions of the Vedas (the Upaniṣads) were known as the Vedānta, and the philosophical schools that based their thought upon the Upaniṣads are also called Vedānta. Since the Upaniṣads do not provide a consistent system, it was necessary to systematize their teachings. Bādarāyaṇa (about 400 BCE) attempted to do so in the form of short aphorisms called *sūtra*s. His work, the *Vedāntasūtra*, is also known as the *Brahmasūtra* because it is an exposition of, and inquiry into, Brahman; or the *Śārīrakasūtra* because it is concerned with the nature and destiny of the embodied soul; or the *Bhikṣusūtra* because those competent to study it are renunciates; or the *Uttara-mīmāṃsāsūtra* because it is an inquiry into the final sections of the Veda. Its first *sūtra* begins, "*athāto brahma-jijñāsā*" (Now, therefore, the inquiry into the real nature of Brahman, the absolute). Together with the *Dharmasūtra* of Jaimini, which is an inquiry into the duties (*dharma*) enjoined by the Vedas, these two investigations form a systematic inquiry into the content and meaning of the entire Veda, and thus these two *mīmāṃsā*s are orthodox schools *par excellence*. Unlike Jaimini, who laid stress on the ritual portions of the Vedas and puts forth a path of ritual action (*karmakāṇḍa*), Bādarāyaṇa emphasized the philosophical portions, the Upaniṣads, and recommends the path of contemplative wisdom (*jñānakāṇḍa*).

There are several Vedāntic schools based on three primary sourcebooks: the Upaniṣads, the *Bhagavad Gītā*, and the *Brahmasūtra*. Together these are known as the triple canon of

Vedānta. The two main schools are unqualified nondualistic, or Advaita (with Śaṅkara, about 650 CE, as its main proponent), and qualified dualistic, or Dvaita (as expounded in Rāmānuja's [about 1027–1147 CE] qualified nondualism [Viśiṣṭādvaita] and Madhva's [about 1199–1276] dualism [Dvaita]). Other theistic Vedāntic *bhāṣyakāras* include Bhāskara (eighth century), Nimbārka (eleventh century), Vallabha (about 1479–1531), and Caitanya (about 1485–1533). No commentary on the *Brahmasūtra* survives before Śaṅkara's *bhāṣya* (about 650–700 CE), though there are stray references in various works to earlier thinkers.

All Vedānta schools agree that the Upaniṣads teach that Brahman is the ultimate principle underlying the physical universe and individual souls. The chief difference among the Vedānta schools is in how the world and the individual souls can be connected with Brahman. Certain passages in the Upaniṣads affirm the nondifference of the world and the individual souls from Brahman, and there are others that speak of their difference from Brahman. The apparently contradictory passages have to be reconciled, and the mode of reconciliation adopted by each school represents its basic philosophical position.

According to Advaita Vedānta, the Upaniṣadic texts teaching nondifference are primary and those teaching difference are secondary, intended only to lead to the real teaching of nonduality. Brahman is the only reality, and the universe and the individual soul have no existence apart from Brahman. In an oft-quoted verse, "Brahman is real, the universe is nonreal, and individuals are not different from Brahman." Further, Brahman, which is the only reality, is beyond all determination, all attributes. It is only due to ignorance that the attributeless Brahman appears as though endowed with attributes. Thus it follows that Advaita asserts that *karmakāṇḍa* and *jñānakāṇḍa* are independent of each other, whereas Viśiṣṭādvaita argues that they jointly constitute a single work, with right action first and contemplative insight after it.

According to the Viśiṣṭādvaita and the Bhedābheda schools, the texts teaching difference and those teaching nondifference are equally important. The universe and the individual souls are therefore different as well as nondifferent from Brahman. Insofar as the world and souls are imperfect, they are dependent and different from Brahman, who is perfect and independent. At the same time, they are nondifferent from Brahman in the sense that they form the body and the attributes of Brahman.

According to Dvaita Vedānta, the texts teaching difference convey the real teaching of the Upaniṣads. The universe and the individual souls are absolutely different from Brahman. However, this does not mean that they are independent realities. Brahman is the only independent reality, and the world and the individual souls, while separate from Brahman, are dependent thereon. The Upaniṣadic texts that teach nondifference are intended only to emphasize the independent character of Brahman.

Other Philosophies

Kauṭilīya's *Arthaśāstra* (about 321–296 BCE) systematized the science of political economy or material prosperity, which is one of the traditional four goals of life—*dharma*, *artha*, *kāma*, and *mokṣa*. The work is mainly concerned with human subsistence, wealth, and property. It offers theories of kingship and realistic statecraft, a guide to relations among states, conditions for the public good, and formation and implementation of policy.

A highly sophisticated philosophy of language developed at least as early as the fifth century BCE with the *Aṣṭadhyāyi* of Pāṇiṇi. The descriptive analytical grammar of Sanskrit in this work, covering the analysis of phonemes, suffixes, sentences, rules of word combination, and the formation of verbal roots, has not been surpassed. After Pāṇiṇi's beginnings, full-fledged linguistic philosophies were formulated by the leading thinker of the grammarian school, Bhartṛhari (400 CE), in his *Vākyapadīya* that analyzed language as a medium that can lead to liberation.

Śaiva schools are philosophical systems within religious traditions that worship Śiva as supreme deity. Śaiva theology and philosophy developed largely outside the Vedic context, relying instead on Tantras and Āgamas. A number of Śaiva schools developed, including Vīraśaivism or Liṅgāyatism, which traces its origin to five great teachers mentioned in the *Svāyambhuvāgama*: Revaṇasiddha, Marulasiddha, Ekorāma, Paṇḍitārādhya, and Viśvārādhya, and to Basava (1106–68 CE), who is the foremost expounder of the system; Śivādvaita of Śrīkaṇṭha (about 1200 CE), whose *bhāṣya* on the *Brahmasūtra* identifies Brahman with Paramaśiva; Śaiva Siddhānta, a dualistic school which incorporated Tamil devotion and Kashmir Śaiva nondualism and whose most important philosophers include Appar, Tiruñāṉacampantar, Sundaramūrti, Māṇikkavācakar, Aruṇanticivāccāriyār, and Meykaṇṭatēvar (about 1200 CE), whose *Civañāṉapōtam* (Sanskrit, *Śivajñānabodham*) is the basic text of the school; and Kashmir Śaivism (also known as Trika, Spanda, and Pratyabhijña), a nondualistic philosophical system attributed to Śiva himself and his *Śivasūtra*. Its most notable exponents include Somānanda (about 900–950 CE), Utpala (about 925–975 CE), Abhinavagupta (about 975–1025 CE), and Kṣemarāja (about 1000–1050 CE). Kashmir Śaivism recognizes the whole cosmos as a manifestation of divine conscious energy and explains how the formless, unmanifest supreme principle, Śiva, manifests as the entire universe.

Tāntric Texts

Like much of traditional Hindu sacred literature, this extensive category is not yet well cataloged or thoroughly studied. The texts are usually in Sanskrit verse and date to about the sixth or seventh century CE. The main body of Tāntric texts is known as Āgama ("tradition") rather than Veda, but is believed by advocates and initiates to be divinely inspired scripture that has been handed down from teacher to pupil. Even naming within this category is complicated. Texts are divided into three main branches according to the deity worshiped. Usually the *āgamas* of the Śaivas are called Āgama; those of the Śāktas, Tantra; and those of the Vaiṣṇavas, Saṃhitā. Vaikhānasa and Pañcarātra Āgamas are Vaiṣṇava scriptures that extol Viṣṇu; Śaiva Āgamas extol Śiva; and Śākta Āgamas extol the Devī. Śākta Tantras are enumerated as sixty-four and grouped into *dakṣiṇa* and *vāma*, or right and left hand. Vaiṣṇava Tantras are said to number one hundred and eight (although more than two hundred are known) and are grouped into Vaikhānasa and Pañcarātra. Those revealed by Sage Vikhanas to his disciples Bhṛgu, Marīci, Atri, and so on, are Vaikhānasa Tantras. Pañcarātra Āgamas are threefold: *divya*, or works directly revealed by Lord Nārāyaṇa; *munibhāṣita*, or works, such as *Bhāradvāja Saṃhitā* and *Pārameśvara Saṃhitā*, handed over to the sages; and *āptamanujaprokta*, or works written by men whose word is trustworthy. The Śaiva Āgamas are fourfold: *Kāpāla*, *Kālāmukha*, *Pāśupata*, and *Śaiva*. Traditionally, twenty-eight Śaiva Āgamas are recognized as forming the core revealed canon, but hundreds of these scriptures are mentioned here and there.

In theory, a Śaiva Āgama consists of four parts: methods of worship, temple construction, and making images (*kriyā*); philosophical doctrines (*jñāna*); meditative practices (*yoga*); and conduct (*caryā*). However, few survived in that complete form. These are divided into three categories: *tantra* that teaches rituals, *mantra* that teaches the *yoga* stage of worship, and *upadeśa* that expounds the existence and nature of the three eternal entities—individual souls, modes of bondage, and the divine lord (*paśu*, *pāśa*, and *pati*).

Āgamas typically are in the form of a dialogue between Śiva and the goddess (Pārvatī or Umā) or between Bhagavān and Śrī or Lakṣmī. They teach practices and use symbols intended to serve as effective means to reach spiritual liberation, and they emphasize the importance of initiation and authority of the *guru*. Philosophical doctrines in the Āgamas vary. Some of them teach nonduality, others qualified nonduality, and still others duality. What they share is an attempt to put desire (*kāma*), in every meaning of the word, in the service of liberation.

• PRACTICES AND INSTITUTIONS

Rituals

The Veda is the earliest and most authoritative surviving source for the practice of sacrificial rituals. It did not require any permanent or immoveable place of worship, any lasting images, or written texts. What is required is one or more qualified priests who have been trained in the proper hymns and procedures. The sacrifice (*homa*, *yajña*) consists of offering into the sacrificial fire materials such as milk, clarified butter, yogurt, rice, barley, and the *soma* plant. Nowadays various plant materials are substituted for the *soma* because its ancient identity has been lost. It is a Vedic ritual assumption that the essence of what is offered is transported through the fire to the selected *deva*(s), or divine energies.

Two types of Vedic ritual were developed: solemn public rites (*śrauta*), "based on the Śruti," and household or domestic rites (*gṛhya*). The *śrauta* rites are the older of the two and require three fires: the householder's fire (*gārhapatya*), round in shape, located in the west, which was mainly used to prepare food for the sacrifice; the fire into which most of the prepared offerings are placed (*āhavaniya*), square in shape, located in the east; and a semicircular southern fire (*dakṣiṇāgni*), used to ward off hostile spirits and to receive offerings to departed ancestors. Between the two main fires was the *vedi*, a ritually protected grass-lined pit in which oblations and sacrificial utensils were placed to preserve their power when not in use. The rites are complicated and require a number of priestly specialists. The most elaborate of the rituals requires four priests (each a specialist in one of the four Vedas). Among the types of *śrauta* rites are the *agniṣṭoma*, a fairly simple one-day *soma* sacrifice; the *agnicayana*, a complex rite that lasts for several days; and the very rarely performed *aśvamedha*, horse sacrifice. The principal deities invoked in the *śrauta* rite are Agni and Soma.

The *gṛhya* rites, on the other hand, require only one fire and are performed by a family man for the welfare of his family. The ancient Vedic householder was expected to maintain a domestic fire into which he made his offerings. The three castes of Vedic-initiated Brāhmaṇa, Kṣatriya, and Vaiśya males, or the "twice-born," were required to perform this ritual daily. However, with the passage of time, householders began to employ a professional priest to perform not only the daily *homa*, but also most other domestic rites on behalf of the family. This eventually led to hiring a priest to administer lifecycle events or sacraments (*saṃskāra*) that mark all the important transitions in an upper caste Hindu male's life from conception to cremation and a woman's transition along with her husband into the married state.

The *saṃskāra*s are rites of passage, rituals that make possible an individual's transition from one stage of life to another. These domestic rites are described in the Gṛhyasūtras, Dharmasūtras, and Dharmaśāstras, but not every regional community or caste celebrates every one of them or attaches the same importance to each of them. Rites exclusively for females are not discussed in the classical texts. Nevertheless, all of the rites of passage are described as "auspicious" moments, auspicious in the sense that they involve the power to produce good fortune, true happiness.

The highly ritualized life of traditional upper caste Hindus is divided into daily ritual actions (*nitya-karma*) that are to be performed every day, occasional ritual actions (*naimittika-karma*) which are occasioned by some special occurrence, and rites for a desired purpose or particular object (*kāmya-karma*). The *saṃskāra*s are transitional rites that acknowledge a series of identities through which one passes in the course of a lifetime. These sacraments sanctify special moments and support social identities. It is thought that they purify the recipient, and without the ritual purification, further action would be ineffective and fruitless. The word "*saṃskāra*" means "perfecting," thus to "do well."

From antiquity, there have been differing opinions about the exact number of rites of passage, with the proposed number ranging from thirteen to forty, but four are usually considered most important: birth, initiation, marriage, and death. The birth of a boy, especially the first child, is considered particularly auspicious. By the birth of a son, a father is said to have repaid the debt to his ancestors and to have enabled his forefathers to attain the world of heaven (*svar*). The birth of a daughter is not inauspicious, but it does create a practical liability in the context of traditional marriage practices in most of traditional India, where a dowry and other continuing expenses for the parents of daughters are expected. For a child of either sex, the exact moment of birth is noted because a person's horoscope is cast from it and is likely to be an important factor in arranging a suitably matched marriage.

The initiation ritual (*upanayana*) for a boy is held at any time between the ages of eight and twenty-four. He is taught the proper way to recite Gāyatrī-*mantra* daily. It is addressed to

Savitṛ, the sun, and is found in the *Ṛg Veda* (3.62.10): "We meditate on the brilliance of the sun; May it inspire our intellect." At this ceremony, he also is given the sacred thread which is the most obvious external sign that he is among the "twice-born" and has entered into high-caste society and the student stage of life. The traditional ideal was that initiation would mark the beginning of a long period of Vedic study under the guidance of a teacher (*guru*) during which the student would live in his teacher's house. It was society's duty to support him as a student. He would receive food from a few households, take it to the *guru*'s wife, and she would apportion and serve it to her husband's students.

Initiation for females, according to Manu, is marriage. The wife serving her husband is equivalent to Vedic study, and housework is equivalent to the fire oblations (*Manusmṛti* 2.67). However, women's puberty rites have been considered an initiatory rite of passage in some communities, too. There is Vedic evidence that prior to about 600 BCE, females as well as males were initiated with the Gāyatrī-*mantra*, were invested with the sacred thread, and studied the Vedas in the house of the *guru*. The two epics include accounts of women involved in lighting and tending the sacrificial fire to make ritual offerings, and many female sages are named in traditional literature. It is not clear why those practices were lost.

Marriage is the next great transition in people's lives. In Hindu tradition, it is expected of all and inaugurates the householder stage of life, in which obligations to family and society are fulfilled. As a householder, it is appropriate to pursue the goals of duty (*dharma*), wealth and worldly success (*artha*), and pleasure (*kāma*). Because of this, it is said that the householder stage is the safest and best fortress from which to engage in the struggle of life. According to the Dharmaśāstra, a person is born with debts to sages, divine beings, humans including ancestors, and animals. By performing domestic duties, having children, and living a righteous life, the husband, along with his wife, repays these debts.

Wedding ceremonies vary greatly from region to region throughout India, but the following practices are usually considered essential. The date for the ceremony is fixed by astrological calculation; the bridegroom is conducted to the home of his future parents-in-law who receive him as an honored guest; during the ceremony, the bridegroom takes the bride by the hand or is linked to her by a cloth and conducts her around the sacrificial fire; prayers and auspicious *mantra*s are uttered; and seven steps are taken by the bride and groom together to solemnize the irrevocability of their union. A traditional marriage is arranged, although Hindu law acknowledges no less than eight forms of marriage: bride given to a priest without dowry, bride given to a priest with dowry, arranged by parents with dowry, arranged by parents, bride price, love marriage, seduction, and forcible abduction. But, as you might expect, in the modern era the last types on the traditional list have been subjected to serious critique. Traits considered for matching a prospective bride and groom typically include same caste and community, compatible horoscope, same region and language, extent of education, age, height, skin color, artistic skills, and socioeconomic status. Matrimonial advertisement pages in newspapers, and now on the Internet, generally include these categories. The marriage celebration itself is an important social occasion and may be quite elaborate and expensive.

At life's end are the rituals marking a death. The traditional funeral method for most Hindus is cremation. Burial is reserved for small children and others who have not been purified by *saṃskāras* or no longer need the ritual fire to be conveyed to the hereafter (such as ascetics, or *sannyāsins*, who have renounced all earthly concerns and great sages, or *ṛṣis*). Features of the rites vary, but typically the eldest son performs the death rituals. With an iron rod he draws three lines on the ground, saying, "I draw a line for Yama, the lord of cremation; I draw a line for *kāla*, time, the lord of cremation; I draw a line for *mṛtyu*, death, the lord of cremation." Some sesame seeds are put into the mouth of the deceased, the body is put on the funeral pyre, and the eldest son then lights it. When the last rite has been performed, the individual has made the full transition through the stages of life and has become a complete or perfected human being, worthy of honor, and thus an ancestral source of blessings for all of their descendants.

Women's Rituals

Many rituals are performed by both women and men, such as singing devotional songs (*bhajan*), formal worship (*pūjā*) that is directed to and through an image of the divine installed in one's home, and visits to temples or pilgrimage sites. However, several rituals are unique to married women with living husbands. Traditionally women would daily light oil lamps in the house and draw designs (*kōlam*, *raṅgolī*) on its threshold. Whenever a female visitor would leave the house, the wife would offer her auspicious items, such as turmeric, red powder (*kumkum*), bananas, coconuts, betel nuts, and/or betel leaves. Rites would be observed on particular days for the welfare of the husband and/or the entire extended family. Many women observe vows (*vrata*) as a way of life that involves routinely undertaking fasts and other ascetic acts aimed at insuring the safety, happiness, and stability of their households. The *vratas* require them to abstain from certain types of foods or pleasures in order to invite blessings of a deity. There are also some *pūjās* that are unique to women, such as the Kedāra Gaurī-*pūjā*, the Varalakṣmī-*pūjā*, and the Sāvitrī-*vrata*. In North India, many women annually perform the rite of *rakṣābandhan* ("tying of the amulet"), which involves tying a cord of protection around the wrists of their brothers.

Temples

In the Indus Valley or Harappā culture, there may have been structures that were set apart for worship, but the Vedas make no reference to enduring temples or other religious buildings. One of the noteworthy differences between ancient Vedic and later Hindu tradition, in fact, is the establishment of permanent temples. Vedic rituals are performed by ritual experts for the benefit of the patron of the sacrifice (*yajamāna*) or the well-being of the entire world. The sacrifice takes place outdoors, where a fire-altar is set up just for the duration of the rites, and primary elements—earth, water, air, and space (instanced in offerings such as wood, milk, clarified butter, and fruits)—are presented through the sacrificial fire. During the Classical period, a transition to permanent structures was underway, with fixed iconographic representations of deities in sculptured images installed in them for formal worship. Put simply, Vedic *yajña* at temporary sites was largely superseded by Hindu *pūjā* at enduring sites, some of which attracted a large enough following from beyond their immediate surroundings to become centers of pilgrimage.

Early stone temples survive from the Gupta Empire (about 300–500 CE), and by the seventh century there are many large temples in various regional styles. Two main styles of Hindu temple architecture are the northern and the southern. A conical dome, or *śikara*, characterizes the northern. The southern has a central shrine that is located in an open courtyard surrounded by a wall with four gates surmounted by a tower (*gopura*) at each of the four cardinal directions. The *gopurams* usually are shaped in stepped layers with images of deities decorating each level. At a major southern temple, they may reach more than two hundred feet in height.

A temple is a place where the deity is both visible and accessible. Professional priests and supporting staff members maintain regular schedules of services, and offerings are accepted and redistributed as tokens of divine grace (*prasāda*). Temple architecture symbolically represents the quest for the divine and ways to diminish the distance between divine and human. Interior spaces of a large temple complex are arranged to encourage movement by the devotee from the outside towards the center through a series of enclosures that become increasingly sacred as one approaches the central sanctuary. At the door to the *sanctum sanctorum*, a priest serves as an enabling intermediary between the devotee and the deity.

According to ancient ritual manuals, a temple should be on a site that has been carefully selected, its structures should follow specified principles of design and proportion, and it should be prepared for worship by ritual purification and installation of consecrated divine images. A correctly designed Hindu temple can function like a model of reality—as a sacred geometric diagram (*maṇḍala*) that represents the cosmos, the human being, and the cosmic *puruṣa* of the Veda. Devotees enter the temple for *darśana*, to be blessed by seeing and by being seen by the deity through the ritually consecrated images and pervading divine presence. Traditionally, the main image resides in the womb-house (*garbha-gṛha*) of temple. One reason the central chamber is called a womb-house is that this is where a devotee is "reborn" and renewed. Śiva temples usually have Śiva-*liṅga* as their central image. Viṣṇu temples have images of Viṣṇu or of his *avatāras*. Devī temples have a personified image or an aniconic representation of the goddess.

Temple Rituals

Unlike the fire-centered Vedic *yajña*, or sacrifice, a temple ritual, or *pūjā*, involves worship directed toward an image. The deity typically is ritually honored as if the worshipers were serving a great king (the Tamil word for temple is *kōyil*, "house of the king"). The deity in its image form is awakened in the morning along with his consort; is bathed, clothed, and fed; is adorned with jewels and garlands of flowers, is established in his shrine to give audience to his subjects, and is praised and entertained throughout the day; and is prepared for sleep at night. Throughout the day, worshipers may have *darśana*, sing devotional songs, offer prayers and gifts, and perform other acts of homage.

Pūjā is usually translated as "worship." It may be performed in a home or temple. It is the core ritual of theistic, devotional, or popular Hinduism in which a *mūrti*, or a correctly designed and consecrated image, becomes the focus for worship and honor of the divine.

Thus, the term "*pūjā*" most often is short for *mūrti-pūjā* and typically is used to denote a ritual that centers on an image of the divine, or an aniconic form of a deity, or some other object that is believed to manifest spiritual power or sacredness. *Pūjā* is done to receive the deity's blessings and to develop one's own inner divinity. All large temples and most domestic shrines contain images. They are anthropomorphic representations of deities that are formed in wood or clay, or are carved in stone or cast in bronze, or more rarely are made of precious stones. Frequently seen examples of aniconic images are, for instance, the *liṅga* for Śiva and *sālagrāma* stone for Viṣṇu.

A *pūjā* involves three key elements: an offering presented to the deity; the auspicious sight (*darśana*) of the deity; and a blessed item of food, or a flower, or some similar article that had been offered to the deity (*prasāda*) and then is redistributed to someone who had come to worship and now may take away with them this tangible blessing from the ritual setting. In addition, three things are usually associated with the worship of a deity: *mūrti* (or *arcā* or *pratimā*), *mantra*, and *yantra*. *Mūrti* is the physical image consecrated for worship. It may be movable or immovable. If immovable, it would be attached to a pedestal and could not be moved once installed. *Mantra* is a set of sacred sounds or words of power. By recalling, contemplating, or uttering *mantra*(s), one invokes the energy of the deity associated with it and invests the atmosphere with a divine presence that envelope the devotee and deity. It is widely believed that a *mantra* must be given during initiation by a *sadguru* if it is to be reliably effective. Two famous *mantra*s are "*oṃ namaḥ śivāya*" (I bow to the indwelling auspicious [one]) and "*oṃ namo nārāyaṇāya*" (I bow to the indwelling divinity in the human). *Yantra*s are sacred geometrical designs in which the deity is said to reside. They are "instruments" or devices that function as the "form body" of a deity. They allow the infinite personal deity to enter into a delimited ritual sacred space for the purpose of worship. Thus, they are regarded as energetic centers or storehouses of divine power. Not only that, they also serve as an abstract reminder of the presence of the deity. Usually they are geometric designs composed of points, circles, squares, triangles, and rectangles. They may be drawn on sand, paper, or wood or are engraved on metal (gold, silver, copper, or a combination of five metals). Crystal *yantra*s are thought to be the most auspicious and powerful of all *yantra*s.

*Pūjā*s take several alternative forms. A simple worship may consist of an offering of turmeric powder, *kumkum*, flowers, sandalwood paste, and incense. Such a *pūjā* requires little time or ritual knowledge. More elaborate types of worship consist of an offering accompanied by a specific sequence of activities (*upacāra*), each of them accompanied by the recitation of specified *mantra*s. These *pūjā*s may vary from sixteen up to one hundred and eight offerings or more, and the name of a *pūjā* may refer to the number of items being offered. The ritual may open with preliminary acts that include a declaration of intention (*saṃkalpa*) to perform the worship, purification of the devotee and the implements used in the *pūjā*, and a request for removal of obstacles to successful completion. What follows may vary in sequence and number of elements but is likely to include invocation, installation of the image; water for washing its feet; water for washing its head, hands, and body; water for the deity to sip; water for bathing the deity; clothing (upper and lower garments); adding the sacred thread; honoring the deity with perfume and flowers or garlands that are offered to the accompaniment of *mantras*; lighting and wafting incense and lights; offering food; prostrating before the image; greeting and circumambulating the deity; and taking leave of the deity.

The ritual sequence in *pūjā* can be interpreted as a process of embodying the deity and disembodying the worshiper. In this process, the image has a crucial role. It provides a fixed, tangible, embodied form by means of which a worshiper comes into contact with a greater being and higher level of reality that may be otherwise inaccessible. In worship the deity "comes down" to the worshiper who becomes transformed, at least temporarily, and eventually may become perfected. A sign of this transformative process is the concluding exchange in which divine grace (*prasāda*) in a form such as colored powder, scented water, or food is distributed to devotees. The *prasāda* is a tangible form of the presence of the deity to whom it was offered, and it is a literal "take-away" from the worship experience. To sum up, worship is a series of acts to respectfully honor a deity as well as an opportunity to learn and practice the qualities of obedience, devotion, surrender, and sacrifice. It can train the mind, encourage generosity, foster patience, and inspire hope.

Festivals

Hindu festivals tend to be combinations of ritual observances that may involve large processions, recitations of poetry and traditional texts, performances of music and dance, and feasting and feeding the poor. Among the many purposes of Hindu festivals are purification to avert malicious influences, strengthening human relations in society, support for passing through times of crisis in the lifecycle, and strengthening the vital powers of nature. They are intended to enable Hindu families and groups to "rise up" or improve hence are called "*utsava*."

Some Hindu festivals (*utsava*) are local, some are regional, and some are all-India occasions. The timing for observation of many of them is determined by phases of the moon, positions of planets, and other factors calculated in the Hindu calendar. All-India festivals include Kṛṣṇa's birthday (Janmāṣṭmī); Rāma's birthday (Rāmanavamī); Gaṇeśa's birthday (Gaṇeśacaturṭhī); and Daśahrā (Dasserā), a ten-day autumn festival to the goddess that includes *navarātri*, or the "nine nights," and the tenth day of *vijayādaśamī*, or "victory" day. Daśahrā is also known as Durgā-*pūjā*, especially in Bengal; other regions celebrate it as the day Rāma defeated Rāvaṇa. Dīvālī (Dīpāvalī) is the autumn new moon festival of lights, celebrated everywhere with lamps placed in windows, around doors, and floated in rivers, as well as with exchange of gifts; Mahāśivarātri is the night of Śiva; Holī is the late winter or early spring festival characterized by exuberance in which people splash each other with colored powder and water; and Rakṣābandhan (Rākhī) is the day when sisters tie colored threads around their brothers' wrists.

Pilgrimages

Pilgrimage to holy rivers and other sacred sites has long been a prominent and integrating feature of Hindu religious life. A pilgrimage is a journey (*yātrā*) to a holy place, a place of "crossing over" (*tīrtha*) where the secular and sacred meet. While all of India is considered a holy land (*puṇyabhūmi*) as a place that affords human beings the opportunity to reach liberation, special places of pilgrimage are found across the entire subcontinent, from the Himālayas in the north to Kanyākumārī in the south. Many of them have been considered sacred for centuries, including the seven holy cities Ayodhyā, Mathurā, Haridvār, Vārāṇasī, Kāñcīpuram, Avantikā (Ujjain), and Dvārakā and the holy rivers Gaṅgā, Yamunā, Godāvarī, Sarasvatī, Narmadā, Kāvēri, and Sindhu. Some are closely associated with divine individuals, such as Ayodhyā with Rāma and the Mathurā region with Kṛṣṇa; others claim the vital presence of a deity such as Vārāṇasī with Śiva; and still others are at the meeting point of two or more rivers, such as Prayāga (Allahabad).

Each pilgrimage site has advocates and supporters who spread word about its overall superiority and the specific benefits that can result from a visit to it. However, the most acclaimed Hindu pilgrimage site is Vārāṇasī (also known as Kāśī in ancient India, and Banaras in modern India). Vārāṇasī is one of the oldest continuously living cities in the world, and for more than twenty-five hundred years it has attracted pilgrims and seekers. It is considered to be the permanent earthly home of Śiva, and countless generations of saints and sages have lived and taught there. The city is located on the banks of the holy river Gaṅgā, at a point where the river takes a broad crescent sweep toward the north. There are some seventy bathing *ghāṭ*s along the river, and bathing in the Gaṅgā, which fell from heaven to earth through Śiva's matted locks according to Hindu tradition, grants purity. The important cremation grounds of Maṇikarṇikā-*ghāṭ* and Hariścandra-*ghāṭ* are located along the river there, and it is widely believed that by dying within the city a Hindu will attain ultimate and final liberation (*mokṣa*).

Forehead Marks

Many Hindus wear a distinctive mark (*tilaka* or *bindī*) on their forehead to indicate their sectarian allegiance. In ancient days, the forehead mark was made of musk (*kastūrī*). When that substance became rare, the mark was made from saffron. More recently, Hindus began to use a red lead power (*sindūr*) or sandalwood paste. These substances are known to have a cooling effect on the body and are believed to help create a calm and quiet mind. Nowadays the forehead mark typically is made from sandalwood paste, or ash (*vibhūti* or *bhasma*), or a red-colored powder (*kumkum*). A white U- or Y-shaped mark with a red line in the middle indicates that the person is a devotee of Viṣṇu (the U represents the feet of Viṣṇu and the red line represents Lakṣmī); followers of Śiva use three white horizontal lines made of ash; and followers of the Devī usually place a large red dot in the middle of the three. That area of the forehead is known by various names, such as the *ājñācakra*, the third eye, or the spiritual eye, and is said to be the location of a major nerve center at a subtle (nonphysical) level of the human body. When worn by women, the *tilaka* is a reminder of wedding vows. Its presence does not indicate for certain that the woman already is married, and if she becomes a widow she no longer will put on a *tilaka*. The religious significance of the *tilaka* is sometimes neglected or forgotten these days, and it may be used only for the sake of fashion rather than for religious reasons. Some women even wear plastic *tilaka*s, available in a wide range of rainbow colors, to match the color of their *sāṛī*.

Oṃ

The most well-known and mysterious of all *mantras* is *oṃ*. It is a sacred syllable composed of three letters (a-u-m) in a single sound along with a fourth, silence. The vowels "a" and "u" coalesce in Sanskrit to become "o." These three letters represent several important triads: three worlds (earthly or human, midregion or natural, and heavenly or divine), three deities (Brahmā, Viṣṇu, and Śiva), three Vedas (*Ṛg*, *Sāma*, and *Yajur*), three elements (fire or Agni, wind or Vāyu, and sun or Sūrya), three twice-born castes (Brāhmaṇa, Kṣatriya, and Vaiśya), and for Vaiṣṇavas it evokes Viṣṇu, Lakṣmī, and the devotee. The *Māṇḍūkya Upaniṣad* identifies *oṃ* with four levels of consciousness: "a" represents the waking state; "u" represents the dream state; "m" represents the deep sleep state; and the fourth (*turīya*) represents the unchanging transcendent state.

> Just as all the leaves of a sprig are held together by its stem, so all words are held together by the sound *oṃ*. The *oṃ* is the entire universe.
>
> (*Chāndogya Upaniṣad* 2.23.3)

> He who knows the *oṃ* and makes the syllable resound, he takes refuge in that syllable, in the immortal and fearless sound. By taking refuge in it, he becomes immortal like the gods.
>
> (*Chāndogya Upaniṣad* 1.4.5)

> *Oṃ* is the bow, the self is the arrow; Brahman, they say, is the target to be pierced by concentration; thus one becomes united with Brahman as an arrow with the target.
>
> (*Muṇḍaka Upaniṣad* 2.2.4)

> The goal that all the Vedas declare, which all austerities aim at, and that humans desire when they lead a life of continence, I will tell you briefly, it is *oṃ*. This syllable *oṃ* is indeed Brahman. This syllable is the highest. Whosoever knows this syllable obtains all that he desires. This is the best support; this is the highest support. Whosoever knows this support is adored in the world of Brahman.
>
> (*Kaṭha Upaniṣad* 1.2.15–17)

> What was, what is, and what shall be—all this is *oṃ*. Whatever else is beyond the bounds of threefold time, that also is only *oṃ*.
>
> (*Māṇḍūkya Upaniṣad* 1)

Oṃ is uttered at the beginning and end of a Hindu prayer, chant, meditation, recitation of a sacred text, and most rituals. With it everything begins and ends. In Hindu teaching, it is not a concept that refers to something else, but is itself the supreme reality in the form of primeval sound.

• ETHICS AND HUMAN RELATIONS

Varṇa

In Vedic society, as we have observed, *dharma* is one of the most pivotal concepts. Another is *varṇa*. It is introduced in the hymn of dismemberment and sacrifice of the cosmic person in the Puruṣasūkta (*Ṛg Veda* 10.90) which is a tradition of origin for the four classes. The highest three of them were known as "twice-born" because their males underwent Vedic initiation, a rite of passage that gave them access to being full members of a ritual-centered society. The *varṇa* system accepts that people differ from one another and assumes that these differences are expressed in their aptitudes and predilections. Kṛṣṇa says in the *Bhagavad Gītā*, "The four castes were created by me according to the division of aptitudes (*guṇa*) and works (*karma*)" (4.13).

The four classes (*varṇa-dharma*) may be based on an organic model of social economy and division of labor. Each class is of equal value to the functioning of the whole, just like the head, the feet, the arms, and the legs are each important to the whole body's harmonious functioning. Functions differ, but the social body is one.

Some modern Hindu scholars theorize that castes were at first correlated with professions and guilds and then later became hereditary. With the passage of time, perhaps the prestige of the priestly class (Brāhmaṇas) turned the system into a closed vertical hierarchy determined by birth. The domain of priests includes what are considered to be the most important goals in life. Priests must be consulted when people are to be married, be buried, or have dealings with ancestors or with divine boons and blessings. However, priestly *dharma* was to protect and preserve the Vedas, to perform rituals, and to teach without charge. It was the duty of the warrior class (Kṣatriyas) to provide simple housing, food, and life's necessities for priests in return for their service to society. When priests began to perform their duties like merchants (Vaiśyas) and to charge for their services, according to this devolutionary theory of Hindu social stratification, *dharma* was broken and castes became rigidly arranged into a hierarchical structure with the Brāhmaṇas at the top and the workers (Śudras) at the bottom. What once may have been a system of functional interdependence that sustained the harmony of the social whole was transformed into a competitive and divisive force that led to the formation of further subdivisions leading to the multiple castes and subcastes that are recognized today. This interpretation of the emergence of increasing caste rigidity has considerable popular support among contemporary Hindus.

Caste as a genetic phenomenon, as an innate status that is inherited and cannot be changed, is not supported by some influential traditional texts. Satyakāma, in the *Chāndogya Upaniṣad*, was accepted as a student by Ṛṣi Gautama, not on the basis of caste (*gotra*), but on the basis of conduct because he spoke the truth, which is a trait of a Brāhmaṇa. Yudhiṣṭhira in the *Mahābhārata* says, "Truth, charity, fortitude, good conduct, gentleness, austerity, and compassion, he in whom these are observed is a Brāhmaṇa; if these marks exist in a Śūdra, then he is a Brāhmaṇa" (3.131.21). Manu says the same.

Modern social scientists distinguish "class" (*varṇa*) from "caste" (*jāti*). The term "*varṇa*" plays a role in Vedic literature, but the term "*jāti*" does not make its appearance until the Dharmaśāstra literature. In its early use there, it is a synonym of *varṇa*. Later commentators began to make a distinction between the four castes (Brāhmaṇa, Kṣatriya, Vaiśya, and Śūdra) and the multitude of birth groups (*jāti*). Remember that the word "*dharma*" means "to uphold, to sustain." The Hindu caste system as it is represented in the cosmogonic hymn (*Ṛg Veda* 10.90) is an organic structure in which the whole is dependent upon the parts fulfilling their duties in an appropriate manner. This recalls Kṛṣṇa's words in the *Bhagavad Gītā* that it is better to do one's duty even if poorly than to do another's duty well.

Āśrama

In addition to the four classes or castes (*varṇa*), there are the four stages of life (*āśrama*). These stages provide a plan for personal development and a structure oriented toward liberation from *karma* and rebirth. The stages are the celibate student (*brahmacarya*), householder (*gṛhastha*), hermit (*vānaprastha*), and renunciant (*sannyāsin*). Ideally, they would be equally divided into four units of twenty-five years each, forming a century of life.

In the first stage of life, a young person studies sacred scriptures, acquires skills necessary to perform ritual functions, achieves stable discipline, and prepares for responsible adult life. Celibacy is mandatory during this period, which ends with marriage. The second stage of life is devoted to producing a family, acquiring wealth, and repaying one's traditionally defined debts to society, ancestors, and the divine. A traditional student's *dharma* is to remain celibate and to study rather than to work for a living, and a householder's *dharma* is to lead a conjugal life with a marriage partner and to work in order to support the family. There are five main traditional duties of the marriage partners in a twice-born household: *brahma-yajña* (sacrifice to Brahman through studying and teaching the Veda); *deva-yajña* (ritual sacrifices to *devas*); *pitṛ-yajña* (ritual sacrifices to departed ancestors); *bhūta-yajña* (taking care of domestic animals); and *manuṣya-yajña* (feeding guests, the homeless, and the destitute). Most people in fact never go beyond these two stages of life. The third stage of life commences when a person "saw their hair turn grey and their skin wrinkled and their children's children" (that is, when one's own children have become householders themselves). When that time arrives, one is enjoined to turn over one's property and wealth to the adult children and retire to the forest to lead a simple life that is now directed more fully to spiritual pursuits. Finally, the stage of total renunciation is when a person becomes an ascetic, owning nothing, with the sky as their roof, the grass as their bed, taking what food that chance may bring, and desiring nothing but liberation and the welfare of all.

This ideal traditional map of the four stages of life is intended to take a person toward the fulfillment of human life by successive steps. As a rule, one should progress through each of the four stages in turn. But in extraordinary cases, tradition reports that some steps may be omitted. For instance, Śuka, Vyāsa's son, was born a *sannyāsin*; Śaṅkara became a *sannyāsin* right from the student stage; and Buddha became a *sannyāsin* from the householder stage.

Puruṣārtha

Another influential group of categories for guidance through life is the traditional set of four aims or goals of living. The first two of the four are *artha* ("what is useful"; wealth) and *kāma* ("what is pleasurable"; desire). As economic and acquisitive aims, they are instrumental or means-oriented values. They may be innate, practical, even necessary, but they cannot yield permanent results since every worldly object is impermanent, changeable, and will pass away. Within their limits the first two are positive values, but a typical problem with them results from attachment and misguided expectations that any temporary objects can produce eternal bliss. The third aim—to maintain *dharma* (righteousness, duty)—is an ethical value. It is both regulative and integrative. Any instrumental value should be limited and guided by the requirements of *dharma*. The fourth and final goal is *mokṣa* (liberation, realization). It is an intrinsic and end value. While the first two goals are means toward an end (that is, comfort and happiness), the third sets boundaries and a developmental direction that is preparation for the last. The fourth and last is neither a means nor a limit but the ultimate goal itself.

Ethics

According to Hindu assumptions, desire or an exertion of the will is what impels every action. The total of such actions constitutes one's conduct and character. Whether such actions are mental, verbal, or physical, the three should be aligned. This is technically known as *trikaraṇaśudhi*, or "one in thought, word, and deed." *Karma* is both "a deed" and the "results of a deed." It is not fate but a perfect conservation of energy. Every action produces an appropriate result and also leaves behind a subtle trace that shapes character. The kārmic past can be determined with precision, but the future remains uncharted because character can be changed even if that may be a remarkably difficult task. The broadest context for thinking about the significance of this in traditional Hindu culture is the totally meaningful cosmos constituted by *karma* in which there are no baseless actions, no meaningless accidents, and no inexplicable or unjustifiable circumstances despite every painfully baffling appearance to the contrary.

There are five cardinal virtues found in Hindu scriptures that are keys to Hindu ethics. Noninjury (*ahiṃsā*) is often stated to be the most important of them. In ancient India, various animals were ritually killed in Vedic rituals, and people were killed by their own rulers in capital punishment and by their enemies in wars. However, the doctrines of *ahiṃsā* and vegetarianism reinforced one another through a common aversion towards killing and eating animals, as well as through the importance placed on the cow. Historically, it was primarily the Jainas and the Buddhists who inspired India to vegetarianism. Contrary to popular stereotypes, many Hindus are not vegetarians. Some eat fish, others chicken or lamb, and a few even eat beef. For the most part, Brāhmaṇas (except in Bengal and Kashmir) are vegetarian, although dietary practices are ever changing.

The five cardinal virtues are duties common to all (*sādhāraṇa-dharma*) and should be cultivated by everyone, irrespective of distinctions of caste or stage of life. How these virtues are identified varies from one scripture to another, and in the sixteenth chapter of the *Bhagavad Gītā* (verses 1–3), there is a particularly long list that includes fearlessness, purity of thought, steadfast in knowledge and devotion, charity, self-control, performance of sacrifice, study of the scriptures, austerity, simplicity, nonviolence, truthfulness, freedom from anger, renunciation, tranquility, aversion to faultfinding, compassion for all living beings, freedom from covetousness, gentleness, modesty, steadiness, courage, patience, fortitude, cleanliness, and freedom from malice and conceit. However, all of these can be considered variations of the five great cardinal virtues: purity, self-control, detachment, truth, and nonviolence.

Yoga or Mārga: Paths to Liberation

Hindu spiritual disciplines (*sādhana*) were traditionally divided into three paths or ways (*mārga*): the path of selfless action (*karma*), the path of devotion (*bhakti*), and the path of knowledge (*jñāna*). Other paths that are influential but may be less well known include *rāja-yoga*, or the path of meditation; *kuṇḍalini-yoga*, or the path of awakening the coiled inner power; *mantra-yoga*, or the path of mystic sounds; *haṭha-yoga*, or the path of physical postures; and *kriyā-yoga*, or the path of transmutative actions. In the *Bhagavad Gītā*, Kṛṣṇa describes the three ways to liberation. Each of these paths can be considered an independent means to the ultimate goal of life, although the way of knowledge and the way of devotion each typically incorporate the other two ways as prerequisites.

Karma-Yoga

The way of action (*karma*) is the path of disinterested service. *Karma* means action or work, and in general all action binds the actor—whether through meritorious acts that produce meritorious results or through unmeritorious acts that produce unmeritorious results. The way of action requires acting in accordance with one's duty without desire or attachment to the fruits or effects of those actions. Neither praise nor blame, neither reward nor punishment, should be of concern. If one acts selflessly, others benefit and one's character becomes ennobled, too. Acting with desire, with expectations or swayed by attraction and aversion, leads to unhappiness and bondage. The way of action seeks to transform all acts, behavior, or work into worship. Every action needs a motive, and by making worthy worship one's motive, all of life becomes divine service.

Bhakti-Yoga

The way of devotion (*bhakti*) is defined by Ṛṣi Nārada in his *Bhaktisūtras* as an intense love for the divine. In the *Bhāgavata Purāṇa*, Prahlāda prays to his lord: "That constant love which the ignorant have for the objects of their senses, let me have that constancy in my love for thee" (canto 7). The great nineteenth-century ecstatic mystic Rāmakṛṣṇa says that the devotional experience of *bhakti* is like "the continuous flow of lamp oil poured from one container to another" that provides an ever-renewing source of light to illumine all of life. *Bhakti* is an acknowledgment of generous divine compassion. Kṛṣṇa says, "Even if an unrighteous person adores me with exclusive devotion, he must be regarded as righteous. . . . My devotee is never lost" (*Bhagavad Gītā* 9.31). Devotion is an emotion (*bhāva*) that is transformed into an essence (*rasa*). It does not stop with mere emotionalism, but leads to training of the will and the intellect.

Devotion is built upon the foundations of action (*karma*) and knowledge (*jñāna*). The first requisite is renunciation of the wrong understanding of self that led one into attachment. This makes it possible to perform disinterested actions without the desire to benefit from them. Then disinterested action helps to purify the mind and make it ready for devotion. The second requisite is right knowledge that enables one to understand oneself as distinct from matter and its effects and to understand the divine being who generously gives and supports life. Then love and devotion grow and reverence increases.

Devotion itself is of two kinds: formal (*prapatti*) and surrender (*śaraṇāgati*). They have been compared to the "monkey way" in which the young cling to their mother's back through their own efforts and the "cat way" in which the mother picks up and carries her young without any effort on their part. The way of formal devotion is like a ladder with four main steps: clear knowledge of the realms of *karma*, *jñāna*, and *bhakti*; the will to undertake spiritual disciplines in their appropriate sequence; the scriptural qualifications of birth; and the patience to endure the ills of one's *karma* until it is exhausted. This is a long gradual path and can be punctuated by challenges and difficulties. Unconditional surrender, on the other hand, preserves the essentials of formal devotion, dispenses with its predisposing conditions, and omits nonessentials. It is the easier and more direct way to liberation. The prerequisite, however, is absolute confidence in the saving grace of the divine lord. The gradual acquisition of merit is not part of this path. All that is needed is unreserved self-surrender to divine grace. Kṛṣṇa's promise is, "Letting go of all duties, take refuge in me alone. I shall deliver you from all unrighteous actions. Do not grieve" (*Bhagavad Gītā* 18.66).

According to the Vaiṣṇava tradition, devotion can assume many forms. The role of the devotee in relation to the divine lord may be one of servant to master (an influential model is Hanumān to Rāma); friend to friend (Arjuna to Kṛṣṇa); parent to child (Kausalyā to Rāma, or Yaśodā to Kṛṣṇa); child to parent (Dhruva to Viṣṇu, or Prahlāda to Viṣṇu); wife to husband (Sītā to Rāma); and lover to beloved (Rādhā to Kṛṣṇa). There are also said to be nine methods of devotion (*navavidhā-bhakti*): hearing about the glory of the divine (*śravaṇa*), singing divine praise (*kīrtana*), contemplation (*smaraṇa*), worshiping the lord's feet (*pādasevana*), worship directed through an icon or image (*arcana*), prostration to the divine (*vandana*), acting as a servant of the divine (*dāsya*), fellowship in the lord's company (*sakhya*), and offering oneself totally (*ātma-nivedana*). In these various ways, *bhakti* transforms self-centeredness into divine-centeredness.

Jñāna-Yoga

According to this way, the path to liberation is in and through knowledge (*jñāna*). The question is, "What is knowledge?" In this context, it is not information as a set of facts about people, places, ideas, or things. Liberating knowledge is about the inner self or immortal soul. The way of knowledge involves a twofold means. The remote means (*antaraṅga-sādhana*) consists of factors that have been prescribed in the scriptural texts as indirectly helpful to prepare for a direct experience of Brahman-*ātman*. They include performing rituals, giving gifts, austerity, and the duties appropriate to one's class and stage in life. Such activities are purifying and provide a foundation for subtle and profound experience.

The fourfold requirement (*sādhana-catuṣṭaya*) that qualifies an aspirant to pursue the path of knowledge, according to Advaita Vedānta, forms the proximate means (*bahiraṅga-sādhana*). The four are discrimination of the eternal from the noneternal; nonattachment to the enjoyment of the fruits of one's actions either in this world or in any other; abundant possession of the six virtues, namely, calmness, equanimity, turning away from sense-objects, forbearance, concentration, and faith; and intense longing for liberation. According to tradition, one who meets the fourfold requirement is qualified to study the Upaniṣadic texts under the guidance of a teacher (*guru*) who is learned in scripture and well established in the truth. In this context, a *guru* is defined as a spiritual master who has attained oneness with the divine and without whom a disciple cannot attain liberation.

The proximate path of knowledge (*jñāna*) consists of three steps: hearing (*śravaṇa*), reflection (*manana*), and contemplation (*nididhyāsana*). Hearing means the proper understanding of the meaning of Vedāntic statements. These are of two kinds: intermediary and major texts. The intermediary texts relate to the nature of the world, while major texts impart the supreme knowledge of nonduality. The intermediary texts impart only a secondary or mediate knowledge of the truth. It is from the major or great texts that the direct experience of the plenary reality may be obtained. This can be expected to occur only after impediments in the form of long-established false beliefs are overcome through diligent reflection and contemplation. After the impediments have been removed, there arises the intuitive experience of nonduality, or *mokṣa*. This is direct knowledge of the self. When ignorance is destroyed, self-realization occurs. Kṛṣṇa says to Arjuna, "Just as fire reduces firewood to ashes, so does the fire of knowledge reduce all ignorance to ashes" (*Bhagavad Gītā* 4.37).

Religious Orders and Holy Persons

While Jainas and Buddhists developed monasticism, there have been ascetics in Hindu tradition as far back as the Vedic period. Many of the Vedic and Upaniṣadic sages were forest-dwellers, and Hindu ascetics have been known by various labels: *śramaṇa* (wanderer), *keśin* (long-haired ascetic), *yati* (wandering ascetic), *parivrājaka* (wanderer), *yogī* and *muni* (silent sage), *tapasvi* (performer of austerities), *sādhu* (holy person), *vairāgī* (renunciant), and *sannyāsin* (renunciant). Contemporary scholars disagree as to whether asceticism was a part of the Vedic (householder) tradition or whether it emerged out of reactions to Vedic ritualism. In other words, is there a conflict between the Brāhmaṇa ritualist and the renunciant? How divided and far apart are the householder and the renouncer?

In general, Hindu renunciants wear ochre robes, have shaven heads or long-matted hair, and perform spiritual practices for the purpose of liberation (*mokṣa*). They live alone on the edges of society, along the banks of rivers or in forests, in mountain caves, or in cremation grounds; or they live in hermitages (*āśrama*) or monasteries (*maṭha*). According to tradition, the great Vedāntic sage, Śaṅkara, founded monasteries in the four corners of India and a renunciate order of monks with ten branches (*daśanāmi*). The ten are associated with different monastic centers: Jyotirpīṭha at Badrināth in the north has the Giri, Sāgara, and Parvata orders; Govardhanapīṭha at Purī in the east has the Āraṇya and Vāna orders; Sāradāpīṭha at Śṛṅgeri in the south has the Bhāratī, Purī, and Sarasvatī orders; and Kālikāpīṭha at Dvārakā in the west has the Tīrtha and Āśrama orders.

Roles for Women

In Hindu tradition, the ideal female is admired and honored, but in practice the human female may not be so well treated. Hindu women have been appreciated as wives but shunned as widows. They have been portrayed as goddesses but also persecuted as seductresses who drain the life from a man. Typical roles that are relevant to understanding representations of females in Hindu tradition would include goddess, wife, widow, lover, consort, courtesan, and prostitute. Females are represented as occupying roles at all levels of reality and relative power from subservient and dependent to dominant and independent; as upholders of tradition or as innovators and modernizers; and as members of matrilineal or patrilineal families. The range is remarkable.

During the Vedic period, women seem to have had considerable freedom and many privileges in the spheres of family, civic life, and religion. The high status of at least some women was correlated with the fact that the performance of Vedic sacrificial rituals depended on the patronage of married householders who sponsored them. A wife was *ardhāṅginī*, a partner to her husband in religious rites. Evidence suggests that in early Vedic times, women in the upper classes may have received the sacred thread, studied the Vedas, and participated in the performance of rituals. Women named in the Vedas as sages include Lopāmudrā, Viśvavārā, Ghoṣā, and Indrāṇī. Early women scholars included Kathī, Kālapī, Bahvici, Gārgī Vācaknavī, and Maitreyī. Biṣpalā was named as a female warrior.

The end of the Vedic period saw great changes in the status of Hindu women. Brāhmaṇical specialization required longer periods of education, marriage at an earlier age was becoming fashionable, and this combination of factors would have allowed fewer women to participate in Vedic learning. As the extent of Vedic teaching and practice increased, memorization took longer and longer, and women needed that time for bearing and nurturing children. With a growing emphasis on ancestral sacrifices that only males were permitted to perform, the preference for male children increased, and the childbearing function of women was regarded as crucially important for propagating the male line. The transition from ritualism to asceticism evidenced in the Upaniṣads appears to have had a negative influence on the status of women in society, too.

The Classical and Medieval periods saw the further development of *strī-dharma*, codes of ideal behavior for Hindu women. During this time, Hindu law books, especially the *Manusmṛti*, defined in detail the roles of women. From then onwards the Hindu woman was to focus on her husband; he was to be her most immediate model and avenue of approach to the divine. Men's religious practices were to be aimed at general prosperity, and women's religious practices were to be aimed at family welfare and domestic prosperity. The *Manusmṛti* prescribed a subservient and dependent status for women:

> By a girl, by a young woman, or even by an old woman, nothing must be done independently, even in her own house. In childhood a female must be subject to her father, in youth to her husband, when her husband is dead, to her sons. A woman must never be independent.
>
> (*Manusmṛti* 5.148)

However, even in the *Manusmṛti* there are both ideological and practical limits to the subservience of women. Manu said that a wife is a physical embodiment of the goddess of good fortune and auspiciousness, that where women are honored the gods will be pleased, and where they are not honored no sacred rite will yield rewards. Manu also states that women's property (*strī-dhan*) is for the woman to retain, use, and bequeath as she may determine. With the Modern period has come an expanding freedom for Hindu women due to India's social reform movements, worldwide consciousness-raising, and female leadership. Positive models for advancing the roles of women also have been developed by observing that some norms for behavior (*varṇāśrama-dharma* and *sva-dharma*) from an earlier era varied from place to place and situation to situation and that some of them no longer suit conditions in the current Kali Yuga.

• MODERN EXPRESSIONS

Hindu Renaissance

What is generally called the Hindu Renaissance was a nineteenth-century movement to remodel society in ways that were inspired by classical Hindu values from an era prior to later foreign invasions and colonialism. British imperial rule, which imagined itself the heir to the Mughal Empire, was culturally traumatic because British Christians, unlike Mughal Muslims from Central Asia, imported into India and imposed radically disruptive economic, political, legal, educational, and social institutions. The introduction of Western shipping, especially in the cities now known as Kolkata (Calcutta), Mumbai (Bombay), and Chennai (Madras), shifted the balance of India's economy from the heartland to the periphery and from old villages and towns to new coastal cities. An agrarian and caste-based society began to give way to capitalist commerce and currency-based values. Western education introduced alien ideas about the conduct of politics and religion and about the course of history and the basis of culture. In the effort to assess and to question these new forces for change, a number of Hindu social and religious reform movements arose. The religious reforms took on nationalist overtones and gave birth to political organizations. A further result was the spread of the modern idea that there is a unified and uniform religion called Hinduism, which emerged as a reinterpretation and hybridization of traditional self-understandings in response to anticolonial nationalist needs and then survived into the contemporary era in independent India as a religious category that has ongoing political overtones and consequences. Hinduism, now understood as a modern world religion, combines continuity of traditional Hindu cultural patterns with their modern adaptation and significant transformation.

Brāhmo Samāj

The Brāhmo Samāj (Society of God) was founded in 1828 in Calcutta by Rammohun Roy (1772–1833), who is sometimes called the father of modern India. As the social and religious expression of a small but influential group of wealthy and Westernized Indians, the Brāhmo Samāj sought to create a purified form of Hinduism that would be free from all of the following: distinctions based on class or caste identities, child marriage, polytheism, temple rituals involving image worship, lack of education for women, and marginalizing of widows.

Roy was born in western Bengal into an orthodox Brāhmaṇa family, and although he outwardly remained a Hindu, wearing the sacred thread and observing many of the customs of orthodox Brāhmaṇas, the theology he proposed was strikingly nontraditional. He was a modern renaissance individual who was liberal in his social and political views and a radical freethinker in religious matters. He spoke five languages: Bengali, Sanskrit, Arabic, Persian, and English; and he was familiar with the Bible, Unitarianism, Islam, Freemasonry, Deism, and Western social life. He was versed in the Hindu scriptures, too. By applying his critical intellect to religious questions, he came to the conclusion that Hinduism, in its ancient and true form, did not contain all the elements he found distasteful in the religion of his time. He believed that if Hindus would read and understand their ancient scriptures, with reason and conscience as their guide, they would discard the distorted superstitions and illegitimate rituals and questionable social practices that somehow became associated with Hindu tradition over the centuries. After his death, Debendranath Tagore (1817–1905), the father of Nobel Prize-winning poet Rabindranath Tagore, became the leader of the Brāhmo Samāj. Under his guidance a less rationalist and more mystical doctrine was developed. The third leader of the Brāhmo Samāj, Keshab Chandra Sen (1838–84), admitted women to membership and abolished caste in the Samāj. As his theology became more eclectic and syncretistic, a schism developed, and the more conservative faction remained under the leadership of Debendranath. In 1881, Keshab founded the Church of the New Dispensation for the purpose of establishing the truth of all the great religions in a single institution that he believed would replace them all. Although the Brāhmo Samāj was an elite movement that never attained the status of widespread acceptance as part of the Hindu mainstream, it made a major contribution to a process of social and religious renewal by drawing attention to the persistence of inhumane practices and the need for education and reform.

Ārya Samāj

At about the time that the Brāhmo Samāj was at its height, Svāmī Dayānanda Sarasvatī (1824–83) founded a very different reform movement in western India. An orthodox Brāhmaṇa from Gujarat, Dayānanda founded the Ārya Samāj (Āryan Society) in 1875. While the Brāhmo Samāj was acknowledging the superiority of Western values, Western science, and Upaniṣadic wisdom, the Ārya Samāj rejected them and instead proposed a “return to the Veda” in its revival movement.

Dayānanda taught that the Vedas (that is, the four *saṃhitās*, or collections) were eternal, literally true, and universally authoritative. They taught monotheism and morality, not polytheism, image worship, or caste discrimination. Those were not Vedic but Purānic and were no more than symptoms of the decline of Vedic society as a result of the destructive Mahābhārata War. To improve society what was needed was to go back to the Vedas rather than to accept Western ways of doing things. He admonished Hindus to be proud of their ancient heritage and to reclaim it, not to be ashamed of it as if it were mere superstition, as Westerners were declaring. To revive the Golden Age, Dayānanda started Vedic-oriented educational institutions throughout India that did not neglect modern knowledge but contextualized it within the framework of Vedic revelation as he understood it. The purpose of the Ārya Samāj was to unify Hindus by a return to a long-forgotten faith in the Vedas as a complete model for human life. His speaking, writing, and debating style was dogmatic and forceful, and it had a major influence in revitalizing the Hindu community in northern India and awakening it to greater self-confidence. His influence continues to be important today through the Ārya Samāj and a family of other social and religious organizations in India.

A few drops of rain do not make a monsoon, although they may herald its imminent arrival. The Brāhmo Samāj and the Ārya Samāj brought about change in a limited segment of the population of eastern and northern India during the colonial era, but also served to awaken Hindus more generally to the need to strengthen their own cultural and social institutions through local self-governance, indigenous education, and social service work for the benefit of the weaker elements of society. The two movements (each in their own way) inspired creative responses to colonial repression and to imposed Western values, awakened Hindus to the importance of cultural self-criticism, and inspired succeeding generations to examine and appreciate the history and sociology of India without automatically accepting images of their heritage that came from foreign sources and failed to serve Hindu and more broadly Indian interests.

Rāmakṛṣṇa Mission

Rāmakṛṣṇa (1836–86) was a great revitalizing influence on modern Hindu religion and culture especially through his "gospel" of the truth of all religions and through his disciple Svāmī Vivekānanda, who gained international respect for the modern resurgence of Hinduism. Rāmakṛṣṇa was born of poor Brāhmaṇa parents in rural Bengal as Gadadhar Chatterjee and was raised in the Vaiṣṇava-*bhakti* tradition. He received training in all sixty-four tāntric spiritual disciplines from the female wandering renunciant Yogeśvarī and was taught nondual Advaita Vedāntic wisdom by the male renunciant Toṭāpurī. He later became known as the goddess Kālī's child due to his repeated experience of ecstatic trances and mystic visions of her and of other deities. His followers considered him to be a divine incarnation (*avatāra*) and a supremely realized self (*paramahaṃsa*), a rare type that nevertheless has graced India for thousands of years. His continuing influence on the way that Indian spirituality in general, and Hindu religion in particular, is understood may be summarized as "all religions are true and are but different paths to the One." This maxim was neither a formal definition nor a mere theory for him, but rather a summary of his own personal experience. Rāmakṛṣṇa practiced a number of different Hindu spiritual disciplines that included various forms of *bhakti* and Tantra as well as *jñāna-yoga*. He tried Christian and Muslim ones, too. He had many visionary experiences, and their effect was to confirm for him that he had reached the goal of each tradition and had found that the goal of each path was the same.

Crucial to Rāmakṛṣṇa's continuing influence after he left his body (*mahāsamādhi*) in 1886 was the articulation by others of his inclusivist viewpoint that integrated the diverse and otherwise competing or even conflicting features of Hindu religion. After he departed, Rāmakṛṣṇa's young monastic disciples gathered in Calcutta, took formal vows of renunciation (*sannyāsa*), and formed the Rāmakṛṣṇa Mission to spread his ideas. Foremost among his disciples was Svāmī Vivekānanda (*née* Narendranath Datta, 1863–1902), a former member of the Brāhmo Samāj. In 1893, Vivekānanda attended, as a Hindu participant, the World's Parliament of Religions in Chicago where he presented the idea that Vedānta was the definitive and most representative form of Hindu religion and that its central philosophy can permit one to see other religions and types of religious experience as valid in their own right, even if all religions and all religious experiences ultimately culminate in an experience of absolute oneness. Vivekānanda, with his powerful personality and stirring oratorical ability, deeply impressed the audience in Chicago. He was invited to lecture in the United States and England for the next four years and then returned to India in 1897, where he participated in the founding of the Rāmakṛṣṇa Mission that became one of the most important educational and service organizations in modern India. The Mission, in addition to its work in education and social service in general, has been particularly active in the field of health care, where it puts into practice its teachings of tolerance and recognition of the inner divinity of all.

Theosophical Society

The Theosophical Society is an international spiritual movement that has exerted considerable influence in India, especially through its centers in Banaras and in Adyar near Madras (now Chennai). Though not strictly Hindu, it is based on a form of "Theosophy" in the sense of "divine wisdom" that was inspired by Western alchemy and occultism and then came to interpret them from an Indo-Tibetan perspective.

The Society was founded in New York City in 1875, by the extraordinary Russian psychic Helena Petrovna Blavatsky (1831–91) in collaboration with Henry Steel Olcott (1832–1907) and William Q. Judge (1851–96). Blavatsky had traveled in Europe, North America, the Middle East, Japan, and India and claimed to have spent seven years studying with Hindu *mahātmā*s, great spiritual teachers, in Tibet. In 1879, she returned to India and founded the world headquarters of the Theosophical Society at Adyar, Madras. Her doctrines quickly took on an Indian character, and she and her followers soon established numerous branches in India and subsequently around the world. Blavatsky's main doctrines appear in her books *Isis Unveiled* and *The Secret Doctrine*.

The Society reached the peak of its influence under its next leader, Annie Besant (*née* Wood; 1847–1933), a reform-minded woman who had been born in London of Irish parents. Under her guidance, many Theosophical lodges were founded in Europe and the United States where they helped to acquaint the West with Hindu philosophy, although in a rather idiosyncratic form. The Society spread the idea that Vedānta is the definitive form of Hinduism; India is the most spiritual land on the planet; and India has the world's oldest and most universal religious teachings. Besant was well known throughout India for her advocacy of Indian Independence. She proposed that her pupil Jiddu Krishnamurti (1895–1985) was the messianic reincarnation of Buddha. He disavowed that identity in 1928, but went on to become a spiritual teacher and educator with an international following.

Aurobindo

Another modern teacher whose doctrines have been influential outside India was Aurobindo Ghose (1872–1950), who has been acknowledged as one of the greatest mystic-philosopher-poet-sages of modern India and one of the most original of its modern Hindu thinkers. His synthetic thought (Integral Yoga) expressed a universal manifestation of the absolute in a series of grades of reality from matter up to the highest absolute spirit. Aurobindo tried to revive and exemplify the ancient ideal of the Vedic sage for the modern world. His thought was highly innovative; of particular note is his idea of the ascent of consciousness into the "supramental," which he presented as a vital historical task and not merely limited to the inner world of an individual, but ultimately involving all of humanity and the entire cosmos.

Aurobindo was sent to England as a child and was educated at Cambridge. Upon his return to India at the age of twenty, he became committed to the Indian Independence movement and was jailed for revolutionary activities. While in prison, he had a profound religious experience that impelled him to withdraw from politics and settle in the French colony of Pondicherry in South India. There he established an *āśrama* and achieved a reputation as a respected sage. His followers saw him as the first incarnate manifestation of the super beings whose evolution he prophesied, and apparently he did not discourage that belief. He was a prolific author and wrote, among his many works, *The Life Divine*, *Sāvitrī*, and *The Secret of the Veda*.

Gandhi and Independence

Mohandas K. Gandhi (1869–1948) was a saint of modern India who made the religion of selfless service and nonviolence his life mission. He was the most important leader in the Indian independence movement and appeared to many to be the very quintessence of the Hindu tradition. His austere celibate life, his undeviating allegiance to truth and nonviolence, and his "fasts unto death" were marks of a life that most Hindus found both appealing and challenging.

He was born into a devout Vaiṣṇava family in Gujarat where he was profoundly affected by Vaiṣṇava devotion and Jaina teachings of nonviolence. While studying law in London, he met Theosophists who introduced him to Edwin Arnold's translation of the *Bhagavad Gītā*, a text that was to form the foundation of his personal philosophy. In London, he also read the Bible and the Qur'ān. Perhaps the most profound impression made upon him during this period was from reading Leo Tolstoy's *The Kingdom of God Is Within You*. Henceforth, Gandhi considered Tolstoy to be his *guru*.

After passing the bar exam, Gandhi went to South Africa to practice law. He began to simplify his life there and started an active but nonviolent resistance movement that he named "Satyāgraha" ("truth-force"). He saw nonviolence as the only appropriate way to express strength that is born of love and truth. In 1915, after successful but incomplete campaigns for equal treatment in South Africa, he returned to India.

Gandhi characterized his life as "experiments with truth." He would say, "my life is my message," and first and foremost he lived the vow that one should never deviate from the truth, not even for the sake of any seeming advantage. Truth formed the cornerstone of Gandhi's religion, and one of the preconditions for finding the truth was self-effacement. Gandhi called it "making oneself a zero." The second principle upon which he based his life was nonviolence, and he termed it the only way to truth. Nonviolence, according to Gandhi, is not merely nonkilling; it means an active love so large that it includes every living being. Nonviolence is a manifestation of truth in action. The third principle Gandhi advocated was sexual continence, including abstaining from everything designed to stimulate the senses, such as alcohol, tobacco, and drugs.

Thus, Gandhi personalized and modernized the ancient Hindu concepts of truth (*satya*), nonviolence (*ahiṃsā*), and sexual continence (*brahmacarya*). Employing these practices, he sought not only to eradicate the exclusion and ill-treatment of people at the lowest level of society who suffered from so-called untouchability, but also to free India from foreign rule. Gandhi renamed untouchables as *harijan*s, "people of god." He gave them equal status in his *āśrama*, though he never sought outright eradication of the caste system. As he said, caste was an occupational division of society based on kinds of labor. Untouchability, on the other hand, was a demeaning classification of people that amounted to a violation of nonviolence.

The Indian nationalist struggle, of which Gandhi was a leading advocate, resulted in India's Independence from British colonial rule in 1947. Thus we see in him a unique mixture of Hinduism and nationalism. He identified truth with God; nonviolence as truth in action; renunciation, especially celibacy, as a tremendous power for spiritual development; the dignity of manual labor; equality for all; and self-sufficiency. He was rooted in his Hindu tradition and lived an unusual, imperfect, but nevertheless challenging exemplary life.

Modern Gurus

The globalization of Hinduism was due initially to Svāmī Vivekānanda's visit to Chicago in 1893, his establishment of the first Vedanta Center in New York City in 1894, and the subsequent founding of the Rāmakṛṣṇa Mission in 1897. Since then many other teachers and organizations have followed. The sage of Arunacala, Ramaṇa Maharṣi (1879–1950), spent virtually his entire life at Tiruvannamalai in Tamil Nadu, yet his teachings, which are a pure, experiential form of Advaita Vedānta, have had a significant and still-increasing influence on Westerners. Among recent independent teachers around the world who claim his influence—just a few from a number that now is approaching a hundred who are reasonably well-known—are Paul Brunton, Douglas Harding, Jean Klein, Nisargadatta Maharaj of Mumbai, H.W.L. Poonja (Papiji), and Eckhart Tolle.

Paramahaṃsa Yogānanda (1890–1952) came to the West and established the Self-Realization Fellowship in the United States, which now has centers around the world. He is the author of the fascinating *Autobiography of a Yogi*, a book that has had a profound influence on an untold number of twentieth-century seekers of spiritual wisdom, most of them unknown but a few of them world changers like Steve Jobs.

During the 1960s, there was a steady flow of Hindu *guru*s to the West, such as Maharishi Mahesh Yogi (1917–2008), the founder of the Transcendental Meditation (TM) movement; the then youthful *guru* Maharaj Ji (*born* 1957, now Prem Rawat) who led the Divine Light Mission; Bhaktivedanta Prabhupada (1896–1977), who took the International Society for Krishna Consciousness (ISKCON or the Hare Kṛṣṇa movement) to the West in 1965; Swami Muktananda (1908–82), the founder of the Siddha Yoga movement; and Bhagwan Shree Rajneesh (1931–80), a controversial tāntric teacher. A number of other *guru*s who have developed large followings in the West include Swami Satchidananda (1914–2002) and Swami Chinmayananda (1916–93), both of them direct disciples of Swami Sivananda (1887–1963) of Rishikesh, Gurumayi Cidvilasananda (female successor to Muktananda), and Mata Amritanandamayi, Sri Ma, and Anandi Ma. Two other Hindu *guru*s who have had an influence on the West, though they never left India, include the joy-permeated mother, Anandamayi Ma (1896–1982) and Satya Sai Baba (1926–2011).

Modern Technology

The Internet has thousands of sites pertaining to Hinduism. Not only are there websites that make available major texts, but there are also new sites coming online daily that offer minor texts, support the work of various sects or temples or *guru*s, or facilitate suitable marriage matches. *Pūjā*s and rituals may be performed online to deities in temples in India no matter where one is physically located. Horoscopes are cast and matched by computers. In fact, India has become the world's second leading producer of computer technicians, and the industry is changing the way one can access and interact with Hindu culture and religion.

New technologies now make available recitations of scriptural texts, singing of devotional songs, and the *darśana* of deities and *guru*s from virtually every library, Internet Center, marketplace, or electronically linked home and at any time of the night or day. What once took place only at specified times in a temple, home, or *pāṭhaśālā* (center of Vedic learning), now can be accessible via computers, digital storage devices, tablets, telephones, televisions, and movie screens. This allows people outside of India to hear and see what once required costly travel. They can also learn the proper performance of particular rituals, such as the annual changing of one's sacred thread and the monthly or annual ancestral rites.

The new technologies are a mixed blessing. They provide instant access, but much of the material could be misapprehended without a living teacher to guide one through it. Initiation is a crucial ingredient for most Hindu religious practices. Without it, the power and authority required to perform a rite correctly and effectively may be lacking.

• TRANSMISSION OF THE TRADITION OUTSIDE OF INDIA

Hinduism has become a world religion and a global phenomenon, with Hindu temples established throughout the world. Beginning from the fifth century, Hindu religion and culture became influential in Southeast Asia, including Indonesia, Malaysia, Singapore, Bali, and Java. Brāhmaṇas and merchants, especially Tamilians from South India, established sea trade and then settled overseas. Local kings modeled themselves on ancient Hindu kings, and Brāhmaṇa priests performed rituals in the courts of local chiefs. The earliest material evidence of Hindu culture in Southeast Asia comes from Borneo, where late fourth-century Sanskrit inscriptions testify to the performance of Vedic sacrifices by Brāhmaṇas. Over time, the civilizations of Southeast Asia developed their own religious forms that added distinctive local elements while preserving traditional Hindu features. Stories from the *Rāmāyaṇa* and the *Mahābhārata* became widely known in Southeast Asia and remain very popular there in local versions.

Hindu religion has spread to other parts of the world, including South and East Africa, the Pacific Islands, South America, the West Indies, North America, Europe, and Australia through migration of Indian populations. This movement took place in two waves. First, during the nineteenth century, empires and nations around the world sought cheap Indian labor and many Indians sought opportunities to work abroad. Most of these first-wave emigrants were indentured laborers. Then in the 1960s and continuing to this day, a second wave of highly educated urbanites seeking greater professional opportunities migrated to the major cities in Europe and North America. This second wave is comprised mainly of professionals, such as doctors, engineers, computer scientists, and university professors.

As immigrant families prospered in the new world, they felt a need for their own religious institutions, temples, teachers, and cultural venues to keep alive their inherited tradition in a land where locals observed no Hindu holidays, had no wandering renunciants, and spoke no Indian languages. Community-inclusive, nonsectarian temples and all-Indian cultural centers became a focal point for preserving Hindu tradition. At first, existing buildings were converted to the purpose, but more recently money has been raised to build temples in traditional architectural styles. New temples now exist around the world that duplicate their counterparts on the subcontinent, complete with the properly designed and consecrated images, trained priests, appropriate rituals, and familiar educational and cultural activities.

As global Hindu religion continues to grow, the greatest challenge it faces is to teach each new generation, wherever born and educated, characteristic elements of traditional behavior and values. In some parts of the world the bonds of the tightly knit Hindu extended or joint family may seem to be less strong, inter-caste and inter-religious marriages may be becoming more generally accepted, and women may be taking up new nontraditional roles. Hindu tradition and the people who observe it have always adapted to changing times and local circumstances, and nevertheless have found it possible to preserve time-honored forms of life.

• RELATIONS WITH OTHER RELIGIONS

Hindus, Jews, and Zoroastrians for the most part have enjoyed peaceful relations and have been largely free from inter-religious conflicts. Perhaps this is because active recruitment and conversion activities tend to be marginal factors in each of the three traditions. Relatively small numbers of participants from generation to generation have been lost from one or another of these traditions to one of the others, even without an active competition among them for participants, but no large population category remains totally free from incidental movement into or out of it over time. Disappointments, disaffection, new opportunities, or affections that lead to new affiliation through friendship or a marriage are possible everywhere.

Jaina Dharma and Buddha Dhamma

Hindu, Jaina, and Buddha Dharma traditions took shape and developed their respective institutions in the same milieu. The three share many assumptions: existence is sorrowful and requires deliverance, rebirth exists due to *karma*, there is an innate moral law, ignorance causes suffering, everything empirical is impermanent, and spiritual practices can remove ignorance and appropriately redirect one's way of living. They differ in the status they give to Vedic tradition. Hindus affirm the authority of the Veda; Jainas and Buddhists do not, and so are heterodox and "outside the Veda." Jaina and Buddhist monastic institutions were established by members of the warrior class who renounced their position in society in order to attain spiritual realization: Vardhamāna (about 599–527 BCE), known as Mahavīra, and Siddhārtha Gautama (about 566–486 BCE), known as Buddha. In the face of those challenges, Brāhmaṇism adapted Vedic institutions and adopted some parts of the new Jaina and Buddhist ones, retaining continuity with Vedic tradition while transforming it into classical Hindu tradition.

Siddhārtha Gautama, though born a Hindu prince, eventually rejected inherited authority and ritual practices, caste, divine sovereignty and grace, and the reality of an enduring self or soul. All of these were either explicit or implicit in Vedic religion and remained so in classical Hindu tradition. As a "reform" movement, Buddhists admitted persons of any age and caste to their practices and the monastic life. Early Buddhist emphasis on the central importance of the monastic order went counter to Hindu emphasis on family life and "non-renunciation" as essential components in the full course of human development, followed only afterward by renunciation in one's elder years. Hindu opposition took the form of lively debate and the interruption of the funding of Buddhist monastic and teaching institutions by royal patronage, but also the incorporation of some elements of Buddhist thought and practice—going so far as to name Gautama the Buddha as the ninth incarnation of Viṣṇu. However, his Hindu status is often accompanied by the cautionary qualification that Viṣṇu assumed this particular incarnation as a means to confuse and destroy enemies of the Veda.

Hindu and Jaina social institutions and ritual practices overlap, but there are some significant differences in how the spiritual plight of living beings and its possible resolution are understood. For Jainas, the twenty-four Tīrthaṅkaras, or "path-makers," of which Mahavīra was the twenty-fourth, are not divine incarnations, but instead are departed ideal exemplars of release from the kārmic problem of worldly living. Jainas view *karma* as a sticky substance that binds the soul to the world, perpetuates harm and violence, and eventually must be radically renounced by heroic or monastic disciplines involving a resolute commitment to nonviolence (*ahiṃsā*). As far as this world is concerned, Jainas typically are carefully vegetarian, are not bound to observe formal Hindu caste distinctions, do not offer sacrifices for ancestors, and do not worship any divine creator, sustainer, or moral governor of the universe.

Muslims and Islam

Relationships between Hindus and Muslims over the centuries have been at times cordial but at other times confrontational. History offers many examples of an explosive as well as a mutually enriching relationship. Muslim armies invaded India in 711 CE, and Muslim rule in most of the subcontinent, except for a few princely states, ended a thousand years later in 1757. Attitudes and administrative policies of Muslim rulers toward Hindus varied. Some, like Fīrūz Tughluq (*ruled* 1351–88) and Awrangzeb (*ruled* 1658–1707), were anti-Hindu and enforced a poll tax on non-Muslims. Others, like the Bengali Sulṭān Ḥusayn Shāh (*ruled* 1493–1519) and Akbar (*ruled* 1556–1605), were positively disposed toward their Hindu subjects. Where royal courts were Muslim, patronage was likely to be diminished or withdrawn from Hindu institutions. A few rulers actually had Hindu temples destroyed and replaced by mosques. One well-known and tragic instance was a mosque in North India dating from 1528, the so-called Bābrī masjid that had been constructed during the reign of Bābur, who was the first Mughal emperor. Hindus have claimed it was built on a site where an earlier Hindu temple had marked the birthplace of Lord Rāma, the seventh *avatāra* of Viṣṇu. In 1992, a group of Hindu militants forcefully tore the unused mosque apart in the hope that eventually they would be able to rebuild a temple on the site. In contrast to such competition for space and conflict over place, many great *sants* (saints) like Kabīr (about 1440–1518) and Shirdi Sāī Bābā (*died* 1918) subordinated the differences between the two communities to a higher reality that surpasses spiritual pretensions and religious institutions.

Hindu and Muslim beliefs and practices are based on fundamentally different assumptions, so Islamic religion could not really be absorbed into Hindu tradition, and neither have Muslims (about 15 percent of India's population) been sufficiently powerful to make India into an Islamic nation. Indian Muslims, with few exceptions, are of native descent, but in theory have become outcastes with whom dealings with Hindus are restricted by formal rules. Therefore, upper caste Hindus and Muslims ordinarily do not intermarry. The teachings of Islam envision a single community with no place for caste distinctions, but in practice some Indian Muslims do observe them. After centuries of living separately but in close proximity,

Hindus and Muslims have found ways to coexist peacefully most of the time, although the Partition of India and creation of Pakistan after Independence from Britain in 1947 has continued to complicate their relationship considerably.

Sikh Dharam

When Hindu and Muslim leaders and institutions were mutually struggling for ideological supremacy in the fifteenth century, Gurū Nānak (1469–1539) discovered a third religious way beyond the polarities of then-dominant traditions. Through disciplined devotional practice of chanting and meditation, a distinctive new path to liberation that retains many affinities with Hindu tradition was revealed to him. Over time, this became what we know today as Sikh Dharam. Sikhs differ from Hindus in rejecting elaborate ritualism, divine incarnations, and status determined by caste. They discourage asceticism, and instead honor and celebrate the values of married family life. They have their own lineage of authoritative teachers, body of scriptures, and set of historically significant places of worship. Their ethos reflects a balance between mystical and martial images and practices.

Christianity

With the ascendancy of British economic power and political authority from about 1757, Hindus faced two centuries of intense challenge from Christianity. As early as the fourth century CE, Syrian Christians had inhabited the Malabar Coast of southwest India and the Portuguese established communities on the northwest coast in the sixteenth century. But those earlier communities had little impact on Hindu tradition, even though they included the presence of missionaries.

Even during the two centuries of British colonial dominance, the greatest effect on Hindus of the Christian presence in India was to motivate changes within Hindu institutions rather than to recruit large numbers of converts. Christians both invited and provoked Hindus into dialogue with other world religions. Christian critiques of Hindu practices inspired Hindus to develop clearer theories of scriptural authority and better definitions of the ideal society. Beginning in the nineteenth century with the Brāhmo Samāj, and continuing to the present, Neo-Vedāntic forms of Hinduism in particular have been used to explain and to justify the seeming "degenerations" such as "idol" worship and caste and gender distinctions based on birth.

Perhaps more than any other world religion, Hinduism frustrates Christians because Hindus can accept that Jesus was an incarnation of the divine, was specially conceived and born of a virgin, and taught deeply appealing ethical principles in the Sermon on the Mount, but at the same time reject Christian claims to have unique knowledge of god and exclusive possession of the true and effective path to salvation. While those theological claims are most often dismissed, the good work of missionaries, who have made significant contributions to social service, education, and health care, is respected and appreciated.

• THE TRADITION IN THE STUDY OF RELIGIONS

Academic study of religion, indeed nearly every sort of research or field of study, tends to be influenced and encroached upon by the agendas, ideologies, and interests of people who want to protect some already entrenched viewpoint or to overthrow that one in favor of some alternative. In the nineteenth century, when a few scholars in universities in Great Britain and elsewhere in Western Europe were working to develop an early version of a "scientific" way to study religions, they were regarded as potential competitors to long-established programs of study in Christian divinity schools, seminaries, and universities. On the other hand, those early scholars of comparative religion (as it was then called) were occasionally granted financial support by agencies or departments within their government. The support was not entirely disinterested philanthropy. At the time, there were administrative responsibilities to manage populations in colonized regions of the world, and colonial management required knowledge. While the academicians may have wished to pursue knowledge independently, as a practical matter they were working in a narrow cultural space that was sandwiched between established and locally dominant religious institutions to the one side and to the other side their imperialist patrons who could make use of any knowledge they created in ways that were beyond their control and served other purposes. It was difficult to keep diplomatic balance and intellectual focus between those competing interests.

India already had seen Christian missionary activity by the seventeenth and eighteenth centuries, and soon saw European traders and colonial administrators in India who doubled as scholars of native legal systems, languages, and social institutions. The Europeans formed "Asiatick" Societies and similar organizations that were open exclusively or primarily to themselves and that provided forums for discussion, debate, and an exchange of knowledge about life on the subcontinent. Then a major project that had been proposed in Oxford, approved in 1879, and received support from the British government's India Council significantly extended the range and depth of study of the religions of India. Between 1879 and 1894, the project published English translations of traditional religious texts in a series called the Sacred Books of the East. Of forty-nine volumes of texts in the series, twenty-one volumes were Hindu texts, twelve volumes were Jaina and Buddhist texts, and eight volumes were Zoroastrian texts. The series had been the idea of Friedrich Max Müller (1823–1900), a German-born scholar of philology and languages at Oxford. He had learned Sanskrit before arriving in Oxford and went on to develop theories about the close relationships of language to mythology and religion. While his theories were a product of his nineteenth century intellectual milieu and tend to be neglected today, his contribution to the study of religions—and particularly to Hindu and other religions of India—continues to be significant.

Hindus and Hindu tradition have maintained an important place in the development of the study of religions long after being given a majority role in the Sacred Books of the East. Questions about "the Hindu case" continue to be raised and debated, but are far from settled today. Among them are the following. Should Hinduism be considered a single religion, a set or a cluster of closely related religions, or not a religion at all but something else entirely? Is social and cultural status as determined by birth (class and caste) an essential component of Hindu religion or separable from it? How fixed or how fluid are the boundaries of the category called Hindu? Can it include people who were not born of Hindu parents, or people who had ancestors who were identified as Hindu but who do not identify as Hindu themselves? Is it ever appropriate to include people who think of themselves as Jainas or Sikhs, for instance, within the definition of Hindu? Why or why not? Who is able to speak meaningfully or authoritatively about being Hindu—what are the requisite qualifications? What methods and theories are legitimate to use in studying Hinduism? In short, the most basic concepts and problems in the academic study of religion—how religion is defined, what are clear instances of a religion in contrast to something else, the connections between social arrangements and religious institutions—attract scholars of religion to carefully consider Hinduism or Hindu tradition as an important case study that is complex and does not yield easy answers.

• DISCUSSION QUESTIONS

1. Are Hindus unique in taking for granted the authority of something (the Veda) about which most of them have little detailed knowledge themselves? From your own experience of the social and natural worlds, what else seems to be widely accepted, affirmed, or believed without being directly known or deeply studied and understood? Are there other things that are accepted mostly or exclusively on the basis of the authority of specialists or experts?
2. What might explain the widespread appreciation for the *Bhagavad Gītā*? Is there a single reason, or are there several reasons why it would appeal to people who have different temperaments and are from a wide range of backgrounds?
3. What resources and methods are available to Hindus who hope to manage or even overcome the daunting consequences of *karma*? What do they require?

BIBLIOGRAPHY

Bailey, Greg, ed. 2017. *Hinduism in India: The Early Period.* New Delhi: Sage Publications.

Basham, A. L. 1967 [1954]. *The Wonder That Was India: A Survey of the Culture of the Indian Sub-Continent Before the Coming of the Muslims.* London: Sidgwick and Jackson.

Davis, Richard H. 2015. *The Bhagavad Gita: A Biography.* Princeton: Princeton University Press.

Eck, Diana L. 1985 [1981]. *Darśan: Seeing the Divine Image in India.* Chambersburg: Anima Books.

Flueckiger, Joyce Burkhalter. 2015. *Everyday Hinduism.* Oxford: Wiley Blackwell.

Frazier, Jessica, ed. 2011. *The Continuum Companion to Hindu Studies.* London: Continuum.

Fuller, C. J. 2004 [1992]. *The Camphor Flame: Popular Hinduism and Society in India.* Princeton: Princeton University Press.

Goodall, Dominic, ed. and trans. 1996 [1966]. *Hindu Scriptures*. London: J. M. Dent.

Haan, Michael. 2005. "Numbers in Nirvana: How the 1872–1921 Indian Censuses Helped Operationalise 'Hinduism'." *Religion* 35, 1: 13–30.

Hawley, John Stratton and Vasudha Narayanan, eds. 2006. *The Life of Hinduism*. Berkeley: University of California Press.

Lipner, Julius J. 1996. "Ancient Banyan: An Inquiry into the Meaning of 'Hinduness'." *Religious Studies* 32: 109–26.

Lipner, Julius J. 2010 [1994]. *Hindus: Their Religious Beliefs and Practices*. London: Routledge.

Mittal, Sushil and Gene Thursby, eds. 2004. *The Hindu World*. London: Routledge.

Mittal, Sushil and Gene Thursby, eds. 2008. *Studying Hinduism: Key Concepts and Methods*. London: Routledge.

O'Flaherty, Wendy, ed. and trans., Daniel Gold, and David Shulman. 1988. *Textual Sources for the Study of Hinduism*. Manchester: Manchester University Press.

Sweetman, Will and Aditya Malik, eds. 2016. *Hinduism in India: Modern and Contemporary Movements*. New Delhi: Sage Publications.

FIGURE 2.1 Icon of Ṛṣabha, the first Tīrthaṅkara (Ādinātha) in a temple in Jaisalmer, Rajasthan.

Image courtesy of robertharding/Alamy Stock Photo.

2

Jaina Dharma

ANNE VALLELY

• THE TRADITIONS DEFINED

A sea of scooters, cars, festooned rickshaws, and garlanded trucks, each blasting their distinctive horns, jostle for openings along the congested streets of suburban Mumbai. Crowds of passersby deftly navigate the traffic, weaving perilously close to the oncoming vehicles, with little more than a raised hand to shield them. Schoolgirls, arms linked, race along the road's edge; skinny boys delivering cups of tea deftly dart through the crowd and disappear; businessmen in suits, hollering into cell phones, hurriedly stride in all directions. Overhead, a kaleidoscope of towering advertisements—heralding Bollywood's newest releases, beauty products, and high-end real estate compete for a piece of the skyline with the less glamorous but more numerous faces of politicians smiling from billboards that line the streets. The humid air joins the cacophony of images and sounds and covers the city like a heavy blanket. In the midst of the din, a group of Jaina renouncers wearing crisp white robes moves deliberately and briskly through the crowd. The clamor intuitively keeps its distance, creating a sanctified space around them. They are a striking sight: their serene expressions and purposeful steps distinguish them from the crowd of preoccupied and harried onlookers. Among the *muni*s is a former businessman. At the age of sixty, he gave up his fortune, his belongings, and his ties to his family to dedicate himself to the rigorous life of a Jaina renouncer. He will never again possess anything. He will spend the rest of his life wandering from town to town, dependent on others for sustenance, without ever calling any place home. His accomplishments as a businessman were many but are dwarfed before his glorious quest for world negation. He has attained the highest goal of Jaina tradition. Even unknown passersby call him "Mahārāja," honoring him for his courage and spiritual wisdom.

World renunciation is the dominant religious ideal in Jainism and, though pursued by a tiny minority, plays an important role in Jaina social life and retains a powerful hold on the popular religious imagination. It is the central motif through which the community defines itself: Jainas are those who uphold the renunciatory ideals of nonviolence, nonattachment, and nonabsolutism. These ideals are evident even in those acts that seem, on the surface, to be a display of the community's worldly engagement and affluence—such as in the sponsoring of elaborate festivals, extravagant rituals, and temple construction or the running of costly hospitals and animal shelters. Here, as with other examples of worldly involvement, the close association with renunciatory ideals is always the professed motive: giving is done in the name of worldly disengagement.

Peering into the world of Jainism is to witness an extraordinary religious expression. The tradition makes the singular and potentially revolutionary claim that nonviolence (*ahiṃsā*) is the only path to salvation and that violence is the root of all human woes. For Jainas, the concept of nonviolence has considerable reach: It extends beyond the human community to include all living beings and censures not only physical violence but also harmful speech and injurious thoughts.

To define oneself as Jaina is to situate oneself within a vibrant moral universe in a highly distinctive way, namely, as a cosufferer with all sentient life. To be Jaina in this religious sense (one could easily define oneself as Jaina in purely social terms that would denote membership within a particular historical community and make no claims to transcendent goals) is to see through the spectacle of worldly existence, with all its intoxicating pleasures and crushing defeats, and to know that one's *jīva* (soul), just like the *jīva*s of all living beings, yearns to be free of it. Importantly, Jainism's other-worldly goals never result in a trivializing of embodied, earthly existence. Instead, the body and by implication, the world, offers the only means for escape from the cycle of births, deaths, and rebirths (*saṃsāra*), serving as a kind of smelter for the *jīva*'s refinement if properly (that is, nonviolently) engaged with.

Irrespective of the considerable differences that exist among the Jaina communities worldwide, all emphasize the centrality of the doctrine and practice of *ahiṃsā* in defining their tradition. Whether they are renouncers, who have given up worldly life to pursue a rigorous path of asceticism, or householders busy with such "worldly" concerns as family and work, Jainas universally share an identity rooted in an ancient ethic of restraint and compassion.

• HISTORY AND COSMOS

Jainism is a tradition that counsels restraint. Like the *śramaṇa*, or world-renouncing, cultures of ancient India (of which it is a celebrated expression), the Jaina tradition views the world as a tempest from which the wise withdraw and from which all eventually yearn to escape. The allures of life, with its fascinations and charms as well as its repulsions, are viewed as little more than a ruse that ensnares us in *saṃsāra.*

There were many world-renouncing groups extant in eastern India during the seventh century BCE, the earliest period for which we have historical record of a distinctively Jaina Dharma. The origin of the renouncer traditions is unknown and may be connected, as many Jainas believe, with the indigenous religions of the Indus Valley civilization (about 3000 BCE).

The *śramaṇa* traditions were united in their repudiation of the Brāhmaṇical orthodoxy and its fixation with upholding cosmic and social order. They rejected the "florid utterances" and rituals of the Vedic priests as being pointless and wasteful. Rather than seeking to support the social order, they renounced it, viewing it, and worldly life in general, as the fundamental adversary to self-realization.

Mokṣa, or liberation, was the goal of the various *śramaṇa* traditions, and their analyses of the causes of bondage shared much in common. All held *karma* to be the primary vice through which the soul is trapped and bound to the worldly realm. Understanding worldly life as a scourge—one that is fundamentally hostile to the realization of the true self—was the necessary precondition to achieving freedom from it. But for those who would later come to be known as "Jainas," knowledge alone would not be sufficient. *Mokṣa* could never be attained through purely psychological efforts, because, for Jainas, worldly bondage is a real condition requiring bodily exertion to undo. Disentangling oneself from *saṃsāra* requires a physical drawing back from all that it constitutes. The path to *mokṣa* for Jainas necessitates a bodily rigor that distinguishes it from other renouncer traditions. As a consequence, asceticism has always been a central and defining aspect of the Jaina path and remains a powerful and central cultural ideal.

The Jaina ideals of nonviolence and nonattachment are best symbolized by the lives of the twenty-four great mythohistorical ascetic teachers called "Jinas"—those "conquerors" who triumphed over worldly, egoist passions and became free. "Tīrthaṅkara" is another common term, used interchangeably with Jina, and means "one who creates a ford" or bridge to cross over the ocean of *saṃsāra*. Although each of the twenty-four Jinas has a distinctive biography, their teachings all identify world renunciation and nonviolence as the path to liberation. The best known and most beloved of the Jinas are those chronologically closest to us—the twenty-third Jina, Bhagavān Pārśvanātha, believed to have lived in the ninth century BCE, and the twenty-fourth Jina, Bhagavān Mahāvīra, a historical figure who lived between 599–527 BCE (according to traditional dating). Scriptures tell us that Mahāvīra's parents were followers in the lineage founded by the twenty-third Jina and that Mahāvīra continued this tradition rather than founded it. Nevertheless, because the historical evidence for Pārśvanātha's existence is less abundant than it is for Mahāvīra, modern historical accounts typically pay him little attention. Instead, they begin with Mahāvīra, the last Jina in the series of twenty-four, sometimes mistakenly referring to him as the "founder" of Jainism. The preceding twenty-two Jinas are beyond historical reach, but that does nothing to diminish their powerful presence within the religious life of the community.

Mahāvīra (an honorific title meaning "Great Hero") was born "Vardhamāna Jñātṛputra" into a ruling clan in the northeastern region of India (near present-day Patna). Indifferent to worldly successes and pleasures, he yearned only to find the truth of existence. With this aim, he renounced worldly life at the age of thirty to become an itinerant renouncer. In his efforts to distinguish between eternal happiness and the fleeting, ephemeral pleasures associated with the body, he renounced all physical comforts and endured deprivations of every kind.

Without assistance from any human or divine being, Mahāvīra waged war on "himself," that is, on his passions and his *karmas*. Like the Jinas before him, he taught that our passions are our fiercest foes, represent the only adversary worth fighting, and must be fought on one's own: no one can assist us in destroying our own *karma*. Rejecting the notion of a creator god as well as the idea of grace, Jainas contend that the battle for spiritual freedom is a solitary one.

In Jainism, harm to others leads to bondage, but waging war on the self is the surest path to salvation. The *Uttarādhyayanasūtra* (9.34–36) states: "Difficult to conquer is oneself; but when that is conquered, everything is conquered."

Mahāvīra was a fearless and heroic combatant who attained his goal of spiritual enlightenment after twelve years, six months, and fifteen days on a path of extreme physical austerity. For this, like the great ascetic teachers before him, he is called "Jina," meaning conqueror, and from which Jainism derives its name.

As mentioned above, Mahāvīra is not understood by Jainas as the founder of Jaina Dharma so much as its restorer. The truths of the tradition are believed to be eternal but in need of rekindling at specified times during the long cycles of time. Jainism shares with most of the religions of India a belief in the repetitive waxing and waning of cosmological time. The universe is understood to move through enormous and fixed cycles, for which there are corresponding physical, social, and moral effects. A full cycle takes eons to complete and is divided into two half-cycles, marked by contrasting trends; one of progress (*utsarpiṇī*) and one of decline (*avasarpiṇī*). Each trend (constituting a half-cycle) is subdivided into six phases, marking the progressive deterioration or amelioration. We are currently living in the fifth phase of the declining half-cycle, called the Kali Yuga (Age of Strife), an inauspicious period characterized by increasing natural and social degeneration. For Jainas, the world around us gives us plenty of evidence of this: the global environmental crises, the disparities between the rich and the poor, the increase in violence on the international scene, the explosion of degenerate diseases, and even the nihilism that marks much of the modern period, all point to an age of decline. The impending sixth phase will be worse still; a time when living creatures will suffer great physical pain and when all decency, as well as the teachings of the Jinas, will disappear.

While the first two and last two phases of the cycle are antipodes—periods of ease counterpoised by periods of misery, the in-between phases (third and fourth) are a mixture. On the downward cycle, the third marks the entry of suffering and is described as "happy-sad" (*sukha-dukha*), followed by a period where suffering comes to dominate, described as "sad-happy" (*dukha-sukha*). These labels describe emotional, subjective states, which are associated with the objective social and physical decline of the eras. Whereas in early periods, individuals live long and peaceful lives without much difficulty, the middle eras introduce the crucial element of pain, strife, and uncertainty. Existence now comes to be marked by ambivalence: joy and loss, health and illness, beauty and ugliness. Interestingly, these eras also witness the emergence of *dharma*, and the association is not accidental: without some degree of suffering, spiritual insight would be impossible; the soul would remain in a state of ignorance if nothing roused it from its delusional slumber.

It is during these liminal phases that the twenty-four great prophetic teachers, or Jinas, appear, prodding the recalcitrant through their teachings and rekindling faith in the eternal truths through their own lived experiences. Their appearance is vital since all that remains to keep the *dharma* afloat in these turbulent times are their teachings. From an early age, Jaina children learn the extraordinary tales of the lives of the Jinas, whose biographies extend over many lives, each a moral tale presaging the next. The children become skilled at making the connections between the Jinas' previous lives and, in so doing, learn the moral law of *karma*. The biographies of the most popular Jinas are highly elaborate and complex, while others include a minimum of detail. But the Jinas all share the characteristic qualities of being deeply compassionate, courageous, and self-disciplined. In the final life of each, the Jina-to-be awakens to the true nature of the soul's anguish in *saṃsāra* and embarks on a path to liberate it. In all cases, this means pursuing the path of worldly renunciation. Throughout history, and continuing to the present day, Jainas who wake up to the reality of the soul and its bondage in worldly life regard the ascetic path the only legitimate one to gain freedom. While most Jainas reject this option for themselves, they accept its logic and honor it as the ultimate path.

Jaina cosmology is a great cosmic drama between sentient, beings and the nonsentient matter that ensnares them, played out against a backdrop of time and space (*arūpa-ajīva*). With no concept of a creator god, the *jīva* (soul or sentient being) and *ajīva* (a nonsentient material component that attaches itself to the soul, also called *karma*) are the key and only players in this drama. *Arūpa-ajīva* denotes that which is neither matter nor sentient, and primarily refers to space and time but also to the cosmic principles that enable activity and inactivity.

The soul in its pure state is said to be god-like: the eternal experiencer of truth, bliss, and omniscience. This is the glory of "self-realization" for which the soul, slumbering through the cycle of births and deaths from beginningless time, has yearned—albeit silently. Deformed by the kārmic matter that encases and defiles it, the soul has, for the most part, remained oblivious to its fate. Only when it awakens to its true spiritual trajectory, a pivotal phenomenon called "*samyag darśana*," or correct vision, does the path to *mokṣa* become a possibility.

The soul, when animated with passions (*saṃjvalana*), involuntarily lures kārmic particles, which become attached to the *jīva*, and obscures its omniscient nature. The bound *karma* distorts the soul and causes further *karma* to be drawn in. Encrusted, the soul is now cast into an endless succession of births and deaths—changing form as a consequence of *karma* but unable to stop the cycle (*saṃsāra*). The human form, like all life forms, is but one "product" or outcome of this soul-matter association. Freedom is possible but difficult to achieve. The connection between *jīva* and *ajīva* is beginningless and is sustained by passions (*kaṣāya*)—attachment, aversion, greed, and envy. With every ungenerous word or deed or harmful thought, new *karma* is drawn in, adding to the old. *Mokṣa* is a longed-for idyllic state of bliss and omniscience, in which the soul has freed itself from captivity. But this can only be achieved when the inflow of new *karma* is permanently blocked and when the blanket of *karma* that encases and oppresses the soul is scuffed out, layer by layer.

Jainas contend that the *jīva* can only be severed from *ajīva* through sustained and rigorous efforts at detachment from worldly life, in other words, through renunciation. Jaina scriptures provide us with detailed analyses of the causes of kārmic bondage and of the mechanisms of release. Consider Mahāvīra's teaching, recorded in the *Ācārāṅgasūtra*, the oldest of the (Śvetāmbara) Jaina scriptures. It states: "All breathing, existing, living, sentient creatures should not be slain, nor treated with violence, nor abused, nor tormented, nor driven away" (1.4.1). Because the normal life of a householder invariably involves at least some degree of attachment (for example, familial bonds) and some forms of violence (for example, that which is involved in feeding oneself), it does not permit attainment of the highest spiritual goals. Such goals can only be achieved through renunciation. Jaina scriptures provide us with detailed analyses of the causes of kārmic bondage and of the mechanisms of release. They represent the most fundamental teachings delivered by Mahāvīra over twenty-five hundred years ago. After he attained a state of enlightenment (*kevala-jñāna*), he quickly attracted many disciples who, under his guidance, formed a unified community.

After his death, Mahāvīra's mendicant disciples assumed leadership of the community, which continued to attract followers. However signs of discord soon appeared, and within two centuries, the once cohesive Jaina community had split into two distinct traditions, each with distinctive scriptures and at odds with the other. The precise causes of the sectarian split remain unexplained, but according to tradition, it was primarily as a consequence of the southward migration by one group of Jainas in the fourth century BCE, in response to a famine in the north. The northern and southern communities then developed in isolation from each other, resulting in inevitable differences. It is claimed that when the southerners eventually returned to the north, they were confronted with a tradition that was alien and intolerable to them. In their absence, recensions of sacred teachings had been made which, in their view, deviated from the practice of Mahāvīra (Jaini 1979: 5). One very evident example of this was the northern monks' practice of wearing garments. For the southern communities, nudity was a fundamental expression of nonattachment for all Jaina mendicants, which Mahāvīra himself had practiced, and was therefore not open to change. The northerners agreed that Mahāvīra practiced nudity, but understood its importance differently. They maintained that after initiating himself as a renouncer, Mahāvīra donned a single robe, but that because he was completely engrossed in his soul and indifferent to his body, he did not notice when it slipped off. On this basis, the northerners concluded that clothing, in and of itself, is not an impediment to spiritual progress. The differences between the two groups—and there were others—crystallized over this issue, and tellingly, the names by which the two came to be known reflect its centrality: the group from the south subsequently came to be called Digambara (meaning "sky clad"), affirming nudity for mendicant males; the group from the north came to be called Śvetāmbara ("white clad"). It is important to bear in mind, however, that what is today presented as the outcome of a portentous debate was more likely the consequence of a gradual change over time. Paul Dundas writes, "archaeological and inscriptional evidence suggests that there was a gradual movement among Jain monks towards a differentiation based on apparel, or the lack of it, rather than any abrupt doctrinal split" (2002: 48).

One of the most interesting differences between the Śvetāmbara and Digambara is over the question of female religiosity, which is itself one aspect of the larger debate on garments.

According to the Digambara, a woman is of inferior religious status to a man because of her flawed physical and emotional nature. As such, she can never achieve *mokṣa*; she would have to be reborn as a male before liberation could occur (Jaini 1991). The Śvetāmbara tradition too considers women's "nature" to be less well suited to renunciation than men's, but not so severely that it excludes them from attaining liberation. This disagreement forms part of the more general dispute over the requirement of nudity for mendicants. Neither group considers nudity an acceptable practice for women, but among the Digambaras, for whom nudity is a requirement for spiritual progress, it serves as the coup de grâce that prevents women from taking full monastic vows. The practical outcome of these theoretical debates is that among the Digambara, men alone are accorded the title (and possess the prestige) of full renouncers. Women, however, are permitted to practice renunciation as *āryikā*s, "noble women," and essentially live as nuns. Among the Śvetāmbara, by contrast, female mendicancy has a long and even illustrious history. According to the scriptures, since the time of Ṛṣabha (Jainism's first Jina of mythic times, also called Ādinātha), nuns (*sādhvī*) have always outnumbered monks by more than two to one. The Jina Mahāvīra is said to have had thirty-six thousand nuns and fourteen thousand monks as disciples (Dundas 1992: 49).

Although Śvetāmbara and Digambara Jainas disagree over the authenticity and interpretation of scriptures, and most importantly over monastic practice, both hold essentially identical views on the soul, the nature of reality, and the need for renunciation.

Both traditions prospered in the centuries following Mahāvīra's death. Royal support was a central factor in their early successes (as it was with the spread of Buddhism). The mutual disregard of the Brāhmaṇa (priestly) caste, by both local kings and *śramaṇa* groups, led to their natural alliance. Jainas, along with other renouncers, proclaimed the superiority of the Kṣatriya (kingly/warrior caste) over that of the Brāhmaṇas. In the centuries straddling the end of the old and start of the new millennium (300 BCE–400 CE), the *śramaṇa* groups were numerous and organized, and with the allegiances they made with local rulers they constituted a "parallel civilization" (Jaini 1991: 275) that rivalled the Brāhmaṇical order. The migration patterns of Jainas during the period reflect this sociopolitical reality, in that they are connected with the granting, and subsequent withholding, of kingly favor. By the fifth century CE, in central and southern India, the Digambaras had become an influential cultural force. And the same could be said of the Śvetāmbara in northern and western India by the seventh century. This period is also marked by a large increase in the number of lay followers, a factor that necessitated the development of scriptures aimed at those on the householder path. The mendicant-scholars' acknowledgment of the lay path as a legitimate (albeit subordinate) one, as well the high degree of lay participation, contributed to the advance of Jainism during its period of royal support and enabled it to survive when that support was withdrawn.

The Golden Age of royal support for Jainas came to a close by the eleventh and twelfth centuries, primarily due to the rise of Hindu theism and of Muslim counterinfluences. An energetic devotional Hindu movement (*bhakti*) had emerged in South India, and by the ninth century CE, with the benefit of royal patronage, it had spread throughout India. From the twelfth century onward, Jainas in the north also came increasingly under the presence of Islam, another centrally theist tradition. These factors may have contributed to a falling out of favor for the Jaina tradition, with its emphasis on asceticism and its denial of a supreme god.

Jainas began to withdraw, socially and geographically, to the western regions of India, from Rajasthan in the north to Karnataka in the south, where they remain concentrated to this day.

Significantly, long after the end of the *śramaṇa* "civilization," when its challenge had become assimilated within Brāhmaṇical orthodoxy, the Jaina Dharma continued to thrive. Buddhism, its closest rival, fared less well in India. It was effectively absorbed within the ecumenical outreach of Hinduism. Śākyamuni Buddha became identified as the ninth *avatāra* of Viṣṇu and was ensconced within Hinduism's pantheon of deities. It remains a curiosity as to how Jainas, who always have been a tiny minority numerically, have managed to retain their distinctive identity and flourish on the Indian subcontinent within the dominant Hindu culture.

• SACRED LIFE AND LITERATURES

The sacred literature of the Jainas is held to derive from the Jina Mahāvīra himself. According to the tradition, Mahāvīra, in his omniscient state (*kevalin*), uttered the sacred sounds that were put to memory by his immediate disciples (called *gaṇadharā*s) and then passed on to subsequent disciples, in an oral tradition that continued uninterrupted until the famine of northern India around 300 BCE. It is said that during this disaster, great numbers of mendicants perished, and with them, much of the oral tradition. The group that fled south (later known as the Digambara) did not fare much better: In the turmoil of famine and flight, they were ill prepared for the arduous task of preserving and transmitting a vast canon. From this point on, the story of the authenticity and preservation of Jaina scriptures becomes a complex and contentious one, with Śvetāmbara and Digambara groups disagreeing over which teachings were faithfully remembered.

The entire Jaina canonical literature, or Āgama, is comprised of three main branches: the Pūrva, the Aṅga, and the Aṅgabāhya. The Pūrvas are concerned with a variety of topics in Jaina metaphysics, cosmology, and philosophy. They constitute the oldest part of the Jaina scriptures, believed to date back to the period of Pārśvanātha, the twenty-third Jina, of the ninth century BCE. The Pūrvas disappeared at the time of the famine, but the essence of their content had been memorized and integrated into later works, a commonly used mnemonic device in oral traditions. It is widely assumed that the content of the Pūrvas were incorporated into a body of literature called the Aṅga ("limbs"), which dates from the time of Mahāvīra.

The works of the Aṅga are concerned with a broad range of topics, including mendicant conduct, heretical philosophical schools, doctrine, religious narratives, and laws of *karma*. The final section of the Aṅga, called the *Dṛṣṭivāda*, is believed to have contained the main teachings of the Pūrvas. Unfortunately, the *Dṛṣṭivāda* suffered the same fate as the Pūrvas and disappeared from the ranks of the Śvetāmbara Jainas.

Digambara Jainas, despite their migration, succeeded in retaining portions of the *Dṛṣṭivāda* and put it in writing around the second century CE. This work, called the *Ṣaṭkhaṇḍāgama*, marks the first written scripture of the Jainas. Not long after, a second Digambara work was produced, compiled from the same sources, and called the *Kaṣāyaprābhṛta*. Significantly, the *Ṣaṭkhaṇḍāgama* and the *Kaṣāyaprābhṛta* constitute the only canonical works the Digambaras recognize as legitimate. They reject the scriptures retained by the Śvetāmbara as inauthentic deviations from the original canon (Jaini 1979: 52).

The Aṅgbāhya is an ancient subsidiary canon that contains some of the most important Jaina scriptures. Comprising thirty-four texts, it includes dialogues on the nature of the soul, ontology, cosmology, astronomy, the time cycles, accounts of the first Jina of our period (Ṛṣabha), monastic discipline, and lectures on a variety of moral themes. The Aṅgbāhya also includes a text called the *Prajñāpanā*, which, according to the Śvetāmbara, contains the essence of the lost *Dṛṣṭivāda* and, through it, the lost Pūrvas. According to the Digambaras, the Aṅgabāhya was lost.

Both the Śvetāmbara and Digambara later produced an enormous post-canonical literature based on the works of their learned *ācārya*s (mendicant-scholars), including works by Jinasena, Hemacandra, Kundakunda, Haribhadra, and Umāsvati. The writings, called Anuyogas, achieved canonical status within their respective traditions and are today considered to be among the most outstanding works of ancient Indian philosophy.

The work of the *ācārya* Umāsvati merits special note. His treatise, the *Tattvārthasūtra*, composed in Sanskrit in the second century CE, is the only Jaina scripture recognized as authoritative by both Śvetāmbara and Digambara Jainas. It effectively integrates the vast canonical teachings to produce a single coherent Jaina philosophy. Lastly, in the mid-1970s, a text called the *Samaṇ Suttaṁ* was produced in an effort to reconcile sectarian differences and foster unity. Compiled by representatives from Jainism's major religious communities, it contains only those scriptural teachings common to all. Today the tradition of writing commentaries on scriptures and creating new philosophical works remains an important and popular practice among mendicant communities as well as among lay disciples and scholars.

The Renouncer Ideal

The sacred life of the Jainas, upon which their literature expounds, is unequivocally associated with the ideal of renunciation. The "sacred" in Jainism denotes the transcendent or other-worldly, and therefore the sacred path is the one that leads us out of the tangle of worldly existence.

The path to *mokṣa* is an arduous one and successes are achieved only gradually. Jaina scriptures present a view of human life as plotted along a ladder of spiritual progress called *guṇasthāna*s (stages of purity). One's place on the ladder reflects one's level of spirituality and spans the scale from the nadir of ignorance to the zenith of enlightenment. The lighter one's kārmic "load," the greater the degree of purity and the more advanced along the *guṇasthāna*s. The lowest state is that of *mithyādṛṣṭi* (the deluded view of reality), where a soul may dwell for countless lives until it acquires *samyag-darśana* (the fourth rung), the correct view of reality. *Samyag-darśana* is not achieved based on study, as this would be completely fruitless for someone in a deluded state. Instead, it is described as arising from a spiritual jolt or an "awakening" that suddenly enables one to see clearly. Though still very much a spiritual neophyte, one who has attained *samyag-darśana* can now begin the difficult but glorious journey to *mokṣa*.

The *guṇasthāna*s are stages of increasing restraint and purification. Lay Jainas, despite being in the possession of *samyag-darśana*, are assumed to be relatively low down on the ladder (usually on the fourth or fifth rung). Those who possess extraordinary mental and physical control, such as the mendicants, are assumed to be on higher rungs. The sixth rung (called *sarva-virata*) is attained when one renounces worldly life and accepts the *mahāvrata*s (great vows, indicating absolute restraint). Of course, such a scheme is overdetermined in its support of renunciation, in that the desire to renounce worldly life is itself read as evidence of a higher stage of purity. The absence of such interest is understood to be an indicator of a low spiritual rung.

A philosophy that emphases the *mokṣa-mārga* (path of renunciation) as the religious ideal and which considers human life in terms of stages of purification may reinforce a view of lay life as a diluted or weaker form of the mendicant path. While the scriptures (and many scholarly works) suggest such a reading, the actual lived practices of lay Jainas do not bear this out. The overwhelming majority of Jainas throughout history have chosen the path of the "householder." Rather than renounce the world, they participate in it unequivocally, actively, and joyfully. In recent years, scholars have been redressing this imbalance in the academic interpretive perspective, for instance, by looking at the significant role that "this-worldly" values as health, happiness, and wealth have played at all times in Jaina social life (Cort 2001; Laidlaw 1995), as well as by exploring the rich devotional forms of religious expression in Jainism (Kelting 2001). Indeed, one of the most intriguing features of the Jaina tradition is the degree to which the laity is so successfully engaged in worldly pursuits. Jainas are well known for their business acumen and, in the main, are an affluent community. But there is no need to exaggerate the "this-worldliness" of the Jainas in response to an earlier overemphasis on Jainism's *śramaṇa* roots. No matter how far removed individual Jainas may be from the mendicant path, in their religious lives they are united in the veneration of the ascetic ideal and of those who embody it, namely, the Jinas and the renouncers. Jaina renouncers seek to follow the path of nonviolence established by the Jinas, and as living exemplars of the tradition's highest ideals, they are highly esteemed and sometimes ritually venerated.

It is worth highlighting that the Jinas, who constitute the focus of Jaina worship, were also once human renouncers—albeit heroic ones who attained liberation and taught the path of release. The ritual of *Jina-pūjā* (also called *Deva-pūjā*) is the primary means by which the Jinas are venerated and is the centerpiece of worship within Jaina communities. Through it, devotees make explicit their goal to emulate the path of nonviolence and detachment that the Jina established. For the image-worshipping majority, the ritual adoration is done before an image of a Jina, typically made of marble or stone. The forms of *Jina-pūjā* can be simple or highly elaborate (as they are during festivals), but the most common form is the *aṣṭadravya* ("eight substances"[1]). As the name implies, the *pūjā* centers around eight substances that are offered to the Jina, each expressing an aspect of the devotee's desire for liberation. For instance, water, which denotes purity and cleanliness, is offered as a symbol of the devotee's desire for spiritual purification; dehusked (nongerminating) rice represents the end of the cycle of births and deaths and symbolizes the devotee's desire for liberation. The offering of flowers or saffron-colored rice symbolizes the beauty of *mokṣa* that the devotee desires, or, alternately, it can symbolize worldly passions that must be renounced. The offering of substances is accompanied by the recitation of *mantras*, as well by an inner state of devotion and reverence called *bhāva-pūjā*.

For the nonimage-worshiping communities, *Jina-pūjā* is exclusively a matter of *bhāva-pūjā*—an interior, contemplative devotional practice done without objects or substances. (The Sthānakavāsī and Terāpanthī communities within the Śvetāmbara fold do not practice image worship.)

One distinguishing feature of *Jina-pūjā* is that it is performed without expectation of any external response: with or without material offerings, *Jina-pūjā* is directed toward beings who have attained the ultimate state of release, and therefore neither reciprocate nor respond to the offerings in any way. Rather than engaging in an exchange, *Jina-pūjā* "makes concrete" one's desire to emulate the path of the Jina and to become free. Jainas perform it as a means to stimulate their own soul towards the path of release.

Despite the tradition's overwhelming celebration of renunciation, it would be a mistake to think that all Jainas are Jina-like, indifferent to worldly pleasures. Indeed, within India, the community is far better known for its business acumen and worldly successes than it is for its ascetic aspirations. Jaina worship allows for the expression of worldly desires, but, fascinatingly, does so in a way that ensures they remain subordinate to the ideals of renunciation. One example of this is revealed through the ritual of *Jina-pūjā*, discussed above. Every Jina has his own male and female attendant deities called *yakṣa* or *yakṣī*—celestial beings who are eager to honor the Jina and who, in temples, are always depicted flanking the Jina image. Whereas the Jina remains unmoved by the prayers of the devotees, the attendant deities are not. When the latter are pleased with the devotees, they shower them with their celestial blessings and protection, even if unsolicited. Among the most popular of these deities are the goddesses Cakreśvarī, Ambikā, and Padmāvatī, *yakṣīs* to the first Jina Ṛṣabha (or Ādinātha), the twenty-second Jina Neminātha, and the twenty-third Jina Pārśvanātha, respectively. In some cases, their popularity is so great that separate temples have been dedicated to them. Jainas, like all peoples everywhere, seek personal well-being and worldly success, and throughout their long history have established a culture that balances the needs for worldly involvement with those of worldly withdrawal, but always within an ideological framework that privileges the latter.

• PRACTICES AND INSTITUTIONS

Since the time of Mahāvīra, Jainism has been identified as a *caturvidhasaṅgha* (fourfold community), comprised of monks, nuns, laymen, and laywomen. The success of Jainism as a minority tradition has depended, in large part, on the steady and clearly defined relationship that exists between these groups and especially between those who renounce the world in pursuit of nonviolence and those who remain "in the world" and support their quest.

Dāna is the institution that sustains the *caturvidhasaṅgha* and is therefore at the very heart of Jaina religious life. It is a simple word that signifies "alms" or "donation" (with which its shares a cognate) but through a distinctively Jaina interpretation, becomes the instrument through which the tradition flourishes.

At its most fundamental level, *dāna* is about providing renouncers with food and water, since they are not permitted to acquire these essentials on their own. The vow of *ahiṃsā* prohibits renouncers from all activities associated with the growing, preparation, and exchange of foods. The basics of their vegetarian diet, namely, plants, fruits, and water, all contain life (*jīva*), and for a Jaina mendicant, harming any of these life forms is prohibited. It is only through the piety of householders that the renouncers remain kārmically unaffected by the violence inherent in the preparation of food.

The householder chops, cooks, and boils and, in so doing, renders the food "*ajīva*" (without life). Whatever food the mendicant consumes must be devoid of all life, so that its ingestion will accrue no new *karma*. The householder, who has not renounced the world and lives "in" society, accepts that a degree of violence is necessary in order to survive. She (it is usually the woman of the home who gives these alms) is happy to provide the renouncers with "leftover" food (it cannot be made expressly for the mendicants, as this would implicate them in the violence of its preparation).

Dāna is an expression of nonreciprocal unilateral giving. Renouncers do not provide religious instruction "in exchange" for sustenance; instead, they adamantly deny any exchange takes place since that would implicate them in the worldly life they have renounced. Jonathan Parry succinctly captures the logic of this denial when he writes, "The reciprocated gift belongs to the profane world; the unreciprocated gift to a quest for salvation from it" (1986: 462).

Dāna, more generally, refers to all forms of religious giving and includes the protection that mendicants provide to all living beings (considered its most sublime expression), as well as the lavish donations given by wealthy families for temple construction. All of these result in the accumulation of spiritual merit (*punya*). Without *dāna*, the religious giving of the householders, the monastic institution, and its associated practices could not exist.

Dāna allows the renouncers to pursue their religious practices in a realm removed from the violence and attachment of worldly life. At the time of their initiation, an ascetic-aspirant receives five great vows (*mahāvrata*). In accepting them, he or she swears to observe nonviolence and to renounce lying, stealing, sexual intercourse, and acquisitiveness or the ownership of possessions.

Each of these vows is all encompassing, and together they are intended to lead to total restraint. For Jainas, both the intention underlying the act (thought, deed, or action) as well as the act itself must be pure. For instance, consuming vegetarian food while having harmful thoughts would still result in the accumulation of *pāpa* (bad *karma*). And *pāpa* would be equally accumulated as a result of the unintentional consumption of nonvegetarian food, though of a "lighter" quantity than if it had been intentionally consumed. Jainism and Buddhism differ on this, with Buddhism giving much importance to the role of intention alone.

The *mahāvrata*s are like an elaborate regulatory grid, limiting worldly involvement and regulating all aspects of one's existence. They leave virtually nothing to chance: they dictate how one sleeps (tranquilly, with little movement), the time one rises (at the auspicious hour of 4 a.m.), what and whether one eats (only vegetarian "*ajīva*" alms, and only if offered), what one wears (simple white cloths for Śvetāmbaras) or does not wear (nudity being a requirement for Digambara renouncers), how one talks (minimally and with restraint), how one walks (barefoot, carefully with eyes on the ground in front of them), where one walks (from town to town continuously, except for the four months of the rainy season), and where one eliminates one's bodily waste (a place devoid of all *jīva*s).

*Mahāvrata*s serve as a comprehensive, all-embracing system designed to impede the acquisition of new *karma* (a process called *saṃvara*) and assist in destroying one's existing *karma* (called *nirjarā*). Everything that a mendicant does—from preaching to studying, from fasting to meditation—is with the aim of furthering the processes of *saṃvara* and *nirjarā*.

The religious life of Jaina householders, whose knowledge of and sympathy with the ascetic path was vital for the continued existence of the monastic institution, has obviously always been less constrained. Until the close of the first millennium, it was probably quite variable (Folkert 1993: 12). During that period, a set of scriptures was developed, called *śrāvakācāra*s, addressing the religious life of householders and closely modeled on the mendicant path. They depicted the ideal lay life as one of gradual progress along a path of increasing restraint, delineated in eleven stages, called *pratimā*, in which the final stage entailed ascetic renunciation.

While some lay Jainas clearly do regulate and interpret their lives according to the *pratimā*, the vast majority do not. The most popular religious practices are those of devotion, *pūjā* (worship), temple rituals, and pilgrimage—which are Hinduism's most popular forms of religious expressions as well. Superficially, there is little to distinguish between Jaina and Hindu popular religion (if we can talk in these generalized terms). But a closer look at lay Jaina religiosity reveals the presence of its *śramaṇa* influences as mediated through forms of religious expression that are more acceptable to householders. Most of the colorful, devotional practices of householders (from home *pūjā*s to far-away pilgrimages) are about celebrating the lives of the Jinas. Intriguingly, the crux of lay Jaina devotional life centers on the worship of heroic ascetics who remain aloof from the cares of the world. The songs and prayers of lay devotees, often expressed in an emotive language of love, do not await response. Instead, they are performed as a type of discipline, with the goal of fostering detachment from worldly life. That reveals the degree to which the renouncer ethos has penetrated the very fabric of Jaina life and is an example of the genius with which Jainism integrates the sober and the joyful, the devotional and the ascetic, the other-worldly and the this-worldly.

• ETHICS AND HUMAN RELATIONS

Jaina tradition is known for its ascetic ideal, its astonishingly beautiful architecture, and its philanthropy, among other things. But perhaps it is most renowned for its ethics. An ethical outlook is the very foundation of a worldview, informing every dimension of what we do, bringing into focus that which is deemed worthy of concern, and allowing us to be blind to other realities. In Jainism, ethics are concerned with the interactions of humans with all living beings; there is virtually no sphere from which humans are free from the obligation of concern. Unlike many ethical traditions that conceive of ethics in terms of human-human relations or human-human-divine relations, Jainas accord the nonhuman a place of tremendous importance. Leading an ethical life is wholly impossible without paying heed and extending compassion to animals, plants, and even the smallest of living beings, most of which seem far removed from the drama of human life. But the Jaina tradition insists that the drama of human life is not fundamentally different from that of other sentient beings, and the path to liberation is a shared one.

According to Jaina tradition, the universe is infused with countless life forms. Humans are but one of its expressions, along with animals, plants, and elemental forms of life. Each life has a soul, and each soul is inherently luminous, although differently encased in kārmic matter. Harm to any other life causes us to be burdened with additional *karma* and to sink deeper in the swamp of bondage. Because of this, the world is akin to a moral theater, where every interaction has ethical implications. Jaina ethics are distinctive in their scope, rigor, and ideal of universal compassion and are encapsulated in the two aphorisms widely invoked by Jainas to define their tradition: *ahiṃsā paramo dharma* ("nonviolence is the supreme path") and *parasparopagraho jīvānām* ("all souls render service to each other").

The desire to lead a life of nonviolence is the impetus underpinning the ascetic imperative in Jainism. Padmanabh Jaini explains how Jaina ethics follow from its worldview:

> This awareness of the basic worth of all beings, and of one's kinship with them, generates a feeling of great compassion (*anukampā*) for others. Whereas the compassion felt by an ordinary man is tinged with pity or with attachment to its object, anukampā is free of such negative aspects; it develops purely from wisdom, from seeing the substance (dravya) that underlies visible modes, and it fills the individual with an unselfish desire to help other souls towards mokṣa. If this urge to bring all tormented being out of saṃsāra is particularly strong and is cultivated, it may generate those auspicious karmas that later confer the status of Tīrthaṅkara upon certain omniscients. When present to a more moderate degree, anukampā brings an end to exploitative and destructive behavior, for even the lowest animal is now seen as intrinsically worthwhile and thus inviolable.
>
> (1979: 150)

Dedication to the ethical principle of nonviolence derives from Jainism's unique cosmology, which emphasizes the common fate of all living beings. For those who are truly awake to the violence inherent in life, there is little choice but to repudiate it thoroughly. Renouncers acquire tremendous respect because they have renounced the world fully to pursue ethical ideals. In so doing, they have seized upon the opportunity that human birth has given them, refusing to fritter it away as do most humans. A life of mendicancy, and the possibility of *mokṣa*, is only available to humans.

Compassion is not directed so much at the suffering *in* social life, but at the suffering *of* social life; it arises from observing worldly life itself. The message of the Jinas is that all human beings are capable of conquering the bondage of physical existence and achieving freedom from the cycle of rebirths (Folkert 1993). *Ahiṃsā*, as Jainas formulate it, is not concerned with social roles and obligations, and its teachings are not designed to remedy social ills so much as escape them. It reveals a perception of the world as inherently corrupt and in need of transcendence; it leads to renunciation and motivation to help individuals out of *saṃsāra*. The highest cultural and religious ideals revolve around nonviolence, nonpossession, and nonattachment; these are embodied in the ascetics.

Jaina ethics are enshrined in the *mahāvrata*s—the five "great vows" that work to "fence in" or limit worldly entanglement. Nonviolence (*ahiṃsā*) is the first and most fundamental vow. It demands that one avoid violence in thought, speech, and action; and it is believed to be the foundation upon which the remaining four derive. They are truthfulness, nonstealing, sexual restraint, and nonpossession.

Although Jainas treat the human incarnation as a privileged one that should not be squandered, they do not believe that humans possess anything unique that would endow them with an innate superiority. There exist five categories of living beings in the Jaina universe, each corresponding with the number of senses they possess. They are arranged according to the following schema (Umāsvāti 1994: 45):

Number and Type of Senses	**Examples of Beings**
1. sensed beings called "*nigoda*s," with touch	earth, water, fire, air
2. sensed beings, with touch and taste	worms, leeches, mollusks
3. sensed beings, with touch, taste, smell	all small insects (ants, fleas)
4. sensed beings, with touch, taste, smell, sight	wasps, flies, mosquitoes
5. sensed beings, with touch, taste, smell, sight, hearing	fish, birds, quadrupeds, humans

The greater the number of senses one possesses, the greater is one's ability to understand worldly existence as a state of bondage in need of escape. But an increase in the number of senses does not mean greater moral worth. Consciousness is the inalienable characteristic of every *jīva*, however undeveloped. It is present even in the *nigoda*s (the least-developed life form); and through progressive development along the *guṇasthāna*, they too may culminate in the supreme state of omniscience. Therefore, human distinction from surrounding life forms is a matter of degree, not of kind, and it is established through ethical behavior. Humans alone can be said to be "ethical." The designation of "ethical" or "unethical" is nonsensical if applied to the behavior of insects, plants, and animals as it is to young children or even adults who lack understanding; its employment hinges upon a level of awareness and responsibility that only the human incarnation possesses. In Jainism, ethical practice is the most compelling and potent manifestation of human potential, and asceticism is its highest expression.

It could be argued that Jainas view the meaning of "the human" in a nonessentialized way that is akin to Jinasena's reinterpretation of the Hindu priestly class "Brāhmaṇa"—that is, as a status achieved on the basis of ethical conduct as opposed to one ascribed at birth. We become truly human only through moral behavior; in its absence, we can claim no special status. Through *ahiṃsa* (restraint, compassion, and nonviolence), human dignity is established in a universe teeming with conscious life.

• MODERN EXPRESSIONS

The developments within Jainism in the modern period are too many and varied for a comprehensive examination here. Nevertheless, an overview is possible, highlighting some significant events and possible trends.

The social identity of lay Jainas derives in large measure from their association with a specific renouncer lineage: Śvetāmbara Jainas are those householders who support and identify with renouncers wearing white robes; Digambara Jainas are those who support and identify with monks whose asceticism necessitates nudity.

In India, sectarian affiliation often plays an important role in determining the boundaries of social engagement (for example, it influences the choices with whom one marries). As a consequence, the minutiae of Jaina philosophical debates, which are of little interest to the majority of lay Jainas, have nonetheless had profound effects on lay social organization and identity. This indeed has been the case since the first split after the death of Mahāvīra. Although the schism between the Śvetāmbara and Digambara was as much a reflection of the different geographic and linguistic regions in which the groups developed as it was an expression of doctrinal dispute, it is not generally understood in these terms. Instead, cultural differences tend to be subsumed within sectarian identity.

Jaina laity, therefore, always has been vulnerable to mendicant rivalries but never passively so. Indeed, it was often educated lay disciples, with a keen knowledge of their scriptures, who would initiate the challenges that led to intermonastic schisms. Ironically, the lofty debates over other-worldly matters are fought and decided on this-worldly terrain. A mendicant who breaks from his order because of a difference of opinion over doctrine or practice needs the support of lay disciples if he (and his challenge) is to survive. The social ramifications of doctrinal disputes can therefore be momentous, leading to the splintering of a previously unified community. Much of Jaina history can be understood in this light.

Jainism experienced a rise in sectarian divisions from the fifteenth century CE onward when it had become well established in the western regions of India and when the pull of Hindu and Muslim theism was waning. Many of the reform movements did not survive their leaders, but several remain active today. The most important among these are the Sthānakavāsīs (about fifteenth century) and the Terāpanthis (about eighteenth century), both of which emerged as reform movements from within the Śvetāmbara tradition. The Sthānakavāsīs rejected the temple and image-worship practices that were ubiquitous at the time, arguing they were harmful accretions that ran counter to the ideals of nonviolence and nonattachment. They developed their own canon and initiated the practice of wearing mouth-shields, a further expression of *ahiṃsā*, with the aim of not harming living beings in the atmosphere. The Terāpanthis emerged as a reform group from within the Sthānakavāsīs. They were critical of what they considered to be the renouncers' laxity in ascetic practice and their ignorance of Jaina scriptures. In particular, they considered the use of *sthānaka*s (temporary dwellings for mendicants) to be contrary to the tenet of nonviolence. Among the Digambara, a similar reform movement in about the sixteenth century led to the emergence of the Digambara Terāpantha, a group that rejects the use of flowers in worship as a form of unnecessary violence. Reform and renewal are an integral part of all vibrant religious and cultural traditions. For most of Jainism's long history, they have tended to come from within the mendicant ranks and then extend beyond them, influencing and altering lay religious practice and organization in novel ways.

The twentieth century saw the emergence of visionaries who sought to reinvigorate the Jaina tradition from a position outside the renouncer path and thereby indirectly challenging the hegemony of the monastic ideal. Shrimad Rajchandra (1867–1901), Kanji Swami (1890–1980), Acharya Sushil Kumarji (1926–1994), Shri Chitrabhanu (1922–) are among the most prominent of these modern, and untraditional, leaders. With the exception of Shrimad Rajchandra, a lay ascetic from Gujarat well known for his influence on the thinking of Mohandas K. Gandhi, the others were once orthodox monks in India who either renounced their mendicancy and returned to lay life or remained as monks but outside the institution of orthodox monasticism. Paul Dundas (1992: 232) has suggested that these accommodations with lay life may provide us a glimpse of Jainism's future, especially as it develops outside of India, where the ideology of the *mokṣa-mārga* has little currency. If so, these lay-ascetic accommodations may be the most recent expressions of the ancient strategy of "cautious integration" that has served Jainism so well in the past. New leaders continue to debate the meaning and scope of renunciation, but, at the same time, live according to the ideals of nonviolence and detachment that underpin it.

Mahāvīra's teachings still have the power to inspire new generations of Jainas and non-Jainas alike, twenty-five hundred years after they were first uttered. Today, especially in the diaspora, many are energetically interpreting the teachings in decidedly sociocentric terms that include such things as social activism, animal-rights consciousness, and environmentalism. Such interpretations are viewed by those who support them not as a departure from the "authentic" Jaina path, but rather as true to the spirit of Mahāvīra. Indeed, one could argue that it has been a quest to uphold this "spirit" that has underpinned every reform and schism in Jaina tradition since its inception. Mahāvīra's insights into the human condition, and the sublime ethic of nonviolence that he taught, makes the path of Jainism a strikingly relevant one in the modern period.

• TRANSMISSION OF THE TRADITION OUTSIDE OF INDIA

Jainas today continue to explore the potentials of *anekāntavāda* for inter-cultural harmony and as a tool for world peace. In 2002, for instance, an international conference was convened in Los Angeles at California State Polytechnic University (Pomona) on the value of *anekāntavāda* for the modern world. Throughout their history, Jainas have had to negotiate with practices that deviate from their accepted beliefs, and they have done so in creative ways that have allowed them to maintain the essence and integrity of their own teachings. Jainas now living outside of India—especially in the UK, the US, and Canada—are involved in their own "negotiations," fully immersing themselves in their new homelands, embracing the English language, and adopting many of the local cultural customs. Nevertheless, their identity as Jainas remains central and is safeguarded in a variety of ways; paramount among these is the maintenance of their distinctive dietary practices (Vallely 2002a,b).

• RELATIONS WITH OTHER RELIGIONS

Jaina aptitude for inter-cultural and inter-religious dealings may be among the most important features of the tradition, as well as a factor in the survival of a distinctive Jaina identity as a heterodox minority in the context of the potentially overwhelming presence of Hinduism. Padmanabh Jaini, an eminent scholar of Jainism and Buddhism, has argued that the Jaina *ācārya*s early recognized their predicament as a minority that was in need of social interaction with non-Jainas but was vulnerable to assimilation. The leaders had the wisdom to prescribe a middle ground. According to Jaini, this resulted in a practice of "cautious integration," the essence of which is captured by the following maxim: "All worldly practices (those not related to salvation) are valid for the Jainas, as long as there is neither loss of pure insight nor violation of the vratas" (*Upāsakādhyayana, kalpa* 477–480; Jaini 1979: 287).

"Cautious integration" involves acceptance of local customs, including language, holidays, dress codes, and cuisine (with the exception of nonvegetarian foods and other prohibited items), as well as the basic framework of the Hindu *saṃskāra*s (lifecycle rituals) such as birth and marriage rites. But perhaps the most conspicuous expression of the practice of cautious integration is seen in the Jaina adoption of the caste system—an ideological construct that runs counter to Jaina teachings. The *ācārya* Jinasena (about ninth century CE) is credited with this adaptation—one that was likely essential for Jainas in order to prosper, given their need for fruitful social integration with the surrounding Hindu populace and the antipathy of Brāhmaṇical society toward any deviation from accepted patterns of social behavior (Jaini 1979: 292). Jinasena succeeded by reinterpreting the meaning of the caste system in terms acceptable to Jainism. Pointedly, he maintained that its genesis was a product of social and political expediency and that it was not of divine origin as the Brāhmaṇas claimed. In addition, he redefined "Brāhmaṇa" to mean an honorable status achieved on the basis of exemplary ethical conduct and not an ascribed status based on one's birth, as was asserted by Hindu orthodoxy.

As ingenious as Jinasena's scheme clearly was, the danger of reading philosophers to understand the social anthropology of a community is that their abstracted ideals may obscure the concrete, often rough-and-ready, lived reality as it exists on the ground. In the case of Jainism, Jinasena's formulations may give the false impression of the existence of an eternally self-contained, clearly demarcated social unit of Jainas interacting with religious others in calculated and careful ways. Such a view would not accurately capture the way most Jainas have, throughout the centuries, lived their lives. Historically, Jaina devotional practices were typically polymorphous and inclusive (Carrithers 2000; Flügel 2005): Being a "follower of the Jina" did not exclude the worship of Hindu gods and goddesses, nor preclude seeking marriage partners from within certain vegetarian Hindu communities. The social integration that Jainas practiced, while cautious, was also open and creative.

The seeds of the shift towards a more exclusivist religious identity began during the nineteenth century when religion became a matter of colonial interest, and eventually, an instrument of colonial control. Jainism did not initially receive recognition as an independent tradition by the British colonial government and was instead classified under the broad category of "Hinduism," which meant that Jaina religious concerns were governed by a religio-legal framework that was often alien to them (for instance, in Jaina rules of inheritance, the widow is heir to her late husband's estate, something not accepted under Hindu law). This lack of sensitivity to Jaina customs led to the emergence of a movement to have Jainism recognized as a legally distinct religion, alongside that of Hinduism, Islam, and Christianity.[2] Initially, the movement grew slowly; before it could persuade the colonial (and then postcolonial) government, it first had to persuade Jainas themselves to dispense with the practice of identifying as "Hindu-Jaina" or of consigning their "Jainness" to caste affiliation.

The movement gained momentum in the decades following independence and has achieved striking success in the new millennium. The 2001 Indian census witnessed the appearance of over a million "new" Jainas over a ten-year period. The spectacular increase in numbers came from a new willingness among the "followers of the Jina" to identify "Jainism" as their primary mark of religious identity, and to do so in a more exclusivist way.

As recently as 2014, the Supreme Court of India voted to grant Jainas minority status and to recognize Jainism as a distinct religion. For many, this ruling came as a long-awaited and momentous victory that will ensure Jainism's recognition as a distinct and major world religion. It is important to note, however, that not all Jainas welcomed the decision; a considerable minority—mainly from within the Śvetāmbara fold (which has a higher percentage of social, including business and marital, integration with Hindu communities) argued that the legal demarcation from Hinduism was unnecessary given the *de facto* recognition that Jainas already possessed and given the obvious successes the community has enjoyed in the absence of such a distinction.

This section began by suggesting that a factor in the survival of a distinctive Jaina identity may have been its aptitude for fluid inter-cultural and inter-religious dealings. That contemporary Jaina communities now possess more robustly defined religious identities will certainly have some impact on the way in which the heterodox minority engages with, and is received by, the diverse religious communities that are its neighbors. But it is far too soon to predict how, and to what extent, these new legal developments will influence social relations with other traditions, and it is unlikely that the familiar and frequent interactions between Jainas and non-Jainas will be affected by them. Instead, the Jaina ethos, characterized by open exchange and nonviolence, is likely to be a far more important factor in this regard.

Indeed, it has often been suggested that the Jaina facility at compromise may be a natural manifestation of its worldview, which rejects dogmatism as a form of ignorance. Jainas have given this worldview formal expression in their philosophical doctrine of *anekāntavāda*, which means "the doctrine of not one-sidedness." *Anekāntavāda* states that all truth-claims are partial and are unavoidably bound to a particular context; ignorance arises if we mistake partiality for truth. Jainas insist that the doctrine of *anekāntavāda* is a natural outgrowth of the principle of nonviolence in thought, action, and speech, and it is a reminder that the imposition of one's views on another (however enlightened one may feel them to be) is a form of ideological violence. Ironically, medieval Jaina *ācārya*-philosophers were not averse to using the philosophical doctrine tactically to dismiss the rival philosophies of Buddhism and Hindu Vedānta as being *ekānta*, or one-sided! Whether or not the motive underpinning the doctrine's use was to draw different viewpoints together or to keep them distinguished, the effect has been to acknowledge a multiplicity of valid perspectives on all matters.

• THE TRADITION IN THE STUDY OF RELIGIONS

The status of the Jainas as a numerical minority in India, a presumption that the Vedas and Sanskrit language held exclusive priority or greater prestige, and a relatively late awareness of the value and extent of Jaina manuscripts had the result that lesser and later attention was accorded to Jaina Dharma in the early decades of the academic study of religion. Long neglected, then grouped with Buddhists as followers of dissenting heterodox and ascetic movements, only slowly did the tradition of the Jainas come to be appreciated by academic scholars as one that merits close and careful study for its own distinctive features.

German philologists or linguists were among the first Europeans to publish on the Jainas. At the time, their efforts were controversial on at least two counts. First, Jaina manuscripts were preserved respectfully but not freely or widely circulated. Second, the acts that are required for the process of printing were considered by Jainas to involve cruelty if not violence. Indeed, the "discovery" and collection of Jaina manuscript texts that eventually made them available to a general readership and for academic study involved significant pressure from outsiders. A striking example was the 1873–74 tour of libraries and repositories in western India made by Georg Bühler (1837–98) accompanied by Hermann Jacobi (1850–1937). Bühler was on assignment from the British colonial government to locate, identify, and catalogue indigenous manuscripts—and to purchase them whenever possible for administrative use or archival collections. Just a few years later in 1879, Jacobi published an ancient manuscript that attested to the separate status of Jaina tradition. It was the *Kalpasūtra* of Bhadrabāhu who lived until about 356 BCE. An English translation by Jacobi was published in the Sacred Books of the East series in 1884. That text was a decisive influence on the establishment of a separate field of Jaina Studies and put Jacobi on an academic rather than administrative basis when he returned to India in 1913–14 to identify additional Jaina manuscripts.

From the mid-twentieth century through to the present, studies based on anthropological and sociological methods that do not take for granted the primacy or defining role of written texts have become an increasingly important corrective and complement to earlier studies. The focus has shifted from "Jainism" in a narrow sense toward the various kinds of lives that Jainas attempt and achieve. Recently this has included studies informed by related fields, such as bioethics and ecology and intergroup relations, to learn what resources might be available from Jaina tradition that could be applied to problems of ethnic and racial relations, as well as the impending climate crisis. Finally, religious studies is a field that repeatedly questions its own categories, and so the reputed "atheism" of Jaina tradition is of continuing interest as a limiting case or test case in debates about how to define religion itself.

• DISCUSSION QUESTIONS

1. For followers of Jaina tradition, what is the dominant or highest religious ideal? In fact, is it the central pursuit or characteristic of the lives of most people? If not, does this seem extraordinary, or does it seem typical of most human beings and their religions? Are there similar patterns that you know about in other religious traditions?
2. What is the meaning of *dāna*, and in what ways has it preserved and maintained Jaina tradition?
3. How have Śvetāmbara and Digambara versions of Jaina Dharma each been a response to the influence of Mahāvīra, and how do the two differ from one another?

• NOTES

1 The eight substances are water, sandalwood, dehusked rice, flowers, coconut, *dīp*, *dhūp*, and *phal*. *Ardhya*, a mixture of the eight *dravya*s, is used as a final offering.

2 The Sikh community was engaged in similar efforts to have their tradition recognized as distinct from Hinduism.

BIBLIOGRAPHY

Babb, Lawrence A. 1996. *Absent Lord: Ascetics and Kings in a Jain Ritual Culture.* Berkeley: University of California Press.

Banks, Marcus. 1992. *Organizing Jainism in India and England.* Oxford: Clarendon Press.

Caillat, Colette and Ravi Kumar. 1981. *The Jain Cosmology*. New York: Harmony Books.

Carrithers, Michael. 2000. "On Polytropy: Or the Natural Condition of Spiritual Cosmopolitanism in India: The Digambar Jain Case." *Modern Asian Studies* 34, 4: 831–61.

Carrithers, Michael and Caroline Humphrey, eds. 1991. *The Assembly of Listeners: Jains in Society*. Cambridge: Cambridge University Press.

Chapple, Christopher Key, ed. 2002. *Jainism and Ecology: Nonviolence in the Web of Life*. Cambridge: Harvard University Press.

Cort, John E. 1990. "Models of and for the Study of Jains." *Method & Theory in the Study of Religion* 2, 1: 42–71.

Cort, John E., ed. 1998. *Open Boundaries: Jain Communities and Cultures in Indian History*. Albany: State University of New York Press.

Cort, John E. 2001. *Jains in the World: Religious Values and Ideology in India*. New York: Oxford University Press.

Dundas, Paul. 2002 [1992]. *The Jains*. London: Routledge.

Flügel, Peter. 2005. "The Inventin of Jainism: A Short History of Jaina Studies." *International Journal of Jaina Studies* (online) 1, 1: 1–14.

Folkert, Kendall W. 1993. *Scripture and Community: Collected Essays on the Jains* (ed. John E. Cort). Atlanta: Scholars Press.

Humphrey, Caroline and James Laidlaw. 1994. *The Archetypal Actions of Ritual: A Theory of Ritual Illustrated by the Jain Rite of Worship*. Oxford: Clarendon Press.

Jaini, Padmanabh S. 1979. *The Jaina Path of Purification*. Berkeley: University of California Press.

Jaini, Padmanabh S. 1991. *Gender and Salvation: Jaina Debates on the Spiritual Liberation of Women*. Berkeley: University of California Press.

Kelting, M. Whitney. 2001. *Singing to the Jinas: Jain Women, Maṇḍaḷ Singing and the Negotiations of Jain Devotion*. New York: Oxford University Press.

Laidlaw, James. 1995. *Riches and Renunciation: Religion, Economy and Society Among the Jains*. Oxford: Clarendon Press.

Parry, Jonathan. 1986. "The Gift, the Indian Gift and the 'Indian Gift'." *Man* (n.s.) 21, 3: 453–73.

Umāsvāti. 1994. *That Which Is: Tattvārtha Sūtra by Umāsvāti: A Classic Jain Manual for Understanding the True Nature of Reality* (trans. Nathmal Tatia). San Francisco: HarperCollins.

Vallely, Anne. 2002a. "Ethical Discourses Among Orthodox and Diaspora Jains." *In* Michael Lambek, ed., *A Reader in the Anthropology of Religion*, 555–69. Oxford: Blackwell Publishers.

Vallely, Anne. 2002b. *Guardians of the Transcendent: An Ethnography of a Jain Ascetic Community*. Toronto: University of Toronto Press.

FIGURE 3.1 The *stūpa*, or reliquary mound, at Sanchi, northeast of Bhopal.

Image courtesy of AJP/Shutterstock.com.

3

Buddha Dhamma

CHRISTINA A. KILBY[1]

THE TRADITIONS DEFINED

At a place called Bodh Gaya in the northern Indian state of Bihar, an ancient fig tree stretches forth its limbs in a gesture of welcome. Under this shade gather people from every region of the globe; the hot air hums with the cadences of their many languages. Some people prostrate, some chant, and others meditate. Monks and nuns, pilgrims and tourists, shaven heads and dreadlocks, bare feet and trekking boots, all intermingle at this sacred heart of Buddhist history. The fig tree, reverently known as the Bodhi Tree or Tree of Enlightenment, marks the site where about twenty-five hundred years ago a man sat in meditation and realized a series of liberating truths. His realization merited him the title Buddha, the "Awakened One," and set in motion a new body of teachings called the *dhamma*.

The original Bodhi Tree died long ago, but tradition holds that one of its branches was saved and planted in Sri Lanka where it flourished until, in the nineteenth century, an offshoot was replanted at Bodh Gaya. Thus, according to these legends, a descendant of the original Bodhi Tree has revived the sacred site of Bodh Gaya and restored its continuity with the past. The story of Buddhism itself follows a similar arc. Buddhism had largely disappeared from India by the thirteenth century CE, but its offshoots survived because missionary monks and merchants carried the Buddhist teachings abroad to Central, East, and Southeast Asia. Bodh Gaya now hosts a complex of temples reflecting the architectures and colors of Bhutan, China, Japan, Myanmar, Nepal, Sri Lanka, Thailand, Tibet, and Vietnam, representing many of the lands beyond India where Buddhism has spread and flourished over the centuries. In the contemporary period, as Buddhist pilgrimage has enjoyed a renaissance, these descendant branches of Buddhism have returned to India to revitalize the place where Buddhism began. Buddhism is "Indian" once again.

This chapter introduces Buddhism as an Indian religion. This means that we shall focus largely on classical Buddhism as it was articulated in Indian languages and within the framework of Indian ideas about the cosmos and human possibilities within it. Yet Buddhism's missionary character—its claim to universal efficacy across geographical, ethnic, and linguistic boundaries and its success in transforming itself in order to effectively cross such boundaries—challenges the conception of Buddhism as an "Indian" religion. Buddhism is the most cosmopolitan of the religions that India has given to the world and has assumed diverse forms in different places. Thus, our chapter will not only introduce the Buddha Dhamma within an Indian historical and philosophical context, but will also consider some of the major manifestations of Buddhism beyond India.

An Insider Definition

If the diversity of forms that Buddhism has taken may occupy the outsider, insiders to the tradition have a clearer understanding of what it means to be Buddhist. For insiders, to be a Buddhist means to take refuge in the Buddha, the *dhamma*, and the *saṅgha*. The Buddha was a man named Gotama (Sanskrit Gautama) who experienced transformative insights concerning the suffering inherent in life and the path to suffering's cessation. Those truths are embodied in his teachings, the *dhamma* (Sanskrit *dharma*), whose living representatives and keepers are the members of his monastic order, the *saṅgha*. When Buddhists go for refuge to the Buddha, they seek the protection and guidance of one who has accomplished total freedom. When they go for refuge to the *dhamma*, they place their confidence in his teachings that show the true path to freedom; and when they go for refuge to the *saṅgha*, they entrust themselves to the respected community of renunciants who embody and transmit the precious teachings.

Buddha

The historical Buddha under whom Buddhists seek refuge was a man called Gotama, later also known as Siddhatta (Sanskrit Siddhārtha), meaning "accomplished one," or as Sākyamuni (Sanskrit Śākyamuni), the "Sage of the Sākya [Clan]." He was one of many wandering teachers who lived in India around the fifth century BCE. This period in Indian history was a time of profound philosophical pursuits that is recalled as an "age of transcendence," when various groups of seekers renounced household life in order to pursue spiritual liberation. The Buddha practiced the path that is in Hindu contexts called *jñāna-mārga*, the path of knowledge, that involves training the body and mind to withdraw from sense objects, thereby purifying one's obscurations and enabling a meditative experience of insight into the nature of ultimate reality (the substance of that insight differs markedly between Buddhism and Hinduism, as we will discuss below).

Several canonical Buddhist texts recall events from Sākyamuni Buddha's life, and the composite story that emerges—enriched with details and flourishes through the centuries—serves as a hagiography that inspires Buddhists everywhere and is a central feature of Buddhist education. Buddhists have faith that the arc of Sākyamuni's life narrative reveals dhāmmic truths. Indeed, the Buddha's major analytical insights arise not from divine revelation, but from experiences, both mundane and transcendental, that he undergoes throughout his life course as a human being. A brief telling of this influential life story follows here.

Sākyamuni Buddha's parents are a king and queen who rule a kingdom in northern India. One night, Queen Māyā has a dream in which a white elephant enters her side, after which she miraculously conceives a child. When ten months have passed, the queen leans against a tree near the town of Lumbinī (in present-day Nepal) and gives birth without pain to an extraordinary child who can already walk and talk. Flowers blossom under his feet as he takes his first steps. Māyā dies within seven days—for her womb is too sacred to be occupied by another—but the baby, raised by his aunt, grows to be strong and healthy.

According to the traditional accounts, Brāhmaṇa priests notice marks on the boy's body that confirm his special identity and portend his future. According to their reading of thirty-two major and eighty minor marks, if the boy adopts a householder's life, he will become a world conqueror—a king. If the child adopts a religious life, he will become a world renouncer—an ascetic who seeks religious truth. As the narrative unfolds, we learn that the child's father, King Suddhodana, is eager that his child inherit his kingdom and become a world conqueror. He makes the decision to shield young Siddhattha from sights and experiences that might awaken the child's spiritual sensibilities.

Siddhatta enjoys a life of luxury in the palace. Presumably, he never witnesses the problems of sickness, old age, or death that ordinary people experience. He grows up to be the strongest, brightest, most attractive man in the kingdom and wins the hand of a lovely maiden named Yasodharā in marriage. Even though he has everything the senses could desire—in addition to a wife, he also has courtesans who please him—Siddhattha grows restless. When he has come of age, despite the restrictions that his father has imposed, he manipulates his charioteer into taking him outside the walls of his palaces. In the next sequence of events, the prince experiences the Four Holy Sights that inspire his renunciation.

On his first journey outside the palaces, Siddhatta sees an old man. The texts portray the old man graphically, as do contemporary temple paintings: he is stooped over a cane, with decaying teeth and sagging skin. Siddhattha is shocked. He asks his charioteer about the old man; the charioteer, incredulous that Siddhatta could be so naive about the realities of time, informs Siddhatta that all humans are subject to aging and decay. On his second journey, Siddhatta sees a sick person, moaning in pain. On his third, he sees a corpse burning upon a funeral pyre. These first three sights teach Siddhatta the painful realities of impermanence. On Siddhatta's fourth journey, he sees a renunciant who has given up the householder life to seek liberation. Siddhatta resolves to do the same.

When he is twenty-nine years old, on the very night that his son is born, Siddhattha's Great Departure takes place. Although most men in the culture of his time would have been thrilled to learn of the birth of a male heir, Prince Siddhattha views the baby as a fetter binding him to the world that he has resolved to abandon and names the child Rāhula, "fetter."

Siddhatta leaves his wife and child, resolving to return after he has discovered the religious truths that he seeks.

Siddhattha cuts his hair, casts off his royal garments, and wanders for six years, studying with various masters and encountering a range of ascetics like himself. One group that Siddhatta joins practices extreme austerities, and as he performs a strict fasting diet, Siddhatta grows emaciated. Some temple images of the Buddha depict his skeletal form during this period of austerities. One day, on the verge of death from starvation, Siddhatta recognizes that his harsh self-denial has brought him no closer to any liberating truth. This moment marks his discovery of the "Middle Way," the ideal of a balance between self-indulgence and self-denial that will characterize many aspects of Buddhist practice and philosophy as the tradition develops. Siddhatta gratefully accepts food offered by a cowherd girl and, with his health restored, dedicates his full efforts to meditation. At the age of thirty-five, he reaches enlightenment under the fig tree in Bodh Gayā.

After his awakening experience, the Buddha teaches and leads a renunciant community for forty-five years. He also guides kings and intervenes in wars. Scriptures recount that he dies at the age of eighty, although they yield conflicting calculations of the dates for his death. Two main streams of textual evidence indicate that he probably died either around 480 BCE or in 383 BCE. After Sākyamuni Buddha's body is cremated, eight kingdoms of central India divide his ashes into eight portions and enshrine each in a reliquary monument called a *stūpa.* Pilgrims have traveled to these monuments to venerate the Buddha's relics since Buddhism's earliest centuries. The centrality of relic veneration in Buddhist traditions suggests the enduring power and presence of the Buddha after his death.

Philosophical speculations on the nature of the Buddha's body have occupied Buddhists in the major schools of Buddhism that developed over the centuries (the origins and characteristics of these schools are discussed below in "History"). In the Theravāda tradition, the Buddha's body was conceived as twofold. Sākyamuni's human body was his "form body" (*rūpakāya*) that now persists only in his corporeal relics. The Buddha's "truth body" (*dhammakāya*) is the collection of teachings through which he can still be encountered. When counseling a dying man who expresses a fervent longing to gaze upon the Buddha's body one last time, Sākyamuni advises the man to seek his presence in the *dhamma* instead: "One who sees the *dhamma* sees me. One who sees me sees the *dhamma.*"

In the Mahāyāna tradition, the body of the Buddha is contemplated on a more cosmic scale. The physical human body of a Buddha like Sākyamuni is understood as an "emanation body" (Sanskrit *nirmāṇakāya*) that has material form; it is only one of three bodies that a Buddha manifests in the world. The second body is the "enjoyment body" (Sanskrit *sambhogakāya*), which is a Buddha's celestial body, composed of light, that is accessible in visions or meditation. The third body, even more transcendent, is the "truth body" (Sanskrit *dharmakāya*), which is more abstract than its Theravādin correlate (*dharmakāya* as "the Buddhist teachings"): it is the formless manifestation of absolute truth, or ultimate reality itself.

Dhamma

The *dhamma* is understood, in different ways, as an enduring form of the Buddha's body. In its most common and accessible usage, however, the *dhamma* is the teaching, the way, and the truth, tangibly manifest in the Buddhist scriptures but transcending any particular language or medium. The *dhamma* is usually characterized as comprising three fundamental teachings, which are also referred to as the "three marks of existence": all phenomena lack essence (*anattā*, "no-soul"); thus, all phenomena are impermanent (*anicca*); and thus, all phenomena are unsatisfactory (*dukkha*).

Competing philosophical systems in India at the time the Buddha lived were based on the premise that each human has a soul (Sanskrit *ātman*) and that each individual soul is identical with the universal divine soul (Brahman); according to these systems, release from *saṃsāra*, the realm of rebirths, requires realization of the unity of the soul with Brahman through *yoga*, or the harnessing of the mind. Buddhism shares with Hinduism and Jainism the idea that the world of rebirth is ultimately unsatisfactory and must be transcended, but unlike its sister Indian traditions, the Buddha Dhamma challenges the very idea of a soul or essential self traversing that world.

Buddhism does not argue that people do not exist; rather, the tradition claims that people and other phenomena do not exist in the solid, independent, and unchanging way in which ordinary minds perceive them. *Kamma* (Sanskrit *karma*), intentional activities, propel consciousness—itself in flux—through *saṃsāra*. Each individual brings with him or her the fruit of kāmmic activities (both wholesome and unwholesome) from previous lifetimes which, the logic of the theory of *kamma* suggests, contributes to our abilities to advance spiritually. Put differently, as consciousness, always changing and responding to new environments, is propelled through *saṃsāra*, it carries with it kāmmic impressions from past experiences that help to determine its future state. In Buddhism, it is consciousness that is reborn from moment to moment and lifetime to lifetime, sometimes allowing for spiritual advancement and sometimes thwarted by negative kāmmic residue.

The Buddha Dhamma teaches that since all phenomena are void of soul, all things are subject to change and thus are impermanent. Because most of us journey through *saṃsāra* unaware that reality is void of stasis, ignorantly behaving as if we and other phenomena have the nature of permanence, we are constantly disappointed by reality, and so existence is characterized by suffering or unsatisfactoriness (*dukkha*). If, on the other hand, we could see reality clearly, we would understand that all things are impermanent and we would be liberated from attachment to the fleeting phenomenal world.

Dukkha, unsatisfactoriness, is the first of the Four Noble Truths that constituted the Buddha's first sermon after his enlightenment. These truths are regarded as the core teaching of the *dhamma*. The truth of *dukkha* means that all experiences, even wonderful experiences, bring pain because they inevitably change or cease; and while some things change rapidly, and other things change slowly, all things nonetheless change. The second of the Four Noble Truths is the cause of *dukkha*—namely, thirsting, craving, or possessive desire, based on our delusion that things (especially ourselves) have permanence. This truth teaches that we would not crave impermanent phenomena, which lead us to disappointment, if we understood the nature of reality. Most significantly, we would not be motivated by the falsely posited "me" or "I" or "mine" that undergirds all desire and possessiveness.

The Third Noble Truth is that the cessation of *dukkha* is possible, and this cessation is known as *nibbāna* (Sanskrit *nirvāṇa*). In other words, there is an end to unsatisfactoriness and the suffering it brings. The path, that leads to this end, the Noble Eightfold Path, is the Fourth Noble Truth. The Eightfold Path is presented as a Middle Way between the two extremes of hedonism and self-denial that the Buddha experienced in his earthly course of life. This Eightfold Path has three divisions—wisdom, ethical conduct, and meditation—each of which is a necessary aspect of training and transformation in Buddhist life. The cultivation of wisdom includes right view and right intention; the cultivation of ethical conduct includes right speech, right action, and right livelihood; and the cultivation of meditation includes right effort, right mindfulness, and right concentration. In this context, "right" is understood pragmatically as that which creates wholesome or positive effects. These eight are not understood as progressive stages of spiritual advancement; rather, each of the eight should be cultivated simultaneously in the life of a Buddhist practitioner.

Saṅgha

There are two main understandings in Buddhist tradition of who comprises the *saṅgha*. Buddhist scriptures describe a "fourfold" *saṅgha* that includes monks, nuns, and male and female followers who have attained a basic level of *dhammic* insight. By this definition, the *saṅgha* includes many followers of the Buddha Dhamma across time and space, regardless of gender or ordination status (or caste, since the Buddha rejected the sanctity of caste distinctions). In a second and more commonly employed sense, however, the *saṅgha* refers specifically to ordained communities of Buddhist monks and nuns, visibly distinct from the rest of society with their shaven heads and monastic robes. This *saṅgha* is afforded special respect because ordained communities provide a model of renunciation and, at least in theory, dedicate their whole lives to preserving and transmitting the teachings. In their midst, the *dhamma* is living and present in this world.

When a male or female Buddhist joins a monastic order, often as a child, he or she first takes novice vows and trains under the supervision of a teacher. In some Theravāda Buddhist cultures, there is a tradition of temporary ordination, in which a boy takes novice vows for a short period of time as part of his maturation to adulthood. In Buddhist cultures more broadly, seeking ordination is a way not only of furthering one's individual progress on the spiritual path, but also of bringing merit to one's family and community. Sometimes ordination is also sought as a means of economic security and educational opportunity. A variety of factors can lead a person to undertake monastic ordination. From a Buddhist perspective, no matter what motivating factors are involved, the very act of taking vows and adopting a life of renunciation is considered meritorious and a personal and social good.

Fully ordained Buddhist monks hold over two hundred vows and fully ordained nuns hold over three hundred vows. These vows, collected in the section of the Buddhist canon called the *Vinaya* ("Discipline"), govern the personal comportment of a monastic (including limitations on sexual conduct and the amassing of personal wealth), the organization and harmony of the monastic community, and procedures for resolving disputes or violations within the order. The monastic vows shape a life of renunciation so that an individual can, ideally, devote his or her whole life to study and meditation in order to reach enlightenment. In reality, many monks and nuns are engaged in performing rituals rather than in advanced study and meditation. Still, for the surrounding lay community, the *saṅgha* serves symbolically as a spiritual ideal, a source of hope and blessing, a field of merit for their donations, and a protective force whose virtue can safeguard the community or the state. In many Buddhist cultures, the *saṅgha* also wields significant political power that it may use either to legitimate or to challenge the authority of a ruling regime. The *saṅgha* is where the spiritual and temporal aspects of Buddhism are most visibly intertwined.

Other categories of renunciant practitioners within Buddhist communities do not fit clearly into the monastic category. In Theravāda and Tibetan Buddhist contexts, the full ordination lineages for nuns were broken, and so alternative patterns of renunciation have developed in which women live as quasi-monastic figures (as in Theravāda Buddhist cultures) or as life-long novices (as has traditionally been the case in Tibet). In both cases, these women renounce family life, take a limited number of vows, shave their heads, and wear robes, but they never receive full ordination and the accompanying recognition and support that fully ordained monks do. In Japan and Tibet, traditions developed in some sects to allow for married monks who transmit the stewardship of their temples and teachings to biological heirs. Tibetan Buddhism also assumes the presence of nonmonastic ascetic personalities, such as the *yogī* or *yoginī*, or householder tāntric priests and their wives or consorts.

The integrity of the *saṅgha*—in terms of both its structural unity and its moral purity—is a frequent concern in Buddhist scriptures. Causing a schism in the *saṅgha* is named as one of several heinous sins for which a terrifying kāmmic retribution in hell inevitably awaits. Sākyamuni Buddha spent much of his long teaching career advising his monastic community on their rules of discipline and adjudicating conflicts so that the community could uphold its high ideals while adapting in a reasonable way to the challenges and failures that its human members would present. Just before his death, as his last words to his monks, the Buddha gives instructions about instituting a hierarchy of seniority within the *saṅgha* and expelling one troublesome member of the community. He then asks his disciples three times whether they have any remaining doubts about the path or the practice; when they do not offer any, he declares with confidence that each member of the *saṅgha* is certainly bound for enlightenment. With these final words, he confirms for future generations that he is leaving behind a *saṅgha* unshakable in its realization of the *dhamma*.

• HISTORY

Despite the scriptures' caution against schisms in the *saṅgha*, the Buddhist community has split into many different branches since the Buddha's death. Some of these sectarian splits were due to differences in philosophical approach or textual interpretation; others resulted from disagreements about the monastic vows and ordination practices; and still others arose as Buddhists adapted new scriptures or religious techniques. Later, as Buddhism took root in lands beyond the Indian subcontinent, the religion responded to the various conditions and concerns of the new regions in which it was established. The history of Buddhism thus evolved from a small community of wandering renunciants to a diverse array of institutions with an equally diverse range of philosophical and ritual orientations.

Early Buddhism

In the first generations after the Buddha's death, the practice of Buddhism was focused on preserving (through recitation and practice) the core doctrines that the Buddha taught. Some of the most important doctrines transmitted in Buddhism's first generations were the doctrine of no-soul (*anattā*); the doctrine that the human person is composed of five aggregates (*khandha*), each of which is impermanent and lacking essence; and the doctrine of interdependent origination (*paṭiccasamuppāda*), which explains how phenomena come into being in dependence upon other phenomena. In order to preserve their understanding of the Buddha's core teachings, monastics convened three Buddhist Councils in the centuries after the Buddha's death. At these councils, members of the ordained *saṅgha* recited the canonical scriptures and arbitrated points of dispute about interpretation.

One famous Buddhist who lived in the third century BCE, as early Buddhism was transitioning into its sectarian phase, was the emperor of India's Mauryan dynasty, Aśoka. During his early reign, Aśoka was responsible for numerous deaths of innocents on the battlefield. He "converted" to Buddhism later in life, eventually renouncing warfare, enacting stricter laws against killing, and establishing humanitarian institutions such as hospitals (for people and for animals) and watering stations for travelers. Aśoka supported the Buddhist *saṅgha* financially and sent Buddhist missionaries across the Indian subcontinent and to Sri Lanka. He also supported non-Buddhist religious groups and expressed an inclusive desire for many religions to be practiced freely in his kingdom. Aśoka's pillars and edicts, still extant at many sites in India and abroad, attest to this period of benevolent Buddhist kingship, which has served as a model for the ideal relationship between *saṅgha* and state in many Buddhist cultures.

Sectarian Buddhism

As the Buddhist monastic community continued to grow and to spread, disagreements about how to properly observe the monastic rules of conduct gradually led to divisions in the *saṅgha*. Some texts recount "eighteen schools" of Buddhism existing during this time, although we have little historical information about most of these groups. Disagreements among these schools about the interpretation of doctrine led them to produce new elaborations of Buddhist thought and the composition of many scholastic texts classified as Abhidhamma. In the first century BCE in Sri Lanka, the Pali language Buddhist scriptures that had been memorized and recited by monastics for centuries were first recorded in writing. The Pali canon, used by the Theravāda school, has been transmitted from its first century BCE redaction.

The robust Buddhist scholasticism and textual legacies that stem from its sectarian period firmly established Buddhism as a philosophical contender in India for over one thousand years. The only school of Buddhism from the sectarian period that survives, however, is the Theravāda.

Theravāda Buddhism

Theravāda Buddhism originated from one of the textually conservative groups from the sectarian period. Subsequently, Theravāda institutions preserve many of the doctrines and practices from early Buddhism and try to follow the teachings preserved in the Pali canon closely. Theravāda Buddhism, like early Buddhism, is centered on the renunciant community. The Theravāda tradition stresses the importance of renouncing householder life so that an individual can devote his or her whole life to study and meditation in order to reach enlightenment; it is usually assumed in Theravādin cultures that only the ordained *saṅgha* have the potential to find enlightenment in this lifetime. Reaching enlightenment requires total detachment from worldly pleasures and intensive dedication to the practice of insight meditation (*vipassanā*, discussed below). The purpose of meditation for Theravāda Buddhists is to realize the liberating truth of no-self; an individual who accomplishes this ultimate goal is called an *arahant* and is freed from future rebirth.

Lay people in the Theravādin world primarily work to earn merit so that in future rebirths, they might meet with favorable circumstances to renounce the world and achieve liberation. For the laity, the *saṅgha* serves as a spiritual example, a source of hope and blessing, a field of merit for their donations, and a protective force whose virtue can safeguard the community or the state. In Theravāda Buddhist cultures, the symbiotic relationship between the *saṅgha* and laity is highly visible, especially as monks make their daily rounds in ochre robes to beg for alms from their lay neighbors.

Over the centuries, Theravāda Buddhism took root in the Bengal region of India as well as in Cambodia, Laos, Myanmar, Sri Lanka, and Thailand. Theravāda Buddhism is still practiced widely in those regions and is often inextricably tied to national identity.

Mahāyāna Buddhism

Around the beginning of the common era, there arose a new form of Buddhism that called itself the Mahāyāna, or "Great Vehicle." Mahāyāna Buddhism emerged alongside the composition of new Sanskrit scriptures, claiming to be the words of the Buddha, that transmitted some of the ideas and doctrines that were already nascent in sectarian Buddhist groups but developed them in significantly new directions.

One of these, the idea of the composite and provisional nature of the material world, grew into a rigorous philosophy of emptiness (Sanskrit *śūnyatā*), or the nonsubstantiality of all phenomena. The Mahāyāna scriptures elaborating on the idea of emptiness called themselves the "perfection of wisdom" (*prajñāpāramitā*), and they became an important genre of *sūtra*s within the Mahāyāna scriptural canon. Other new scriptures, drawing on earlier speculations about the transcendent identity of the Buddha, portrayed the Buddha as a cosmic savior figure reigning over celestial realms; the path to enlightenment that a Buddha follows over many lifetimes as a *bodhisattva* was elaborated into ten distinct stages and seen as the cumulative development of six "perfections" or virtues: generosity, diligence, effort, patience, concentration, and wisdom.

Furthermore, in Mahāyāna thought the *bodhisattva* path is understood not only as the path that Sākyamuni followed but also as a path to be replicated by ordinary practitioners—lay or ordained. This innovative promise of the potential for all human beings, even lay people, to achieve Buddhahood sets Mahāyāna Buddhism apart from the Theravāda. In Mahāyāna Buddhism, the ideal practitioner is not a monastic who practices in solitude into order to become an *arahant*, but rather a *bodhisattva* who practices over many lifetimes to perfect the characteristics that will bring full Buddhahood. The *bodhisattva* also commits to serving others along the way, engaging in worldly activities so that every other being can be liberated, too. Mahāyāna Buddhists appeal to the help of Buddhas or celestial *bodhisattva*s, such as Mañjuśrī, known for his wisdom, or Avalokiteśvara, known for his compassion; they also seek visions of these *bodhisattva*s in their meditations.

In the first centuries of the common era, Mahāyāna Buddhism spread along the Silk Road to Central Asia and China, and from there to Korea in the fourth century and Japan in the sixth century. Vietnam, though primarily supporting Mahāyāna Buddhism because of its connection with China, has seen some Theravāda influence from its Southeast Asian neighbors. Some of the Mahāyāna traditions developed in these regions have been highly intellectual, others have focused on particular forms of intensive practice, and still others have emphasized popular forms of devotion. Two of the most influential schools in the Mahāyāna world include the Pure Land school, in which followers chant the name of Amitābha Buddha in order to claim his promise that they can be reborn in his pure land where they will be enlightened, and the Chán (Chinese; Japanese Zen) school, which focuses on practices such as "just sitting" in meditation and contemplating paradoxical statements (Chinese *gōng'àn*, Japanese *kōan*) that are designed to confound the dualistic mind.

Tāntric Buddhism

By the seventh century, Tāntric—a ritual system of visualizations, symbols, and *mantras*—was well established in certain Hindu communities in the Indian subcontinent. Tāntric practitioners sought to harness the psycho-physiological energies of the subtle body and ritually activate them in order to experience liberation. Tāntric Buddhism is seen by its practitioners as a method to embrace the energies of *saṃsāra* and establish them, nondually, as the ground of *nirvāṇa*. Sometimes Buddhist Tāntric practice involves antisocial behavior, such as breaking taboos and purity laws in shocking ways and appealing to wrathful manifestations of enlightened beings to accomplish one's aims. Other times, Tantra is not socially or doctrinally transgressive, instead offering an orderly and elegant way of envisioning worlds as *maṇḍala*s governed by benevolent Buddhas; this "right-handed" style of Tantra was integrated into the monastic curricula of large Buddhist universities.

Tāntric Buddhism was transmitted from India to Nepal, the Himālayas, and Tibet in a series of encounters from the seventh century to the twelfth century (by this time, Mahāyāna Buddhism was already established in East Asia, so East Asian Mahāyāna Buddhism has been less influenced by Tantra). Tibet, Mongolia, and several areas of southern Russia—Buryatia, Kalmykia, and Tuva—also inherited Tāntric Buddhism. Tāntric Buddhism today coexists in these regions with more mainstream Mahāyāna texts, doctrines, and practices; it is envisioned as a faster but more dangerous way to accomplish what Mahāyāna Buddhism achieves gradually through more conventional means.

Buddhism Beyond India

Each of the three major schools of Buddhism visible in the world today—Theravāda, Mahāyāna, and Tantra—are rooted in Indian texts and practices. However, as Buddhist traditions have flourished abroad, they have evolved beyond their Indian roots in significant ways. Geographical and climate diversity have precipitated some of these changes. In Tibet, for example, the climate is too severe and the population density too sparse for monastics to wander daily to beg for alms. Instead, lay people in Tibet are likely to visit monasteries and to donate large stocks of barley, butter, or tea on each visit. Other differences in Buddhist expression across Asia reflect the diverse aesthetic and architectural styles of different regions; a Japanese temple with its subdued, naturalistic color scheme and carefully arranged gardens contrasts markedly with a Tibetan temple, outfitted in vibrant technicolor and surrounded by an untamed natural landscape.

Perhaps more unexpectedly, Buddhism has frequently adapted to local customs and beliefs concerning the spirit world: ghosts, landscape deities, ancestral spirits, and so forth. In Thailand, Buddhist monks are frequently employed in ritual activities to drive away ghosts and propitiate local spirits. Even though Buddhism teaches no-soul (*anattā*), Buddhist monks in Thailand perform rituals to call back people's souls that have wandered outside their bodies, causing distress for the humans involved. In Tibet, Tāntric Buddhist rituals are used to subdue antagonistic landscape deities who hamper the establishment of Buddhist institutions like temples, *stūpa*s (Pali *thūpa*), or meditation sites; sometimes, such rituals serve to "convert" local spirits to Buddhism by binding them with oaths to protect the religion. In some cases, local Tibetan spirits even join the Buddhist pantheon and receive veneration.

In China, where the Confucian virtue of filial piety has historically been a pillar of society, Buddhism met with a challenge. The institution of monasticism demanded that sons and daughters abandon their parents and their filial duties to care for them as they aged and to propagate the family lineage, a prospect deeply unsettling to Chinese sentiments. In response, Buddhists in China developed merit-making rituals designed to help repay the kindnesses of one's parents and to aid their favorable rebirth—and in particular, to assure that monks' parents would not be reborn as hungry ghosts (see "Cosmos" below). These ceremonies helped portray Buddhist ordination as an opportunity to serve one's parents rather than abandon them and aided in Buddhism's success in the Chinese cultural context.

While a study of Buddhism's diverse adaptations across Asia could span many volumes, the above examples serve as a brief glimpse of Buddhism's flexibility as a religion. The fact that Buddhist scriptures were meant to be translated, not ossified in Pali or Sanskrit, is a fitting analogy for Buddhism's mandate as a missionary religion that should adapt to the needs and dispositions of its different audiences. The Mahāyāna Buddhist doctrine of skillful means (Sanskrit *upāya*), which teaches that the Buddhist message can be strategically reworked—or even deliberately misconstrued—if it brings about a spiritual result for its audience, provides an additional justification for Buddhism's creative adaptation across linguistic, geographic, and cultural boundaries.

• COSMOS

Cosmic Space

According to Buddhist tradition, the appearance of Buddhism in history is not a function of geography or culture but is part of a larger cosmic scheme. The division of the Buddhist scriptures called the Abhidhamma provides the most systematic account of Buddhist understandings of the nature of the cosmos, and its imagery continues to exert a strong influence in shaping the worldview of contemporary Buddhists. According to the Abhidhamma, *saṃsāra*—the cycle of births, deaths, and rebirths that forms the basis of ancient Indian cosmology—contains many thousands of world systems, each of which contains thirty-one levels of existence into which beings may take birth. There are three main subdivisions of these thirty-one levels. From lower to higher, representing a gradation from gross to subtle, these subdivisions are the Realm of the Five Senses, the Realm of Pure Form, and the Formless Realm. The Realm of Five Senses, which is the abode of human beings and others with consciousness and five physical senses, is the realm about which Abhidhamma texts have the most to say.

In the center of the Realm of Five Senses rises a massive mountain called Meru. On its slopes lie several levels of deities, whose rebirth is the result of wholesome *kamma*. Below Mount

Meru are various hells, which are places of pain and torture inhabited by beings whose unwholesome *kamma* from past activities is coming to fruition. Mount Meru is surrounded by concentric rings of mountains and oceans, beyond which lie four continents. Humans and other animals populate these lands, as do wandering spirits called hungry ghosts who suffer from appetites that they are never able to satiate. One of the four continents, Jambudvīpa (traditionally identified as India), is a sacred land where fully enlightened beings are born and preach the *dhamma*. The Buddhist *maṇḍala*, with its tiered mountain in the center, concentric rings, and gates in the four directions, is a representation of the sacred geography of this universe centered on Mount Meru.

Rebirth into any of the levels of the cosmos—and into the body of a hell-being, hungry ghost, animal, human, or deity—is taught to be the result of a being's intentional activities in the past; Buddhism's cosmic geography reflects a moral hierarchy. This moral hierarchy is not fixed, however. Each rebirth, whether pleasant or painful, is merely temporary because eventually one's kāmmic balance will eventually shift and drive a new rebirth. As beings transit physically from place to place, they also journey mentally through the thirty-one meditative states identified by Buddhist tradition. Thus, the Buddhist cosmos is a map of states of consciousness as well as of territories in a cosmic moral geography. It encompasses all of the modes and realms of existence that it is possible for beings to experience based on their dispositions, tendencies, and voluntary actions.

In Buddhist cosmology, the human being is the only creature in the entire cosmos, including all of its many heavens and hells, that has the ability to attain release from rebirth by reaching enlightenment, or *nibbāna*, the "blowing out" of ignorance, hatred, and greed. Unlike lower beings, humans have the capacity to reason, which enables them to discern the nature of the unsatisfactoriness of existence and to understand and practice its remedy. Unlike the gods, humans experience enough suffering to motivate their renunciation of *saṃsāra* and their search for release.

Buddhism does not posit a single divine judge that presides over human destiny. In Buddhism, each being is the architect of her own future, and her volitional activities alone determine where she will be reborn. In other words, Buddhism places ethical responsibility squarely on the shoulders of individuals, whose meritorious activities determine their happiness not only in the present lifetime, but also in many lifetimes to come.

Cosmic Time

Theravāda conceptions of cosmic time are laid out in a canonical text called the *Cakkavattisutta*. This particular *sutta* (Pali *sutta* or Sanskrit *sūtra*), which means "thread"—that is, a treatise, discourse, or sermon—describes how each world system goes through vast periods of generation, development, decline, and destruction. Within the life cycle of each universe are smaller cycles in which the lifespan and virtue of its inhabitants wax and wane.

Buddhists today believe that they are living in the dispensation (*sāsana*) of a Buddha, a fully enlightened or awakened being who "sets the wheel in motion," as tradition teaches. This means that he promulgates the *dhamma*, often represented in Buddhist art by an eight-spoked wheel. Though Buddhist tradition testifies that ordinary people can be enlightened, only a Buddha is considered to be "fully" enlightened. Unlike those who attain enlightenment because they hear the *dhamma* after it has been discovered and taught by another, a full Buddha discovers the truth for himself and then teaches it to others. This distinction makes possible the understanding that certain eras in history are more sacred than others are because they are marked by the historical appearance of a full Buddha.

In the Theravāda tradition, the dispensation of each Buddha lasts five thousand years. Theravāda Buddhists marked the halfway point of the Buddha's dispensation with religious celebrations in 1954. According to traditional thinking, it is a great boon to be born in an age such as ours in which the Buddhist teachings are known. Although we are not contemporaries of Sākyamuni Buddha, we are living in his *sāsana*, which means that during this time period the *dhamma* is alive and available to beings who seek it. Those who will be living at the end of this dispensation will not be so lucky; moral depravity in this dispensation will result in a shortening of the human life span, until people will live only ten years. Human society will become so morally bankrupt that people begin murdering each other; parents kill their children, and children kill their parents. Even the *dhamma* taught by the Buddha will be forgotten, another sign of future depravity. Then a righteous king will reinstate morality and herald the new dispensation of a fully enlightened being: the next Buddha, Metteyya (Sanskrit Maitreya). Tradition teaches that Metteyya is now passing through a series of rebirths in order to develop the virtues necessary for enlightenment.

• LITERATURE

The Buddhist Canons

Buddhists have historically used the criterion of "Buddha's word" (*buddhavacana*), meaning that a text either was spoken by the Buddha or accurately reflects his teachings, in order to authenticate a text as "scripture." However, there is no single canon of scriptures that all Buddhists view as authoritative. Three different Buddhist canons govern respectively the three major schools of Buddhism (Theravāda, Mahāyāna, and Tantra). Each canon follows the same traditional division into "three baskets" (*tipiṭaka*), which include the monastic codes (*Vinaya*), the Buddha's sermons and discourses (*Sutta*), and later systematic and scholastic works (*Abhidhamma*). Commentarial works and other scholastic treatises supplement these three baskets and, even though they may not qualify as "Buddha's word," can be viewed as canonical to varying degrees.

While there is much shared content among the three canons, each of the three canons has a unique origin and history. None of the three canons is a translation of one of the others (although each has been translated to some extent into other languages and is considered just as valid in translation). Furthermore, each canon is voluminous in size—ranging from forty volumes to over one hundred.

As we have learned (see "History" above), Theravāda Buddhism is based on a canon of scriptures in the Pali language. Pali is an ancient Indian vernacular that served primarily as a liturgical language; early Buddhist scriptures were recorded in Pali as a way of rejecting Brāhmaṇa priests' claims of the inherent sanctity of Sanskrit (this chapter prioritizes the use of Pali terminology in order to reflect Buddhist views on language). The Pali canon preserves many doctrinal teachings from early Buddhism, as well as rules of monastic discipline and some of the scholasticism of the sectarian Buddhist period.

The Mahāyāna schools of East Asia rely on a Chinese canon composed mainly of translations of Sanskrit texts, which include many Mahāyāna scriptures. Mahāyāna *sūtras* claim, as do the Pali *suttas*, to be "Buddha's word," although they often appeal to the authorship of cosmic Buddhas rather than of the historical Sākyamuni. As cosmic teachings, Mahāyāna scriptures frequently claim to possess their own spiritual powers, ask to be worshiped, and give instructions for doing so.

The Tāntric schools of Tibet and Inner Asia base their thought and practice primarily on Tibetan translations of Sanskrit texts (some shared in common with the Chinese canon, some distinct). These texts include many Mahāyāna scriptures and commentaries, as well as Tāntric ritual texts. One unique aspect of the Tibetan canon is its inclusion of revelations called "treasure texts" (Tibetan *gter ma*), which are believed to have been hidden by past enlightened beings and then retrieved at auspicious moments in history from their hiding places in the earth, sky, or minds of future disciples.

Although scholars may speak of the "Pali canon," the "Chinese canon," or the "Tibetan canon," each of these collections not only differs markedly from the other two, but also exists in multiple versions or redactions. In effect, the "Buddhist canon" is more of an ideal form than a single identifiable collection of texts.

Jātaka Tales

Within the canon, one genre of literature that is particularly well known and beloved in the lay community is the life story of the Buddha Sākyamuni, detailed above (see "Buddha"). Yet the story of a Buddha's life, preserved in texts such as the Pali *Mahāpadānasutta*, actually begins not with his birth as Siddhatta, but with the string of previous lifetimes through which he perfects the virtue and wisdom necessary for enlightenment. In the Theravāda scriptures, the future Buddha appears as a human (but never as a female); as an animal, including a lion, a monkey, and a variety of snakes; and sometimes as a deity. These tales of the Buddha's previous lives, called Jātakas, are beloved stories within Buddhist cultures and serve as pedagogical tools for educating children (and adults) in particular Buddhist virtues. Moral teachings associated with the lives of the Buddha are reproduced iconically on the walls of Buddhist temples throughout the contemporary Buddhist world and have been the artistic theme of many ancient reliquaries that have been excavated throughout India, Sri Lanka, and Southeast Asia.

One of the most well-known Jātaka tales describes Gotama Buddha's previous birth as a prince who, while playing in the forest, chances upon a tigress with a new litter of cubs, all on the verge of starvation. Out of compassion for the tigress, too weak to feed her own precious offspring, the prince pricks his arm and allows the tigress to drink his blood. As she regains her strength, her appetite grows and she devours the prince limb by limb. In another birth, as a prince named Vessantara, the future Buddha gradually gives away everything that he has, including his wife and children, as he perfects the virtue of generosity. The story of Vessantara figures in some of the larger merit-making ceremonies in order to encourage lay generosity toward the *saṅgha.*

While Jātaka stories such as these may appear extreme, unrealistic, or perhaps even unadvisable—sacrificing one's human body for an animal, or "giving away" one's wife and children into servitude—their hyperbolic nature serves to stun the listener and inspire her toward some of Buddhism's highest ideals, even if only a nearly enlightened being could (or should) enact them to their fullest extent.

• ETHICS AND HUMAN RELATIONS

Buddhist ethics and the human relationships that they govern can be conceived of in many ways: in terms of the law of kāmmic cause and effect, in terms of the interdependent nature of all that exists, or even in terms of particular virtues, such as compassion or generosity, that are necessary correlates to spiritual progress. Here I will provide a brief overview of Buddhist ethics by appeal to a different framework: vows. In Buddhism, vows are more than rules that regulate life; they are also expressions of personal intention and objects of meditative contemplation. Different types of vows govern the ethical lives and relationships of different categories of Buddhists.

The Five Precepts

The ideal Buddhist layperson, especially in the Theravādin world, makes a lifetime commitment to the Three Refuges and then adopts Five Precepts. These precepts are taught by the Buddha as five restraints: from injury to creatures, from stealing, from lying, from sexual misconduct, and from the occasion of sloth from liquor. Formulated as restraints rather than as positive imperatives, the structure of the precepts presumes that because of the dissatisfactory nature of *saṃsāra,* it is not always possible to accomplish good; what is possible is to refrain from intentionally causing harm. In reality, of course, Buddhists do not hold these precepts perfectly, but the ideals that the precepts convey form the foundational Buddhist conceptions of ethics and virtue.

In the larger context of Buddhist practice, where wisdom, ethical conduct, and meditation are interwoven parts of the Eightfold path, the ethical precepts are not ends in themselves; rather, they are steps leading to *samādhi* (concentration, mental purity), a prerequisite for wisdom and necessary if one is to reach *nibbāna*. In the Theravādin worldview, once one attains *nibbāna* and becomes an *arahant*, it is impossible to behave in an unethical fashion. Observing the precepts prepares the way for enlightenment, which is an ethical state as well as a psychological one.

Monastic Discipline

When a Buddhist undergoes ordination, he or she typically takes ten novice vows. These vows add five ascetic commitments to the five lay precepts described above. They commit the novice monastic to refraining from eating after noon, indulging in music or dancing, wearing ornaments, using high chairs and soft beds, and handling money. These ten vows illustrate the Buddhist value of detachment from sense pleasures as a prerequisite to deeper practice and integration within a renunciant community.

When a monastic takes full ordination, he or she accepts a much larger number of vows. Though the exact number varies according to one's ordination lineage, fully ordained monks take over two hundred and fully ordained nuns take over three hundred vows. These vows govern more than what might appear as "ethics," though they do govern human relatedness. Many of the vows commit the monastic to refraining from various types of pleasurable indulgence and from harmful or divisive behavior, while other vows concern the public comportment of monastics and the public image of the *saṅgha*. Here, we see that part of the ethical responsibility of the *saṅgha* is to model restrained and upright behavior for the lay community and to avoid subjecting the *saṅgha* to doubt or distrust. The monastic vows are classified according to their level of seriousness and include instructions about whether and how a violation can be amended so that the violator can remain part of the community.

In Mahāyāna texts, an additional enumeration of vows called the "Bodhisattva Precepts" is presented. These precepts include the five lay precepts discussed above, as well as proscriptions against broadcasting the faults of others, disparaging others while praising oneself, stinginess, anger, and disrespecting the Three Refuges. In one school of Mahāyāna Buddhism (the Tendai school in Japan), these ten Bodhisattva Precepts replaced the Vinaya rules for ordained monks.

The Bodhisattva Vow

For Mahāyāna Buddhists, the highest spiritual commitment is to work not only for one's own eventual Buddhahood, but also for the Buddhahood of all beings in *saṃsāra*. One commits to this ideal by taking a *bodhisattva* vow. A *bodhisattva* vow can be taken by lay people or monastics in a ritual ceremony, and the vow is believed to extend into the practitioner's future lifetimes (while the monastic discipline only applies to one's current lifetime). Mahāyāna monastics usually take the Vinaya vows as prerequisite to the *bodhisattva* vow to reflect their view that the monastic discipline, which enables personal liberation, is simply a first stage of practice that culminates in a higher vocation of liberating others.

Tāntric Vows

Within Tāntric Buddhist contexts, when a disciple receives a tāntric teaching, he or she receives certain vows (*samaya*) that govern the disciple's relationship to the *guru* and to the practice received. Keeping one's commitment pure, through refraining from disparaging one's teacher, teachings, and fellow disciples and through protecting the sanctity and secrecy of the practice, is considered necessary for the practice to bear fruit. In Tāntric Buddhist thought, the powerful blessing of the *guru*—accessed through pure commitment—is the instrument that enables a quick enlightenment, and so tāntric vows primarily concern the way a disciple relates with wholehearted devotion to the teacher, rather than how a disciple relates to the rest of the world.

• PRACTICES AND INSTITUTIONS

Dāna

The central religious practice of the Buddhist laity is *dāna*, generosity. Buddhist scriptures delineate three types of gifts: gifts of material, gifts of the *dhamma*, and gifts of fearlessness. Material gifts include food or any material possession needed or desired by another; the highest of material gifts is the gift of one's own body, sacrificed for the well-being of others, an act that the Jātaka tales often depict from the Buddha's previous lifetimes. The gift of the *dhamma* is the gift of Buddhist teachings, and it is this gift that characterizes Sākyamuni Buddha's generosity to the world. The gift of fearlessness, a category shared with other Indian religions, is the offering of refuge and protection to those fleeing hardship. This gift falls within the moral domain of the righteous Buddhist king or, by extension, a Buddhist government.

For lay Buddhists, *dāna* is primarily practiced by giving food or other appropriate donations to the monastic *saṅgha*. As in Jainism, the Buddhist practice of *dāna* joins the lay and monastic communities in an interdependent relationship. While the *saṅgha* relies on the laity for their daily material sustenance—the food they eat and the robes they wear—the laity rely on the *saṅgha* as a supreme field of merit in which their kāmmic seeds of generosity can flourish, securing for them the promise of well-being in this life and in future lives. In many Buddhist cultures, *dāna* is a daily performance, as monastics make their rounds among the nearby villages with their begging bowls and lay people line up to offer them food from their pots.

Chanting

On a full-moon day, at daybreak, a group of lay Theravāda Buddhists seat themselves before a *bhikkhu* (monk) draped in saffron. Under his direction, they chant the Three Refuges followed by the Five Precepts. People will bustle about the temple all day, but the sound of chanting permeates the space and serves as an anchor where the intentions of all present are united in devotion. After they return home, many lay Buddhists also chant the refuges and other prayers at home shrines.

For lay and monastic Buddhists, like practitioners of other Indian religions, chanting is a common practice and integral part of religious life. In Buddhism, chanting serves both as a form of merit making and as a form of meditation. Chanting requires the alignment of body, speech, and mind in a way that focuses the practitioner's attention on a noble aspiration, blessing, or vow. Chanting also manifests the original oral character of the Pali *sutta*s—teachings spoken by the Buddha and recited by his disciples for centuries. When monks or nuns chant their Vinaya vows, their chant unites them in common purpose and mutual obligation.

Pilgrimage

In the Buddha's last sermon before his death, he advises his followers to make pilgrimage to four sites: the sites of his birth (Lumbinī), his enlightenment (Bodh Gayā), his first sermon (Sarnātha), and his passing away (Kusinārā). He also instructs that his followers should cremate his remains and erect *stūpa*s as sites of worship so that devotees can offer reverence, establish firm faith, and be reborn in heavenly realms. Pilgrimage is a popular form of merit making. It is also a brief experiment in renunciation as pilgrims forsake the comforts and certainties of home in order to dedicate their efforts toward remembering great teachers and paying homage to the places those teachers have blessed with their presence.

Buddhist pilgrimage to the Indian sites associated with Sākyamuni Buddha's life has enjoyed a strong revival since the early twentieth century, both in response to archaeological discovery and restoration of these sites and to Buddhism's modern renaissance in India. Other regional and local pilgrimages have also developed beyond India in the lands where Buddhism spread; pilgrimages to famous temples, sacred mountains, meditation caves, or sites associated with exemplary Buddhist masters or their miracles are common throughout the Buddhist world, from Japan to Sri Lanka to Tibet.

Meditation

Buddhist meditation traditions are rooted in ancient Indian practices shared with other contemplatives in the *jñāna-yoga* tradition. Myriad forms of meditation are taught in Buddhist scriptures: from meditating on the breath, the parts of the body, the feelings, or the nature of impermanence itself to elaborate visualizations of Buddhas and *bodhisattvas*, hells, and pure lands. Some meditations are used to observe physical or mental phenomena, while other meditations are used to cultivate particular mental attitudes; for example, the Four Immeasurables are Buddhist meditations that cultivate loving kindness, compassion, sympathetic joy, and equanimity. Meditation practices serve not only to develop right view, mindfulness, and wisdom, but also to form self-aware ethical agents who can relate to others in wholesome ways.

Buddhists divide their many forms of meditation into two main categories: calming (*samatha*) and insight (*vipassanā*). These can be understood as two purposes of meditation rather than two discrete forms of meditation. The goal of calming meditation, a practice that Buddhists recognize among non-Buddhist contemplatives as well, is to develop single-pointed concentration and mental tranquility. The scriptures teach that physical and mental benefits, and even superpowers, can result from the dedicated practice of calming meditation. The goal of insight meditation is to lead to enlightenment—*nibbāna*—by enabling pure insight into the nature of reality and its three marks (impermanence, unsatisfactoriness, and no-soul).

For Buddhists, only insight meditation can liberate, and only Buddhism offers this practice. While most Buddhist schools understand insight meditation as an analytical process, some schools (such as Chán/Zen) teach that because insight is ultimately nonanalytical and nondual, it should be cultivated with nonanalytical methods. Practices such as "just sitting" (Japanese *zazen*) and meditation on *kōans*, which are paradoxes that are designed to create a break with the analytical mind, developed according to this understanding of insight. In any Buddhist context, however, insight into the three marks of reality cannot liberate if such insight is merely achieved intellectually. Only a deep and intuitive grasp of these Buddhist truths will transform the life and outlook of the practitioner, accomplishing the end of suffering.

Historically, meditation has not been practiced by the majority of Buddhists. Most lay people have focused their energies on merit making in order to secure the kāmmic circumstances for enlightenment in a future lifetime, rather than meditating in order to develop enlightened wisdom in the present lifetime. Even many Buddhist monks and nuns have, through the centuries, spent more of their time reciting texts and performing rituals than engaging in meditation. Modern expressions of Buddhism, however, have seen lay people engage in meditation in greater numbers. For example, in Myanmar, a mass lay meditation movement occurred as a form of resistance and resiliency in the face of military dictatorship. Buddhist converts across the modern world are often attracted to Buddhism because of its meditation practices, and so modern converts tend to engage in meditation much more seriously than lay Buddhists have in Buddhism's earlier history.

Temples and Images

A Buddhist temple is a venue for the performance of religious rituals and veneration of Buddha images. It is often attached to a monastic residence so that temple caretakers are readily at hand. There is no consistent division in Buddhism between temples and monasteries; some small temples will be cared for by one or two resident monks, while larger monastic complexes may include several temples for worship. Temples can be located in bustling inner cities, in rural farming villages, or in mountainside clefts. Their settings are often geomantically determined and ritually demarcated as sacred space.

Buddha images are constructed by means of a careful iconometric process and with appropriate ritual steps. In each of the major Buddhist traditions, Buddha images are consecrated through a final ritual that enlivens the image ("opens its eyes") with the power and presence of the Buddha. Buddha images are considered supports or aids for worship and meditation; the more, the better. The production of Buddha images is a common form of merit making that lay people may sponsor.

Any visitor to a Buddhist temple, or *vihāra*, on full-moon days—the most active dates of the Buddhist religious calendar—witnesses Buddhists paying respects and making offerings to images of the Buddha. A Buddhist shrine does not have an inner sanctum, as Hindu temples do, where the deity is said to "reside." Instead, the shrine room is normally open and approachable from all sides within an image hall, and because neither caste nor gender bars one from Buddhist worship, anyone may enter. Usually a lay Buddhist will present before the Buddha image an offering, which may include incense or flowers, bowls of water, sweets or ritual cakes, or tea. This ritual is also conducted at domestic shrines, a common feature of many homes in the Buddhist world.

In addition to its ritual and devotional functions, a temple can also serve as a hub for secular activities within a Buddhist community. In Theravādin Buddhist cultures, where lay Buddhists provide the monastics with their daily midday meal, they may also meet friends at the monastic compound, use the library for their studies, and seek the advice of monks. In other Buddhist contexts, temples have provided social services, such as guesthouses for pilgrims or homes for the elderly or mentally ill.

Stūpas and Relics

*Stūpa*s are ancient Indian reliquary mounds that have formed centers for Buddhist devotion and pilgrimage since Buddhism's earliest years. Imbuing the landscape with Buddhist symbolism, they are viewed as representations of the enlightened mind of the Buddha, and the relics they contain represent either the Buddha's body (corporeal relics) or speech (scriptures). In early Buddhism, *stūpa*s were managed by lay organizations separate from the monastic *saṅgha* and served as centers for worship, pilgrimage, and education—especially about the life of the Buddha, which relief carvings at *stūpa*s often depict. The prominence of the Buddha at *stūpa*s, present through his remains as well as through his life stories, may have led to the development of practices of visualization of the Buddha that became important features of Mahāyāna Buddhism. Because many Mahāyāna scriptures refer to *stūpa*s and are oriented toward lay rather than monastic practice, there appears to have been a close connection between the religious activities occurring at *stūpa*s and the rise of Mahāyāna Buddhism.

*Stūpa*s have traditionally gained their power and sanctity from the relics they contain. The Buddhist textual tradition as well as lived practices testify to a long history of expectation among Buddhists that the Buddha is in some way still accessible after his death. Theravāda Buddhism describes three categories of "relics" of the Buddha: relics of use (such as an umbrella or begging bowl), bodily relics, and relics of remembrance (a statue or painting). While relics associated with Sākyamuni Buddha are especially prized, relics of other famous masters are treasured as well, so there is no shortage of relics in the Buddhist world. In Tibetan Buddhism, relics are believed to physically reproduce themselves as a way of spreading blessing and power.

Nuns and Other Female Renunciants

Though Sākyamuni Buddha establishes an order of nuns as part of the *saṅgha*, he does so with a mysterious warning. If women are ordained, he cautions, the lifespan of the *dhamma* will decrease by half. Despite this prophecy, Sākyamuni agrees to ordain the first group of nuns at the earnest bequest of the woman who raised him, his aunt Pajāpatī. An early collection of enlightenment songs, the *Therīgāthā* (Songs of the Female Elders), provides moving glimpses into the lives of Buddhism's earliest nuns and their journeys through grief, aging, insight, and freedom.

The *bhikkhunī* (fully ordained nun) lineage ceased to exist in Sri Lanka by the twelfth century CE; history is silent about nuns in all Theravādin cultures by the fourteenth century. Although there are lineages of fully ordained nuns in Southeast and East Asian Mahāyāna communities, it is likely that the full ordination lineage for women was never introduced into Tibet.

As a result of the loss of nuns' ordination lineages in the Theravāda and Tibetan traditions, aspiring female monastics in these schools have adopted lives of renunciation and spiritual practice without achieving formal status. Although their monastic dress, their places of residence, their meditation practices, and the vows that govern their lives separate them from ordinary laywomen, these women are not officially recognized as members of the *saṅgha*. Each Theravādin culture, according these women a kind of special status, calls them "mothers" (female ascetics in Hinduism are also commonly referred to as *mātājī*, "mother"). Although "mother" is a cultural appellation of respect, the term "mother" is nonetheless fraught with ambiguities when applied to monastic women aspiring to lead lives of renunciation.

In Tibet, the women who live in monastic communities have typically received novice ordination, but not full ordination. Just like monks, these nuns wear maroon robes and shave their heads, but their limited spiritual status means that they are considered less worthy fields of merit than are their monk counterparts. As a result, nuns receive fewer material and educational resources for their growth; their relative poverty forces them to undertake farm work or difficult ritual services (such as extreme fasting) in order to provide for their basic needs. Despite these hardships and prejudices, which are operative at different degrees in the various Tibetan sects, many Tibetan Buddhist nuns have achieved high levels of education, meditative realization, administrative power, and social prestige. Other Tibetan women have lived as nonmonastic tāntric practitioners who do not need to participate in the status system of the monastic establishment.

One of the most significant movements in contemporary Buddhism is a revival of *bhikkhunī* ordination in the Theravāda and Tibetan Buddhist traditions, elevating the status of these female renunciants and restoring the Buddha's original plan for a fourfold *saṅgha* (monks, nuns, laymen, and laywomen). The traditional monastic view has been that the order of nuns cannot be revived if there are no other ordained nuns in the lineage who can perform the initiation, which is a requirement of the *Vinaya*. However, many Buddhist leaders have come to support the revival of *bhikkhunī* lineages in Theravāda and Tibetan Buddhism. These supporters argue that *bhikkhunī* can receive ordination from nuns in Mahāyāna communities who, although they carry a different ordination lineage than those of the Theravāda or Tibetan Buddhists, are fully ordained in an unbroken lineage, and therefore meet the requirements of the *Vinaya* for conducting new ordinations.

In 1996, through the efforts of Sakyadhita International Association of Buddhist Women, the Theravāda *bhikkhunī* order was historically re-established when eleven Sri Lankan women received full ordination in Sarnath with the support of Sri Lankan monks and Korean nuns. Since that time, hundreds of Sri Lankan *bhikkhunī* have been ordained with the cooperation of nuns in various Mahāyāna communities. A similar effort is currently underway in the Tibetan Buddhist tradition. In March 2017 in Bodh Gaya, nineteen Tibetan nuns received novice vows with the support of the Tibetan Karmapa Lama and Taiwanese nuns; they will receive full ordination vows in two years.

These historic ordinations have fundamentally reshaped the global Buddhist *saṅgha* after many centuries of fracture and have secured new possibilities for Buddhist women to pursue lives of renunciation, teaching, and service to others.

Reincarnate Lamas

Buddhism assumes a world in which beings are reborn, propelled by *kamma*, until reaching enlightenment. Tibetan Buddhism, derived from Indian Tāntric Buddhism and now practiced in communities across the Tibetan Plateau, the Himālayas, and parts of Central Asia, is the only Buddhist tradition to actively identify certain persons as *bodhisattva*s who have intentionally taken rebirth into particular circumstances in order to continue their efforts in teaching and service to others. The doctrinal term used to describe these beings is "emanation body" or *tulku* (Tibetan *sprul sku*, or Sanskrit *nirmāṇakāya*), which refers to the physical body of a Buddha like Sākyamuni. Tibetan Buddhists also use the term *lama*, the Tibetan translation for the Sanskrit *guru*, to refer to these highly revered individuals.

The recognition of individuals as reincarnations of past masters and emanations of *bodhisattva*s has grown into a religious institution that is central to Tibetan Buddhism. Reincarnate *lamas* can amass wealth and estates that are inherited by the next recognized incarnation; in this, they provide a model for succession and inheritance within celibate monastic institutions. Reincarnate *lamas* also serve as symbolic connections between figures from the past and present, often stretching across ethnic and national boundaries. The Dalai Lama, who is the highest ranking incarnate *lama* in one Tibetan Buddhist sect (the *dGe lugs pa*), is the most famous modern example of a reincarnate *lama*; Tenzin Gyatso, who was awarded the Nobel Peace Prize and has given numerous talks and rituals around the world, is the fourteenth incarnation in the Dalai Lama *tulku* line.

• MODERN EXPRESSIONS

Buddhist Modernism

Buddhism's rekindling in modern India has been fed by several different flames, but in each of these instances the form of Buddhism in play is what may be called "Neo-Buddhism" or "Buddhist Modernism." These terms refer to a postcolonial expression of Buddhism that first emerged in Sri Lanka in response to the British colonial presence and its denigration of Buddhism as a backward, superstitious form of idol worship. Reacting against that colonial ideology and adopting some of its biases, Theravāda leaders (both monastic and lay) led a revival of Buddhism that championed the Western Enlightenment ideals of rationality, morality, and humanistic social reform. The Buddhist Modernism movement spread to India, where it came to influence not only South Asian Theravāda Buddhists, but also Tibetan Buddhists traveling to India for pilgrimage.

One major hallmark of Buddhist Modernism has been an appeal to the legitimating role of science, seen most clearly in the archaeological excavations of Buddhist sites and historical-critical research on Buddhist texts. Buddhist Modernists have also framed their tradition as empirically based, atheistic, and consonant with the discoveries of modern neuroscience. Now, Buddhist Modernism also includes Engaged Buddhism (social activism based on Buddhist principles), which has taken many forms in the global Buddhist diaspora.

Two important Buddhist organizations were founded in 1891 as expressions of Buddhist Modernism. The first was the Maha Bodhi Society, founded in Sri Lanka by Theravāda Buddhist reformer and visionary Anagārika Dharmapāla (an Indian branch of the society was founded one year later in Calcutta). The primary goal of the Maha Bodhi Society was to reclaim legal control of the site of Bodh Gaya for Buddhists. They published pamphlets, books, and a journal; they constructed temples, monasteries, schools, and pilgrim guesthouses; and they undertook social projects and site restoration work. The Mahabodhi Temple is the grandest monument standing at Bodh Gaya today.

Also founded in 1891 in Calcutta was another Neo-Buddhist society, the Bauddha Dharmankura Sabha (later called the Bengal Buddhist Association). This was also a Theravāda Buddhist revival group inspired by the movement in Sri Lanka. Like the Maha Bodhi

Society, its members included Indian and European elites and its aim was to reclaim legal control over Buddhism's historical sites in India. The legacy of these two groups in reviving and maintaining Buddhist pilgrimage sites is strong today.

Ambedkarite Buddhism

Buddhist Modernism laid the groundwork for a new expression of Indian Buddhism a few decades later. After India gained Independence in 1947, a highly accomplished low-caste activist named Bhimrao Ramji Ambedkar (1891–1956) became disillusioned with prospects for the abolition of caste and all discrimination based on birth. Ambedkar was one of India's most remarkable twentieth-century leaders. From humble beginnings in western India, he obtained a legal education in London, earned a doctoral degree at Columbia University in New York, became an expert in constitutional law, and participated in writing the Constitution of India. Through the twenty years leading to Independence, he was a prominent public spokesperson for untouchable and low-caste rights and, at times, an opponent of Mohandas K. Gandhi over how to resolve problems of caste-based discrimination. After India gained its freedom, Ambedkar found in the teachings of the Buddha—one of the great spiritual luminaries of his own country—a rational and effective basis for universal human equality. In 1950, he addressed a conference of the World Fellowship of Buddhists in Sri Lanka and in the next few years attended their meetings in Rangoon. He established the Buddhist Society of India in 1955 and then converted to Buddhism by taking the Three Refuges and the Five Precepts in a large public ceremony held in Nagpur in October 1956. More than three hundred thousand others in attendance followed his example and became Buddhists at the same time. Mass conversions to Buddhism among low-caste Hindus still occur periodically as a form of social protest and activism.

In India today, there are about two million Ambedkarite Buddhists. The Neo-Buddhism inspired by Ambedkar continues to be a factor in efforts to improve social and economic mobility for low castes. In general, this means that Ambedkarite Buddhism plays a role in politics, and at times the result is inter-caste and inter-religious conflict. For instance, low-caste or Dalit Buddhists have become involved in ongoing campaigns to reassert Buddhist control over historically significant sacred sites, such as Sarnath and Gaya. These new Buddhist movements mirror recent Hindu movements to regain control of sites operated by other religious groups, such as the Hindu campaign for removal of a Muslim mosque at Ayodhya. These site-specific examples of religious politics have generated conflicts among various Buddhist groups and have often pitted Indian Neo-Buddhists against Tibetan Buddhists.

Tibetan Buddhism in Exile

In 1950, the People's Liberation Army of Maoist China invaded Tibet. The Fourteenth Dalai Lama, Tenzin Gyatso, fled Tibet in 1959 and was granted asylum in India. By the time a wave of eighty thousand Tibetans arrived in India following the Dalai Lama as refugees, the Buddhist sites of modern India had already been inscribed with historical meaning for twentieth-century Buddhists, but the ritual revival of Buddhism in India was only beginning.

In Tāntric Buddhism, the power of place is believed to be extremely potent. A place's power can be installed by the ritual activity of an accomplished practitioner or by the perceived traces of the presence of an enlightened being. Geomantic analysis, a sacred way of reading the landscape, can help recover the power of sites that have been forgotten or consecrate new sites for sacred purposes. One of the most prominent ways that Tibetan Buddhists have contributed to the modern revival of Buddhism in India is through the ritual reactivation of Buddhist sites' sacred power. The most vivid example of this kind of ritual activity is the Dalai Lama's Kālacakra Tantra empowerment given at Bodh Gaya in 1985. With a quarter of a million participants, this empowerment ceremony was the largest known Tibetan Buddhist ritual gathering in history. Subsequent Kālacakra empowerment ceremonies have made the circuit of other holy sites in India, including Amarāvatī, where the *Kālacakra Tantra* was believed to have been taught by the Buddha. These tāntric rituals are believed to reinstate ancient sites with spiritual power that can be harnessed by other pilgrims and meditators who visit them. The Kālacakra ceremony has also been refashioned by the Tibetan exile community as a "Kālacakra for World Peace," a fitting marker of the internationalized character of modern Buddhism in India as well as of modern interpretations of Buddhist social ethics.

The charismatic leadership of the Fourteenth Dalai Lama has garnered the Tibetan exile community in India international attention. Today over one hundred thousand Tibetan refugees live in India, but the Tibetan presence in India looms much larger. Tibetan Buddhists (including both ethnic Tibetans and Western converts, some of Hollywood fame) have sponsored the construction of numerous monasteries and temples, which have dramatically increased Buddhist pilgrimage and tourism in India. The Central Institute of Higher Tibetan Studies, a Buddhist university founded in 1967 as a partnership between the Fourteenth Dalai Lama and Jawaharlal Nehru, has further underscored Tibet's role in the preservation and revitalization of Buddhist traditions that were once lost in India. Today, whether through ritual activity or through institution building, Tibetan Buddhists are playing a major role in the Buddhist revival in India.

• RELATIONS WITH OTHER RELIGIONS

Hinduism and Jainism

The relationship between Buddhism and its sister religions in India has been marked by a relatively peaceful coexistence within a pluralistic society. Just as Hindus consider Buddhists to be heterodox for rejecting the authority of the Vedas, Buddhist texts construe Hindus as philosophically errant for their beliefs in the existence of a soul, the permanence of phenomena, and so forth; yet this philosophical difference has resulted in very little violent conflict between Hindus and Buddhists in Indian history. Hindus came to absorb the Buddha into their sacred history by naming him as an *avatāra* of Viṣṇu. On the other hand, the Ambedkarite Buddhist movement could be viewed as a dimension of conflict with Hinduism, insofar as Ambedkarite Buddhists use conversion as a form of protest of Hindu caste traditions.

Buddhism has even more in common with Jainism, its fellow reform movement from India's "age of transcendence." While Buddhists view Jainas as heterodox for their belief in an eternal soul, there is little history of conflict between Buddhists and Jainas other than competition for patronage. Although both Buddhism and Jainism emphasize renunciation, Buddhists advocate a Middle Way between self-denial and self-indulgence, while in the Jaina tradition the monastic lifestyle is more strictly ascetic.

Islam

Buddhism's use of images, its valorization of the renunciant lifestyle, and its rejection of the idea of an eternal God all contrast sharply with the central beliefs and practices of Islam. On the surface, the two religions have little in common, other than the fact that both are missionary religions that spread across Asia through the trade routes, in part by means of the basic literacy that each tradition encouraged. When the Ṭālibān destroyed the historic rock-cut Buddha images in Bamiyan, Afghanistan, it seemed very clear that Islam is inherently intolerant of Buddhism and an enemy of the religion. The historical narrative that Buddhism's decline in India was sealed by the destruction of incoming Muslim armies further reinforces this belief.

Although it is true that Mughal armies destroyed the last Buddhist monasteries in India in the thirteenth century, it is not true that violence has marked the majority of Muslim-Buddhist interactions in India. Umayyad Muslim rule in India in the eighth century was characterized by tolerance and protection for the Buddhist population, who were given official *dhimmī* status as an authentic minority religion, on par with other "people of the Book" (Arabic *ahl al-kitāb*). Much of Indian history, and world history, has involved peaceful coexistence between Muslims and Buddhists as members of multireligious societies.

As Buddhism has contributed to the formation of national identity (and subsequently, nationalism) in Southeast Asian cultures, the nominally nonviolent religion has sometimes been leveraged as a tool for oppressing and killing Muslim citizens. The most vivid contemporary example of Buddhist persecution of Muslims stems from an ongoing conflict in Myanmar, where Buddhist monastic authorities have directed much of the marginalization and terrorization of Rohingya Muslims.

Christianity

In the nineteenth century, during the time of European colonization in South Asia, the encounter between Buddhism and Christianity was highly contentious and predominantly marked by European cultural chauvinism. Interestingly, a few Europeans took up the cause of Buddhism as part of the Buddhism Modernism revival movement. Foremost among these was Henry Steel Olcott (1832–1907), an American who had served as a colonel in the Civil War and afterward became closely involved with Helena Petrovna Blavatsky (1831–91) and the establishment of the Theosophical Society. Olcott and Blavatsky visited India and Sri Lanka in 1879–80, and Olcott made further visits up to 1883, during which he deeply involved himself with the Buddhist revival and created a Buddhist catechism based on the Christian model. The colonial legacy in South Asia, therefore, influenced the emergence of a modern Buddhism in direct conflict with Christianity but also borrowing some of Christianity's forms and values.

The groundwork for later forms of inter-religious dialogue and cooperation between Buddhists and Christians was laid in part by the writings and influence of a (Christian) Catholic Trappist monk named Thomas Merton (*died* 1968), who formed personal friendships with the Fourteenth Dalai Lama and the Vietnamese Zen monk Thich Nhat Hanh, two of the most famous Buddhist figureheads in the modern world. Merton was an early and influential proponent of inter-religious dialogue in its modern manifestation. Today, the Dalai Lama and Nhat Hanh continue to build on Merton's initiatives by encouraging a harmonious relationship between Buddhism and Christianity. They are careful to acknowledge the distinctness of each tradition, but cite shared ethical values as well as similar contemplative traditions as the bases for mutual cooperation between Buddhists and Christians.

• DISCUSSION QUESTIONS

1. Who was the historical Buddha?
2. In as concise a way as you can manage, what are the basic differences among the main schools, sects, or branches of Buddhist tradition?
3. Do Hindu, Jaina, and Buddhist traditions differ from one another in their answers to a key question: What is the source of suffering, can suffering be overcome, and what is required to overcome it? If so, in what ways do they differ?

• NOTE

1 The late Dr. Tessa Bartholomeusz (1958–2001) authored the first edition of this chapter, published in *Religions of South Asia*, ed. Mittal and Thursby (2006). Some of her words—and much of her wisdom—remain in this revised edition. Dr. Bartholomeusz's deep knowledge of Sri Lankan Buddhism, as well as her acute insights into the intersections of gender and violence with Buddhism, continue to shape the field of Buddhist Studies and to inspire an increasingly humane engagement with the communities we study. This chapter owes much to Dr. Bartholomeusz, as well as to one of her teachers and mine, Dr. Karen Lang.

BIBLIOGRAPHY

Bartholomeusz, Tessa J. 1994. *Women Under the Bō Tree: Buddhist Nuns in Sri Lanka*. Cambridge: Cambridge University Press.

Bartholomeusz, Tessa J. 2002. *In Defense of Dharma: Just-War Ideology in Buddhist Sri Lanka*. London: RoutledgeCurzon.

Bond, George. 1988. *The Buddhist Revival in Sri Lanka: Religious Tradition, Reinterpretation, and Response*. Columbia: University of South Carolina Press.

Collins, Steven. 1982. *Selfless Persons: Imagery and Thought in Theravāda Buddhism*. Cambridge: Cambridge University Press.

Collins, Steven. 1990. "On the Very Idea of the Pali Canon." *Journal of the Pali Text Society* 15: 89–126.

Cone, Margaret and Richard F. Gombrich, eds. and trans. 1977. *The Perfect Generosity of Prince Vessantara: A Buddhist Epic*. Oxford: Clarendon Press.

Coningham, Robin A. E. 1995. "Monks, Caves and Kings: A Reassessment of the Nature of Early Buddhism in Sri Lanka." *World Archaeology* 27, 2: 222–42.

Gethin, Rupert. 1998. *The Foundations of Buddhism*. Oxford: Oxford University Press.

Gombrich, Richard. 1966. "The Consecration of a Buddhist Image." *The Journal of Asian Studies* 26, 1: 23–36.

Gombrich, Richard F. 1988. *Theravāda Buddhism: A Social History from Ancient Benares to Modern Colombo*. London: Routledge & Kegan Paul.

Gombrich, Richard F. and Gananath Obeyesekere. 1988. *Buddhism Transformed: Religious Change in Sri Lanka*. Princeton: Princeton University Press.

Hirakawa, Akira. 1990. *A History of Indian Buddhism from Śākyamuni to Early Mahāyāna* (trans. and ed. Paul Groner). Honolulu: University of Hawaii Press.

Huber, Toni. 2008. *The Holy Land Reborn: Pilgrimage and the Tibetan Reinvention of Buddhist India*. Chicago: University of Chicago Press.

Huntington, Susan. 1990. "Early Buddhist Art and the Theory of Aniconism." *Art Journal* 49, 4: 401–8.

Jondhale, Surendra and Johannes Beltz, eds. 2004. *Reconstructing the World: B.R. Ambedkar and Buddhism in India*. New Delhi: Oxford University Press.

Kalupahana, David J. 1976. *Buddhist Philosophy: A Historical Analysis*. Honolulu: University of Hawaii Press.

Kapstein, Matthew T. 2000. *The Tibetan Assimilation of Buddhism: Conversion, Contestation, and Memory*. New York: Oxford University Press.

Keown, Damien. 2013 [1996]. *Buddhism: A Very Short Introduction*. Oxford: Oxford University Press.

Lopez, Donald S., ed. 2004. *Buddhist Scriptures*. New York: Penguin Books.

Mitchell, Donald W. and Sarah H. Jacoby. 2013 [2002]. *Buddhism: Introducing the Buddhist Experience*. Third edition. New York: Oxford University Press.

Prothero, Stephen. 1996. *The White Buddhist: The Asian Odyssey of Henry Steel Olcott*. Bloomington: Indiana University Press.

Reynolds, Frank E. 1997. "Rebirth Traditions and the Lineage of Gotama: A Study in Theravāda Buddhology." *In* Juliane Schober, ed., *Sacred Biography in the Buddhist Traditions of South and Southeast Asia*, 19–39. Honolulu: University of Hawaii Press.

Reynolds, Frank E. and Jason A. Carbine, eds. 2000. *The Life of Buddhism*. Berkeley: University of California Press.

Robinson, Richard H., Willard L. Johnson, and Thanissaro Bhikkhu (Geoffrey DeGraff). 2005 [1970]. *Buddhist Religions: A Historical Introduction*. Belmont: Thomson Wadsworth.

Schopen, Gregory. 1990. "The Buddha as Owner of Property and Permanent Resident in Medieval Indian Monasteries." *Journal of Indian Philosophy* 18, 3: 181–217.

Schopen, Gregory. 1991. "Archaeology and Protestant Presuppositions in the Study of Indian Buddhism." *History of Religions* 31, 1: 1–23.

Seneviratne, H. L. 1978. *Rituals of the Kandyan State*. Cambridge: Cambridge University Press.

Smith, Bardwell L., ed. 1978. *Religion and Legitimation of Power in Sri Lanka*. Chambersburg: Anima Books.

Tambiah, S. J. 1970. *Buddhism and the Spirit Cults of North-East Thailand*. Cambridge: Cambridge University Press.

Thapar, Romila. 1973 [1963]. *Aśoka and the Decline of the Mauryas*. New Delhi: Oxford University Press.

Thapar, Romila. 1978. *Ancient Indian Social History: Some Interpretations*. New Delhi: Orient Longman.

Trainor, Kevin. 1997. *Relics, Ritual, and Representation in Buddhism: Rematerializing the Sri Lanka Theravāda Tradition*. Cambridge: Cambridge University Press.

Warder, A. K. 1970. *Indian Buddhism*. New Delhi: Motilal Banarsidass.

Williams, Paul with Anthony Tribe. 2000. *Buddhist Thought: A Complete Introduction to the Indian Tradition*. London: Routledge.

Wilson, Liz. 1996. *Charming Cadavers: Horrific Figurations of the Feminine in Buddhist Hagiographic Literature*. Chicago: University of Chicago Press.

Zelliot, Eleanor. 2004. "B. R. Ambedkar and the Search for a Meaningful Buddhism." *In* Surendra Jondhale and Johannes Beltz, eds., *Reconstructing the World: B. R. Ambedkar and Buddhism in India*, 18–34. New Delhi: Oxford University Press.

FIGURE 4.1 Shrī Harmandir Sāhib (also known as Shrī Darbār Sāhib, or the Golden Temple) in Amritsar.

Image courtesy of Elena Mirage/Shutterstock.com.

4

Sikh Dharam

PASHAURA SINGH

• THE TRADITIONS DEFINED

Sikh religion originated in the Punjab ("five rivers") region of northwest India more than five centuries ago. With unflinching faith in divine unity, it stresses the ideal of achieving spiritual liberation within a person's lifetime through meditation on the divine Name. It is also oriented toward action, encouraging the dignity of regular labor as part of spiritual discipline. Family life and social responsibility are important aspects of Sikh teachings. Notably, the Sikh tradition is the youngest of independent religions of India, where the Sikhs are about 2 percent of India's more than one billion people. What makes Sikhs significant in India is not their numbers but their contribution in the political and economic spheres. The global population of the Sikhs is about twenty-five million, which is more than the worldwide total of Jewish people. About twenty million Sikhs live in the state of Punjab, while the rest have settled in other parts of India and elsewhere. These include substantial communities of Sikhs established in Southeast Asia, Australia, East Africa, United Kingdom, mainland European countries, and North America through successive waves of emigration. In the last century, about a half million Sikhs immigrated to the United States of America.

• COSMOS AND HISTORY

Origins of the Tradition

Sikh religion is the newest of the world religions, with origins not in a distant prehistory that can never be fully recovered, but instead in a period of rich historical sources. As a consequence, scholars of Sikh Studies are able to explore issues of scriptural authority, social history, gender, diaspora, and national and religious identity from perspectives that scholars of other religions often lack. The Sikh tradition is rooted in a particular religious experience, piety, and culture and is informed by a unique inner revelation of its founder, Gurū Nānak (1469–1539), who declared his independence from the other thought forms of his day. He tried to kindle the fire of autonomy and courage in those who claimed to be his disciples (*sikh*, "learner"). Notwithstanding the influences he absorbed from his contemporary religious environment, that is, the devotional tradition of the medieval poet-saints (*bhagat/sant*) of North India with which he shared certain similarities and differences, Gurū Nānak laid down the foundation of distinctive teaching, practice, and community from the standpoint of his own religious ideals. It is instructive to note that the medieval poet-saints who advocated *nirguṇa bhakti* (devotion to the unqualified God) came to be called Sants in academic discourse in the twentieth century. Many of these Sants were of low-caste origins. The teachings of Gurū Nānak align in some significant ways with those of the Sants, while adding a distinctive level of sophistication and coherence. For instance, Gurū Nānak's understanding of the divine Name (*nām*), Word (*shabad*), Preceptor (*gurū*), and Order (*hukam*) carry us beyond anything that the works of earlier Sants offer in any explicit form (McLeod 1968: 161). A significant number of selected compositions of fifteen poet-saints were included in the Sikh scripture, where they are referred to as *bhagat*s (the Punjabi variation of *bhakta*s, or devotees), including the works of the Ṣūfī Muslim saint Farid (1173–1265), although the text itself gives him the title of Shaikh, not Bhagat. Rejecting the ascetic streak and misogynistic bias of some of these religious figures of North India, Gurū Nānak had a strong sense of mission that compelled him to proclaim his message for the ultimate benefit of his audience and to promote socially responsible living in a familial context. The Sikh tradition that developed from his teachings was faced with the problem of defining itself over and against the existing and known religious traditions in the Punjab. Mostly, these traditions were of Hindu, Muslim (particularly Ṣūfī), or Nāth origins. Throughout his authentic compositions available in the Sikh scripture, Gurū Nānak made a very clear distinction between his own teachings and practices and the teachings and practices of other paths.

Nānak was born to an upper-caste professional merchant (Khatrī) family of the village of Talwandī, present-day Nankana Sahib in Pakistan. Much of the material concerning his life comes from hagiographical *janam-sākhī*s (life-narratives). His life may be divided into three distinct phases: his early contemplative years, the enlightenment experience accompanied by extensive travels, and a foundational climax that resulted in the establishment of the first Sikh community in western Punjab. In one of his own hymns he proclaimed:

> I was a minstrel out of work; the Lord assigned me the task of singing the divine Word day and night. He summoned me to his Court and bestowed on me the robe of honor for singing his praises. On me he bestowed the divine Nectar (*amrit*) in a cup, the nectar of his true and holy Name.
>
> (*Ādi Granth* p. 150)

This hymn is intensely autobiographical, explicitly pointing out Gurū Nānak's own understanding of his divine mission, and it marked the beginning of his spiritual reign. He was then thirty years of age, had been married to Sulkhanī for more than a decade, and was the father of two young sons, Shrī Chand and Lakhmī Dās. He set out on a series of journeys to both Hindu and Muslim places of pilgrimage in India and elsewhere. During his travels, he came into contact with the leaders of different religious persuasions and tested the veracity of his own ideas in religious dialogues.

At the end of his travels, in the 1520s, Gurū Nānak purchased a piece of land on the right bank of the Rāvī River in central Punjab and founded the village of Kartārpur ("Creator's Abode"). There he lived for the rest of his life as the "Spiritual Guide" of a newly emerging religious community. His charismatic personality and teaching won him many disciples, who received the message of liberation through religious hymns of unique genius and notable beauty. They began to use these hymns in devotional singing (*kīrtan*) as a part of congregational worship. Indeed, the first Sikh families who gathered around Gurū Nānak in the early decades of the sixteenth century at Kartārpur formed the nucleus of a rudimentary organization of the Nānak Panth, the "path of Nānak," referring to the community constituted by the Sikhs who followed Gurū Nānak's path of liberation. He explicitly refers to his path as the Gurmukh Panth to distinguish it from the Brāhmaṇical, the ascetical, and the Islamic traditions of his day. In his role as what the sociologist Max Weber called an "ethical prophet," Gurū Nānak called for a decisive break with existing formulations and laid the foundation of a new, rational model of normative behavior based on divine authority. The authenticity and power of his spiritual message ultimately derived not from his relationship with the received forms of tradition, but rather from his direct access to Divine Reality through personal experience. Such direct access was the ultimate source of his message and provided him with a perspective on life by which he could fully understand, interpret, and adjudicate the various elements of existing traditions. Throughout his writings, he conceived of his work as divinely commissioned, and he required that his followers obey the divine command (*hukam*) as an ethical duty.

Gurū Nānak prescribed the daily routine, along with agricultural activity for sustenance, for the Kartārpur community. He defined the ideal person as a Gurmukh ("one oriented towards the Gurū"), who practiced the threefold discipline of "the divine Name, charity, and purity" (*nām-dān-ishnān*). Indeed, these three features, *nām* (relation with the Divine), *dān* (relation with the society), and *ishnān* (relation with the self), provided a balanced approach for the development of the individual and the society. They corresponded to the cognitive, the communal, and the personal aspects of the evolving Sikh identity. For Gurū Nānak, the true spiritual life required that "one should live on what one has earned through hard work and that one should share with others the fruit of one's exertion" (*Ādi Granth* p. 1245). In addition, service (*sevā*), self-respect (*pati*), truthful living (*sach achār*), humility, sweetness of the tongue, and taking only one's rightful share (*hak halāl*) were regarded as highly prized ethical virtues in pursuit of liberation. At Kartārpur, Gurū Nānak gave practical expression to the ideals that had matured during the period of his travels, and he combined a life of disciplined devotion with worldly activities set in the context of normal family life. As part of Sikh liturgy, Gurū Nānak's *Japjī* (Meditation) was recited in the early hours of the morning and *So Dar* (That Door) and *Ārtī* (Adoration) were sung in the evening.

Gurū Nānak's spiritual message found expression at Kartārpur through key institutions: the *saṅgat* ("holy fellowship"), where all felt that they belonged to one large spiritual fraternity;

the *dharamshālā*, the original form of the Sikh place of worship; and the establishment of the *laṅgar*, the interdining convention which required people of all castes to sit in status-free lines (*paṅgat*) to share a common meal. The institution of *laṅgar* promoted the spirit of unity and mutual belonging and struck at a major aspect of caste, thereby advancing the process of defining a distinctive Sikh identity. The Nāth Yogīs and the Sants did repudiate the caste system and removed themselves from its authority, but they could not organize a communal situation of open commensality in direct opposition to this convention. Evaluating the rejection of caste by members of the Sant tradition, for instance, Jagjit Singh concludes that the "anti-caste movements like those of Kabir and other Bhaktas, whose departure from caste ideology had been confined to the ideological plane, remained still-born in the field of social achievement" (1985: 46). The egalitarian ideal of the institution of *laṅgar* was the decisive factor in breaking the traditional order in which the society was organized based on the taboos of pollution and purity within the hierarchical caste system. Finally, Gurū Nānak created the institution of the Gurū ("Preceptor"), who became the central authority in community life. Before he passed away in 1539, he designated one of his disciples, Lehnā, as his successor by renaming him Aṅgad, meaning "my own limb." Thus, a lineage was established, and a legitimate succession was maintained intact from the appointment of Gurū Aṅgad (1504–52) to the death of Gurū Gobind Siṅgh (1666–1708), the tenth and the last human Gurū of the Sikhs.

Successors of Gurū Nānak

The early Sikh Gurūs followed a policy of both innovation and preservation. The second Gurū, Aṅgad, consolidated the nascent Sikh Panth in the face of the challenge offered by Gurū Nānak's eldest son, Shrī Chand, the founder of the ascetic Udāsī sect. Gurū Aṅgad further refined the Gurmukhi script for recording the compilation of the Gurū's hymns (*bāṇī*). The original Gurmukhi script was a systematization of the business shorthands (*laṇḍe/mahājanī*) of the type Gurū Nānak doubtless used professionally as a young man. This was an emphatic rejection of the superiority of the Devanagri and Arabic scripts (along with Sanskrit and the Arabic and Persian languages) and of the hegemonic authority they represented in the scholarly and religious circles of the time. The use of the Gurmukhi script added an element of demarcation and self-identity to the Sikh tradition. In fact, language became the single most important factor in the preservation of Sikh culture and identity and became the cornerstone of the religious distinctiveness that is part and parcel of the Sikh cultural heritage.

A major institutional development took place during the time of the third Gurū, Amar Dās (1479–1574), who introduced a variety of innovations to provide greater cohesion and unity to the ever-growing Sikh Panth. These included the establishment of the city of Goindwāl, the biannual festivals of Dīvālī and Baisākhī that provided an opportunity for the growing community to get together and meet the Gurū, a missionary system (*mañjī*) for attracting new converts, and the preparation of the Goindwāl *pothī*s, collections of the compositions of the Gurūs and some of the medieval poet-saints.

The fourth Gurū, Rām Dās (1534–81), founded the city of Rāmdāspur, where he constructed a large pool for the purpose of bathing. It was named Amritsar, meaning "the nectar of immortality." To build an independent economic base, the Gurū appointed deputies (*masand*) to collect tithes and other contributions from loyal Sikhs. In addition to a large body of sacred verse, he composed the wedding hymn (*lāvāṅ*) for the solemnization of a Sikh marriage. Indeed, it was Gurū Rām Dās who for the first time explicitly responded to the question "Who is a Sikh?" with the following definition:

> He who calls himself Sikh, a follower of the true Gurū, should meditate on the divine Name after rising and bathing and recite *Japjī* from memory, thus driving away all evil deeds and vices. As day unfolds he sings *gurbāṇī* (utterances of the Gurūs); sitting or rising he meditates on the divine Name. He who repeats the divine Name with every breath and bite is indeed a true Sikh (*gursikh*) who gives pleasure to the Gurū.
> (*Ādi Granth* pp. 305–6)

Thus, the liturgical requirements of the reciting and singing of the sacred word became part of the very definition of being a Sikh. The most significant development was related to the self-image of Sikhs, who perceived themselves as unique and distinct from the other religious communities of North India.

The period of the fifth Gurū, Arjan (1563–1606), was marked by a number of far-reaching institutional developments. First, at Amritsar he built the Harimandir, later known as the Golden Temple, which acquired prominence as the central place of Sikh worship. Second, he compiled the first canonical scripture, the *Ādi Granth* (Original Book), in 1604. Third, Gurū Arjan established the rule of justice and humility (*halemī rāj*) in the town of Rāmdāspur, where everyone lived in comfort (*Ādi Granth* p. 74). He proclaimed, "The divine rule prevails in Rāmdāspur due to the grace of the Gurū. No tax (*jizya*) is levied, nor any fine; there is no collector of taxes" (*Ādi Granth* pp. 430, 817). The administration of the town was evidently in the hands of Gurū Arjan, although in a certain sense Rāmdāspur was an autonomous town within the context and the framework of the Mughal rule of Emperor Akbar. Fourth, by the end of the sixteenth century the Sikh Panth had developed a strong sense of independent identity, which is evident from Gurū Arjan's assertion "We are neither Hindu nor Musalmān" (*Ādi Granth* p. 1136).

Fifth, dissensions within the ranks of the Sikh Panth became the source of serious conflict. A great number of the Gurū's compositions focus on the issue of dealing with the problems created by "slanderers" (*nindak*), who were rival claimants to the office of the Gurūship. The Udāsīs and Bhallās (Gurū Amar Dās' eldest son, Bābā Mohan, and his followers) had already established parallel seats of authority and had paved the way for competing views of Sikh identity. The rivalry of these dissenters was heightened when Gurū Arjan was designated for the throne of Gurū Nānak in preference to his eldest brother, Prithī Chand, who even approached the local Mughal administrators to claim the position of his father. At some point, Prithī Chand and his followers were branded *miṇā*s ("dissembling rogues").

Finally, the author of *Dabistān al-Mazāhib* (The School of Religions), a mid-seventeenth-century work in Persian, testifies that the number of Sikhs had rapidly increased during

Gurū Arjan's period and that "there were not many cities in the inhabited countries where some Sikhs were not to be found." In fact, the growing strength of the Sikh movement attracted the unfavorable attention of the ruling authorities because of the reaction of Muslim revivalists of the Naqshbandiyya Order in Mughal India. There is clear evidence in the compositions of Gurū Arjan that a series of complaints were made against him to the functionaries of the Mughal state, giving them an excuse to watch the activities of the Sikhs. The liberal policy of Akbar may have sheltered the Gurū and his followers for a time, but in May 1606, within eight months of Akbar's death, Gurū Arjan was tortured to death by the orders of the new emperor, Jahāngir. The Sikh community perceived his death as the first martyrdom, which became a turning point in the history of the Sikh tradition.

Indeed, a radical reshaping of the Sikh Panth took place after Gurū Arjan's martyrdom. The sixth Gurū, Hargobind (1595–1644), signaled the formal process when he traditionally donned two swords symbolizing the spiritual (*pīrī*) and the temporal (*mīrī*) investiture. He also built the Akāl Takht (Throne of the Timeless One) facing the Harimandir, which represented the newly assumed role of temporal authority. Under his direct leadership, the Sikh Panth took up arms in order to protect itself from Mughal hostility. From the Sikh perspective, this new development was not taken at the cost of abandoning the original spiritual base. Rather, it was meant to achieve a balance between temporal and spiritual concerns. A Sikh theologian of the period, Bhāī Gurdās, defended this martial response as "hedging the orchard of the Sikh faith with the hardy and thorny *kīkar* tree." After four skirmishes with Mughal troops, Gurū Hargobind withdrew to the Śivalik Hills, and Kīratpur became the new center of the mainline Sikh tradition. Amritsar fell into the hands of the *miṇā*s, who established a parallel line of Gurūship with the support of the Mughal authorities.

During the time of the seventh and eighth Gurūs, Har Rāi (1630–61) and Har Krishan (1656–64), the emphasis on armed conflict with the Mughal authorities receded, but the Gurūs held court and kept a regular force of Sikh horsemen. During the period of the ninth Gurū, Tegh Bahādur (1621–75), however, the increasing strength of the Sikh movement in rural areas again attracted Mughal attention. Gurū Tegh Bahādur's ideas of a just society inspired a spirit of fearlessness among his followers: "He who holds none in fear, nor is afraid of anyone, Nānak, acknowledge him alone as a man of true wisdom" (*Ādi Granth* p. 1427). Such ideas posed a direct challenge to the increasingly restrictive policies of the Mughal emperor, Awrangzeb (*ruled* 1658–1707), who had imposed Islamic laws and taxes and ordered the replacement of Hindu temples by mosques. Not surprisingly, Gurū Tegh Bahādur was summoned to Delhi by the orders of the emperor, and on his refusal to embrace Islam he was publicly executed in Chāndnī Chowk on November 11, 1675. The Sikhs perceived his death as the second martyrdom, which involved larger issues of human rights and freedom of conscience.

Tradition holds that the Sikhs who were present at the scene of Gurū Tegh Bahādur's execution shrank from recognition, concealing their identity for fear they might suffer a similar fate. In order to respond to this new situation, the tenth Gurū, Gobind Siṅgh, resolved to impose on his followers an outward form that would make them instantly recognizable. He restructured the Sikh Panth and instituted the Khālsā ("pure"), an order of loyal Sikhs bound by a common identity and discipline. On Baisākhī Day 1699 at Anandpur, Gurū Gobind Siṅgh initiated the first "Cherished Five" (*pañj piāre*), who formed the nucleus of the new order of the Khālsā. The five volunteers who responded to the Gurū's call for loyalty, and who came from different castes and regions of India, received the initiation through a ceremony that involved sweetened water (*amrit*) stirred with a two-edged sword and sanctified by the recitation of five liturgical prayers.

The inauguration of the Khālsā was the culmination of the canonical period in the development of Sikhism. The most visible symbols of Sikhism known as the five Ks—namely, uncut hair (*kesh*), a comb for topknot (*kaṅghā*), a short sword (*kirpān*), a wrist ring (*kaṛā*), and breeches (*kachh*)—are mandatory to the Khālsā. Gurū Gobind Siṅgh also closed the Sikh canon by adding a collection of the works of his father, Gurū Tegh Bahādur, to the original compilation of the *Ādi Granth*. Before he passed away in 1708, he traditionally terminated the line of personal Gurūs and installed the *Ādi Granth* as the eternal Gurū for Sikhs. Thereafter, the authority of the Gurū was invested together in the scripture (*Gurū Granth*) and in the corporate community (Gurū Panth).

Evolution of the Panth

The historical development of the Sikh Panth took place in response to four main elements. The first of these was the ideology based on religious and cultural innovations of Gurū Nānak and his nine successors. This was the principal motivating factor in the evolution of the Sikh Panth.

The second was the rural base of the Punjabi society. Gurū Nānak founded the village of Kartārpur to sustain an agricultural-based community. It is located on the bank of the river Rāvī, providing extremely fertile soil for agriculture. Gurū Nānak's father, Kālū Bedī, and his father-in-law, Mūlā Chonā, were village revenue officials (*paṭvārī*) who must have been instrumental in acquiring a parcel of land at Kartārpur. Since the Mughal law recognized Gurū Nānak's sons as the rightful owners of their father's properties, Gurū Aṅgad had to establish a new Sikh center at Khudūr. It confirmed an organizational principle that the communal establishment at Kartārpur could not be considered a unique institution, but rather a model that could be cloned and imitated elsewhere. Similarly, Gurū Amar Dās founded the city of Goindwāl. Interestingly, the location of Goindwāl on the right bank of the Beās River was close to the point where the Mājhā, Mālvā, and Doāba areas converge, making it a central location in the Punjab. This may help account for the spread of the Panth's influence in all three regions of the Punjab. Gurū Rām Dās founded the city of Rāmdāspur (Amritsar). During the period of Gurū Arjan, the founding of the villages of Tarn Tāran, Shrī Hargobindpur, and Kartārpur in the rural areas saw a large number of converts from local Jāṭ peasantry. Further, Gurū Tegh Bahādur's influence in the rural areas attracted more Jāṭs from the Mālvā region, and most of them became Khālsā during Gurū Gobind Siṅgh's period. It may have been the militant traditions of the Jāṭs that brought the Sikh Panth into increasing conflict with the Mughals, a conflict that shaped the future direction of the Sikh movement.

The third factor was the conflict created within the Sikh community by dissidents, which originally worked to counter and then, paradoxically, to enhance the process of the crystallization of the Sikh tradition. Gurū Nānak's son, Shrī Chand, was the first dissident who lived a life of celibacy. Although he failed to attract much support from early Sikhs, he created his own sect of Udāsīs (renunciants). This group was closer to the Nāth Yogīs in its beliefs and practices. Similarly, the followers of Mohan (Gurū Amar Dās' elder son), Prithī Chand (*miṇā*), Dhīr Mal (Gurū Har Rāi's elder brother, who established his seat at Kartārpur, Jalandhar), and Rām Rāi (Gurū Har Krishan's elder brother, who established his seat at Dehrā Dūn) posed a challenge to the mainline Sikh tradition. All these dissidents enjoyed Mughal patronage in the form of revenue-free grants (*madad-i-māsh*). Their pro-establishment stance triggered the mainline tradition to strengthen its own resources.

Finally, the fourth element was the period of Punjab history from the seventeenth to the eighteenth centuries, in which the Sikh Panth evolved in tension with Mughals and Afghans. All four elements combined to produce the mutual interaction between ideology and environment that came to characterize the historical development of Sikhism.

Worldview

The nature of the Ultimate Reality in Sikh doctrine is succinctly expressed in the Mūl Mantar ("seed formula"), the preamble to the Sikh scripture. The basic theological statement reads as follows:

> There is one Supreme Being ("1" *Oaṅkār*), the Eternal Reality, the Creator, without fear and devoid of enmity, immortal, never incarnated, self-existent, known by grace through the Gurū. The Eternal One, from the beginning, through all time, present now, the Everlasting Reality.
>
> (*Ādi Granth* p. 1)

The numeral "1" at the beginning of the original Punjabi text represents the unity of Akāl Purakh (the "Timeless One," God), a concept that Gurū Nānak interpreted in monotheistic terms. It affirms that Akāl Purakh is one without a second, the source as well as the goal of all that exists. He has "no relatives, no mother, no father, no wife, no son, and no rival who may become a potential contender" (*Ādi Granth* p. 597). It should always be kept in mind that the vital expression of the One is through the many, through infinite plurality of the creation, as is evident from Gurū Arjan's saying, "Unity becomes plurality, and plurality eventually becomes unity" (*Ādi Granth* p. 131). This particular understanding of the One in the Sikh tradition provides a distinctive meaning to "monotheism," different from what is normally construed to be in Semitic traditions. The Sikh Gurūs were fiercely opposed to any anthropomorphic conceptions of the divine. As the creator and sustainer of the universe, Akāl Purakh lovingly watches over it. As a father figure, he runs the world with justice and destroys evil and supports good (*Ādi Granth* p. 1028). As a mother figure, the Supreme Being is the source of love and grace and responds to the devotion of her humblest followers. By addressing the One as "Father, Mother, Friend, and Brother" simultaneously, Gurū

Arjan stressed that Akāl Purakh is without gender (*Ādi Granth* p. 103). Paradoxically, Akāl Purakh is both transcendent (*nirguṇa*, "without attributes") and immanent (*saguṇa*, "with attributes"). Only in personal experience can he be truly known. Despite the stress laid on *nirguṇa* discourse within the Sikh tradition, which directs the devotee to worship a nonincarnate, universal god, in Sikh doctrine god is partially embodied in the divine Name (*nām*) and in the collective Words (*bāṇī*) and the person of the Gurū and the saints. In sum, Sikh doctrine invokes a Divine Reality that is at once transcendent and immanent, personal and impersonal, and both having and not having attributes.

Gurū Nānak's cosmology hymn in *Mārū Rāg* addresses the basic questions about the genesis of the universe:

> For endless eons, there was only darkness. Nothing except the divine Order (*hukam*) existed. No day or night, no moon or sun. The Creator alone was absorbed in a primal state of contemplation. . . . When the Creator so willed, creation came into being. . . . The Un-manifested One revealed itself in the creation.
>
> (*Ādi Granth* pp. 1035–36)

Gurū Nānak maintained that the universe "comes into being by the divine Order" (*Ādi Granth* p. 1). He further says, "From the True One came air and from air came water; from water he created the three worlds and infused in every heart his own light" (*Ādi Granth* p. 19). Gurū Nānak employed the well-known Indic ideas of creation through five basic elements of air, water, ether, fire, and earth. As the creation of Akāl Purakh, the physical universe is real but subject to constant change. It is a lush green garden (*jagg vaṛī*), where human beings participate in its colorful beauty and fragrance (*Ādi Granth* p. 118). For Gurū Nānak the world was divinely inspired. It is a place that provides human beings with an opportunity to perform their duty and achieve union with Akāl Purakh. Thus, actions performed in earthly existence are important for "all of us carry the fruits of our deeds" (*Ādi Granth* p. 4).

For the Gurūs, human life is the most delightful experience that one can have with the gift of a beautiful body (*Ādi Granth* p. 966). It is a "precious jewel" (*Ādi Granth* p. 156). Indeed, the human being has been called the epitome of creation: "All other creation is subject to you, [O Man/Woman!], you reign supreme on this earth" (*Ādi Granth* p. 374). Gurū Arjan further proclaims that human life provides an individual with the opportunity to remember the divine Name and ultimately to join with Akāl Purakh (*Ādi Granth* p. 15). But rare are the ones who seek the divine Beloved while participating in worldly actions and delights.

The notions of *karma* (actions) and *saṃsāra* (rebirth or transmigration) are central to all religious traditions originating in India. *Karma* is popularly understood in Indian thought as the principle of cause and effect. This principle of *karma* is logical and inexorable, but *karma* is also understood as a predisposition that safeguards the notion of free choice. In Sikh doctrine, however, the notion of *karma* undergoes a radical change. For the Sikh Gurūs, the law of *karma* is not inexorable. In the context of the Gurū Nānak's theology, *karma* is subject to the higher principle of the "divine Order," an "all-embracing principle" that is the sum total of all divinely instituted laws in the cosmos. The law of *karma* is replaced by Akāl

Purakh's *hukam*, which is no longer an impersonal causal phenomenon but falls within the sphere of Akāl Purakh's omnipotence and justice. In fact, the primacy of divine grace over the law of *karma* is always maintained in the Sikh teachings, and divine grace even breaks the chain of adverse *karma*.

• SACRED LIFE AND LITERATURES

Sacred Life

The Sikh view of sacred life is intimately linked with the understanding of the nature of *gurmat* ("Gurū's view or doctrine") whereby one follows the teachings of the Gurūs. Gurū Nānak employed the following key terms to describe the nature of divine revelation in its totality: *nām* (divine Name), *shabad* (divine Word), and *gurū* (divine Preceptor). The *nām* reflects the manifestation of divine presence everywhere around us and within us, yet the people fail to perceive it due to their *haumai*, or self-centeredness. The Punjabi term "*haumai*" ("I, I") signifies the powerful impulse to succumb to personal gratification so that a person is separated from Akāl Purakh, and thus continues to suffer within the cycle of rebirths (*saṃsāra*). Akāl Purakh, however, looks graciously upon the suffering of people. He reveals himself through the Gurū by uttering the *shabad* that communicates a sufficient understanding of the *nām* to those who are able to "hear" it. The *shabad* is the actual "utterance," and in "hearing" it a person awakens to the reality of the divine Name, immanent in all that lies around and within.

The institution of the Gurū carries spiritual authority in the Sikh tradition. In most of the Indian religious traditions, the term "*gurū*" stands for a human teacher who communicates divine knowledge and provides his disciples with a cognitive map for liberation. In Sikhism, however, its meaning has evolved in a cluster of doctrines over a period of time. There are four focal points of spiritual authority, each acknowledged within the Sikh tradition as Gurū: doctrine of eternal Gurū; doctrine of personal Gurū; doctrine of Gurū Granth; and doctrine of Gurū Panth. First, Gurū Nānak uses the term "Gurū" in three basic senses: the Gurū is Akāl Purakh; the Gurū is the voice of Akāl Purakh; and the Gurū is the Word, the Truth of Akāl Purakh. To experience the eternal Gurū is to experience divine guidance. In Sikh usage, therefore, the Gurū is the voice of Akāl Purakh, mystically uttered within human heart, mind, and soul (*man*).

Second, the personal Gurū functions as the channel through whom the voice of Akāl Purakh becomes audible. Nānak became the embodiment of the eternal Gurū only when he received the divine Word and conveyed it to his disciples. The same spirit manifested itself successively in his successors. In Sikh doctrine, a theory of spiritual succession was advanced in the form of "the unity of Gurūship" in which there was no difference between the founder and the successors. Thus, they all represented one and the same light (*jot*) as a single flame ignites a series of torches.

Third, in Sikh usage, the *Ādi Granth* is normally referred to as the *Gurū Granth Sāhib*, which implies a confession of faith in the scripture as Gurū. As such, the *Gurū Granth*

Sāhib carries the same status and authority as did the ten personal Gurūs from Gurū Nānak through Gurū Gobind Siṅgh, and therefore, it must be viewed as the source of ultimate authority within the Sikh Panth. In actual practice, it performs the role of Gurū in the personal piety and corporate identity of the Sikh community. It has provided a framework for the shaping of the Sikh Panth and has been a decisive factor in shaping a distinctive Sikh identity. The *Gurū Granth Sāhib* occupies a central position in all Sikh ceremonies, and its oral/aural experience has provided the Sikh tradition with a living presence of the divine Gurū. Indeed, the *Gurū Granth Sāhib* has given Sikhs a sacred focus for reflection and for discovering the meaning of life. It has functioned as an ultimate source of authority within the Sikh tradition. In a certain sense, Sikhs have taken their conception of sacred scripture farther than other people of the Book, such as Jews and Muslims.

Finally, the key phrase Gurū Panth is normally employed in two senses: first, the Panth of the Gurū, referring to the Sikh community, and second, the Panth as the Gurū, referring to the doctrine of Gurū Panth. This doctrine fully developed from the earlier idea that "the Gurū is mystically present in the congregation." At the inauguration of the Khālsā in 1699, Gurū Gobind Siṅgh symbolically transferred his authority to the Cherished Five when he received initiation from their hands. Thus, the elite corps of the Khālsā has always claimed to speak authoritatively on behalf of the whole Sikh Panth, although at times non-Khālsā Sikhs interpret the doctrine of Gurū Panth as conferring authority on a community more broadly defined. As a practical matter, consensus within the Sikh community is achieved by following democratic traditions.

In order to achieve a state of spiritual liberation within one's lifetime, one must transcend self-centeredness created by the influence of *haumai*. In fact, *haumai* is the source of five evil impulses traditionally known as lust (*kām*), anger (*krodh*), covetousness (*lobh*), attachment to worldly things (*moh*), and pride (*haṅkar*). Under the influence of *haumai*, a person becomes "self-willed" (*manmukh*)—one who is so attached to his passions for worldly pleasures that he forgets the divine Name and wastes his entire life in evil and suffering. This self-willed condition can be transcended by means of the strictly interior discipline of *nām simaran*, or "remembering the divine Name." This threefold process ranges from the repetition of a sacred word, usually Wāhigurū (Praise to the Eternal Gurū), through the devotional singing of hymns with the congregation to sophisticated meditation on the nature of Akāl Purakh. The first and the third levels of this practice relate to private devotions, while the second refers to corporate sense. On the whole, the discipline of *nām simaran* is designed to bring a person into harmony with the divine Order. The person thus gains the experience of ever-growing wonder (*vismād*) in spiritual life and achieves the ultimate condition of blissful "equanimity" (*sahaj*) when the spirit ascends to the "realm of Truth" (*sach khaṇḍ*), the fifth and the last of the spiritual stages, in which the soul finds mystical union with Akāl Purakh.

The primacy of divine grace over personal effort is fundamental to Gurū Nānak's theology. There is, however, neither fatalism nor any kind of passive acceptance of a predestined future in his view of life. He proclaimed, "With your own hands carve out your own destiny" (*Ādi Granth* p. 474). Indeed, personal effort in the form of good actions has a place in Gurū Nānak's view of life. His idea of "divine free choice," on the one hand, and his emphasis on the "life of activism" based on human freedom, on the other, reflect his ability to hold in tension seemingly opposed elements. Gurū Nānak explicitly saw this balancing of opposed tendencies, which avoids rigid predestination theories and yet enables people to see their own "free" will as a part of Akāl Purakh's will, as allowing Sikhs the opportunity to create their own destinies, a feature stereotypically associated with Sikh enterprise throughout the world. Sikhism thus stresses the dignity of regular labor as an integral part of spiritual discipline. This is summed up in the following triple commandment: engage in honest labor (*kirat karnī*) for a living, adore the divine Name (*nām japanā*), and share the fruit of labor with others (*vaṇḍ chhakaṇā*). The formula stresses both the centrality of meditative worship and the necessity of righteous living in the world.

Scriptures and Other Literature

The *Ādi Granth* is the primary scripture of the Sikhs. It contains the works of the first five and the ninth Sikh Gurūs, four bards (Sattā, Balvaṇḍ, Sundar, and Mardānā), eleven Bhaṭṭs (panegyrists associated with the Sikh court), and fifteen Bhagats ("devotees" such as Kabīr, Nāmdev, Ravidās, Shai<u>kh</u> Farīd, and other medieval poets of *sant*, *ṣūfī*, and *bhakti* origin). Its standard version contains a total of 1,430 pages, and all correspond exactly in terms of the material printed on individual pages. The text of the *Ādi Granth* is divided into three major sections. The introductory section includes three liturgical prayers. The middle section, which contains the bulk of the material, is divided into thirty-one major *rāg*s, or musical patterns. The final section includes an epilogue consisting of miscellaneous works that could not be accommodated in the middle section.

The second sacred collection, the *Dasam Granth*, dates from the 1690s and is attributed to the tenth Gurū, Gobind Siṅgh. His *Zafarnāmā* ("Letter of Victory") was added in the eighteenth century. The sequence of its compositions was fixed in late nineteenth century. Its modern standard version of 1,428 pages consists of four major types of compositions: devotional texts, autobiographical works, miscellaneous writings, and a collection of mythical narratives and popular anecdotes. Currently, a heated debate is going on over the authorial "legitimacy" of the *Dasam Granth* text. There is an anti-Dasam Granth lobby, claiming that major portions of the text are at odds with the *Ādi Granth* and that it should not be authoritative for Sikhs. They are throwing the baby out with the bath water! In opposition to this group, Sikh institutions have offered a strong rebuttal to their polemic arguments by acknowledging the *Dasam Granth* as a secondary Sikh scripture. There is an urgent need to move beyond polemics and locate its text in the context of courtly culture of late seventeenth century Punjab in Mughal India.

The works of two early Sikhs, Bhāī Gurdās (about 1553–1636) and Bhāī Nand Lāl Goyā (1633–1715), make up the third category of sacred literature. Along with the sacred compositions of the Gurūs, their works are approved in the official manual of the *Sikh Rahit Maryādā* (Sikh Code of Conduct) for singing in the *gurdwārā*s.

The last category of Sikh literature includes three distinct genres: the *janam-sākhīs* (birth narratives), the *rahit-nāmās* (manuals of code of conduct), and the *gur-bilāses* (splendor of the Gurū) literature. The *janam-sākhīs* are hagiographical accounts of Gurū Nānak's life, produced by the Sikh community in the seventeenth century. The *rahit-nāmās* provide rare insight into the evolving nature of the K͟hālsā code in the eighteenth and nineteenth centuries. The *ur-bilāses* mainly focus on the mighty deeds of two warrior Gurūs, Hargobind and particularly Gobind Siṅgh.

• INSTITUTIONS AND PRACTICES

The K͟hālsā and the Rahit

From the perspective of ritual studies, three significant issues were linked with the first *amrit* ceremony. First, all who chose to join the order of the K͟hālsā through the ceremony were understood to have been "reborn" in the house of the Gurū, and thus to have assumed a new identity. The male members were given the surname Siṅgh ("lion"), and female members were given the surname Kaur ("princess"), with the intention of creating a parallel system of aristocratic titles in relation to the Rājput hill chiefs of the surrounding areas of Anandpur. Second, the Gurū symbolically transferred his spiritual authority to the Cherished Five when he himself received the nectar of the double-edged sword from their hands, and thus became a part of the K͟hālsā Panth and subject to its collective will. In this way, he not only paved the way for the termination of a personal Gurūship, but also abolished the institution of the *masands*, which was becoming increasingly disruptive. Several of the *masands* had refused to forward collections to the Gurū, creating factionalism in the Sikh Panth. In addition, Gurū Gobind Siṅgh removed the threat posed by the competing seats of authority when he declared that the K͟hālsā should have no dealings with the followers of Prithī Chand (*miṇā*), Dhīr Mal, and Rām Rāi. Finally, Gurū Gobind Siṅgh delivered the nucleus of the Sikh Rahit (Code of Conduct) at the inauguration of the K͟hālsā. By sanctifying the hair with *amrit*, he made it "the official seal of the Gurū," and the cutting of bodily hair was thus strictly prohibited. The Gurū further imposed a rigorous ban on smoking.

All Sikhs initiated into the order of the K͟hālsā must observe the Rahit as enunciated by Gurū Gobind Siṅgh, and subsequently elaborated. The most significant part of the code is the enjoinder to wear five visible symbols of identity, known from their Punjabi names as the five Ks (*pañj kakke*). These are unshorn hair (*kesh*), symbolizing spirituality and saintliness; a wooden comb (*kaṅghā*), signifying order and discipline in life; a miniature sword (*kirpān*), symbolizing divine grace, dignity, and courage; a steel "wrist-ring" (*kaṛā*), signifying responsibility and allegiance to the Gurū; and a pair of short breeches (*kachh*), symbolizing moral restraint. Among Sikhs, the five Ks are outer symbols of the divine Word, implying a direct correlation between *bāṇī* ("divine utterance") and *bāṇā* ("K͟hālsā dress"). The five Ks, along with a turban for male Sikhs, symbolize that the K͟hālsā Sikhs, while reciting prayers, are dressed in the word of God. Their minds are thus purified and inspired, and their bodies are girded to do battle with the day's temptations. In addition, Khālsā Sikhs are prohibited from the four cardinal evils (*chār kurahit*): "cutting the hair, using tobacco, committing adultery, and eating meat that has not come from an animal killed with a single blow."

Worship, Practices, and Lifecycle Rituals

The daily routine of a devout Sikh begins with the practice of meditation upon the divine Name. This occurs during the *amritvelā*, the "ambrosial hours" (that is, the last watch of the night, between 3:00 and 6:00 in the morning), immediately after rising and bathing. Meditation is followed by the recitation of five liturgical prayers, which include the *Japjī* of Gurū Nānak. In most cases, the early morning devotion concludes in the presence of the *Gurū Granth Sāhib*, in which the whole family gathers to receive the divine command (*vāk laiṇā*, or "taking God's Word") by reading a passage selected at random. Similarly, a collection of hymns, *Sodar Rahiras* (Supplication at That Door), is prescribed for the evening prayers, and the *Kīrtan Sohilā* (Song of Praise) is recited before retiring for the night.

Congregational worship takes place in the *gurdwārā*, where the main focus is upon the *Gurū Granth Sāhib*, installed ceremoniously every morning. Worship consists mainly of the singing of scriptural passages set to music, with the accompaniment of instruments. The singing of hymns (*kīrtan*) in a congregational setting is the heart of the Sikh devotional experience. Through such *kīrtan*, the devotees attune themselves to vibrate in harmony with the divine Word, which has the power to transform and unify their consciousness. The exposition of the scriptures, known as *kathā* ("homily"), may be delivered at an appropriate time during the service by the *granthī* ("reader") of the *gurdwārā* or by the traditional Sikh scholar (*gyanī*). At the conclusion of the service all who are present join in reciting the *Ardās* ("Petition," or Sikh Prayer), which invokes divine grace and recalls the rich common heritage of the community. Then follows the reading of the *vāk* (divine command) and the distribution of *kaṛāh prasād* (sanctified food).

At the end of congregational worship, everyone shares in the *laṅgar* prepared and served by volunteers as part of the community service expected of all Sikhs. All present, Sikhs and non-Sikhs alike, sit together to share a traditional vegetarian meal—usually flat bread, bean stew, and curry. This custom is a powerful reminder of the egalitarian spirit that is so central to Sikhism. It is worth mentioning that approximately one hundred thousand people share meals every day at the largest community kitchen of Gurū Rām Dās Laṅgar at the Golden Temple in Amritsar. An interesting story relates to recent event of the potential failure of the Oroville Dam emergency spillway on the evening of February 12, 2017, when Sikh volunteers invited the 188,000 evacuees who were forced to leave their homes to come to their *gurdwārā*s for a nice vegetarian meal and a rest on the floors of their prayer halls. Several *gurdwārā*s in the surrounding Northern California area, including Sacramento, Roseville, Turlock, and Tracy, also publicly invited anyone in need to come to their houses of worship.

The central feature of the key lifecycle rituals is always the *Gurū Granth Sāhib*. When a child is to be named, the family takes the baby to the *gurdwārā* and offers *kaṛāh prasād*. After offering thanks and prayers through *Ardās*, the *Gurū Granth Sāhib* is opened at random and a name is chosen beginning with the same letter as the first composition on the left-hand page. Thus, the process of *vāk laiṇā* (divine command) functions to provide the first letter of the chosen name. The underlying principle is that the child derives his or her identity from the Gurū's word and begins life as a Sikh. To a boy's name the common surname Singh is added, and to a girl's name Kaur is added at the end of the chosen name. In some cases, however, particularly in North America, people employ caste names (for example, Ahluwalia, Dhaliwal, Grewal, Kalsi, Sawhney, or Sethi) as the last elements of their names, and for them Singh and Kaur become middle names. In addition, the infant is administered sweetened water that is stirred with a sword, and the first five stanzas of Gurū Nānak's *Japjī* are recited.

A Sikh wedding, according to the Anand (Bliss) ceremony, also takes place in the presence of the *Gurū Granth Sāhib*, and the performance of the actual marriage requires the couple to circumambulate the sacred scripture four times to take four vows. Before the bridegroom and the bride make each round, they listen to a verse of the *lāvāṅ*, or "wedding hymn" (*Ādi Granth* pp. 773–74), by the fourth Gurū, Rām Dās, as given by a scriptural reader. They bow before the *Gurū Granth Sāhib* and then stand up to make their round while professional musicians sing the same verse with the congregation. During the process of their clockwise movements around the scripture, they take the following four vows: first, to lead an action-oriented life based upon righteousness and never to shun the obligations of family and society; second, to maintain a bond of reverence and dignity between them; third, to keep enthusiasm for life alive in the face of adverse circumstances and to remain removed from worldly attachments; and finally, to cultivate a "balanced approach" (*sahaj*) in life, avoiding all extremes. The pattern of circumambulation in the Anand marriage ceremony is the enactment of the primordial movement of life, in which there is no beginning and no end. Remembering the four marital vows is designed to make the life of the couple blissful.

The key initiation ceremony (*amrit saṅskār*) for a Sikh must take place in the presence of the *Gurū Granth Sāhib*. There is no fixed age for initiation, which may be done at any time the person is willing to accept the Khālsā discipline. Five Khālsā Sikhs, representing the collectivity of the original Cherished Five, conduct the ceremony. Each recites from memory one of the five liturgical prayers while stirring the sweetened water (*amrit*) with a double-edged sword. The novice then drinks the *amrit* five times so that his body is purified from the influence of five vices; and five times the *amrit* is sprinkled on his eyes to transform his outlook toward life. Finally, the *amrit* is poured on his head five times to sanctify his hair so that he will preserve his natural form and listen to the voice of conscience. Throughout the procedure, the Sikh being initiated formally takes the oath each time by repeating the following declaration: *Wāhigurū jī kā Khālsā! Wāhigurū jī kī Fateh*! (Khālsā belongs to the Wonderful Lord! Victory belongs to the Wonderful Lord!). Thus, a person becomes a Khālsā Sikh through the transforming power of the sacred word. At the conclusion of the ceremony, a *vāk* is given and *kaṛāh prasād* is distributed.

Finally, at the time of death, both in the period preceding cremation and in the postcremation rites, hymns from the *Gurū Granth Sāhib* are sung. In addition, a reading of the entire scripture takes place at home or in a *gurdwārā*. Within ten days of the conclusion of the reading, a *bhog* ("completion") ceremony is held, at which final prayers are offered in memory of the deceased.

• ETHICS AND HUMAN RELATIONS

The *Ādi Granth* opens with Gurū Nānak's *Japjī*, where the fundamental question of seeking the divine Truth is raised as follows: "How is Truth to be attained, how the veil of falsehood torn aside?" Gurū Nānak then responds: "Nānak, thus it is written: submit to the divine Order (*hukam*), walk in its ways" (p. 1). Truth obviously is not obtained by intellectual effort or cunning but only by personal commitment. To know Truth one must live in it. The seeker of the divine Truth, therefore, must live an ethical life. An immoral person is neither worthy of being called a true seeker, nor capable of attaining the spiritual goal of life. Any dichotomy between spiritual development and moral conduct is not approved in Sikh ethics. In this context, Gurū Nānak explicitly says: "Truth is the highest virtue, but higher still is truthful living" (*Ādi Granth* p. 62). Indeed, truthful conduct (*sach achār*) is at the heart of Sikh ethics.

The central focus in the Sikh moral scheme involves the cultivation of virtues such as wisdom, contentment, justice, humility, truthfulness, temperance, love, forgiveness, charity, purity, and fear of Akāl Purakh. Gurū Nānak remarked, "Sweetness and humility are the essence of all virtues" (*Ādi Granth* p. 470). These virtues not only enrich the personal lives of individuals, but also promote socially responsible living. The Gurūs laid great stress on the need to earn one's living through honest means. In particular, living by alms or begging is strongly rejected. Through hard work and sharing, Sikh ethics forbids withdrawal from social participation. The Sikh Gurūs offered their own vision of the cultivation of egalitarian ideals in social relations. Such ideals are based on the principle of social equality, gender equality, and human brotherhood/sisterhood. Thus, it is not surprising that any kind of discrimination based on caste or gender is expressly rejected in Sikh ethics.

The key element of religious living is to render service (*sevā*) to others in the form of mutual help and voluntary work. The real importance of *sevā* lies in sharing one's resources of "body, mind, and wealth" (*tan-man-dhan*) with others. This is an expression toward fellow beings of what one feels toward Akāl Purakh. The service must be rendered without the desire for self-glorification, and in addition, self-giving service must be done without setting oneself up as a judge of other people. The Sikh Prayer (*Ardās*) holds in high esteem the quality of "seeing but not judging" (*dekh ke anādith karnā*). Social bonds are often damaged beyond redemption when people, irrespective of their own limitations, unconscionably judge others. The Sikh Gurūs emphasized the need to destroy this root of social strife and enmity through self-giving service.

Finally, Sikhism is dedicated to human rights and resistance against injustice. It strives to eliminate poverty and to offer voluntary help to the less privileged. Its commitment is to the ideal of universal brotherhood, with an altruistic concern for humanity as a whole (*sarbatt dā bhalā*). In a celebrated passage from the *Akāl Ustat* (Praise of Immortal One), Gurū Gobind Siṅgh declared that "humankind is one and that all people belong to a single humanity" (verse 85). Here it is important to underline the Gurū's role as a conciliator who tried to persuade the Mughal emperor Bahādur Shāh to walk the ways of peace. Even though Gurū Gobind Siṅgh had to spend the major part of his life fighting battles that were forced upon him by Hindu hill *rājā*s and Mughal authorities, a longing for peace and fellowship with both Hindus and Muslims may be seen in the following passage from the *Akāl Ustat*:

> The temple and the mosque are the same, so are the Hindu worship [*pūjā*] and Muslim prayer [*namāz*]. All people are one, it is through error that they appear different. . . . Allāh and Abhekh are the same, the Purāṇa and the Qur'ān are the same. They are all alike, all the creation of the One.
>
> (verse 86)

The above verses emphatically stress the irenic belief that the differences dividing people are in reality meaningless. In fact, all people are fundamentally the same because they all are the creations of the same Supreme Being. To pursue this ideal, Sikhs conclude their morning and evening prayers with the words "Says Nānak: may thy Name and glory be ever triumphant, and in thy will, O Lord, may peace and prosperity come to one and all."

Society: Caste and Gender Issues

Gurū Nānak and the succeeding Gurūs emphatically proclaimed that the divine Name was the only sure means of liberation for all four castes: the Khatrī, originally the Kṣatriya (warrior), the Brāhmaṇa (priest), the Śūdra (servant/agriculturalist), and the Vaiśya (tradesman). In the works of the Gurūs, the Khatrīs were always placed above the Brāhmaṇas in the caste hierarchy while the Śūdras were raised above the Vaiśyas. This was an interesting way of breaking the rigidity of the centuries-old caste system. All of the Gurūs were Khatrīs, which made them a top-ranking mercantile caste in Punjab's urban hierarchy, followed by Arorās (merchants) and Āhlūwālīās (brewers). In the rural caste hierarchy, an absolute majority (almost two-thirds) of Sikhs are Jāṭs (peasants), followed by Ramdasīās (artisans), Ramdāsīās (cobblers), and Mazhabīs (sweepers). Although Brāhmaṇas are at the apex of the Hindu caste hierarchy, Sikhs place Brāhmaṇas distinctly lower on the caste scale. This is partly because of the strictures the Sikh Gurūs laid upon Brāhmaṇa pride and partly because the reorganization of Punjabi rural society conferred dominance on the Jāṭ caste.

Doctrinally, caste has never been one of the defining criteria of Sikh identity. In the Sikh congregation, there is no place for any kind of injustice or hurtful discrimination based upon caste identity. In the *gurdwārā*, Sikhs eat together in the community kitchen, share the same sanctified food, and worship together. The *Sikh Rahit Maryādā* explicitly states, "No account should be taken of caste; a Sikh woman should be married only to a Sikh man; and Sikhs should not be married as children." This is the ideal however, and in practice most Sikh marriages are arranged between members of the same endogamous caste group. Caste, therefore, still prevails within the Sikh community as a marriage convention. Nevertheless, inter-caste marriages take place frequently among urban professionals in India and elsewhere.

The Sikh Gurūs addressed the issues of gender within the parameters established by traditional patriarchal structures. In their view, an ideal woman plays the role of a good daughter or sister and a good wife and mother within the context of family life. They condemned both women and men alike who did not observe the cultural norms of modesty and honor in their lives. It is in this context that images of the immoral woman and the unregenerate man are frequently encountered in the scriptural texts. There is no tolerance for any kind of premarital or extramarital sexual relationships, and rape in particular is regarded as a violation of women's honor in Punjabi culture. Rape amounts to the loss of family honor, which in turn becomes the loss of one's social standing in the community. The notion of family honor is thus intimately linked to the status of women.

The issue of gender has received a great a deal of attention within the Sikh Panth. It is notable that the Sikh Gurūs offered a vision of gender equality within the Sikh community and took practical steps to foster respect for womanhood. They were ahead of their times when they championed the cause of equal access for women in spiritual and temporal matters. Gurū Nānak raised a strong voice against the position of inferiority assigned to women in society at the time:

> From women born, shaped in the womb, to woman betrothed and wed; we are bound to women by ties of affection, on women man's future depends. If one woman dies he seeks another; with a woman he orders his life. Why then should one speak evil of women, they who give birth to kings?
>
> (*Ādi Granth* p. 473)

He sought to bring home the realization that the survival of the human race depended upon women, who were unjustifiably ostracized within society. Gurū Nānak's egalitarian ideas about women set him far apart from medieval poet-saints of North India, particularly Kabīr, who described woman as "a black cobra," "the pit of hell," and "the refuse of the world" (*Kabīr Granthāvalī* 32.2, 30.16, 30.20). Gurū Amar Dās abolished the customs among women of the veil and of *satī* (self-immolation) and permitted the remarriage of widows. He further appointed women as Sikh missionaries. Indeed, Sikh women were given equal rights with men to conduct prayers and other ceremonies in *gurdwārās*. In actual practice, however, males dominate most Sikh institutions, and Sikh women continue to live in a patriarchal society based on Punjabi cultural assumptions. In this respect, they differ little from their counterparts in other religious communities in India. Although there is a large gap between the ideal and reality, there is clear doctrinal support for the equality of rights for men and women within the Sikh Panth. Consequently, Sikh women have been asserting themselves with growing success in recent years.

• MODERN EXPRESSIONS

The modern religious and cultural transformation within the Sikh tradition took place during the colonial period at the initiatives of the Siṅgh Sabhā (Society of the Siṅghs). This reform movement began in 1873 at Amritsar. The principal objective of the Siṅgh Sabhā reformers was to reaffirm the distinctiveness of Sikh identity in the face of the twin threats posed by the casual reversion to Hindu practices during Sikh rule and the explicit challenges from actively proselytizing religious movements such as Christian missionaries and the Ārya Samāj (Society of the Āryas). The Tat Khālsā (Pure Khālsā), the dominant wing of the Siṅgh Sabhā movement, succeeded in eradicating all forms of religious diversity by the end of the nineteenth century and established norms of religious orthodoxy and orthopraxy. The reformers were largely successful in making the Khālsā ideal the orthodox form of Sikhism, and they systematized and clarified the Khālsā tradition to make Sikhism consistent and effective for propagation.

Indeed, the Tat Khālsā ideal of Sikh identity, which was forged in the colonial crucible, was both old and new. It was forged in the crucible of colonial encounter. In addition to the economic and military policy of the British, there were other elements that meshed together to produce a great impact on the emerging Sikh identity. These additional elements in the larger colonial context were new patterns of administration, a new technology, a fresh approach to education, the entry of Christian missionaries, and the modernist perspective based on the scientific paradigm of the Enlightenment. All these factors produced modern Sikhism, characterized by a largely successful set of redefinitions in the context of the notions of modernity and religious identity imposed by the dominant ideology of the colonial power closely associated with Victorian Christianity. As such, modern Sikhism became a well-defined "system" based on a unified tradition, and the Tat Khālsā understanding of Sikh identity became the norm of orthodoxy.

Among the twenty-five million Sikhs in the postmodern world, however, only approximately 15 to 20 percent are *amrit-dhārīs* (initiated), those who represent the orthodox form of the Khālsā. A large majority of Sikhs, however, about 70 percent, are *kesh-dhārīs*, that is, those who "retain their hair" and thus maintain a visible identity. These Sikhs follow most of the Khālsā Rahit without having gone through the initiation ceremony. The number of Sikhs who have shorn their hair, and are thus less conspicuous, is quite large in the West in general, and in particular in North America and the United Kingdom. Popularly known as *monā* (clean-shaven) Sikhs, they retain their Khālsā affiliation by using the surnames Singh and Kaur. These Sikhs are also called *ichhā-dhārīs* because they "desire" to keep their hair but cut it under some compulsion. They are frequently confused with *sahaj-dhārī* (gradualist) Sikhs, those who have never accepted the Khālsā discipline. Although *sahaj-dhārī* Sikhs practice *nām simaran* and follow the teachings of the *Ādi Granth*, they do not observe the Khālsā Rahit and in general do cut their hair. The number of *sahaj-dhārīs* declined during the last few decades of the twentieth century, although they have not disappeared completely from the Sikh Panth. Finally, there are those who violate the Khālsā Rahit and cut their hair after initiation. These lapsed *amrit-dhārīs*, who are known as *patit* or *bikh-dhārī* (apostate) Sikhs, are found largely in the diaspora. There is thus no single way of being a

Sikh, and the five categories of Sikhs are not fixed permanently. Punjabi Sikhs frequently move between them according to their situation in life.

• TRANSMISSION OF THE TRADITION OUTSIDE OF INDIA

There are now more than two million Sikhs who have settled in foreign lands as a result of successive waves of emigration over the past hundred years. It is not surprising to find the establishment of more than five hundred *gurdwārā*s in North America and the United Kingdom alone. The recent years have witnessed among the Sikhs of North America a revived interest for their inherited tradition and identity. This awakened consciousness has produced a flurry of activities in children's education. Sikh parents realize that worship in *gurdwārā*s is conducted in Punjabi, which scarcely responds to the needs of children born in North America. At schools, these children are being trained to be critical and rational, and they are therefore questioning the meaning of traditional rituals and practices. Traditionally trained *granthī*s and *gyanī*s are unable to answer their queries. Moreover, without adequate knowledge of Punjabi, the language of the *Ādi Granth*, the new generation of Sikhs is in danger of being theologically illiterate.

Moreover, a steady process of assimilation is in progress among second- and third-generation Sikhs. Western culture has added new challenges and obstructions to the Sikh tradition. This situation has created new responses from the Sikh community. Many Sikh parents have started home-based worship in both Punjabi and English to meet new challenges from the diaspora situation. They have introduced another innovative feature in the form of Sikh Youth Camps to pass on the Sikh traditions to the children. These camps last one or two weeks. Through them, a spiritual environment is created which provides the children with continuous exposure to Sikh values and traditions.

Finally, in the 1970s a group of Caucasian Americans and Canadians converted to the Sikh faith at the inspiration of their *yoga* teacher, Harbhajan Singh Khalsa (Yogi Bhajan), who founded the Sikh Dharma movement. These so-called white, or *goṛā*, Sikhs, male and female alike, wear white turbans, tunics, and tight trousers. They live and raise families in communal houses, spending long hours in meditation and chanting while performing various postures of Tāntric Yoga. They have thus introduced the Sikh tradition into a new cultural environment. Most Punjabi Sikhs have shown an ambivalent attitude toward these converts. On the one hand, they praise the strict K͟hālsā-style discipline of the white Sikhs; and on the other hand, they express doubts about the mixing of the Sikh tradition with the ideals of Tāntric Yoga.

In sum, Sikhism is considered a world religion because it has adherents from all over the world. It is no longer limited to Punjab and Punjabi culture. The second generation of "white" (*goṛā*) Sikhs is fully trained at Miri Piri Academy (MPA) at Amritsar in the living traditions of Sikhism, Sikh music, and martial arts along with their normal educational curriculum. They are further exposed to the refined forms of folk traditions of Punjabi culture, such as *bhaṅgṛā* and *giddhā*. Most remarkably, the Chaṛhdī Kalā Kīrtan Jathā (High Spirited Group of Devotional Singh) is a group of three musicians—Jugat Guru Singh Khalsa, Sada Sat Simarn Singh Khalsa, and Hari Mander Jot Singh Khalsa—who are trained in classical *rāga*s of the *Gurū Granth Sāhib* at MPA. They have traveled extensively, sharing, teaching, and inspiring Sikh congregations around the world. Indeed, with the coming of a millennial generation of white Sikhs, Sikhism has indeed become a world religion. In other words, these non-Punjabi Sikhs "present a challenge to the Punjabi Sikhs to move from a parochial, context-based religion to a universal, text-based religion" (Leonard 1999: 276).

• RELATIONS WITH OTHER RELIGIONS

The ability to accept religious pluralism is a necessary condition of religious tolerance. Religious pluralism requires that people of different faiths be able to live together harmoniously, which provides an opportunity for spiritual self-judgment and growth. It is in this context that Sikhism expresses the ideals of coexistence and mutual understanding. Sikhism emphasizes the principles of tolerance and the acceptance of the diversity of faith and practice. It is thus able to enter freely into fruitful inter-religious dialogue with an open attitude. Such an attitude signifies a willingness to learn from other traditions and yet to retain the integrity of one's own tradition. It also involves the preservation of differences with dignity and mutual respect.

The Sikh Gurūs were strongly opposed to the claim of any particular tradition to possess the sole religious truth. Indeed, a spirit of accommodation has always been an integral part of the Sikh attitude toward other traditions. The inclusion of the works of the fifteen medieval non-Sikh saints (*bhagat bāṇī*, "utterances of the Bhagats"), along with the compositions of the Gurūs, in the foundational text of the Sikhs provides an example of the kind of catholicity that promotes mutual respect and tolerance. For instance, the Muslim voice of the devotee Shai<u>kh</u> Farīd is allowed to express itself on matters of doctrine and practice. This is the ideal Sikhs frequently stress in interfaith dialogues.

The presence of the *bhagat bāṇī* in the Sikh scripture offers a four-point theory of religious pluralism. First, one must acknowledge at the outset that all religious traditions, have gone through a process of self-definition in response to changing historical contexts. Thus, in any dialogue the dignity of the religious identities of the individual participants must be maintained. One must be able to honor a commitment as absolute for oneself while respecting different absolute commitments for others. For this reason, the quest for a universal religion and the attempt to place one religious tradition above others must be abandoned. Second, the doctrinal standpoints of different religious traditions must be maintained with mutual respect and dignity. Third, all participants must enter into a dialogue with an open attitude, one that allows not only true understanding of other traditions, but also disagreements on crucial doctrinal points. Finally, the "other" must somehow become one's "self" in a dialogue, so that the person's life is enriched by the spiritual experience.

• RECENT DEVELOPMENTS WITHIN THE TRADITION

The most significant issue confronting Sikhs around the world is the tendency to associate their tradition with violence. The use of warrior imagery to evoke the valor of the Sikhs has been standard since colonial times. Relatively little attention has been directed to the other dimensions of the Sikh tradition. What is expected of the Sikh warriors is not violence but militancy in the sense that they are prepared to take active and passionate stand on behalf of their faith. In 1973, for instance, the main political party of the Sikhs in Punjab, the Akali Dal (Army of the Immortal), passed Anandpur Sahib Resolution, demanding increased autonomy for all the states of India. Over the following years, relations with the Indian government became increasingly strained as a result. In an apparent attempt to sow dissensions within the ranks of the Akali Dal, the Congress government encouraged the rise of a charismatic young militant named Jarnail Singh Bhindranwale (1947–84). But this strategy backfired in the spring of 1984, when a group of armed radicals led by Bhindranwale decided to provoke a confrontation with the government by occupying the Akāl Ta<u>kh</u>t (Throne of the Immortal) building in the Golden Temple Complex in Amritsar. The government responded by sending in the army. The assault that followed—code-named "Operation Blue Star"—resulted in the deaths of many Sikhs, including Bhindranwale, as well as the destruction of the Akāl Ta<u>kh</u>t and severe damage to the Golden Temple itself. A few months later, on October 31, 1984, Prime Minister Indira Gandhi was assassinated by her own Sikh bodyguards. For several days, unchecked Hindu mobs in Delhi and elsewhere killed thousands of Sikhs. It took more than a decade to contain separatist violence, and the main Sikh political party (Akali Dal) reasserted its right to work within the democratic framework for greater justice and transparency. In the end, peaceful process has proved more effective than violent struggle.

On September 15, 2001, an American Sikh became the first victim of the racial backlash that followed the 9/11 terrorist attacks. Balbir Singh Sodhi was shot dead in Phoenix, Arizona, by a self-described "patriot" who mistook him for a Muslim. It is painfully clear that too many people in the West simply do not know who Sikhs are. On Sunday morning, August 5, 2012, a gunman burst into the Sikh *gurdwārā* in Oak Creek, Wisconsin, and opened fire, killing five men and one woman, ambushing one police officer and injuring three others. During an exchange of gunfire, he eventually died of a self-inflicted gunshot wound to the head after he was shot by another police officer. The dominant narrative that has emerged in both media coverage and public discourse since then has been one of mistaken religious identity. It presumes that the killer, identified as a white supremacist named Wade Michael Page, may have shot the Sikhs because he ignorantly believed they were Muslim. To a certain extent, such a storyline seems accurate because hundreds of times since the terrorist attacks of 9/11, Sikhs have been the victims of horrific attacks like this. The perpetrators of such crimes have invariably assumed that because Sikh men wear turbans and have beards they are Muslims, even specifically Ṭālibān. How terrible it is that it has taken the slayings in Wisconsin to serve as a national teachable moment about Sikh beliefs and practices.

The early twenty-first century continues to be a very exciting time for Sikh Studies. Within the last generation, scholars have begun to question the prevailing attitudes towards the study of Sikhism in both the West and India itself to the point that this least examined and perhaps most misunderstood of South Asia's religious and cultural traditions now occupies seven academic chairs within the United States of America and one in Canada, with more proposed in the University of California system. It should therefore elicit no surprise that undergraduate and graduate courses in Sikh Studies, particularly Sikh history and religion, have been increasing dramatically over the last two decades, a rise which corresponds in part to Sikh immigration into Canada, the United States, and the United Kingdom.

Finally, Sikhism has had and continues to have a seemingly unending number of dominant, institutional, regional, national, and local expressions of faith in constant dynamic relationship with one another, continually influencing each other and defining and redefining what it has meant and continues to mean to be a Sikh in different places around the globe. Most instructively, the Sikh community has always been involved in the process of "renewal and redefinition" throughout the world. In fact, the question "Who is a Sikh?" occupies much of the attention in the online discussion among the various Sikh networks, although the debate frequently becomes acrimonious. Each generation of Sikhs has to respond to this question in the light of a new historical situation and to address the larger issues of orthodoxy and orthopraxy. Unsurprisingly, the diaspora Sikhs have to respond to these issues from their own particular situation in different cultural and political contexts. In fact, they rediscover their identity in cross-cultural encounters, as well as through their interaction with other religious and ethnic communities. They have to face new challenges, which require new responses. It is no wonder that they are starting to provoke fresh responses to the notions of self, gender, and authority in the postmodern world. On the whole, the process of Sikh identity formation is an ongoing phenomenon of a dynamic nature.

• DISCUSSION QUESTIONS

1. How many sources of authority in religious matters are there in Sikh tradition? What are they, and are some more important or authoritative than others?
2. What is the meaning of the term "Guru" in Sikh tradition? How does this meaning differ from the usual meaning of the same term when it appears in other contexts?
3. What are the main kinds of spiritual discipline or religious practice encouraged or required in Sikh tradition?

• BIBLIOGRAPHY

Cole, W. Owen. 1982. *The Guru in Sikhism*. London: Darton, Longman, & Todd.

Cole, W. Owen. 1984. *Sikhism and Its Indian Context, 1469–1708: The Attitude of Guru Nanak and Early Sikhism to Indian Religious Beliefs and Practices*. London: Darton, Longman, & Todd.

Grewal, J. S. 1991. *The Sikhs of the Punjab*. Cambridge: Cambridge University Press.

Grewal, J. S. 1998. *Contesting Interpretations of the Sikh Tradition*. New Delhi: Manohar.

Leonard, Karen. 1999. "Second Generation Sikhs in the US: Consensus and Differences." *In* Pashaura Singh and N. Gerald Barrier, eds., *Sikh Identity: Continuity and Change*, 275–97. New Delhi: Manohar.

McLeod, W. H. 1968. *Guru Nanak and the Sikh Religion*. Oxford: Clarendon Press.

McLeod, W. H. 1989. *The Sikhs: History, Religion, and Society*. New York: Columbia University Press.

McLeod, Hew [W. H.] 1997. *Sikhism*. London: Penguin.

McLeod, W. H. 1999. *Sikhs and Sikhism: Gurū Nānak and the Sikh Religion; Early Sikh Tradition; The Evolution of the Sikh Community; Who is a Sikh?* New Delhi: Oxford University Press.

McLeod, W. H. 2003. *Sikhs of the Khalsa: A History of the Khalsa Rahit*. New Delhi: Oxford University Press.

Oberoi, Harjot. 1994. *The Construction of Religious Boundaries: Culture, Identity, and Diversity in the Sikh Tradition*. New Delhi: Oxford University Press.

Singh, Harbans. 1983. *The Heritage of the Sikhs*. New Delhi: Manohar.

Singh, Harbans, ed. 1992–98. *The Encyclopaedia of Sikhism*. 4 volumes. Patiala: Punjabi University.

Singh, Jagjit. 1985. *Perspectives in Sikh Studies*. New Delhi: Guru Nanak Foundation.

Singh, Nikky-Guninder Kaur. 1993. *The Feminine Principle in the Sikh Vision of the Transcendent*. Cambridge: Cambridge University Press.

Singh, Nripinder. 1990. *The Sikh Moral Tradition: Ethical Perceptions of the Sikhs in the Late Nineteenth/Early Twentieth Century*. New Delhi: Manohar.

Singh, Pashaura. 2000. *The Guru Granth Sahib: Canon, Meaning, and Authority*. New Delhi: Oxford University Press.

Singh, Pashaura. 2003. *The Bhagats of the Guru Granth Sahib: Sikh Self-Definition and the Bhagat Bani*. New Delhi: Oxford University Press.

Singh, Pashaura. 2006. *Life and Work of Guru Arjan: History, Memory, and Biography in the Sikh Tradition*. New Delhi: Oxford University Press.

Singh, Pashaura. 2015. "Framing the Dasam Granth Debate: Throwing the Baby Out With the Bath Water!" *Sikh Formations: Religion, Culture, Theory* 11, 1–2 (Encountering Sikh Texts, Practices and Performances: Essays in Honour of Professor Christopher Shackle, edited by Pashaura Singh and Arvind-pal Singh Mandair): 108–32.

Singh, Pashaura and Louis E. Fenech, eds. 2014. *The Oxford Handbook of Sikh Studies*. New York: Oxford University Press.

Part II

What India Has Received From the World

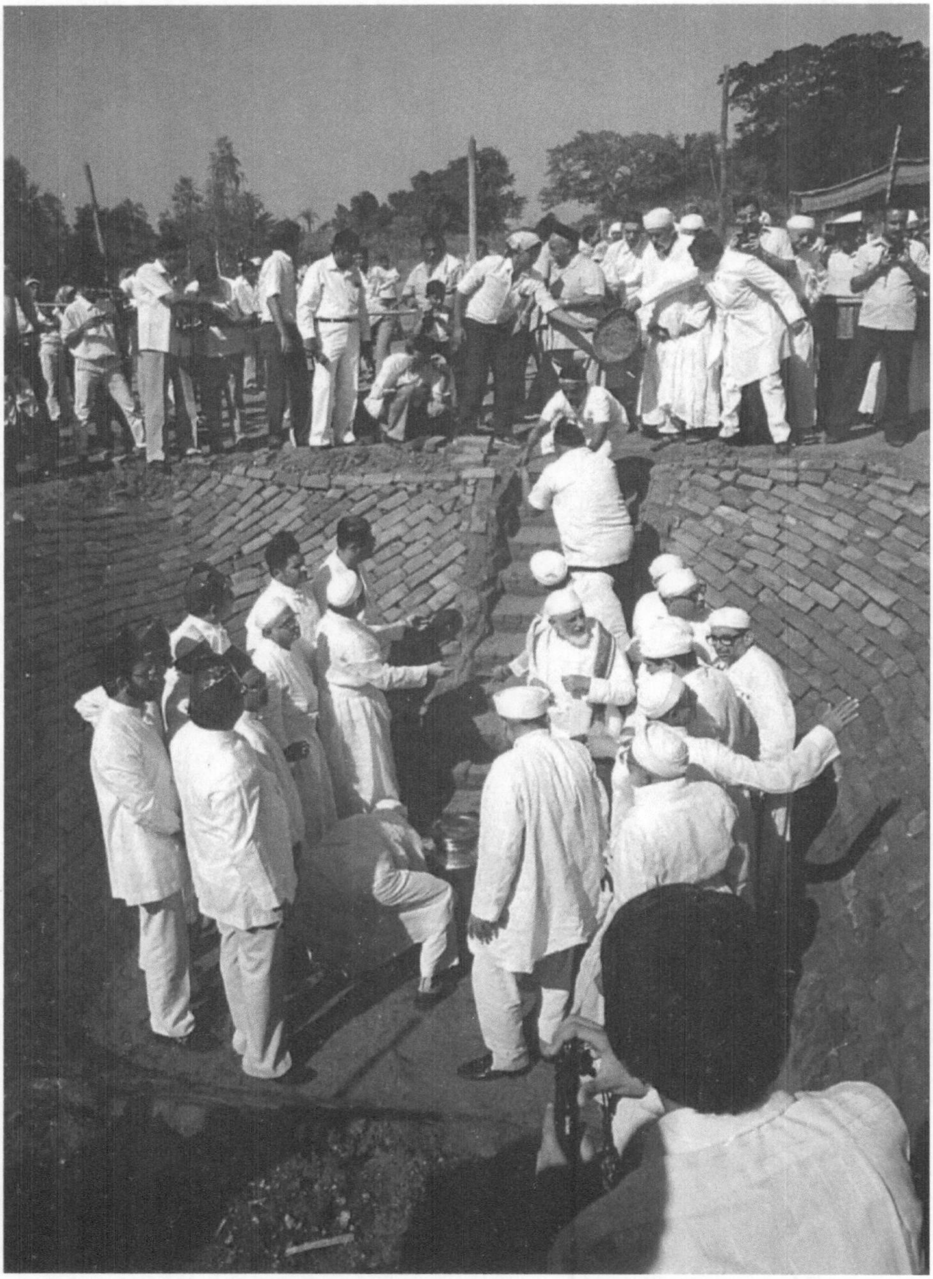

FIGURE 5.1 Installation of the foundation for a new fire temple at the site of the first Parsi landing in Gujarat.

Image courtesy of T. M. Luhrmann.

5

Indian Zoroastrian Traditions

T. M. LUHRMANN

• THE TRADITIONS DEFINED

Zoroastrianism is an ancient religion based on the teachings of the prophet Zarathustra or (in the Greek) Zoroaster. Its most distinctive elements are the strong dualism inherent in a basically monotheistic theology and the role of fire, which is used to represent divinity and is enshrined in temples as the focus of religious prayer. Originally a Persian spirituality, Zoroastrianism's modern adherents are small in number but can be found all over the globe. They are probably concentrated in India, and in particular in Bombay (now Mumbai). There do appear to be modern Zoroastrians in Iran, but recent census figures (which report as many as twenty-five thousand Iranian Zoroastrians) are thought to be misleading, and the only late twentieth-century scholarship of Iranian Zoroastrianism (Boyce 1977; Fischer 1973) describes the remnants of Zoroastrian practice in rural areas. In any event, it is in India that modern Zoroastrianism has had its most recent impact and acquired a distinctive form, associated with a remarkable group of people, the Parsis, whose history is inseparable from that of Mumbai itself.

• COSMOS AND HISTORY

Zarathustra is thought to have lived in the middle of the second millennium BCE, though there is a good deal of debate about this; the suggested date is based on the similarity of the language in the teachings ascribed to Zarathustra (the *Gāthās*, which are included in a longer sacred text, the *Avesta*) with the language of the *Ṛg Veda*, which is thought in this analysis to date from around the same period (Boyce 1975, 1979). This dating also makes Zarathustra a rough contemporary of the patriarch Abraham. He seems to have been born into a nomadic people; many passages in the words attributed to him speak of herding cattle. These nomads probably descended from the Indo-Iranian people who had roamed the southern steppes in the fourth millennium BCE. By the third millennium, they seem to have separated into two cultures, but even a thousand years later they shared much in common, and the tone and ethos of the two great traditions echo each other across their texts.

The religion that holds Zarathustra's words as its central teaching shares much with its Indo-Iranian past, and Zarathustra may have been a priest in the early Indo-Iranian religion. That religion put fire and water at the center of its practice, as does Zoroastrianism, and its central concept seems to have been *aša* (Vedic Sanskrit *ṛta*, later *dharma*) that also remains central in Zoroastrian theology. To the Indo-Iranians, *aša* was thought to be something akin to natural law, the order of the universe in which the sun rises and the seasons turn in their regular and expected manners. Ritual sacrifice seems to have been thought to strengthen this process and was made daily to both fire and water. Fuel, incense, and animal fat were given to the fire, along with frequent blood sacrifice of an animal; but to the water, the milk, sap, and leaves of a sacred plant were offered. Scholars think that this is the sacred plant mentioned as *soma* in the Vedas and *haoma* in the *Avesta*; it may have been the stimulant *ephedra*. The pre-Zoroastrian texts speak of one wise lord, with two somewhat lesser lords, and an array of abstract personifications of natural elements and human aspirations, like prayer and friendship.

Tradition says that Zarathustra was born laughing and that he left home at twenty to seek the truth. Revelation came to him at thirty, when he stopped at the side of a river and was led into the presence of Ahura Mazdā (God) and five other radiant beings. Exactly how he understood these beings is uncertain—the texts that preserve his teachings are obscure. But his teachings are usually taken to have transformed the Indo-Iranian tradition by elevating Ahura Mazdā, the one wise lord, into a role of singular importance. Ahura Mazdā becomes the one uncreated God, existing eternally, who has created all other gods and all that is good. This last point becomes the issue of greatest acrimony in the interpretation of the ancient texts, because Zarathustra does speak of two fundamental spirits that are utterly opposed and between whom humans must choose. At least to some extent, Ahura Mazdā is a more limited lord than, for example, the Abrahamic deity at the center of Jewish, Christian, and Muslim traditions. But even the God of Hebrew scripture struggles with the presence of other gods. Zarathustra's vision of Ahura Mazdā has a radical uniqueness: Ahura Mazdā is the source of all good, who creates from himself the other deities mentioned in the Indo-Iranian texts. Far more clearly than in the Abrahamic traditions, Zarathustra sees that the one God cannot remove the misery from human life:

> To all of you the soul of the cow [thought to represent the vision of the good, the human ideal] lamented: "For whom did ye shape me? Who fashioned me? (For) the cruelty of fury and violence, of bondage and might, holds me in captivity. I have no pastor other than you. . . ." To him they replied through truth: "There is no help free of enmity for the cow."
>
> (*Yasna* 29.1, 3; Insler 1975: 29)

The text then goes on to explain the presence of two spirits, utterly opposed, between whom the gods did not all choose wisely. "Since they chose the worse thought, they then rushed into fury, with which they have afflicted the world and mankind" (*Yasna* 30.6; Insler 1975: 33).

It is evident even from these early, obscure texts that Zoroastrianism is a doctrine in which moral issues are very clear and very important. God is good, rational, and knowable; he is truth. He is also purity. Evil is the lie, and all acts which are irrational and hurtful are the acts of evil. A human being is essentially good—this is a striking difference from many other religious traditions—but he or she can choose to be influenced by Ahriman, the evil spirit. The central story of the religion is that the human individual participates in a battle between good and evil in which his own freely chosen actions determine the outcome. It is usually accepted that God will ultimately win this cosmic war but only through human initiative.

Zarathustra also seems to have taught that each human being is judged at the end of life. Upon death, the soul comes to a bridge over a chasm, the Činvat Puhl, and a woman representing the person's life deeds beckons the soul to cross over. She is either old and ugly or young and beautiful, as the soul has acted in the world; and as the soul steps upon the bridge, it either widens to allow passage into the paradise beyond or shrinks to force the soul to fall to hellish depths. And yet regardless of the outcome, at the end of time all souls will be redeemed and the earth will emerge in godly bliss. It is said that Zarathustra was the first to teach the doctrines of an individual judgment, the first to teach of heaven and hell, the first to teach of the resurrection of the body and of everlasting life. It is sometimes said that Zoroastrianism is a source from which similar Jewish and Christian teachings are derived (Russell 1987). Then as now, God is represented by fire. He is not fire personified, and contemporary Zoroastrians are quick to point out that they do not worship fire. They use fire to represent God, more or less as the cross represents Jesus. It is not quite clear when the first fire temples were built; Herodotus refers to Persian fire worship, and it may have been that there were very early temples.

Tradition says that for ten years Zarathustra was unable to find any converts among his own people, except for one lone cousin. So he left his people and, after some wandering, came to the court of King Vīštāspa, who accepted his teachings after Zarathustra cured the ruler's beloved horse of illness. Historical records first mention Iranians centuries later, in the ninth century BCE. As described by Herodotus, these are the Medes, who were established in western Iran. They overthrew the Assyrian empire in 614–12 BCE and extended their presence over the Iranian peoples to the east and southwest. Zoroastrianism seems to have spread quickly during their sixty years of rule.

In 549 BCE, the Persian people from the southwest, under Cyrus, an Achaemenian and the current Medean king's son-in-law, overthrew the king and established the first Persian Empire. He went on to conquer Asia Minor and Babylonia (and her subject territories) and brought eastern Iran also under his control. In all likelihood, Cyrus and his people were Zoroastrians. The classical historian Herodotus assumed that they were and said of them,

> They do not believe in gods of human form, as the Greeks do. They offer sacrifices to Zeus, going up into the highest mountains and calling the whole circle of the heaven Zeus. They sacrifice, too, to the sun, moon, and earth and to fire, water, and winds. . . . The Persians welcome foreign customs more than any other people.
>
> (Herodotus 1.131, 135)

The Persian Empire fell to Alexander in 331 BCE, but a Zoroastrian state emerged again within a hundred years, as a Zoroastrian lineage (descending from Arshak or Arsaces) established rule from the border of India to the western boundary of Mesopotamia. In 224 BCE, that lineage was overthrown by another, which established the Sassanian dynasty in Iran. It was during Sassanian times that the canonical body of Zoroastrian religious texts was written down for the first time. These texts—the *Avesta*, which included the seventeen hymns attributed to Zarathustra and called the *Gāthā*s—seem to have been transmitted orally until an alphabet was invented for them in this period. Over the next thousand years, even past the Islamic conquest, additional religious texts emerged, written in another language (Pahlavi or Middle Persian) that served as commentaries on the original Zoroastrian texts. The theology in these later texts is far crisper than it is in Zarathustra's elliptical verses, and much of the theological debate in modern Parsi circles is in effect an argument about whether the Pahlavi version of the theology is what Zarathustra really meant.

Zoroastrianism arrived in India when some Zoroastrians left their homeland, probably for reasons of religious freedom, and landed on an island off the coast of Gujarat early in the tenth century CE. They then made their way to the mainland and settled in areas still associated with the religion: Sanjan, Navsari, and Surat. A famous tale tells of the local king on the mainland hesitant to accept the newcomers. He presented a cup of milk, full to the brim, to explain that the land was already too densely settled; the Parsi leader added a pinch of sugar without spilling a drop and said that his people would only make the land sweeter. Strict rules about endogamy and the prohibitions on non-Parsi presence in fire temples that continue to be observed in India may date from this period, as such restrictions are not found today in Iran.

Parsis lived quietly in Gujarat for seven hundred years. When the British arrived, they began to function in the role of financial mediators and traders. They grew quite wealthy, moved to Bombay, and became the most Westernized "native" community in India. A 1905 Parsi commentator makes this revealing comment in a book on Indian cricket, which Parsis dominated for many years.

> A Parsi in England feels quite at home. He knows well the history and tradition of its people, and is no stranger to their manners and games. He esteems their sports, liberties and literature. Many a wealthy and educated Parsi now-a-days takes an annual holiday to England, just as a Mahommedan or a Hindu goes to Mecca or Benares.
>
> (Patel 1905: 47)

Mecca for the Muslims, Benares for the Hindus; a Parsi, J.M.F. Patel suggests without irony, goes on pilgrimage to London. This process of Westernization has had significant implications for the Zoroastrian religion, for while few Parsis converted to Christianity, their ritual-rich religion shifted to a much more secularized vision. Only in recent years, as the community begins to face the prospect of dying out altogether, have Parsis begun to emphasize the satisfactions of ritual practice and the virtues of involvement in the religious life.

• SACRED LIFE AND LITERATURES

As a textual tradition, Zoroastrianism is based on a messy compilation of texts, many of which are missing and few of which have unambiguous translations. The *Avesta* is the oldest collection and the chief source for the spiritual tradition. The texts are composed in two otherwise unrecorded eastern Iranian languages: the "Gathic" Avestan, similar to the language of the *Ṛg Veda*, and "Younger" Avestan. The Gathic Avestan takes its name from the primary texts of the language, the *Gāthās*, seventeen hymns composed by the prophet and embedded in a longer collection of verses called the *Yasna*, which forms the basis of priestly worship. The *Gāthās* are both passionate and abstract, with frequent references to the "soul of the cow" and cattle herding. They are also difficult to interpret. As one scholar remarks, "Because of their relative brevity and the almost total lack of other earlier or contemporary works of Old Iranian literature, the Gāthās of Zarathustra are truly a text bound with seven seals" (Insler 1975: 1). Other material in the *Avesta* includes hymns to individual deities (the Yašts), a selection of texts addressing purity laws (the *Vendīdād*), and a variety of other prayers. A selection of this material has been assembled in a collection called the "Khordeh Avesta," which is used by many Parsis as a book of common prayer.

None of these texts was written down before the fifth century CE, and even then many were lost. The earliest extant manuscript now dates from 1323 CE. In fact, during the Sassanian period, the *Avesta* was much larger and included a wide range of material: life and legends of the prophet, treatises on cosmogony, books of law, and so forth. All known copies were destroyed in the series of Islamic conquests, although one late Persian book (the *Dīnkard*) gives a detailed summary of the contents: from this, scholars infer that roughly one quarter of the total remains. It remains, however, because it was the quarter in most constant devotional use, and the texts survived from memory.

In addition, there is a variety of commentaries (*Zend*) that survive, written in Pahlavi. (The *Avesta* with its interpretations is often described as the "Zend-Avesta.") Among the important texts are the *Bundahišn*, a text on creation whose theology is far clearer than that in the *Gāthās*. Another is referred to as the *Zādspram*, named for the priest thought to be its author, which includes materials on the prophet's life. His life story can also be found in the *Dīnkard*, which also includes a massive amount of other religious material. Most of these texts date from the ninth century. There are also writings in other tongues, among them modern Persian and Old Gujarati, which are thought to retranslate older texts but which have not been deeply analyzed by scholars. A collection known as the "Persian Rivāyats" consists of Iranian priests' answers to Parsi priests' questions on ritual and spiritual matters between the fifteenth and eighteenth centuries. There is also a considerable Parsi literature in English and Gujarati that dates from the nineteenth and twentieth centuries.

The central textual challenge around which many community theological debates have been organized is the role of dualism and the degree of God's power in the universe. The most famous passage in the *Gāthā*s is this:

> Truly there are two primal Spirits, twins, renowned to be in conflict. In thought and word and act they are two, the good and the bad. . . . And when these two Spirits first encountered, they created life and not-life, and that at the end the worst existence shall be for the followers of falsehood (drug), but the best dwelling for those who possess righteousness (asha).
>
> (*Yasna* 30.3; Boyce 1979: 20)

Mary Boyce, a leading Western scholar and translator of Zoroastrian texts, argued that these words indicate that early Zoroastrianism was dualistic. There are two spiritual beings, one good, one bad, utterly opposed to each other and apparently equally powerful. Many of the Pahlavi texts that date from much later are unambiguously dualistic. The ninth-century *Bundahišn*, for example, explains that in the beginning there were both God (Ahura Mazdā) and evil (Ahriman), both uncreated, both infinite, with a void between them. God knew that evil must be destroyed but that it could not be destroyed by spirit, being spirit; and so God created the material world as a trap for the evil—in the same manner, says the text, as a gardener sets a trap for the vermin in his garden. By entering the world, evil loses its impregnable spiritual state and becomes something of a parasite, dependent upon the world for its existence. Human beings are created to choose between good and evil in this material world and, by choosing, deprive the evil of substance and force it to struggle in the futile effort to escape. Death, pain, and suffering have an independent and external cause.

However, many Parsis vehemently disagree with this interpretation (and indeed within the non-Parsi scholarly community there are widely divergent views on what is called the "continuity thesis"—the thesis that the theology in the *Gāthā*s is the same as that expressed by the *Bundahišn*). In fact, among contemporary Indian Zoroastrians, one can find an array of theological positions. Most Parsis seem to accept the version of Zoroastrian theology that was articulated during the nineteenth century in response to Protestant missionaries who derided the community's "dualism" as superstitious and polytheistic. The most famous of these missionaries, John Wilson, gave a much-quoted speech in 1839 upon his conversion of two Parsi boys. In it he denounced "the monstrous dogma of two eternal principles, which, though not unknown to the ancient Persians, is altogether unreasonable, as inconsistent with the predominance of order, regularity, and goodness in the system of the universe, and altogether impious" (Wilson 1847: 65–6). The written Parsi response was that there is no external evil and that there is no other God than Ahura Mazdā. The evil spirit is a metaphor that refers to an individual's bad thoughts. As Aspandiarji Framjee wrote in 1841: "Hormazd [Ahura Mazdā] . . . is omniscient and omnipotent. . . . Hormazd is pure; and holy; He is formless, self-existent and eternal. . . .

He keeps no partner or companion in His works" (1841: i). A more modern writer who was a Parsi jurist wrote: "There is no Dualism in our religion in the proper sense. . . . In course of time, it was forgotten that the Evil Spirit was the creation of Ahura-Mazdā Himself and it was raised almost to the level of a rival of Ahura-Mazdā" (Vimadalal 1967: 64–5). It is a typical point of view today that the so-called dualism merely denotes the tendency in the modern mind to deviate from the path of righteousness.

In this modern version of Parsi Zoroastrianism, the central text is understood to be the *Gāthās*, Zoroastrianism is understood to be an ethical system compatible with science, and ritual practice becomes attenuated to the vanishing point. By the turn of the nineteenth into the twentieth century, many Parsis had begun to argue that ceremonies are distractions from the real religion, which is the rational, ideal union of scientific secularism and spirituality. As a 1918 essay on "the advancement of religion" put it:

> We now turn to the highest stage of religious culture. The mental caliber of the people of this stage [in which she includes modern Parsis] does not require the props of religious rites and ceremonies for the maintenance of religious sentiment, but is strong enough to presume that sentiment without this aid.
>
> (Engineer 1918: 10)

Probably as a consequence of this emphasis on science and rationality, the ritual practice and textual understanding in much of the contemporary community has become quite limited. A visitor to the community may well be struck by the large number of Parsis who report dissatisfaction with their own knowledge of the faith and who find their own religiosity anemic. Many Parsis as a result have become more engaged with Hindu or Hinduized spiritualities or with other faiths such as Christian Science.

• INSTITUTIONS AND PRACTICES

Like many ancient religions, Zoroastrianism is primarily a purity religion (see Choksy 1989; Modi 1885). The extensive ritual practice prescribed by the religion is premised on the need to remove badness or evil by washing, removing, flicking away, and making sacred. Orthodox rules around purity are among the most stringent in all religious practice. Traditional rules governing menstruation, for example, forbid the woman from touching anything not made of iron. She may not sleep in the house as usual, but on an iron cot in a special room for the purpose and often outside of the main living area; she may not wear her common clothes; she may not touch anything except through iron implements; and she must take a ritual bath upon completion of her menses. Few follow these restrictions so strictly these days, but those who are orthodox will sleep in a separate bed and often have separate clothes for the duration. And Parsis are perhaps most widely known for the rituals in which they dispose of the dead without defiling earth, water, or fire. Corpses are left exposed to the air to allow them to be eaten by vultures. The buildings where they are left awaiting this fate are called "Towers of Silence." Intense arguments surround the practice, some within the

Mumbai community praising the ecological wisdom of the method and others condemning it as barbaric.

The basic ritual act in the religion involves wearing the *sudreh* and *kustī*, the sacred shirt and thread, with which both male and female children are invested somewhere around the age of seven in an elaborate and expensive ceremony (the *navjote*). These items are regarded as basic indications of Zoroastrian identity, and attempts to find out how observant someone is will begin by questioning whether they wear the *sudreh-kustī* and then whether they perform their *kustī* prayers. These are prayers that are supposed to be said upon awakening (although there can be some variations on the normal procedure), before meals, after excreting, and before any other prayers (for thanksgiving, worship, requests for intervention, and so forth: books of prayers and sacred verses suitable for prayers may be easily purchased). The *kustī* prayers involve the recitation of Avestan and Pahlavi verses while untying the *kustī* thread wrapped around the waist, using it to shake off or drive away impurity (or evil), and retying it. As one unties the *kustī*, one says,

> Protect us from the foe, O Mazda and Spenta Armaiti! Begone, daevic Drug! Begone the one of Daeva-origin, begone the one of Daeva-shaping, begone the one of Daeva-begetting! Begone, O Drug, crawl away, o Drug, disappear, O Drug! In the north you shall disappear. You shall not destroy the material world of Asha!
>
> (Boyce 1984: 58)

All Zoroastrian prayers are spoken in the ancient tongues; this presents a considerable challenge for the modern community, as very few individuals actually learn to understand the prayers they memorize. A 1987 dissertation sampled two hundred Parsis enrolled as college students in two Bombay colleges. Ninety percent of them said that they wore their *sudreh-kustī* all the time, and 89 percent said their *kustī* prayers at least once a day. A full 70 percent said that they have "no understanding at all" of what they prayed (Taraporewalla 1987). There is a widespread perception in the community that the level of understanding of the religion and interest in following its edicts is declining among the young, although the trend may have reversed in recent years.

Those who consider themselves observant (probably calling themselves "orthodox") may perform a variety of other practices. They may say obligatory prayers, covering their heads and softly reciting the ancient verses in a singsong voice for an hour or more. They may carry incense around the house, reciting one of the standard prayers (the Ašem Vohū) after the house is swept and clean. They may rise in the morning, bow to the sun, and rub their hands over their face when the sun has touched it. On festive occasions, they may offer milk baths (such as for a child's birthday) and prepare a festive tray, with an oil lamp, red vermillion powder, betel nuts and leaves, almonds, turmeric sticks, and other items, which is presented to the recipient as he or she stands on a small wooden platform, facing east. And there are many other rituals, chosen to bless a new house, to express joy, to commemorate the dead, and to protect during a journey. But Zoroastrianism is fundamentally a solitary religion. There are occasional public rituals, for lifecycle events (the *kustī* ceremony or *navjote*) or even just thanksgiving (the *jašan*), where white-clothed priests sing the prayers in lowered monotones, and there is a sacred well in the city of Mumbai, close to a frenetic commuter rail station, where people gather to pray. But they pray alone.

Ideally, the good Zoroastrian visits a fire temple once a day. These temples (*agiari*) are the primary religious institutions of the religion and are considered the seat of religious power. In contemporary Mumbai, there are forty-four fire temples, each with an ever-burning fire fed on sandalwood by white-frocked priests. Some of these are highly sacred, in temples designated Ātaš Behrāms: these fires have been consecrated from fire taken from sixteen sources (lightning being one) and purified ninety-one times. Others are less so, but in all, the maintenance of purity is what gives the fires their sacred quality. Each fire sits inside a special area that may be entered only by the priests, and the priests themselves acquire their role only through elaborate ceremonies designed to remove the dross of the everyday. They too must be purified before they enter the temple. While in the temple, lay Parsis typically pray (again by themselves) and offer sandalwood by purchasing it from a vendor and giving it to the priest to burn on the fire.

In addition to the fire temples in Mumbai, there are fire temples throughout India in places settled by Parsis. Among the most important are those fire temples established in the earliest places of Parsi settlement in Gujarat, with the holiest being the fire temple in Udwada, a little town on the coast.

• ETHICS AND HUMAN RELATIONS

The central concept in Zoroastrian spirituality is *aša*. Variously translated as truth, righteousness, or natural law, it can also be understood as purity: the absence of the lie, which is evil, or *druj*. I.J.S. Taraporewalla, a much-admired priest and translator of the *Gāthās*, asks, "And what then is this *asha*? Scholars translate it variously as 'Purity,' or 'Righteousness' or 'Truth,' but it is far more than any of these words in their *ordinary sense*. It is the Eternal Truth, the One Reality" (1965: 21; emphasis in original). Most devotions end with the *Ašem Vohū*, an Avestan prayer embedded in the *Yasna*. In translation it reads, "Asha is good, it is best. According to wish it is, according to wish it shall be for us. Asha belongs to Asha Vahista" (Boyce 1984: 57).

By the end of the nineteenth century in India, this emphasis on *aša* had become entrenched in community imagination and practice as an absolute prohibition against lying. The general resonance of the word "truth" in the contemporary community would be hard to overestimate; it carries the penumbra of meanings that *aša* does. What is good is true, and what is true is good. Parsis pride themselves on their truthfulness and not infrequently contrast their honesty with the dishonesty of non-Parsis. Indeed, the community has an admirable reputation for honesty in modern India. This commitment to honesty had clear business advantages during the colonial period, and at least by the late nineteenth and early twentieth centuries, the concept of truth took on this aspect of business reliability for the Parsis.

The business heroes of the eighteenth and nineteenth centuries are presented as gaining commercial credit through their uprightness and truthfulness; contemporary Parsis describe their truthfulness as a commercial asset. Parsis often tell the story that all the banks in Bombay used to employ Parsis as bank tellers because "in earlier days" Parsis always spoke the truth. These days, many Parsis will say, the importance of truth both within the community and without has declined.

The community is also famous for its charity. Charity has always been a religious virtue of the community, commended in the holy texts. But during the colonial period, charitable activity became the primary indicator not only of religious goodness, but also of political and economic power, the means through which a secularized, progressive, Westernized Parsi achieved recognition. Much of earlier Bombay was built with charitable Parsi funds, the more so as the British colonial government began to confer knighthood on those who were outstandingly benevolent. Between 1820 and 1940 the Parsis built over one hundred sixty fire temples; in the same period they erected over forty *dharmšālā*s (rest houses, used to house the poor) and *bāg*s (low-income housing) and donated funds to three hundred and fifty schools, libraries, educational centers, hospitals, clinics, and wards. Parsis in general provided funds in such amounts that the total recorded Parsi charities reported annual incomes of well over one million rupees during the first forty years of the twentieth century (Hinnells 1996; Lala 1981, 1984).

• MODERN EXPRESSIONS

The two most interesting modern expressions of Zoroastrianism can be said to be responses to the somewhat dry, highly rationalized form of the religion that emerged as the dominant spirituality from the colonial encounter. The first is an esoteric version of Zoroastrianism produced in the late nineteenth century as a result of theosophy's attempt to win followers in India (see Luhrmann 2002). This is Elm-e ḵošnūm, an extremely intricate interpretation of rituals and texts. It holds that the words of the *Gāthā*s themselves have a magical, divine power when spoken and that those words have hidden meanings understood only by those with higher knowledge. Followers of Elm-e ḵošnūm also emphasize the *Gāthā*s among the Zoroastrian texts but are much more ritualistically inclined than most Parsis. They tend to be what others would call orthodox, meaning that they follow the extensive purity rules which are meant to govern the pious Zoroastrian's life and that they practice a wide variety of the rituals associated with maintaining purity and godliness.

The Bombay Theosophical Society was founded in 1879 and immediately proved attractive to Zoroastrians. Fifty percent of its original members were Parsi. Theosophy was a Western occult religious philosophy that was rich in magical symbolism, but it presented itself as a scientific and pragmatic approach to nature. "TRUTH," its founder proclaims in her magnum opus, "high-seated upon its rock of adamant, is alone eternal and supreme. We believe in no Magic which transcends the scope and capacity of the human mind"

(Blavatsky 1960, 1: v). Yet theosophists—she argued—were able to contact great souls ("*mahātmā*s") who existed on other spiritual "planes." The teachings these *mahātmā*s delivered enabled theosophists to peer beyond the veil of mere human philosophy into the real. That reality was fundamentally Hindu (at least, Hinduism, as understood in Theosophy, contained the closest representation of the true facts of the spiritual world) and included reincarnation, spiritualism, mesmeric magnetism, and a range of techniques for contacting and manipulating spiritual matter.

And, in fact, Zarathustra was the source of it all.

> The secret doctrines of the Magi, of the pre-Vedic Buddhists, of the hierophants of the Egyptian Thoth or Hermes, and of the adepts of whatever age and nationality, including the Chaldean kabalists and the Jewish *nazars*, were *identical* from the beginning.
> (Blavatsky 1960, 2: 142; emphasis in original)

Blavatsky goes on to say that Zarathustra was really the first, or one of the first, names of these powers and that "all these gods, whether of the Zoroastrians or of the *Veda*, are but so many personated *occult powers* of nature" (Blavatsky 1960, 2: 143; emphasis in original). In 1882, Henry Steel Olcott, an American and one of the great theosophical figures, gave a lecture in Bombay in which he argued that Zoroastrianism was more true, more real, than the mystifications of other upstart religions (such as Christianity) and could be said to contain the deepest truths of all religions. Some fifteen hundred listeners, most of them Parsi, received him with prolonged cheering. Colonial-era Bombay was not the only place, nor Parsis the only group, from which Theosophy gained adherents. For some time, the date of Olcott's arrival in Sri Lanka was even celebrated as "Olcott Day." But Theosophy had different kinds of impact in different settings. In Sri Lanka, Olcott's influence seems to have led to the revival of a more restrained, inwardly directed Buddhism. (Gombrich and Obeyesekere 1988 describe the Buddhism he helped to produce as "Protestant Buddhism.") The Zoroastrianism Olcott encountered, however, was the child of late nineteenth-century rationalization. It had already been Protestantized (at least, that is one description of the faith that emerged from the colonial encounter; see Luhrmann 2002), and the result was somewhat sterile. Theosophy encouraged an occult, symbolic reading of the *Gāthā*s and yet described that approach as scientific.

In 1914, a deeply respected priest, M. N. Dhalla, educated in the Western scholarly approach to religion at Columbia University in New York City, published his magisterial understanding of the faith. *Zoroastrian Theology* argued that the Zoroastrian religion was a wonderful philosophy encumbered by unnecessary and superstitious rituals. Three years later, Phiroze Masani replied with *Zoroastrianism Ancient and Modern* a ringing denunciation of Dhalla's "cruel and obnoxious ideas." His is a colorful book—one subtitle chapter, for instance, reads "Bosh about animal-slaughter from foreign writers"—and in it Masani introduced Elm-e ḵošnūm. Students of this esoteric Zoroastrianism resist the association with Theosophy, but Ḵošnūm is ideologically quite similar to theosophy and followed directly in its wake. The teachings of Ḵošnūm were said to have come from great master souls, hidden in caves and mountaintops behind a spiritual magnetic veil, and protected from death by its energies. Those souls revealed themselves to a shy Parsi boy, who then reluctantly shared their wisdom with others.

Ḵošnūm holds that Zarathustra was not a man (as Dhalla had suggested), but an angel who came down to earth in human form. The words he spoke, then, have a magical character, and Ḵošnūmist Zoroastrians believe that when they speak those words properly, their vibrations will change the world. Ḵošnūm also teaches that certain words in the *Avesta* have hidden meanings, accessible only to those with esoteric knowledge. So Ḵošnūmist lectures are elaborate textual interpretations. The lecturer will take a prayer, or a portion of a sacred text, and explain its hidden significance. The style has the same flavor as the arcana of kabbalistic interpretation. For example, Masani disputes Dhalla's claim, made on the basis of analysis of variations in linguistic style within the ancient texts, that the only portion of the *Avesta* that should be attributed to Zarathustra is the *Gāthās*:

> Perhaps the writer of the book [Dhalla] may go further and say that the word "Yazata" is also not to be found in the Gathas and that therefore all the Yazatas are of a later growth. But the former use of "Vispe" meaning "all" and the superlative degree "Mazishtem" meaning "the greatest" with Srosh suggest a latent force of the word "Yazata" which the adjectives "Vispe" and "Mazishtem" must qualify, and we find the forms Yazai and Yazemnaongho in the Gathas formed from the same verb Yaz from which the noun Yazata is derived.
>
> (Masani 1917: 36)

This is heady stuff for those who previously found their religion bland. It seems to promise higher knowledge and deeper insight. Masani goes on to explain that all the *Avesta* is inspired Zoroastrianism, that all of its rituals are necessary and practically effective (except for the animal sacrifice, which he abhors; real Zoroastrians, he explains, are vegetarian, a view of Zoroastrianism unique to Ḵošnūm), and that true Zoroastrian priests have magical powers exceeding those of a *yogī*. It is also scientifically true: "The fight of Zoroaster with the Daevas is not an allegorical story, but a scientific fact based on the most abstruse laws of vibration, colour and magnetic electricity" (Masani 1917: 395).

Among Parsis, Ḵošnūm evokes some of the same response that the occult does in the West. Those not drawn to it sometimes deride it as lowbrow and unscholarly. Also, lectures on Ḵošnūm are often given in Gujarati (practitioners say that Gujarati has a more powerful vibration than English), and as a result, many Parsis find lectures difficult to follow (in one survey, 44 percent of the elders and 52 percent of the youth said that they thought only in English [Writer 1993: 253]). Yet Ḵošnūm is the intellectual home for many of the more politically powerful orthodox members of the community. Ḵošnūmist founded and now run the Council of Vigilant Parsis, a politically effective vehicle for orthodox reform that can initiate meetings attended by hundreds. And many Parsis read Ḵošnūmist material, even if they do not attend the lectures and even if they feel embarrassed about some of the

Ḳošnūmist claims. Above all, Ḳošnūm advocates the full practice of Zoroastrian rituals, including the menstruation prohibitions, as spiritually meaningful as well as practically effective. That message is compelling for those who are drawn to religious practice but who do not understand the tradition in which they were raised.

The desire to reach out to Zoroastrians who want more from their religion but feel ignorant also inspired a second and possibly more powerful (because more proselytizing) theological innovation. This is an orthodox movement that has emerged under the leadership of a man who studied with Mary Boyce and who returned to Bombay during a time of community unease. He started a revitalization movement, directed at Parsi youth, which promised to take the community back to its roots and to teach it the "true" Zoroastrian religion. Khojeste Mistree led a series of lectures and discussions in the late 1970s that were received in the community as if, many people said, he was a rock star. He spoke about why the religion was personally meaningful and explained the prayers and rituals. Hundreds of people attended the lectures. Khojeste became famous, and he and his students formed a religious institution called Zoroastrian Studies. His teachings are widely used within the community and abroad. Yet while widely known, they are also controversial.

Zoroastrian Studies was not simply a new way to teach the theology with which most Parsis grew up and knew vaguely. Instead, Zoroastrian Studies taught a theology founded on the Boyce continuity thesis that argued that the dualism obvious in the later Pahlavi texts reinstates the theology of the *Gāthā*s and argued that all Zoroastrian religious texts must be regarded as spiritually salient. Mistree believed passionately that this theology was not only the original Zoroastrian theology, but also the most sensible religious theology available, and that Zoroastrianism was unique in solving the puzzle of human pain with logic and wisdom:

> If good and evil do come from the same source, why would Zarathushtra so emphatically have declared their different sources and irreconcilable natures? Can a perfect, all-good Being (God) remain perfect, if part of the nature of that Being is deemed to be evil? In Zarathushtra's mind the answer was clearly "NO!" . . . The great strength of Zoroastrian doctrine lies in the fact that the agency which perpetrates excess or deficiency by way of poverty, chaos, disease and eventually death, is not that which is ordained by God but that which is perpetrated by the antagonistic spirit of evil.
>
> (Mistree 1982: 50)

The claim that Zoroastrianism was special, and that what was special about it was its theology, was deeply appealing even to those who could not quite accept it. "He would explain the *sudreh-kustī*," one Parsi remarked, "and why you should wear it, and you might accept the idea of the *sudreh-kustī* keeping away evil and not quite accept evil as he saw it and still be excited by his teaching."

Mistree saw his task as not just explaining the religion, but helping Parsis to recreate themselves as a community. He called his teaching text *Zoroastrianism: An Ethnic Perspective* and presented it as a tool to help Zoroastrians learn about themselves. He began his teaching in a period in which there were legitimate fears that the community might disappear altogether. By the time he began to teach, one in five Parsis was over sixty-five, and figures suggested that 20 percent of the community never married and that of those who did marry, one in six marriages was an intermarriage. (When a Parsi female marries a non-Parsi, her children are not accepted as Parsi.) Given the absolute refusal to accept conversion, the community was at serious risk. Mistree hoped to inspire people to save the community by teaching them what was worth saving. The route he chose was orthodoxy, but it was orthodoxy recognizably different from Ḵošnūm. It did share similarities: Mistree encouraged a far stricter use of ritual than most Parsi practices, as Ḵošnūmists do, and, like them, he opposed intermarriage and conversion. But, unlike them, he explicitly opposed the Protestantized dualism common in the community, in which the evil principle is subordinated to the good, not equal (or nearly equal) to it, and he did so with the tools of Western scholarship. Far more than the Ḵošnūmists, he emphasized that Zoroastrianism was different from Hinduism and Christianity (and, by implication, from Islam). He explained that Parsis should not believe in reincarnation because reincarnation was a Hindu concept and that they should not believe in the absolute omnipotence of God because that was a Christian concept. And he explicitly presented his theology and practice as a means to revitalize a community he saw at risk of assimilating out of recognition. It is this emphasis on anti-assimilation, intended for people too comfortable with themselves rather than for the dispossessed, that makes this orthodoxy seem more like other new orthodoxies among successful diaspora groups (for example, American Jews) and less like communal revivalism common in South Asia.

Perhaps the most interesting feature of Zoroastrian Studies is that it teaches an orthodox Zoroastrianism which is unlike any other Zoroastrianism and, for that matter, unlike religion as experienced by most South Asians. This is because it has been shaped by the needs that gave rise to it, and those needs are deeply modern and specific to a community that fears its own extinction through dissolution into the larger society in which its members are embedded.

The new orthodox Zoroastrianism has the following characteristics (Luhrmann 1996). First, it has a theological focus, far more so than a religion whose members do not need to rediscover it afresh. Unlike many religious practitioners, those who go through training in Zoroastrian Studies gain a significant appreciation for their own religious texts. They do not simply learn to do the rituals and prayers; they learn about the religion by reading the religious texts and talking about them with each other. Even those who come through the training may remark privately that they do not care about the theology by saying that they do not care about "Bundahišn this" and "Pahlavi that"—naming the specific sources they have studied in class. Mistree held classes for his own inner circle, often consisting of text-based theological discussions.

Second, the focus of the teaching is not to convey knowledge for its own sake, but to invest the texts, their theology, and their rituals with personal significance. This is done in a deliberate, self-conscious, and intimate manner. After teaching on a theological text, Mistree would often lead a guided meditation on the text, so that students would have their own experience of Zoroastrian imagery. When people told me why they found the Zoroastrian Studies approach so appealing, they cast their story in terms of the personal relevance of its theology. One woman, for example, told me that she had been raised in an orthodox family, and she had followed the rigid laws governing menstruation and purity for many years. But when she was nineteen, her mother died. She said that she fought with God, telling that he could not take her mother away; and yet he did, and for her it was terribly difficult to come to terms with a God who was supposed to be your protector, whom she had obeyed so earnestly, and who had then betrayed you. When she went to one of Mistree's classes, she was beside herself with excitement.

> I remember clearly the scene that evening, [my son] as a small child on the sofa, as if someone had come in with a new discovery, although all the time it had been there. It was such a relief to know, looking at the dirt and sickness, that God was not responsible.

Third, this inner experience of the religion as personally meaningful is considered in these classes to be more important than the actual knowledge of the texts or the practice of the ritual. After all, you will only be motivated to follow the religion (and to marry a Parsi) if its rules become emotionally salient to you. Nonetheless, it is a striking shift, for the texts and practice of this ancient religion scarcely mention a personal relationship to divinity. Zoroastrian Studies is more interested in getting Parsis to feel committed to their ethnicity than it is in producing orthodoxy: The orthodoxy is a means to an end, and not the reverse. Mistree travels widely and has lectured in many communities where intermarriage is inevitable (a Parsi child may be the only Parsi in his town, for example). There he has urged people to accept a "two model, one community set up," so that progressive and orthodox can accept each other and tolerate each other's strategies for preserving the faith and its people. The goal of the many tapes, books, and classes that Zoroastrian Studies produces is to "catch" people before they leave the faith and to keep them attached to it as best they can.

Fourth, there is an explicit recognition on the part of Zoroastrian Studies that while being born Parsi just happens, being Zoroastrian is a conscious choice. This is not to say that members of Zoroastrian Studies seriously fear that many Parsis will convert out of Zoroastrianism. They know, however, that many Parsi find other faiths more gripping because they know so little about their own. They believe that the job of an organization like Zoroastrian Studies is to make the religion seem different from other religions and more desirable to those born Parsi. And they were the first to see this need so plainly. So Zoroastrian Studies makes Zoroastrianism fun. It organizes field trips with a group of youths and makes sure there is time to party. It printed a children's book on Zoroastrianism with bright, cheery pictures. Out of necessity, the group sees itself as selling something to people who must be persuaded that they want to buy. Their job is to reach out to those previously uncommitted to the faith and to draw them in. The religion they teach may be ancient, but the manner in which they teach it is very modern.

• TRANSMISSION OF THE TRADITION OUTSIDE OF INDIA

Parsi Zoroastrianism has spread widely across the globe, particularly after Indian Independence, when some worried that the Parsi role in non-British India would be much reduced. There are over ten thousand Parsis in North America and over five thousand in Britain, and there are Parsi communities in Australia, Hong Kong, East Africa, and in many other places (Rivetna 2013).

While Parsis tend to concentrate in particular cities in a country (for example, London, Toronto, Houston, Chicago, and Los Angeles), individual families can be found in many settings. Even the Parsi concentrations are not numerous enough to enable Parsis to socialize with the same exclusivity that they might in Mumbai. As a result, the Zoroastrian experience in these settings is quite different than it is in Mumbai. There is often no fire temple, no *dokhmā*, and no opportunity for the large festival gatherings that mark the Zoroastrian year. Instead, Parsis organize large semi-professional gatherings called "congresses," which in North America meet on an annual basis. They also have organizations that set dates for community dinners and get-togethers. At the 1994 North American Zoroastrian Conference, one woman said,

> When you come to this country, there is a common pattern. First you shun all community events. You think of them as boring and unsophisticated. And then after so many people have asked you about Zoroastrianism, and you feel embarrassed but also curious, after you have come to terms with being different, you begin to attend the dinners and congresses and parties, and they do not seem silly but comfortable. And you begin to learn from the congresses how to verbalize what it is to be Zoroastrian.

In these settings so removed from Mumbai, Parsis have to confront the fact that each has a different sense of what it is to be Parsi. In the congresses, for instance, there are "youth" groups where young men and women literally sit in a circle and discuss their experience of Zoroastrianism. They discover that it is different for each—a human phenomenon, but one rarely confronted in so explicit a manner. They also confront the inevitability of changes in the tradition. In Houston, it is not possible to demand that your child marry a Parsi. You might go to great effort to introduce your children to other Parsi young adults, and even to send them together on skiing trips and rafting adventures, but if an American-raised Parsi child is the only Parsi in his or her high school or college class, the chance that he or she will marry a Parsi is small. So the dilemmas that seem great conundrums in Mumbai disappear, and the question becomes how to retain any sense of being Zoroastrian at all. Here Mistree's teachings become important, and the style he has adopted has been adopted also by other approaches to the faith. Parsis have constructed teaching texts and take-home study courses to instruct people in their religion, and in North America they have become much more tolerant of spouses from outside who marry into the community, learn about the religion, and may even convert. They also have come to accept the *navjotes* (initiation ceremonies) of those children born of one Parsi parent and one non-Parsi parent.

In North America, these adaptations are made more complicated (or easier, depending on one's perspective) by the fact that Parsis are not the only Zoroastrians. There are in North America many Iranians of Zoroastrian descent who arrived around the time of the fall of the Shāh of Iran. As it happens, some of these Zoroastrians have been quite wealthy and have funded the building of fire temples and community centers. But Iranian Zoroastrianism has a different ethos from Parsi Zoroastrianism. It is less exclusive: There are far fewer restrictions on intermarriage, conversion, and the presence of non-Zoroastrians in fire temples. Iranian Zoroastrians often speak Farsi, and not English, as their first language, and their English is often poor. The tensions between the two communities have been at times considerable, and some community organizations have split along ethnic lines.

• RELATIONS WITH OTHER RELIGIONS

It has been argued that postexilic Judaism owes much to Zoroastrians through Jewish appreciation for Cyrus, who freed them, and that Judaic concepts of heaven, hell, and even of a messiah can be attributed to their enthusiasm for Cyrus' ideas (Boyce 1979). Some even argue that because Zarathustra was the first to teach the doctrines of an individual judgment, the first to teach of heaven and hell, the first to teach of the resurrection of the body and of everlasting life, Zoroastrianism is the source of those concepts in Judaism, Christianity, and Islam (Russell 1987).

In turn, Islam has been the source of most of the trouble Zoroastrianism has had as a religion. Tolerated and harassed at different stages by Muslim Persians, the religion has survived in Iran until the present day but in very small numbers. There are no known historical records that unambiguously demonstrate that the Parsi migration to India was because of religious persecution, but it is commonly assumed that people were motivated to leave Persia in numbers to preserve their right to practice their faith.

Meanwhile, in contemporary India there seems to be relatively little anti-Parsi feeling from Hindus and Muslims. This may be the consequence, at least in part, of the remarkable charitable activity of the community. Parsis built hospitals and schools and provided other institutional resources that they shared with members of all religions. It is true that when the Prince of Wales came to Bombay in 1921, Indian nationalists boycotted his arrival as Parsis came out to greet him, and urban riots in the wake of the visit left fifty-three people dead. But in general, there seems to have been little tension over the last century between Parsis and other religious communities.

• THE TRADITION IN THE STUDY OF RELIGIONS

In the nineteenth century, the study of Zoroastrianism was used in the argument against evolutionary arguments that suggested a purely human origin to the belief in God. The discovery of a monotheistic religion that was demonstrably ancient suggested to some Englishmen that religion could not have followed the evolutionary development postulated by anthropologists, and thus could not be explained as a psychological phenomenon. As one stated:

> (The Gâthâs) present truths of the highest moral and spiritual significance, in a form which constantly reminds us of the Pentateuch and the Prophets. . . . They are absolutely irreconcilable with the theory which regards all spiritual and soul-elevating religions as evolved by a natural process from a primitive naturalistic polytheism: they support the view, which alone supplies a true, rational, and adequate account of the movements of human thought, according to which religious beliefs were first set in motion by communications from God.
>
> (Cook 1884: iv, cited in Bilimoria and Alpaivala 1898: 79–80)

The early German translations of the texts did indeed have a Christian feel, and some Western scholars of the nineteenth century went so far as to say that Zoroastrianism was the earliest monotheism and a source for both Christianity and Judaism. Many argued that Zoroastrianism was ethically superior to other faiths (see the collection gathered in Bilimoria and Alpaivala 1898). Meanwhile, in popular elite European culture, Zarathustra became a figure associated with mystic wisdom. The nineteenth-century classicist and philosopher Friedrich Nietzsche borrowed the name of Zarathustra because of its aura, as did Theosophy and other Western esoteric movements.

More recently, academic scholarship has struggled with the attempt to understand the difficult texts and the relationship between the Pahlavi and Avestan materials. The scholarship is deep but limited to a small handful of people who have sufficient knowledge of the languages to engage with the texts. Important scholars include Mary Boyce, Jamsheed K. Choksy, Ilya Gersevitch, Helmut Humbach, Stanley Insler, James R. Russell, Alan Williams, and R. C. Zaehner.

• DISCUSSION QUESTIONS

1. Is the traditional story of the life of Zarathustra similar in any ways to the traditional account of the life of the historical Buddha? If so, how does it differ in terms of life events, discoveries, degree of success, and analysis of human nature?
2. What does it mean to say that Zoroastrian tradition is primarily a purity religion? Do you know of any "purity" elements in any other religious traditions?
3. What is the place or significance of fire in Zoroastrian religious life?

• BIBLIOGRAPHY

Bilimoria, Ardeshir N. and Dinshah D. Alpaivala. 1898. *The Excellence of Zoroastrianism: (The Religion of the Parsis)*. Bombay: Printed at the Jamsetjee Nesserwanjee Petit Parsi Orphanage Captain Printing Works.

Blavatsky, Helene P. 1960 [1877]. *Isis Unveiled: A Master-Key to the Mysteries of Ancient and Modern Science and Theology*. 2 volumes. Pasadena: Theosophical University Press.

Boyce, Mary. 1975. *A History of Zoroastrianism*. Volume 1: *The Early Period*. Leiden: E. J. Brill.

Boyce, Mary. 1977. *A Persian Stronghold of Zoroastrianism*. Oxford: Oxford University Press.

Boyce, Mary. 1979. *Zoroastrians: Their Religious Beliefs and Practices*. London: Routledge & Kegan Paul.

Boyce, Mary, ed. and trans. 1984. *Textual Sources for the Study of Zoroastrianism*. Manchester: Manchester University Press.

Choksy, Jamsheed K. 1989. *Purity and Pollution in Zoroastrianism: Triumph Over Evil*. Austin: University of Texas Press.

Cook, F. C. 1884. *The Origins of Religion and Language*. London: John Murray.

Desai, Boman. 2001 [1988]. *The Memory of Elephants*. Chicago: University of Chicago.

Dhalla, Maneekji Nusservanji. 1972 [1914]. *Zoroastrian Theology: From the Earliest Times to the Present Day*. New York: AMS Press.

Engineer, B. A. 1918. "Advancement of Religion: An Article Contributed to the Dastur Hoshung Memorial." Bombay: K. R. Cama Oriental Institute. Typescript.

Fischer, Michael Max Jonathan. 1973. "Zoroastrian Iran Between Myth and Praxis." Ph.D. Dissertation, University of Chicago.

Framjee, A. 1841. *The Hadie Gum Rahan: Or, a Guide to Those Who Have Lost Their Way, Being a Refutation of the Lecture Delivered by the Rev. John Wilson*. Bombay: Bombay Samachar Press.

Gombrich, Richard and Gananath Obeyesekere. 1988. *Buddhism Transformed: Religious Change in Sri Lanka*. Princeton: Princeton University Press.

Hinnells, John R. 1996. *Zoroastrians in Britain: The Ratanbai Katrak Lectures, University of Oxford 1985*. Oxford: Clarendon Press.

Hinnells, John R. 2005. *The Zoroastrian Diaspora: Religion and Migration*. New York: Oxford University Press.

Hinnells, John R. and Alan Williams, eds. 2007. *Parsis in India and the Diaspora*. New York: Routledge.

Insler, S. 1975. *The Gāthās of Zarathustra*. Tehran-Liège: Bibliothèque Pahlavi.

Kreyenbroek, Philip G., in collaboration with Shehnaz Neville Munshi. 2001. *Living Zoroastrianism: Urban Parsis Speak About Their Religion*. London: Routledge.

Lala, R. M. 1981. *The Creation of Wealth: A Tata Story*. Bombay: IBH Publishing.

Lala, R. M. 1984. *The Heartbeat of a Trust: Fifty Years of the Sir Dorabji Tata Trust*. New Delhi: Tata McGraw-Hill.

Luhrmann, T. M. 1996. *The Good Parsi: The Fate of a Colonial Elite in a Postcolonial Society*. Cambridge: Harvard University Press.

Luhrmann, T. M. 2002. "Evil in the Sands of Time: Theology and Identity Politics Among the Zoroastrian Parsis." *The Journal of Asian Studies* 61, 3: 861–89.

Masani, Ervad Phiroze Shapurji. 1917. *Zoroastrianism Ancient and Modern: Comprising a Review of Dr. Dhalla's Book of Zoroastrian Theology*. Bombay: Ervad Phiroze S. Masani.

Mistree, Khojeste P. 1982. *Zoroastrianism: An Ethnic Perspective*. Bombay: Zoroastrian Studies.

Modi, Jivanji Jamshedji. 1885. *The Religious System of the Parsis: A Paper*. Bombay: Modi.

Patel, J. M. Framjee. 1905. *Stray Thoughts on Indian Cricket*. Bombay: Times Press.

Ringer, Monica M. 2011. *Pious Citizens: Reforming Zoroastrianism in India and Iran*. Syracuse: Syracuse University Press.

Rivetna, Roshan. 2013. "The Zarathusthi World—2012 Demographic Picture: The Numbers Game." *FEZANA Journal* 27, 3: 25–35. Available at: https://fezana.org/fjissue/FEZANA_2013_03_Fall.pdf.

Russell, James R. 1987. *Zoroastrianism in Armenia*. Cambridge: Harvard University Department of Near Eastern Languages and Civilizations and National Association for Armenian Studies and Research.

Taraporewalla, D. 1987. "The Knowledge of Religion Among Parsi Zoroastrians in Bombay." Ph.D. Dissertation, University of Bombay.

Taraporewalla, I. J. S. 1965 [1926]. *The Religion of Zarathushtra*. Bombay: B. I. Taraporewalla.

Vimadalal, Jal Rustamji. 1967. *What a Parsee Should Know*. Bombay: Vimadalal.

Williams, Alan, Sarah Stewart, and Almut Hintze, eds. 2016. *The Zoroastrian Flame: Exploring Religion, History and Tradition*. London: I. B. Tauris.

Wilson, John. 1847 [1839]. *The Doctrine of Jehovah Addressed to the Pársís: A Sermon Preached on the Occasion of the Baptism of Two Youths of That Tribe, May MDCCCXXXIX*. Edinburgh: William Whyte & Co.

Writer, Rashna. 1993. *Contemporary Zoroastrians: An Unstructured Nation*. Lanham: University Press of America.

Zaehner, R. C. 1961. *The Dawn and Twilight of Zoroastrianism*. New York: Putnam.

FIGURE 6.1 Torah scroll in the Bene Israel synagogue at Alibag, south of Mumbai.

Image courtesy of Shalva Weil.

6

Indian Judaic Traditions

SHALVA WEIL

THE TRADITIONS DEFINED

Judaism is a universal monotheistic religion with a belief in a transcendent creator of the world. Its fundamental orientation is practical and this-worldly with no official body of dogma. However, it possesses an orthodox system of codification, based on the Pentateuch and the books of the Prophets and the Hagiographa (the Writings) and embodied in the rabbinical traditions of Judaism. It thus rests on the Written Law and the authority of the Oral Law, notably the Talmud, and its codifications. These laws, such as *kashrut* (dietary laws), are designed to elevate the Jew and distinguish him or her from animals, as well as to define his or her religion vis-à-vis peoples from other religions.

Judaism places emphasis on the observance of the commandments, between man and God and between man and man. The religion is organized around Jewish liturgy, the festivals, and the rituals that mark the lifecycle. Jewish themes span the creation of the universe, God's covenant with the patriarchs (Abraham, Isaac, and Jacob), the liberation from bondage in Egypt, the revelation at Mount Sinai, Israel as a homeland, and the future Redemption in the messianic age. Judaism also incorporates more mystical traditions, as exemplified by Hasidic and kabbalistic practices, which are not necessarily accepted by the mainstream.

Judaism has never been a significant religious force in South Asia, and there has never been more than a miniscule number of Jews there. Judaism, a monotheistic and iconoclastic religion, has even appeared to be in opposition to the dominant religion of Hinduism with its emphases on "polytheism" and iconcentrism, although in recent years similarities are being expounded. Judaism is practiced in a community with a minimum of ten men, namely, a *minyan* (quorum), and does not encourage individual, other-worldly expressions of spirituality. In the orthodox and the conservative traditions, a person is Jewish matrilineally, the religion being defined by the mother. In the reform and the liberal branches of Judaism, a person can be Jewish patrilineally, too. A person can become Jewish through conversion, but Judaism is a nonproselyting religion and does not encourage converts.

Ancient South Asian Jewish communities have been found only in India, where three different Jewish communities flourished: the Bene Israel of Maharashtra, the Cochin Jews of Kerala, and the "Baghdādī" Jews of Calcutta and Bombay. At their peak in 1947, these Jewish communities numbered a mere twenty-three thousand souls (Reissner 1950), but their contribution to India was outstanding in the academic, literary, and military fields (Roland 2009). Today, an estimated thirty-five hundred Jewish members of all three communities remain, while larger Indian Jewish diasporas flourish abroad. In addition, some groups, primarily in the states of Mizoram and Manipur in northeast India, are claiming that they are descendants of the "Lost Israelites." Based on this claim, several thousand have now migrated to Israel. In the past decade, new Judaizing groups in India have emerged, including a group in Andhra Pradesh (Egorova and Perwez 2013).

European Jews reached India at different points in history. Jews arrived with the Portuguese and established communities in Goa. In the second half of the twentieth century, Jews from Germany, Austria, Poland, and other European countries found a temporary haven in India after the Holocaust. Today, India is a popular destination for Jewish and Israeli commercial travelers and transients.

• COSMOS AND HISTORY

Judaism is based on the study and interpretation of texts and praxis within Jewish communities. As far as we know, Jewish communities per se were not established in South Asia until relatively late (although Judaism may have reached the Malabar Coast in the first century), but there is evidence of Jewish contact with local inhabitants in South Asia long before. Linguistic evidence confirms the possibility of early commercial connections between Israel and South Asia from the time of the Bible, where in the book of Kings, the ships of King Solomon (about tenth century BCE) transported cargo with *kofim* (Hebrew; apes), *tukim* (peacocks), and *almag* (sandalwood). These words of Dravidian origin (*almag* is said to be *valgum*) found in the Hebrew Bible confirm the possibility that early traders brought back items of South Indian origin to build the Temple. There is no evidence that the Jewish traders or King Solomon's henchmen set up Jewish communities.

Travelers' tales in the Talmud mention trade with India (Hoddu) and include specific Indian commodities, such as ginger and iron, but although they refer to Hindus and Jews, they make no reference to Indian Jews. In the book of Esther, the kingdom of King Ahaseuerus stretched from Hoddu, generally accepted to be India, to Kush, which is usually said to be Nubia or Ethiopia.

From the ninth century CE, Jewish merchants known as Raadanites traded from the Middle East to South Asia and back. Documents discovered in the Cairo Genizah describe trade in spices, pharmaceuticals, textiles, metals, gold, silver, and silks from the eleventh to the thirteenth centuries between Arabic-speaking Jews from Fustat, Aden, and their Hindu partners in India (Goitein and Friedman 2007). However, the evidence does not indicate that Judaism was disseminated.

In the seventeenth century, Jewish merchant centers were established in Madras, Calicut, and other places. In addition, an independent Jewish traveler, Hazrat Saeed Sarmad, carried on trade between Armenia, Persia, and India and practiced Judaism until he renounced a materialistic life to become a Hindu *sādhu*. Awrangzeb, the Mughal emperor of India, executed Sarmad in 1659 (Ezekiel 1966).

During the nineteenth century, Jewish emissaries traveled to Asia from Palestine and other Jewish centers to make contact with Jews in far-flung places, often in the belief that the scattered Jews were members of the legendary ten lost tribes. According to the Bible, the tribes of the Kingdom of Israel were conquered by the Assyrian kings from 722 BCE on and were exiled to "Halah, Habor, the cities of Medes, and the river Gozan." There has been speculation over the years that the tribes wandered to Hindu Kush and India and possibly further afield and that the river Gozan mentioned in the Bible may in fact be the Ganges.

Three established communities of Jews practiced Judaism as a religion in India: the Bene Israel, the Cochin Jews, and the Baghdādīs. Before Partition, the Bene Israel had synagogues in Karachi (today Pakistan), Aden, and Rangoon, Burma. The Baghdādīs established Jewish communities wherever they handled their commerce in Burma, Singapore, Malaya, Hong Kong, China, Thailand, and elsewhere.

According to the Bene Israel tradition, the ancestors of their community were members of the lost tribes of Israel who had stayed in the Kingdom of Israel. They set sail around the year 175 BCE from Israel to escape persecution by enemy conquerors. Their ship capsized off the coast of Konkan, south of present-day Mumbai. The survivors lost all their possessions, including their holy books. Welcomed by the local Hindus, the Jews took up the occupation of pressing vegetable oil. They were called Shanwār Telīs ("Saturday Oilmen") because they refrained from work on Saturday in accordance with the dictates of the Jewish religion. They remembered the Jewish prayer "Hear, O Israel!" declaring monotheism; they observed some of the Jewish holidays and fasts; and they circumcised their sons as commanded by the Jewish religion. However, they did not know the Oral Law, had no rabbis, and were isolated from the practices and customs of mainstream Jewry.

From the eighteenth century on, the Bene Israel began a lengthy process of bringing their practices in line with other Jewish communities in the world. This process was aided by their contact with the British in India, the resulting move to Bombay and other cities, and access to the English language and higher education. The ultimate outcome of their identification with world Jewry was the gradual emigration of the majority of the Bene Israel community to the Jewish state in Israel during the last half of the twentieth century.

The Jewish settlement of the Cochin Jews on the Malabar Coast is ancient. One theory holds that they arrived with King Solomon's merchants, as mentioned above, although there is no corroboration that a community was actually established. Another account, repeated in South Indian legends, claims they arrived in the first century CE, when Saint Thomas (*died* 53 CE), the disciple of Jesus, supposedly brought Christianity to India. Records noting that the ruler Bhāskāra Ravi Varman (962–1020 CE) granted seventy-two privileges to the leader of the Jews, Joseph Rabban, document the Jewish settlement in Kerala. In 1344, the Jews moved from Cranganore to Cochin.

During the Portuguese period and after Vasco da Gama (about 1460–1524) led an expedition via the Cape of Good Hope to India in 1497–98, some Jewish traders from Europe and elsewhere settled in Goa and Cochin. On the Malabar coast, they set up New Christian communities (Tavim 2003); some joined the Paradēśi (Malayalam; foreigner's) Jewish community, whose synagogue was established in 1568. One member of that community, who rose to prominence under Dutch rule, was Ezekiel Rahabi (1694–1771); he acted as the principal merchant for the Dutch in Cochin and signed his memoranda in Hebrew. The Paradēśi synagogue celebrated its quarter centenary in the presence of Prime Minister Indira Gandhi in 1968.

The Malābārī Jews, who claim original settlement in the area, lived in five major settlements—Cochin, Ernakulam, Chendamanglam, Mala, and Parur—where they established seven synagogues and led a full Jewish community life. After the establishment of the State of Israel in 1948, most of the Jews from Cochin, motivated by Zionism, immigrated as a community to Israel in 1954.

From the eighteenth century on, Jews from Baghdad and other cities in Iraq shifted their enterprises to India and other South Asian centers. One of the founders of the Bombay community was Joseph Semah, who arrived in India in 1730 from Surat; another was Shalom Cohen, a merchant who settled in Calcutta in 1798. Other Jews, who established thriving businesses in the East, as far afield as Singapore, Hong Kong, and Shanghai, as well as magnificent Jewish community structures, followed the Jewish merchants, who escaped deteriorating conditions in Iraq. The "Ba<u>gh</u>dādīs," as they became known, kept up family and trade ties with other members of their community throughout South Asia. One of the most prolific families was the Sassoon family, who arrived in Bombay in 1832. After the withdrawal from India of the British, with whom the Ba<u>gh</u>dādī Jews had associated as non-native Indians, many of them decided to immigrate to England and other English-speaking countries and a few to Israel.

• SACRED LIFE AND LITERATURES

Sacred life among Jews is all-encompassing, covering both lifecycle events and the rhythm of the festivals. All three groups of Indian Jews adhere to the monotheistic nature of Judaism and observe the major festivals and commandments. Some of the sacred life of the Indian Jews is unique, however, influenced by Hindu and Muslim practices. This is particularly the case with the Bene Israel of Maharashtra, who led an integrated life in Indian society, distinguished from their neighbors only by their belief and practice of the Jewish religion.

Even among the Cochin Jews and the Ba<u>gh</u>dādīs, Indian Judaism developed special traits, such as partaking of Indian delicacies on particular festivals or the observance of specific wedding or burial customs, which reflect the influence of local customs.

The most important Jewish festivals for the Bene Israel are Rosh Hashana (New Year), Yom Kippur (Day of Atonement), Simhat Torah (Rejoicing of the Torah), and Pessach (Passover). On Rosh Hashana, the whole community appears in its finery in synagogue, and between Rosh Hashana and Yom Kippur it is customary to visit friends and family. The day after Yom Kippur is known as Shila San, or "Festival of Stale Things," a festival not observed by members of other Jewish communities, when Bene Israel members visit relatives, offering them *gharrie*s, a type of doughnut made of rice and wheat flour, yeast, and overripe cooked scrapings of cucumber fried in oil.

On Yom Kippur, known as the "The Festival of the Closing of the Doors," members of the Bene Israel community, dressed exclusively in white, arrive in synagogue before dawn so as to avoid contact with other (polluting) people on the way (Weil 1994).

On Simhat Torah, the Bene Israel celebrate by dancing merrily in the synagogue; they auction off all the *aliyoth* (literally "going up" to the Torah), as well as the four species used in ritual worship on the festival of Tabernacles (of which Simhat Torah is a culmination), and the right to pull down the fruits hanging in the synagogue *sukka* (tabernacle).

On Pessach, Bene Israel make *matzot*, the traditional unleavened bread eaten by Jews on this festival, made from rice rather than wheat. Some whitewash their houses and tin all their copper pots.

In addition, the Bene Israel observe particular folk customs, such as hair-shaving ceremonies for babies, pilgrimages, and special ways of celebrating the festivals, often adapted from local customs. An unusual feature of Bene Israel religious worship is the intensive belief in the popular Jewish prophet Eliyahoo Hannabi (the prophet Elijah), reminiscent of saint worship in Hinduism and Islam, although also known in Judaism. Elijah is invoked on all auspicious occasions, including circumcisions and purification after childbirth. Whereas Jews in other Jewish communities in the world believe that Elijah ascended to heaven from a site somewhere near present-day Haifa in Israel, the Bene Israel fervently believe that he departed on his chariot from a village called Khandalla in the Konkan. Bene Israel go on pilgrimage to the site, where they point out the footprints of Elijah's horses. There, they make wishes for the redemption of vows or pray for thanksgiving (Weil 2009).

Lifecycle rituals also include some unique elements. For example, the evening before the marriage ceremony, the *mehndī* (henna) ceremony takes place simultaneously in the houses of the bride and groom, who wear flowers tied round their heads, and have henna daubed ritually on their forefingers. A dish called *melida* is prepared, composed of rice flour and sugar covered with fruit and decorated with a rose in the center, while frankincense is burned by the side. The *melida* is blessed and distributed, and the prophet Elijah is invoked.

Among the Cochin Jews, the rituals of the annual cycle, as well as the lifecycle, are imbued with sacred vitality. During Rosh Hashana, the men wear white shirts, sometimes with a pale-colored design, and the women wear long white *luṅgī*s; fresh skullcaps for men and new kerchiefs for women and girls are prepared. After prayers on Rosh Hashana, blessings over the fruits and vegetables follow Kiddush, the sanctification of the wine. The practice of this custom is more elaborate than in other Jewish communities around the world. On the eve of Yom Kippur, between the last meal and the beginning of prayers at the synagogue, all family members ask forgiveness from each other, as is customary in many Jewish communities; then children go to the elder members of the extended family, bending to the ground with both hands to touch their bare feet and kissing their fingertips (a distinctly Indian custom) as the elders put their hand on the children's head and bless them.

On the festival of Succot (Tabernacles), the community erects a booth (Hebrew *sukka*; Malayalam *paṇḍāl*) in the synagogue grounds, which is a temporary structure, covered with palm leaves, commemorating the temporary shelters in which the Israelites lived during their forty-year sojourn in the Sinai Desert. In the Cochin Jewish community, every family covers the *paṇḍāl* with plaited coconut palms and decorates it with leaves, flowers, fruits, and jasmine garlands. On Simhat Torah, a temporary ark, *manara* (Malayalam), is constructed in front of the *heichal* (Hebrew), the ark, of the synagogue, and the Torah scrolls, with silver or gold metal cases, are displayed in it. During the morning and afternoon prayers, there are seven circumambulations around the downstairs pulpit while young men carry the Torah scrolls. The liturgy, texts, and melodies are performed in local Shingli style to the accompaniment of singing, handclapping, and dancing, with everyone partaking of alcoholic drinks and refreshments. According to Cochin custom, the most recently married bridegroom should read the beginning of the new cycle of the Torah, since symbolically every Jew should be "wedded" to the Torah.

The cleaning of the house for Pessach (Passover) and the preparation of special unleavened foods and hand-made *matzot* kept Jewish families busy for months before the festival. Forty-nine days, ritually counted every night, link the festivals of Pessach and Shavuot (Pentecost), the day on which the Jews received the Torah from God on Mount Sinai. On this day, the special Cochin Shingli liturgy is recited, in addition to the prayers in the traditional prayer book. At the synagogue, adults shower the children with sweets and tiny Indian baked sweet balls called *chukunda.*

Among the many unique Jewish customs of the Cochin Jews, outstanding is the wedding ceremony, when the groom himself recites the benedictions. In other Jewish communities, the rabbi or guests recite these blessings. Under the *chupa* (bridal canopy), he holds a gold chalice containing wine in which the wedding ring, tied to a loop made with seven strings, is immersed. He himself states that he is betrothed to his bride according to the laws of Moses and Israel. He drinks from the cup, which he gives to his bride, and places the ring on the index finger of her right hand, with the words "Behold, thou art consecrated to me." A young boy then reads the *ketuba* (marriage contract), according to Shingli custom (Hallegua 2009).

Among the Baghdādī Jews, sacred life was influenced by Muslim practice in Iraq, as well as by new customs adopted in India. A complex number of rituals were devised for the protection of the mother and child around birth, including wearing charms and hanging amulets at the baby's bedside. Nutmeg, garlic, a small blue bead, and God's name might be pinned onto the baby to safeguard him or her. Sometimes, when an elderly person died, a piece of the shroud was used to make a garment for the newborn child, to ensure that he or she live a long life. On the fifth night after birth, the baby was held in the arms of a female relative and an ornamental *pañjā* (hand) was daubed in saffron on the wall of the room to keep evil spirits away. In India, the children tossed a large sheet on which sweets, chocolates, peanuts, sunflower seeds, dried dates, popcorn, and roasted chickpeas were placed and shouted *shasha* (a nonsense word) as they shook the sheet. They then put the sweets and seeds into little bags and distributed them to the offspring of family and friends. A party used to be held the night before the circumcision at which *mezammerim* (singers) sang Hebrew and Arabic songs, learned men read out portions of the kabbalistic book, the *Zohar*, and a musician entertained the guests on a harmonium while guests were entertained at a dinner party. At the circumcision ceremony, at home or in the synagogue, the godmother, *takhdumai*, carried the baby boy into the room and handed him over to the godfather, *sandak*, who then took a seat on Elijah's chair with the baby on his lap. While the women were shouting "Kilililee, kilililee," the *mohel* (ritual circumciser) performed the operation (Cooper and Cooper 2009). Baghdādī Jews developed a large repertoire of Shbahoth (songs of praise or devotional hymns) in the Babylonian Jewish tradition, which they sang on the Sabbath, festivals and lifecycle ritual occasions (Manasseh 2012).

In the past, marriages were arranged. Once the girl's family had accepted the proposal from the boy's father, the contract was formalized, and the engagement was known as *bāt pakkā*, a Hindi designation, indicating that negotiations had been completed. The groom's family gave the bride a small gift of jewelry such as gold bangles. Some time after the *bāt pakkā*, the marriage was held in the synagogue. Prior to the wedding, a henna party for the bride known as the *khadbah*, a word of Arabic origin, was held. On the morning after the wedding, the bride's mother sent a tray of sweetmeats, including *badām jalkī* (almond rings), to her daughter and son-in-law. During the rest of the week, the bride's family hosted the *sheva brachot* (Hebrew; seven blessings). On the Saturday after the wedding, the bride's mother gave a party for the women celebrating the consummation of the marriage and her daughter's initiation as a woman.

The sacred literature of South Asian Jews is based on the Bible, the books of the Prophets and the Writings. Portions of these books are recited in the sacred language Hebrew every week in synagogues around the world. The Bene Israel, who constituted the largest Jewish group in South Asia, were ignorant of the Oral Law and the interpretations of the Bible developed by other Jewish communities and only became aware of them relatively late in history. Nevertheless, they read out the Portion of the Week in Hebrew and recited prayers in Hebrew in the synagogue. Primarily the Christian missionaries translated the Bible and some other holy books for them in the nineteenth century into vernacular languages such as Marathi (Numark 2010). Ironically, missionary activity resulted in a rapprochement of the Bene Israel to Judaism and not to Christianity. The missionaries reinforced the Bene Israel's Jewish identity by establishing schools for the Bene Israel children, educating them in English language, and translating the Jewish Prayer book and other religious works from Hebrew into Marathi. This encouraged the Bene Israel to translate their holy books into Marathi. In 1846, an illustrated Passover Haggada telling the story of the exodus of the Children of Israel from Egypt appeared in Marathi.

In Cochin, the Jews, who were in touch with Portuguese and Dutch Jewry, pray from the standard Jewish Sefardi (Spanish and Portuguese) prayer book used by Sefardi communities all over the world. (The Ashkenazi Jews who originated in Germany and Europe have their own prayer book, which is similar but contains some variations.) In addition, they knew the Oral Law and the interpretations on the texts, but they never produced their own rabbis. They also recited special prayer songs, composed in Shingli, which may be associated with Sri Lanka but is generally believed to be Cranganore in Kerala. The identities of most of the composers, as well as the exact dates of authorship, are unknown, but the musical heritage is preserved by all of the different communities of Cochin Jews. The great Paradēśi *paytan* (devotional composer) Isaac Hallegua composed an ode to his baby daughter Dolly, who died in their summer home in Alwaye at the beginning of the twentieth century (Weil 2010).

The Baghdādī Jews had a strong tradition of scholarship from Iraq, which produced many of the world's greatest rabbis and *halachic* (Jewish legal) decisions. They ordered their lives around Jewish legal response and produced many books of Jewish interest. In particular, they delved into Jewish mysticism and read the *Zohar*, a kabbalistic text, on ritual occasions. In Calcutta and in Bombay, the Baghdādī Jews operated several presses, both translating holy texts into Hebrew and publishing original works. Many of these were written in Judeo-Arabic, the Baghdādī Jews' dialect.

Oral tradition bolstered the written word in keeping alive the sacred life of India's Jews. Between the Bene Israel, the *kīrtana* (Sanskrit; literally "poet," "seer") is just one form of communication, along with ballads, folksongs, and short songs, which served as an educational tool repeating refrains from the Bible. The *kīrtana* was aimed at simple people and had a popularist character. The Bene Israel probably adopted it sometime at the end of the eighteenth century. During the nineteenth century, it gained in popularity and consisted of the presentation of biblical stories composed in Marathi verse, the vernacular of the Bene Israel, and sung to Hindi tunes by the *kīrtanakāra* (lead singer of the *kīrtana*), usually with musical accompaniment. By the end of the nineteenth century, a special Bene Israel *kīrtana* group had formed in Bombay. Associated with this group was Benjamin Samson Ashtamkar, still today remembered by Bene Israel as the greatest *kīrtanakāra*, who composed many biblical and apocryphal *kīrtana*s.

Cochin Jewish Malayalam folksongs, traditionally sung by Jewish women in Kerala, cover biblical, wedding, historical, and ritual themes (Weil 1982). In the Song of Everayi, the narrator tells of one Ephraim the Mudaliyar, accompanied by Rabbi Abraham the Dutch, who began his sojourn to Cochin in Jerusalem, stopping in Egypt and Yemen and ending up in Paloor Bay in Kerala with a carpenter who constructed the synagogue. The Malayalam song apparently reiterates the route the ancient Israelites took to Cochin (Jussay 1986). Today the Cochin Malayali women's tradition is being revived in Israel in an international project (see Johnson 2002; Zacharia and Gamliel 2005).

• INSTITUTIONS AND PRACTICES

The heart of any Jewish collectivity is the Jewish community and communal institutions. The South Asian Jewish communities are no exception. In 1796, the first Bene Israel synagogue, Shaar Harahamim (the Gate of Mercy) was consecrated at Mandvi in Bombay by Commandant Samaji Hasaji Divekar as a thanksgiving for his escape from death while a prisoner of Ṭipū Sulṭān during the Second Anglo-Mysore War. In 1843, some Bene Israel broke away from that synagogue to establish the city's second synagogue, the Shaarei Ratson (Gates of Desire), also known as the New Synagogue. More than thirty synagogues and prayer halls have since been built in India.

As a result of the opportunities offered to the Bene Israel by the British in the army and the railways, at the end of the nineteenth century, Bene Israel families began to immigrate to other centers as far as Burma and Aden. Groups of Bene Israel lived in the hill stations along the railways lines; a large community was settled in Karachi. In 1856, the Bene Israel began settling in Poona, and the Baghdādī Jews and the Bene Israel concentrated in neighborhoods like Rasta Peth and the adjoining Nana Peth. The lane in which the Succoth Shelemo (Tabernacle of Solomon) synagogue was erected in 1921 is called Israel Alley. In 1934, another Bene Israel synagogue was built in Ahmedabad. In 1956, the Judah Hyam Prayer Hall was opened in New Delhi to cater for the needs of Jews in the capital city. Today, only a few of these are able to maintain a regular *minyan* (quorum) on the Sabbath, and in the villages outside Mumbai several beautiful synagogues rarely open for prayers during the year. All synagogues in India, except the Jewish Religious Union, which was affiliated with the British Liberal Union, follow the orthodox tradition, despite their overt affiliation to different synagogue movements outside India. The Jewish Religious Union was founded in Bombay in 1925 by Jerusha Jhirad, a Bene Israel gynecologist, who in 1966 received the distinguished Padma Shri award for outstanding services in the field of social welfare. In the 1950s, this synagogue commissioned liberal rabbis from abroad to minister to the congregation. The Bene Israel themselves never produced a rabbi of their own in India, although individuals versed both in Sefardi and Bene Israel liturgy acted as *hazzanim* (cantors) in the synagogues. Recently, an Israeli-trained Bene Israel rabbi serves in Mumbai.

A variety of sports clubs, Zionist organizations, and charitable and credit associations operated in Bombay, Poona, and other centers over the years. The Stree Mandel, which was established in 1913 as a women's organization, is still active today. In 1875, the Bene Israel Benevolent Society for Promoting Education established Israelite School, an English-language primary school that developed into a high school in 1892. In the 1930s, the school became known as the Elly Kadoorie School after its Baghdādī benefactor and taught its pupils, most of whom were Jewish, Hebrew as well as English and Marathi. Today the school has become a Marathi-language school in which less than twenty of the twelve hundred pupils are Jewish. The Israelite School Old Students' Union, which later became known as the Maccabean Fellowship, was established in 1917. The Jacob Sassoon Free School's pupils were in the past nearly all Jewish. The Bombay ORT school for boys was established in 1962, and the school for girls in 1970. The ORT schools provide technical and vocational training for Bene Israel students, many of whom immigrated to Israel with a basic knowledge of Hebrew.

The Bene Israel in India today represent a vibrant, if small, community. Owing to large-scale emigration, communal activity has declined, and Bene Israel newspapers and periodicals, once prolific, are now published infrequently, and internet newsletters are taking over. Notwithstanding, consolidation has taken place between the different Indian Jewish communities; in 1979 the Council of Indian Jewry was established to represent the interests of all Indian Jews. Due to lack of numbers, members of the Bene Israel and Baghdādī communities and Jews of other origins are forced to cooperate in order to maintain communal institutions. Annually, the Mumbai Jewish community now bakes communal *matzot* together and distributes them to all members.

The Cochin Jews were organized in eight communities, each around its own synagogue, which acted a social control device that determined the fate of its members. In extreme cases, where social taboos were ignored, the congregation could excommunicate a member. One of the earliest records of the division in the community was recorded in 1344, when some of the Jews from Cranganore moved to Cochin, three years after the port of Cranganore was silted up and Cochin was founded. The divisions between the Paradēśi Jews and the other Malābārī are well documented (Segal 1967). In addition to synagogue services, many social activities were organized around the synagogue compound. In particular, Zionist meetings were held with emissaries who arrived from Palestine before and after the establishment of the State of Israel.

Baghdādī Jewish institutional life was founded in Calcutta by the first settlers and enhanced by members of the Sassoon and Elias dynasties. In 1832, the prince of the Exilarch, David Sassoon (1792–1864), while fleeing with his family from the persecutions of the Daud Pasha of Baghdad, arrived in Bombay. He established the Magen David synagogue in 1861. Jacob Sassoon constructed the magnificent Knesseth Eliyahoo synagogue in 1884. In addition, the Sassoon families donated to hospitals, schools, libraries, and more. In Calcutta, the Baghdādī constructed as many as eight synagogues with more than one hundred Torah scrolls in the city. In the summer, in the heyday before Partition, they set up home-away-from-home with sports clubs, Jewish scouts, and prayer meetings in Darjeeling, the mountain resort famous for aromatic tea; and in the winter, in Madhapur, a railway junction town frequented by Anglo-Indians.

• ETHICS AND HUMAN RELATIONS

India has been the model host country for different communities of Jews, who have never suffered from anti-Semitism at the hands of their fellow citizens (except during a brief period in South India under the hands of the Portuguese).

Since the Indian Jews were so well integrated into society and not persecuted, they developed caste-like traits, defining their place in society. They were thus influenced in their external relations with other Hindus, Muslims, and Christians, and they were affected internally. Thus, the Bene Israel, although "out-of-caste," were incorporated in the villages as Shanwār Telīs or "Saturday Oilmen," and many rose during the nineteenth and twentieth centuries in the hierarchy to "clerk caste" or middle class. Internally, they were divided into subcategories, reminiscent of subcastes, made up of "White" and "Black" Jews, designated *goṛā* or *kālā*. Traditionally, these two groups never intermarried and never interdined, although the distinctions have all but faded in recent years. The Cochin Jews, similarly, appear to have been influenced by the hierarchical system of society. They are divided into "White" or "Paradēśi" Jews nonindigenous to Kerala and Malābārī "Black" Jews who claim that they were the original inhabitants. Members of the two tiny groups have never intermarried; they were organized in separate communities with their own synagogues; and in the past, interaction was restricted in different spheres between them. In addition, the Paradēśi Jews had manumitted slaves known as *meshurarim*, with whom they did not intermarry and who did not have rights to go up and read from the Torah (Daniel and Johnson 1995). The beginning of the struggle against this state of affairs began with A. B. Salem, a lawyer, who became the leader of the *meshurarim* and fought for equal rights for this group. Today these divisions have disappeared, and members of the Paradēśi community have married with the *meshurarim*, particularly after the transplantation of the majority of the community to Israel.

The Baghdādī Jews, in their turn, mixed with the British Rāj and, as non-Indians, were accepted in their clubs and social circles. Baghdādī Jews would not pray in the synagogues of the Bene Israel, whom they did not regard as full Jews, possibly imitating the caste-like divisions in Indian society. Again, declining numbers have changed this situation, and today there are no Baghdādī Jews left to run the synagogue services in Mumbai, so a Bene Israel *hazan* (cantor) is employed.

Since Jewish doctrine emphasizes, "Jews are responsible for one another," they build strong communities in which the synagogue is the center. The mutual responsibility of Jews for one another extends to charity and justice. For example, the Home for Destitutes and Orphans, which today caters for a handful of elderly people, was established in its present form in Bombay in 1934. The home had its precursor in the Bene Israel Benevolent Society of 1853, one of the earliest Bene Israel voluntary organizations of which we have record. Beyond the Jewish community, Jews also believe that they should contribute on a humanitarian basis to others less fortunate than themselves. The Bene Israel and Cochin Jewish communities extended charity and education to their members and were well respected in the larger society.

The Baghdādī Jews, who included among their ranks wealthy dynasties such as the Sassoons, not only established strong Jewish communities in Bombay, Calcutta, Rangoon, and other cities in South Asia, but also looked after poorer Jews and contributed to the wider society. In Mumbai, by way of example, David Sassoon established the David Sassoon Mechanics Institute, the David Sassoon Library and Reading Room, the David Sassoon Industrial and Reformatory Institution, the Clock Tower at the Victoria Gardens (now the Veermata

Jijamata Udyan), and the statue of the Prince Consort at the Victoria and Albert Museum (now the Bhau Daji Lad Museum) (Weil 2014). In the 1860s, David Sassoon contributed to an old age home for the destitute, the David Sassoon Infirm Asylum Niwara, and to the Sassoon Hospital in Pune, which was completed after his death in 1867. Today the Sassoon Hospital is the largest district hospital for Pune District, incorporating in its compound the Sir Jacob Sassoon European Hospital, opened in 1909, and the Rachel Sassoon Hospital. In Mumbai, David Sassoon's son Albert contributed towards the Elphinstone Technical High School, which was also called the Sassoon Building; Sir Jacob Sassoon built the Sir Jacob Sassoon High School (1903) at Byculla, which many Bene Israel children attended; Sir Jacob was also the largest single donor towards the famous Mumbai monument, the Gateway of India, constructed in 1924; and his brother Edward Elias (1853–1924) invested in the E.E.E. Sassoon High School (Lentin 2009).

Special mention must be made of the way the Jewish communities and Indian society at large received refugees from the Holocaust and offered them a haven (see Bhatti and Voigt 1999).

Today, despite their miniscule numbers, the Jews of India are remembered for the just treatment meted out to other Jews and their contribution to others, which can still be viewed in surviving institutions in several cities.

• MODERN EXPRESSIONS

The Indo-Judaic tradition in South Asia has largely come in line with the form of Judaism practiced in Israel and in other Jewish communities. Synagogue attendance is dwindling in India as intermarriage with members of other religions is rising, and there are fewer and fewer who know how to lead a prayer service. In Mumbai, the Bene Israel are concentrated in the suburb of Thane and in a few other pockets of religious life, where regular prayers continue unabated. Several Bene Israel synagogues are neglected or being closed. In 2017, in Mattancherry, Kochi, only five Jews remain in Jew Town and a few Malābārī Jews reside dispersed in different locations in Kerala. However, synagogues are turning into museums in the villages of Chennamamgalam and Parur. In Kolkata, where only a few Jews still reside, memories of Baghdādī religious life in India are being collected and preserved (www.jewishcalcutta.in).

Today, the Jews of India can be divided into two subgroups: those who stay because of their overriding attachment to India, and those who will immigrate to Israel and reunite with their families and the majority of their community. The former group includes Indian nationalists, non-Zionists, and those who are too old to envisage emigration. The latter group includes Zionists and realists, who see the eventual future of the Indian Jewish community in Israel, in spite of hundreds of years of harmonic coexistence with the non-Jewish population of India. There are many visits between the two countries, as Indian Jews and young Israeli backpackers go back and forth to India and other popular destinations among post-army youth. The Lubavitcher Hasidic movement (Chabad) holds an annual communal *seder* (meal at which the exodus from Egypt is recounted) at Passover for Israeli and Jewish backpackers in Kathmandu, Nepal. They have established hostels all over India. Unfortunately, in 2008, the Mumbai Chabad House, along with other famous sites, was targeted by terrorists emanating from Pakistan, killing the rabbi and his wife and four other Jews.

Over the past fifty years, small groups of Indians in different parts of India have identified with Jews, although none of them is accepted officially as a Jew unless they convert to Judaism in cooperation with recognized Jewish religious authorities. The most prominent group, collectively known as the Shinlung, claims Ten Lost Tribe descent (Weil 2003). This group, composed of Kukī and other tribes from Mizoram and Manipur states with an offshoot in Tiddim, Burma, has adopted some Judaic practices since the 1960s. These people, who today call themselves the "Children of Menasseh," have set up Jewish prayer halls and observe certain Jewish customs (Samra 2012). In the last decade, over two thousand people from Manipur and Mizoram have immigrated to Israel and converted to orthodox Judaism there. Groups claiming to descend from the Ten Lost Tribes also have emerged in Andhra Pradesh and other regions of India (Egorova and Perwez 2013).

• TRANSMISSION OF THE TRADITION OUTSIDE OF INDIA

The Indo-Judaic religious tradition has survived in diasporic communities of Indian Jews primarily in Israel. In 1947, the British pulled out of India, and the following year, the State of Israel was declared. Today, due to natural increase, over seventy thousand Bene Israel reside in Israel; almost the entire community of Cochin Jews live in Israel, where they number some seven thousand; and some one thousand Baghdādī Jews are also found in Israel. The Baghdādī Jews identified with their British rulers, so when the British Rāj disintegrated in Asia, most Baghdādīs preferred to immigrate to England, Australia, and North America, where they created new diasporic communities. Many Baghdādī Jews write with nostalgia of their previous homes in India and, tracing their family histories over decades and continents, describe the new environment they created in other countries (see, for example, Silliman 2001).

The process of emigration and the adaptation of the Bene Israel in their new homeland in Israel entailed many changes in religious life. At first, the Bene Israel were not accepted as "full Jews" in Israel, and they were only recognized as such after a two-year struggle with demonstrations and strikes in 1962–64. Their nonacceptance by other Jews is still a bitter memory today. In Israel, the Bene Israel adapted some of their traditions and took on others. For example, instead of visiting the Elijah site in the Konkan, the Bene Israel in Israel visit Mount Carmel. They have also adopted many items from the Oral Law, which they did not know years back. However, a surprising number of Indian traditions live on, such as the pre-wedding *mehaṁdī* ceremony and the *melida.* The younger generation of Indians define themselves as Israelis tend to classify themselves as "secular" or "religious" Israelis, but the majority say they are "traditional."

In Israel, the Bene Israel organize as a community, spinning family and ethnic ties tighter and tighter. While there is increasing marriage with other Jews in Israel, the majority are still endogamous, that is, contracted within the ethnic community. Marriage is sometimes negotiated across national borders; social relationships and political orientations are conducted irrespective of territorial blocks (Weil 2012). The Bene Israel communicate with kin and friends through email and electronic media. Films, videos, and YouTube reformulate the cultural traditions of the Indian diaspora and "market" Indian cinema and music over the screen. The older generation of Bene Israel in Israel, as well as new immigrants, read and write in Marathi newspapers like *Mai Bolli*; telephones and the Internet speed up the ever-present communication. Every year, along with regular young Israeli backpackers, hundreds of Bene Israel go to India in organized groups to pray in the synagogues there and buy the latest Indian fashion and jewelry. These "Indian" tourists to India return with suitcases stuffed with spices, gold, silks, and scarves, as well as letters and gifts for friends and relatives who could not make the journey. They then "return" to their Israeli homeland with tangible pieces of their previous "homeland"—India. In addition, they keep up ties between Israel and other smaller Bene Israel "diasporas" in the United Kingdom, Canada, United States, and Australia.

The Cochin Jews live primarily in agricultural settlements in Israel, and while there is no wider Cochin Jewish "diaspora," Cochin Jews also increasingly move between Israel and India, particularly in the last decade. In Israel, where there are Cochin Jewish synagogues, such as the synagogue at the *moshav* (agricultural settlement) called Nevatim, Cochin Jews pray according to Shingli rites and enact their religious ceremonies according to Cochin custom, but they are also influenced by general Israeli trends; most are exogamous, marrying Jews of other ethnic origins. At Nevatim and Givat Koach, there are Cochin Jewish heritage museums, and at the Israel Museum in Jerusalem, there is a reconstructed Malābārī Kadavambagum synagogue imported from Cochin itself.

• RELATIONS WITH OTHER RELIGIONS

Judaism is an endogamous religion, and it is prohibited to marry members of other religions (unless they convert, which is not encouraged). Since Hindus (and members of other religions in India) were unable to marry people of other castes, this arrangement was convenient, and intermarriage with non-Jews was practically unknown in the past. Today, with the liberalization and globalization in India, intermarriage is occurring more frequently in urban centers such as Mumbai, although it is still frowned upon by the Jewish community and is certainly not the norm.

Hinduism and Judaism have elements in common as orthopraxies that have developed complicated systems of law, purity codes, and dietary restrictions that serve to define the religio-ethnic boundaries of the community. Nevertheless, unique customs adapted from Hindu practices characterize the Judaism of the Indian Jews, including the pre-wedding henna ceremony among the Bene Israel, the rites of and belief in the prophet Elijah, and the festival of Shila San on the day after Yom Kippur, when the souls of the ancestors departed and alms were given to the poor. According to some authorities, Cochin Jews isolated themselves from the non-Jewish world during the eight days of Passover, imitating the Brāhmaṇas' asceticism in Hinduism by reasserting their purity, nonpollution, and high-caste status in Indian Kerala culture. Added to other high-caste behaviors of endogamy and dietary restrictions and using a sacred language, Hebrew, Cochin Jews maintained their distinct identity while adopting some Hindu royal and ascetic symbols into their Jewish tradition (Katz and Goldberg 1993).

In Kerala, Cochin Jews also shared common characteristics with the more numerous Christians by virtue of their minority status vis-à-vis the Hindus. Two basic patterns of interrelationship between Christians and Jews in India can be discerned: the symmetrical pattern, whereby there is an equal and corresponding relationship between members of the two religions; and the asymmetrical pattern, where an unequal distribution pertains (Weil 1982). In the case of the Cochin Jews and the Canaanite Christians who are South Indian Christians tracing descent from Thomas of Cana, the symmetrical pattern dominates. Both groups share a common local tradition, customs, folktales and songs, and lifestyle.

The asymmetrical pattern is based upon unequal access to resources between Christianity and Judaism stemming from the fact that Christianity is intrinsically an active missionizing religion, which attempts to bring Jews and members of other religions to the Christian fold. During the nineteenth century, American and British missionaries worked among the Bene Israel and the Cochin Jews but had remarkably few successes with either group, despite the fact that the missionaries translated holy texts into the vernacular and set up Christian schools for village Bene Israel.

Today a kind of "New Age" spirituality, mixing elements in Judaism, and particularly kabbalism, with Hinduism and Buddhism, is popular among Israeli travelers to South Asia. They visit *āśrama*s in India, Tibet, and Nepal and delve into mysticism, which is all part of what Rodger Kamenetz (2007) called "the 'Ju-Bu' phenomenon." There have been several Jewish-Buddhist meetings held in the presence of the Dalai Lama in Dharmasala, in Jerusalem, and elsewhere, and a scholarly interest in Buddhism on the part of Israelis (Shulman and Weil 2008).

• THE TRADITION IN THE STUDY OF RELIGIONS

Indo-Judaic Studies have been slow to develop, but this state of affairs is changing as the field is beginning to receive legitimation and to make its mark on the academic map internationally. The expansion of the field can be related to the influence of what Yair Sheleg (2000) calls the "new spirituals," who incorporate elements of Hindu practice, such as meditation, with Jewish practice and learning. It can also be attributed to the establishment of Israeli diplomatic relations with India in 1992 and to the informal meetings and lectures organized by voluntary organizations such as the Israel-India Cultural Association, the official friendship organization between the two countries founded in Israel in 1992, and its successor the Israel-India Friendship Association, which mainly deals with commercial issues.

Indians, as well as Israelis and diasporic Jews, have entered the scholarly arena of Indo-Judaic Studies. C.R. Das (1996) edited a special issue of *Eastern Anthropologist* on Indian Jews; Margaret Abraham published an article on the Indian Jews in Israel (1995); Singh wrote a book on Indians in Israel (2010). The Israeli journal *Pe'amim* published new research in Hebrew on Indian Jews and Indian Jewish texts, and the Ben-Zvi Institute hosted several seminars on the subject. David Shulman and Shalva Weil (2008) brought together a group of Israeli scholars who have published on India. In 1995, the American Academy of Religion set up its Comparative Studies in Hinduisms and Judaisms Consultation, and in 1997 its Hinduisms and Judaisms Group. The academic discipline received a deep boost with the publication of Hananya Goodman's edited volume, *Between Jerusalem and Benares: Comparative Studies in Judaism and Hinduism* (1994), a pioneering effort, which brought together a group of scholars to investigate what Goodman calls the "resonances" between the great Judaic and Hindu traditions. Similarly, the publication of Barbara A. Holdrege's monumental *Veda and Torah* (1996), which provided equal space and importance to Hinduism and Judaism alike, was a milestone. Holdrege succeeded in imparting the contextuality and textuality of both religions, and instead of characterizing the Hindu and Jewish traditions as opposite ends of the spectrum of the world's religions, she argued that the Brāhmaṇical and rabbinic traditions were both "embodied communities." Both religions study texts that codified their norms in the form of scriptural canons; both represent ethnocultural systems concerned with peoplehood, identity, and tradition, particularly as it is transmitted through family, ethnicity, and culture; and both represent religions of orthopraxy with complex legal systems and laws about purity and impurity, although in the final analysis, the comparisons are "political" (Holdrege 2007).

The *Journal of Indo-Judaic Studies*, established in 1998, has consistently published interesting and important articles on comparative religion, Indian Jews, history of commerce between the Middle East and India, India and the Holocaust, and more. Books and journal articles on South Asian Jews, including information on newly emerging groups who want to affiliate with Judaism, continue to be published at steady pace. The volume *India's Jewish Heritage: Ritual, Art and Life-Cycle* (Weil 2002) is already in its third edition (2009). In 2002, an international conference was held at Oxford University entitled "A Perspective from the Margins: The State of the Art of Indo-Judaic Studies," at which some twenty scholars from three continents convened to discuss issues related to the emerging Indo-Judaic Studies arena (Katz, Chakravarti, Sinha, and Weil 2007). From 2014 through 2017, the Indira Gandhi National Centre for the Arts in New Delhi organized several conferences and exhibitions on the history and significance of India's Jews. In 2017, the first university course in India on India's Jews was offered at Jawaharlal Nehru University and was taught by Shalva Weil. Today, the study of Indo-Judaic traditions is neither rare nor exotic.

• DISCUSSION QUESTIONS

1. It is not easy to determine when and where the earliest practicing Jewish religious communities were established in India, but three have become significant subjects of scholarly study. What are the three, and how are their stories or their self-understanding as Indian communities different from one another?
2. What are the main elements of a practicing Jewish religious community, wherever in the world it may be resident, and how would their practices tend to keep them separate or to

connect them to surrounding cultures that are informed by other religious traditions—particularly in India?

3. What concerns or factors have led to a significant decline in the number of Jews in India in recent decades? What do you imagine may be the most likely future for Jewish institutions in India?

• BIBLIOGRAPHY

Abraham, Margaret. 1996. "Ethnicity and Marginality: A Study of Indian Jewish Immigrants in Israel." *Comparative Studies of South Asia, Africa and the Middle East* 15, 1: 108—23.

Bhatti, Anil and Johannes H. Voigt, eds. 1999. *Jewish Exile in India 1933–1945*. New Delhi: Manohar.

Cooper, John and Judy Cooper. 2009 [2002]. "The Life-Cycle of the Baghdadi Jews of India." *In* Shalva Weil, ed., *India's Jewish Heritage: Ritual, Art and Life-Cycle*, 100–9. Mumbai: Mārg Publications.

Daniel, Ruby and Barbara C. Johnson. 1995. *Ruby of Cochin: An Indian Jewish Woman Remembers*. Philadelphia: The Jewish Publication Society.

Das, C. R. 1996. "Israel's Jews from India." *The Eastern Anthropologist* 49, 3–4: 317–48.

Egorova, Yulia and Shahid Perwez. 2013. *The Jews of Andhra Pradesh: Contesting Caste and Religion in South India*. New York: Oxford University Press.

Ezekiel, I. A. 1966. *Sarmad (Jewish Saint of India)*. Punjab: Radha Soami Satsang Beas.

Ezra, Esmond David. 1986. *Turning Back the Pages: A Chronicle of Calcutta Jewry*. 2 volumes. London: Brookside Press.

Goitein, S. D. and Mordechai A. Friedman. 2007. *India Traders of the Middle Ages: Documents From the Cairo Geniza: "India Book," Part One*. Leiden: Brill.

Goodman, Hananya, ed. 1994. *Between Jerusalem and Benares: Comparative Studies in Judaism and Hinduism*. Albany: State University of New York Press.

Hallegua, Samuel H. 2009 [2002]. "The Marriage Customs of the Jewish Community of Cochin." *In* Shalva Weil, ed., *India's Jewish Heritage: Ritual, Art and Life-Cycle*, 60–7. Mumbai: Mārg Publications.

Holdrege, Barbara A. 1996. *Veda and Torah: Transcending the Textuality of Scripture*. Albany: State University of New York Press.

Holdrege, Barbara A. 2007. "Beyond Hegemony: Hinduisms, Judaisms, and the Politics of Comparison." *In* Nathan Katz, Ranabir Chakravarti, Braj M. Sinha, and Shalva Weil, eds., *Indo-Judaic Studies in the Twenty-First Century: A View From the Margin*, 77–92. New York: Palgrave Macmillan.

Isenberg, Shirley Berry. 1988. *India's Bene Israel: A Comprehensive Inquiry and Sourcebook*. Berkeley: Judah L. Magnes Museum.

Johnson, Barbara C., ed. 2002. *Oh Lovely Parrot: Jewish Women's Songs from Kerala* (trans. Barbara C. Johnson and Scaria Zacharia). Jerusalem: Jewish Music Resource Center.

Jussay, P. M. 1986 [1982]. "The Songs of Evarayi." *Pe'amim* 13: 45–160.

Kamenetz, Rodger. 2007 [1994]. *The Jew in the Lotus: A Poet's Rediscovery of Jewish Identity in Buddhist India*. New York: HarperCollins.

Katz, Nathan. 2000. *Who Are the Jews of India?* Berkeley: University of California Press.

Katz, Nathan and Ellen S. Goldberg. 1993. *The Last Jews of Cochin: Jewish Identity in Hindu India*. Columbia: University of South Carolina Press.

Katz, Nathan, Ranavir Chakravarti, Braj M. Sinha, and Shalva Weil, eds. 2007. *Indo-Judaic Studies in the Twenty-First Century: A View from the Margin*. New York: Palgrave Macmillan.

Lentin, Sifra Samuel. 2009 [2002]. "The Jewish Presence in Bombay." *In* Shalva Weil, ed., *India's Jewish Heritage: Ritual, Art and Life-Cycle*, 22–35. Mumbai: Mārg Publications.

Manasseh, Sara. 2012. *Shbaḥoth—Songs of Praise in the Babylonian Jewish Tradition: From Baghdad to Bombay and London*. Surrey: Ashgate.

Narayanan, M. G. S. 1972. *Cultural Symbiosis in Kerala*. Trivandrum: Kerala Historical Society.

Numark, Mitch. 2010. "Hebrew School in Nineteenth-Century Bombay: Protestant Missionaries, Cochin Jews, and the Hebraization of India's Bene Israel Community." *Modern Asian Studies* 46, 6: 1764–1808.

Parfitt, Tudor. 2002. *The Lost Tribes of Israel: The History of a Myth*. London: Weidenfeld & Nicolson.

Reissner, H. G. 1950. "Indian-Jewish Statistics (1837–1941)." *Jewish Social Studies* 12: 349–66.

Roland, Joan G. 1989. *Jews in British India: Identity in a Colonial Era*. Hanover: University Press of New England.

Roland, Joan G. 2009 [2002]. "The Contributions of the Jews of India." *In* Shalva Weil, ed., *India's Jewish Heritage: Art, Ritual and Life-Cycle*, 110–21. Mumbai: Mārg Publications.

Samra, Myer. 2012. "The Bnei Menashe: Choosing Judaism in North East India." *The Journal of Indo-Judaic Studies* 12: 45–56.

Segal, J. B. 1967. "The Jews of Cochin and Their Neighbours." *In* H. J. Zimmels, J. Rabbinowitz, and I. Feinstein, eds., *Essays Presented to Chief Rabbi Israel Brodie on the Occasion of His Seventieth Birthday*, 381–97. London: Soncino Press.

Sheleg, Yair. 2000. *The New Religious Jews: Recent Developments Among Observant Jews in Israel*. Jerusalem: Keter Publishing House Ltd. [In Hebrew]

Shulman, David and Shalva Weil, eds. 2008. *Karmic Passages: Israeli Scholarship on India*. New Delhi: Oxford University Press.

Silliman, Jael. 2001. *Jewish Portraits, Indian Frames: Women's Narratives From a Diaspora of Hope*. Hanover: University Press of New England.

Singh, Maina Chawla. 2010. *Being Indian, Being Israeli: Migration, Ethnicity and Gender in the Jewish Homeland*. New Delhi: Manohar.

Tavim, José Alberto Rodrigues da Silva. 2003. *Judeus e cristãos-novos de Cochim. História e memória (1500–1663)*. Braga: Edišões APPACDM.

Weil, Shalva. 1982. "Symmetry between Christians and Jews in India: The Cnanite Christians and the Cochin Jews of Kerala." *Contributions to Indian Sociology* 16, 2: 175–96.

Weil, Shalva. 1994. "Yom Kippur: The Festival of Closing the Doors." *In* Hananya Goodman, ed., *Between Jerusalem and Benares: Comparative Studies in Judaism and Hinduism*, 85–100, 293–95. New York: State University of New York Press.

Weil, Shalva. 2003. "Dual Conversion Among the Shinlung of North-East India." *Studies of Tribes and Tribals* 1, 1: 43–57.

Weil, Shalva, ed. 2009 [2002]. *India's Jewish Heritage: Ritual, Art and Life-Cycle*. Mumbai: Mārg Publications.

Weil, Shalva. 2010. "The Place of Alwaye in Modern Cochin Jewish History." *Journal of Modern Jewish Studies* 8, 3: 319–35.

Weil, Shalva. 2012. "The Bene Israel Indian Jewish Family in Transnational Context." *Journal of Comparative Family Studies* 43, 1: 71–80.

Weil, Shalva. 2013. "Indian Jews." *In* David Biale, ed., *Oxford Bibliographies Online: Jewish Studies*. Available at: www.oxfordbibliographies.com/view/document/obo-9780199840731/obo-9780199840731-0046.xml?rskey=2WwgWt&result=133&q=indian+jews#firstMatch.

Weil, Shalva. 2014. "The Legacy of David Sassoon: Building a Community Bridge." *Asian Jewish Life* 14: 4–6. Available at: http://asianjewishlife.org/pages/articles/AJL_Issue_14_Apr_2014/AJL_Issue14_Feature_David_Sassoon.html.

Zacharia, Scaria and Ophira Gamliel, eds. and trans. 2005. *Karkulali-Yefifiah-Gorgeous!: Jewish Women's Songs in Malayalam With Hebrew Translations*. Jerusalem: Ben-Zvi Institute.

FIGURE 7.1 Church of St. Francis of Assisi in Velha Goa.

Image courtesy of akg-images/Pictures From History.

7

Indian Christian Traditions

M. THOMAS THANGARAJ AND
RAKESH PETER DASS

• THE TRADITIONS DEFINED

At the center of a small movement that later became Christianity was a Jewish teacher known as Jesus of Nazareth. It started in the ancient Roman provinces of Judaea and Samaria near the eastern edge of the Mediterranean Sea in the first century of the common era, and so early stories and claims of Christians emerged in the shadow of Judaism and Roman rule. First-century Jewish life in Judaea was marked by a variety of social unrests against perceived economic, political, and social oppression under Roman governments (Horsley 2014). These unrests were inspired by a sense of loss of self-rule and the desire to re-establish a Davidic kingdom. As a result, stories told by early Christians (who were mostly Jews) about Jesus of Nazareth were shaped in the crucible of Jewish ideas about the creator, a messiah, and the restoration of God's (Davidic) kingdom. Jesus' declarations about a kingdom very different from the Roman administration caused enough social and political problems to lead to his trial, indictment, and crucifixion as a criminal. Crucifixion was the standard Roman punishment for serious crimes. After Jesus' death, his disciples claimed that he had been resurrected from the dead on the third day and showed himself to several of them. These disciples began to proclaim his resurrection as good news in and around Jerusalem, and traveling from Jerusalem to different parts of the Greco-Roman world of their day, they established Christian communities that included both Jews and Gentiles.

As the Christian movement grew in different places, diversity and disagreements emerged. In its first three centuries, it was a faith on the margins in the Roman world that suffered persecution and produced many martyrs. In the fourth century, the Roman emperor

Constantine adopted Christianity as a means to consolidate his empire—Constantine preferred Christianity but never made it the "official" or "established" religion of the empire (Chadwick 1993: 127). It was at the behest of Constantine that the early Christians first got together to define themselves and their faith. The first ecumenical Council of Nicaea in 321 CE led to the first empire-wide creed (or statement of faith) of early Christians. About two hundred and twenty bishops gathered for this council, the vast majority of them Greek bishops, with only seven or eight participants from the Latin West (Chadwick 1993: 130). While influential, such creeds were not universally accepted by Christians, and Christian history has produced communities that are both creedal (adhere to a creed) and noncreedal (do not find creeds necessary).

From the middle of the third century CE, western and eastern Christian communities grew apart politically (Fisher 2014: 327), with western churches centered on Rome and eastern churches centered on Constantinople (modern day Istanbul). The first major theological disagreement within Christianity emerged in the fifth century among Eastern Orthodox churches. The Council of Chalcedon in 451 CE declared Jesus of Nazareth to be fully human and fully divine. Many eastern churches rejected this declaration and formed the Oriental Orthodox churches. This Orthodox debate concerned the nature of Jesus. Eastern Orthodox communities claimed Jesus had "two natures": divine and human. Oriental Orthodox communities claim Jesus had "one nature": divine.

The second major Christian disagreement emerged in the eleventh century when the eastern (Orthodox) and western (Roman) churches separated over doctrinal issues in 1054 CE. Eastern-western debates in the eleventh century concerned the monarchy of God the Father with divisions emerging over the question of whether God the Father and God the Son were co-monarchs. The next major debate within Christianity occurred in the sixteenth century, when the sermons and writings of reformers like Martin Luther and John Calvin led to the emergence of Reformation or Protestant churches across Europe. These reformation debates concerned vehement disagreements over issues like the sale of salvation (indulgences), interpretation of scripture, and the place of the papacy within Christianity. As a consequence of this history of debates and divisions, modern Christianity is characterized by four major "historical" churches: Eastern Orthodox, Oriental Orthodox, Roman Catholic, and Protestant. To this list, we could also add more recent Pentecostal and nondenominational churches.

While these institutional differences stem from different and many times divergent claims regarding statements of faith (creeds), theology (doctrines), practices (like sacraments), and church policy, Christian beliefs and practices also share certain typical features (Lakoff 1987, cited in Flood 1996: 7). In other words, patterns of claims and practices can be discerned within the story of Christianity.

Christians source their beliefs and practices to the teachings and acts of Jesus of Nazareth and his followers. Christian claims regarding Jesus generally address the nature of Jesus and the work of Jesus. Many Christians consider Jesus to be divine, whereas other Christians have argued he was a human who had a special relationship with God (Song 1999: 294).

Christians further claim that Jesus' death on the cross and resurrection has saved people from the effects of sin (generally considered a broken relationship with God). Stories about Jesus and the subsequent work of his followers were codified by early Christians in the first few centuries CE and compiled in a collection of books (Bible) in the latter half of the fourth century, probably around 382 CE (Cross and Livingstone 2005: 200). Over centuries, different Christian communities have developed different sets of books as "canonical" or standard (from the Greek word for "measuring rod" or "rule"): The Roman Catholic Church accepts the Hebrew Scriptures (the "Old" Testament), Greek Scriptures (the "New" Testament), and a set of secondarily canonical books (the Apocrypha). Eastern Orthodox Churches accept the Hebrew and Greek scriptures and certain Apocryphal books. Protestant/Reformation churches generally exclude the Apocryphal books altogether.

In addition to the centrality of Jesus and scriptures, typical Christian life also includes certain teachings and actions. Typical teachings include the idea of love (loving God and one's neighbor), the kingdom of God (which is considered egalitarian in nature), the victory of light over darkness, and spreading the message of Jesus (evangelism). Typical Christian practices include worshiping God (including prayers), gathering for worship, engaging with scriptures (through study and sermons), caring for those in need, and taking part in ritualized symbolic actions called sacraments. Important sacraments include baptism (the rite of initiation), Eucharist or Lord's Supper or Mass (the rite of thanksgiving), ordination (the rite of priestly consecration), and marriage (the rite of human union).

Baptism involves consecrating an adult or infant with water as a way to invite the person into membership of the Christian community. In the Eucharist, baptized Christians gather around the Lord's table to share in the body and blood (represented in bread and wine) of Jesus called Christ. The rite of ordination involves the laying of hands by church clergy on new pastors to mark the succession of priesthood and the calling out of Christians to serve as pastors in Christian communities. The rite of marriage invokes the eternal bond between Jesus Christ and his Church in the coming together of two persons in the bond of marriage. While baptism, Eucharist, ordination, and marriage represent sacraments found in most Christian communities, some Christian communities have additional sacraments (Roman Catholics count seven), some less (Protestants count only baptism and Eucharist), and some count none (nonsacramental communities include the Salvation Army and Quakers).

Along with the centrality of the life and teachings of Jesus, the importance of Hebrew and Greek scriptures, certain teachings, and recognizable practices, prototypical Christian life also includes the commemoration of certain religious events or festivals each year. Chief among them are Advent and Christmas, Lent and Holy Week (including Good Friday and Easter), and Pentecost. Celebrated in November–December, Advent ("coming" in Latin) marks the season that anticipates the birth of Jesus of Nazareth. This birth is celebrated by Christians on December 25 each year and called Christmas. The next major Christian anniversary is the Lent–Holy Week. Lent is a season of preparation for the Holy Week. During Lent, most Christians practice repentance and sacrifice to recall the sacrifice of Jesus. Holy Week, a seven-day festival usually celebrated in March, April, or May (depending on whether a sonar, lunar, Julian, or Gregorian calendar is used), begins with Palm Sunday, includes Good Friday, and culminates in the celebration on Easter Sunday a week later. During Palm Sunday, Christians recall the arrival of Jesus of Nazareth in Jerusalem to celebrate the Jewish Passover. Good Friday recalls the trial, crucifixion, and death of Jesus. Easter Sunday commemorates Christian claims that Jesus rose from the dead and appeared to his followers. Roman Catholic churches celebrate Easter on a different date than Orthodox churches do because the former follow the Gregorian calendar while the latter follow the Julian one. Pentecost, the next major Christian anniversary, falls fifty days after Easter and commemorates the arrival of the Spirit among early Christians. In many churches, Pentecost marks the commencement of evangelism by the followers of Jesus. If you visit churches during these festivals, you may also observe the use of different colors on the altar, or on the priest's vestments, or in the attire of the worshipers. Among Lutheran churches, for instance, one may find blue during Advent, white during Christmas, purple and scarlet during Lent, white and gold during Easter, and red during Pentecost.

Since its emergence two thousand years ago, Christianity has been characterized by persistent diversity and ongoing debates. The diversity within Christianity (like that within other religious traditions) is itself a reflection of the development of Christian claims and practices in the context of many locations, cultures, religions, and communities. One early strand of Christianity that developed when Christianity was still spreading in the Middle East (and many centuries before it had reached modern Europe) can be found in modern-day India.

It is believed that Saint Thomas, one of the disciples of Jesus, traveled to India and established churches in India during the very first century of Christianity. Although not all historians agree on the veracity of this claim, there is even today a Christian tradition in India that traces its beginnings to the arrival of Thomas in South India. It is certain, however, that Christianity was a part of the religious landscape of India from the fourth century onwards, if not before.

According to the 2011 census, 2.3 percent of the population of India is Christian. The percentage has fluctuated between 2.3 and 2.6 for several decades. Some statisticians include those Indians who are called "crypto-Christians" due to their secret admiration and devotion to Christ without membership in a Christian church, and thus put the number of Christians closer to 5 percent of the population. There has not been any significant increase in the number of Christians in India during the twentieth century, though there were mass conversions to Christianity in earlier centuries. Christians in India belong to all the four major ecclesial traditions, namely, Eastern Orthodox, Oriental Orthodox, Roman Catholic, and Protestant. The Indian Orthodox Church, Orthodox Syrian Church of the East, Armenian Apostolic Church, Chaldean Syrian Church, and a few other smaller Orthodox groups carry on the Orthodox traditions. These churches are mostly based in the southern state of Kerala. Roman Catholics comprise nearly half of the Christian population in India. They are spread throughout India. Protestants are divided into nearly one thousand denominations. Some of these denominations had their beginnings in Europe or North America, while others are indigenous churches established either by individual charismatic leaders or by groups of local Christians. The Church of South India, a union of former Anglicans, Presbyterians,

Methodists, and Congregationalists, has a membership of around three million. The Church of North India, a similar union of major Protestant churches, is one and a half million strong.

Christians are not evenly distributed in the Indian landscape. The states of Kerala, Tamil Nadu, and Andhra Pradesh together account for a vast majority of India's Christians (*World Christian Encyclopedia* 2001). There is also a concentration of Christians in the northeastern part of India—in the states of Nagaland, Meghalaya, and Mizoram. The Christian population is significantly smaller in the northcentral and western parts of India.

There are many types of Christians in India with varied historical and theological lineages that are shaped by the diverse range of languages, cultures, and customs that have constituted and continue to make up the Indian subcontinent. When speaking of Christians of India, then, it is fair in a sense to ask whether one should speak of Indian Christianity or Indian Christianities. While "Indian Christianity" as a term has a uniting function, it is important to note that behind this term sits the persistent diversity of Christian beliefs and practices. Indian Christianity derives its multiplicity and variety not only from its denominational differences, but also from the regional and linguistic peculiarities that have shaped it (more on this below). Christianity as it is practiced in Nagaland in the northeast, for instance, is significantly different from that in Tamil Nadu in the south because of the differences in local culture and language. These differences are manifested in worship patterns, liturgical practices, and church architecture and in the observation of individual rituals, rites of passage, and family ceremonies such as weddings and funerals. Thus, descriptions of Christian traditions in India are dependent on regional, linguistic, denominational, and social groupings.

• COSMOS AND HISTORY

As it was mentioned earlier, there is a strong historical tradition claiming that Saint Thomas, the disciple of Jesus, came to India during the first century and established churches. Historical scholarship on the Thomas tradition is complex, and the available evidence includes both contradictory and corroborative elements. For instance, there is evidence both of Thomas' maritime arrival and of his "overland" arrival. Yet, retellings of the Thomas tradition from ancient India exist in oral traditions, songs, plays, and inscriptions that echo patterns in the historical narratives of many other religious communities. Thomas tradition sources generally fall under two categories: northern (external) evidence and southern (internal) evidence. Most corroborative of the Thomas tradition within the northern evidence are historical artifacts (like coins) that confirm that Gundaphar (Gondophares in Greek) ruled a kingdom spread across modern-day western India, southern Pakistan, and southern Afghanistan. According to the apocryphal *Acts of Thomas*, the apostle reached India through Gundaphar's court, where he found India's first converts. The southern, internal evidence is more substantial and involves a body of narrative accounts, songs, palm-leaf manuscripts, and lineages of apostolic succession (Frykenberg 2008: 91–115). There is also a tradition, less historically justifiable, that there was a community of Christians on the western coast due to the evangelistic efforts of Bartholomew.

The Christian community that claims its connection to the work of Saint Thomas had lively connection with the East Syrian or Persian Christians. For all practical purposes, it was a Syrian Orthodox church. Its membership included both Persians and local inhabitants. During the Middle Ages, a Latin mission was established in Quilon, but it did not last for long. These Latin Christians had good relations with the Saint Thomas Christians, and various visitors during this period noted their existence, often referring to them as "Nestorians."

The arrival of the Portuguese opened a new page in the history of Christianity in India. In 1498, Vasco da Gama reached India via the Cape of Good Hope in Africa, and thus established a route to India from Europe that enabled trade between India and Portugal. The Portuguese kings were interested, in addition to trade, in the spread of Christianity in India. Their zeal for the spread of Christianity led to their securing the right of ecclesiastical administration in the lands conquered or to be conquered in Africa and Asia. This is known as the Portuguese "*padroado*," or the right of patronage (Thekkedath 1982: 5). Goa, a town on the western coast of India, was made a bishopric, and Franciscans and Dominicans carried on the mission. The initial history of the encounter between Portuguese and Syrian Christians was one of friendly relations. Soon the Portuguese had established their churches and bishoprics firmly on the western coast of India. It was at this time that King John III of Portugal appealed to the pope to send missionaries to India. So Francis Xavier (1506–52), a Jesuit priest, was sent to India as a missionary. Xavier was able to convert to Christianity a large number of people belonging to the fisher caste, primarily on the eastern coast of India. He was able to build the Roman Church in India on firm grounds with an increasing membership.

The initial friendly relations between Syrian Christianity and Western Catholicism were to be marred by differences in beliefs, practices, and especially ecclesial governance. While Syrian Christians continued to recognize the patriarch of the East, Portuguese Catholics demanded allegiance to the pope in Rome. There were also differences among them with regard to the number of sacraments, the manner of giving communion, and priestly celibacy. These differences led to hostility, and finally at the Synod of Diamper by Roman Catholics, held in 1599, a permanent divide between Syrian Christians and Western Catholics was created. The synod declared a clear renunciation of the power of the patriarch and the beliefs and practices of the Syrian Church. The struggle between these two groups of Christians went on until 1653, when the majority of Syrians rebelled unsuccessfully against the Roman authority and Portuguese hierarchy. Some of those who revolted resumed Roman obedience, while a minority persisted as an Eastern Orthodox tradition.

The Roman Catholic missions flourished in the centuries that followed. Akbar (1556–1605) the Mughal emperor became interested in Christianity and welcomed Jesuits in his court. He also hoped for a new religion, called Tawḥīd-I Ilāhī (divine unity), combining elements from the existing three religions: Hinduism, Islam, and Christianity. The Jesuits withdrew from the court once such a new religion was envisaged. Another notable missionary among the Jesuits was Roberto De Nobili. De Nobili came to Madurai, South India, in 1606 and began his work among the higher caste groups in and around that city. He separated himself from the existing Catholic mission, adopted the lifestyle of a Hindu monk, mastered Sanskrit and

Tamil, and was able to attract several to the Christian faith. De Nobili had a vision of generating a Christian faith that was rooted in the local Hindu cultural ethos and practices, including the caste system. He published several works in Tamil and wrote hymns in both Tamil and Telugu. Although De Nobili's work was successful in the initial stages, he came into conflict with the Roman authorities with regard to his views of enculturation and his evangelistic methods. Another notable Jesuit missionary was Constant Joseph Beschi, who published both poetic and prose works in Tamil during the period 1711–42. These were missionaries who attempted to free Christianity in India from the "reproach of foreignness."

The Protestant mission in India began with the arrival of two German missionaries, Bartholomäus Ziegenbalg and Heinrich Plütschau, who were sent by King Frederick IV of Denmark. They arrived in the coastal town of Tranquebar (Tharangampadi), south of Madras on July 9, 1706. They proceeded to learn Portuguese and Tamil, since these were the two languages that were dominant at that time in South India. Ziegenbalg had a keen mind to grasp the languages of India and began translating the Bible into Tamil. He was able to establish congregations in and around Tranquebar, and thus began the Protestant expansion in India. He was to be followed by several missionaries from the West, representing the various denominational and national missionary societies. The establishment of various Protestant mission societies in the West (such as the Society for the Propagation of the Gospel and the Church Missionary Society [both of the Church of England], the Baptist Missionary Society, the London Missionary Society, and others) led to the arrival of many more Western Protestant missionaries in India. Thus, Protestant Christianity grew in India, with several denominational and national linkages with the West. One of the leading figures in the Protestant missionary activity of the nineteenth century was William Carey, who established the Serampore Mission near Calcutta and promoted the cause of Christianity in many ways. He was involved in translating the Bible into several Indian languages, founding the first institution of higher learning in India (Serampore College), and working with the Hindu reformers and the British rulers to ban the practice of *satī* ("the voluntary burning alive of widows on the funeral pyres of their husbands").

While the Protestant expansion was taking place in India, the Roman Catholic tradition experienced its own parallel expansion. In addition to establishing parishes and dioceses in India, the Roman Catholic Church was heavily involved in founding and maintaining educational institutions around the country. Various religious orders were involved in medical, technical, and other differing forms of service.

The further history of Orthodox (Syrian) Christianity in India is marked by the development of a schism that led to the formation in 1887 of the Mar Thoma Church. The Church Missionary Society's missionaries were invited by Mar Dionysios II to teach in their seminaries and bring about a revival in the Syrian Church. Their involvement in the life of the Syrian Church led to the formation of a reformed party by a group of Syrian Christians under the leadership of Abraham Malpan. They ultimately left the Syrian Church and formed the Mar Thoma Church.

One of the remarkable features in the history of Christianity in India is the movement toward unity among mainline Protestants in the twentieth century. It began with a call in 1919 by a few church leaders, who met in the town of Tranquebar and issued what is now called the Tranquebar Manifesto. Conversations toward unity continued from then on between the Anglican, Methodist, Presbyterian, and Congregationalist churches in South India and ultimately led to the formation of the Church of South India, an organic union of all four denominational traditions, on September 27, 1947. Similar conversations took place between Protestant churches in North India, which led to the formation of the Church of North India in 1970. There are continuing conversations even today among the three churches—Church of South India, Church of North India, and Mar Thoma Church—toward a conciliar formation of a church of India. The Lutherans, Baptists, American Methodists, and others remain as churches in their own right. The attempts to broaden the unity among Protestants have not led to further mergers, though there is a spirit of ecumenical collaboration.

Ecumenical cooperation is seen clearly in the work of the National Council of Churches in India, which came into being in 1912 under the name National Missionary Council of India. The goals of the National Council of Churches include unity, witness, service, and practice. The Council offers a "common platform" toward greater church fellowships (unity). In collaboration with state and other actors, it seeks to "further the rule of law, secularism, and human rights" as a united, prophetic, Christian voice in the nation (witness). Through its actions and words, it seeks to promote and develop "just and inclusive communities" in India (service). Finally, as part of its attention to church practice in nation, it seeks to enable its member churches and institutions to reflect "global standards of good governance, inclusion and equity" (http://ncci1914.com/). The National Council has also been instrumental in cross-regional and global ecumenical work. It has been a founding member of the Christian Conference of Asia—which promotes ecumenical unity, witness, and service across the Asia-Pacific region—and a leading member of the World Council of Churches. Ecumenical Christians in India have particularly been on the forefront of developing and leading interfaith relations within churches around the world. Stanley J. Samartha of India, for instance, was appointed the first director of the new subunit on "Dialogue with People of Living Faiths and Ideologies" by the World Council of Churches in 1971. The contribution of Indian Christians to global Christianity regarding interfaith relations has been a reflection of the multireligious context in which Indian Christianity took birth and has developed throughout its history.

Since Vatican II, the Roman Catholic churches in India have been working together with Protestant churches in matters of common concern. When the Eastern Orthodox churches joined the World Council of Churches in 1961 during its assembly in New Delhi, an intentional collaboration between Protestants and Eastern Orthodox Christians in India gained importance.

• SACRED LIFE AND LITERATURES

The sacred life of Indian Christians is guided by several elements, chief of which is corporate worship. Here again, a variety of expressions abound. The Eastern Orthodox churches formed their liturgical practices in the Syrian tradition, with Syriac as their liturgical language. This was to be followed later by the use of Latin rites among some Syrian Christians and the use of the local language Malayalam. The Divine Liturgy (liturgy used during the celebration of the Eucharist) takes precedence in the life of Orthodox Christians in India.

The Roman Catholic churches initially adopted the Latin liturgical traditions and in their contacts with the Syrian Christians developed Syrian rites as well. However, Vatican II brought a significant change in the worship life of the Roman Catholic churches in India. These changes included the use of vernacular languages for liturgy, the employment of local musical traditions, and the adoption of Indian architectural patterns in the building of churches. There have been genuine attempts to present Christian worship through local cultural idiom.

Protestants brought the worship patterns of the varying Western Protestant denominations. These were adapted to the local settings through the incorporation of local languages, cultural practices, and music. However, there remained a domination of Western liturgical elements in Protestant worship. As a scholar of Indian Christianity remarked in 1969: "There is no doubt that to an outside observer the Church in India seems to be dominated by western attitudes and modes of thought" (Boyd 1979: 1–2). Over the centuries, the Protestants themselves have gone through a liturgical renewal and now adopt local religo-cultural practices for Christian worship. The formation of the Church of South India in 1947 led to a process of forming Christian worship in an ecumenical mode that is inclusive of the various Protestant traditions. *The Book of Common Worship*, published in 1963, is the outcome of such an attempt. The most recent attempt at a truly Indian liturgy is exemplified in the alternate version of Eucharist liturgy published in 1985. It "attempts to express an understanding of worship that is more Indian than our traditional Christian worship forms" and encourages people to conduct the service in as authentic an Indian style as possible. The liturgy is organized around five stages: entry (*praveśa*), awakening (*prabodha*), recalling and offering (*smaraṇa-samarpaṇa*), sharing in the body and blood of Christ (*darśana*), and blessing (*preṣaṇa*). The language of the liturgy is guided by concerns of both enculturation and the liberation of the oppressed. Another attempt at a truly ecumenical, Indian, and vernacular Christian expression is the common hymnbook for many Hindi-speaking congregations, *Ārādhănā ke Gīt* (Songs of Worship). Under production since 1967 and revised and updated many times since then, the hymnbook has been a joint effort of the Madhya Pradesh Christian Council and the Methodist Church in Southern Asia.

Apart from the Orthodox, Roman Catholic, and mainline Protestant churches, Pentecostal and nondenominational churches have had their own modes and methods of enculturation of Christian worship. For example, Pentecostal churches were among the first to exploit the emerging light music tradition of India (a mixture of Western and Indian musical traditions) for their worship and piety.

What is common to these Christian churches is the conscious and intentional attempt to develop and practice the worship of the Christian community in linguistic and cultural forms. The story of Christianity in India is a story of languages. Languages, and the cultures that house them, have played an important role in shaping religious identity in India (see, for instance, King 1994; Guha 2008; Orsini 2009), and, like other religious traditions in the country, Indian Christianity has been shaped by the languages in which it has been expressed and brought to life.

Christian literature in Hindi, one of India's official languages, typifies the desire of Indian Christians to be "Indian" and "Christian" in the context of a multireligious society, in which Christians are a minority and desire to contribute to national and social development. Hindi Christian literature tries to balance these positions and interests through a two-pronged strategy of differentiation and cross-over appeals (Peter Dass 2017: 95–96). On the one hand, Hindi-using Christians have sought to differentiate Christian ideas from those of their Hindu and Muslim neighbors. This strategy is most evident in Hindi Christian descriptions of the incarnation of the Word of God, a central claim of Christianity. Eschewing the option of using the Hindu idea of *avatār*s (Hinduism recognizes multiple *avatār*s or incarnations of Viṣṇu), Hindi Christian authors have proposed a Hindi neologism, *dehădhāran* (to "take a body"). The neologism has primarily served to mark the Christian idea of incarnation as different from that of *avatār* (on the problems with using *avatār* to translate incarnation, see, for instance, Dayal 2005). On the other hand, Christian literature in Hindi, including Hindi translations of the Bible, is also populated by polytradition words (words that function across multiple religious traditions). Hindi-language Christian poems reflect a comfort with *prabhu* and *parameśvar*, words commonly used within Hinduism (Arya 2003). Different versions of the Hindi-language Bible continue to use *mandir* (temple) and *pavitr* (holy), terms commonly used by Hindus to describe important aspects of their religious life. Further, Hindi-language hymns are replete with words like *īmān* (faith), *pāk* (pure), *darśan* (vision), *mandir* (temple), *bhakti/bhakt* (devotion/devotee), and *dharm* (religion or faith) that are commonly used in Indian Muslim and Hindu communities.

The sacred life of Indian Christians is also shaped by home-based religious practices. Indian Christians have adapted several of the Hindu rites of passage into their own religious life. These practices vary according to region and denominational affiliation. Christian weddings take on several local cultural practices that are Hindu in origin. Indigenous elements are more conspicuously present in worship settings outside the church building. The prayer meetings held in people's homes, lyrical or musical preaching performed during festive occasions, prayer services at homes related to rites of passage, such as puberty, marriages and funerals, and other such home-based worship services bear clear marks of indigenous elements and influence. In addition to Christmas and Easter, most Christian congregations celebrate church anniversary fesitvals that commemorate the building of the church in that place and harvest festivals in which people bring their farm products to offer to the church as a mark of their gratitude and thanksgiving to God. These are occasions for much more celebrative worship services. The form and nature of these worship services differ from region to region and according to earlier denominational links. Although there have been attempts, especially in theological seminaries, to celebrate the Hindu festivals, such as Dīvālī, Poṅgal, Onam, and others, most Christians tend to see these as beyond the appropriate boundaries of Christian life and witness.

There are several major community events that shape the sacred life of Indian Christians. The Mar Thoma Church has conducted an annual revival meeting since 1895, called Maramon Convention, in which thousands of Mar Thoma Christians and others gather for several days of preaching, prayer, and celebration. The Syrian Orthodox churches have their own celebrations and events. The celebration of the sainthood of Saint George is one such event (Dempsey 2001). The Roman Catholic churches have adapted the Hindu festival processions for their own festivals. The Hindu practice of pulling the temple chariot along the streets of the town on festive occasions has been adapted by Roman Catholic churches for festivals connected with local Roman Catholic shrines. Protestants have generally shied away from close similarities to Hindu festivals but rather have celebrated the church anniversaries, Christmas, and Easter with a few elements that have Hindu cultural roots, for example, the wearing of new clothes for Christmas.

One way to describe the sacred life of Indian Christians is through the categories of distinction and familiarity. In forming their sacred life, Indian Christians seek to be distinct from their Hindu and Muslim neighbors. Therefore, the use of Western or Eastern music, Byzantine and Latin church architecture, and other such distinct Christian practices function to highlight their difference from their non-Christian neighbors. At the same time, Indian Christians are keen to locate their sacred life squarely in the cultural and religious ethos of India, and therefore see themselves as indigenous and "Indian"—categories that are broadly conceived.

As far as sacred literature in concerned, the Bible occupied a central place in the religious life of Indian Christians since the arrival of Protestant missionaries from the West. The Orthodox traditions within India did not pay attention to the translation of the Bible into local languages. Therefore, the sacred text for the Orthodox is the liturgical practices rather than a written document such as the Bible. A Malayalam translation of the Bible was available to the Eastern Orthodox Christians only through the work of the Protestant missionaries in the nineteenth century. The Roman Catholic missions in India were slow to engage in the translation of the Bible into local languages, yet they produced other Christian literature in local languages right from the beginning of their mission. As early as 1616, Thomas Stephens, a Roman Catholic missionary who worked among the Konkani people, published a magnificent Marathi poem of 10,962 verses on Biblical history to take the place of the Hindu Purāṇas (Neill 1984: 241). Other Roman Catholic missionaries wrote extensively in local languages in both poetry and prose yet were hesitant to translate the Bible into local languages. Some even actively opposed the Protestant translations of the Bible. For example, Abbé J. A. Dubois (1977: 65–8) objected that the translations offered by the Protestant missionary societies were of a very low literary quality and that the Bible was not easily comprehensible or appealing to Hindus if it was simply translated and given to them.

The translation of the Bible into the local languages of India was a high priority in the activity of the Protestant missionaries. The first Protestant missionary, Bartholomew Ziegenbalg, translated the New Testament into Tamil within five years of his arrival in India. A major turnout of translations happened with the work of William Carey at Serampore. As Robin H.S. Boyd writes, "He [Carey] and his colleagues eventually set up at Serampore what might almost be called a Bible factory with different linguistic departments, and succeeded in translating the Bible, in whole or part, into more than thirty languages" (1979: 15–16).

The relationship between the Bible and the Hindu scriptures has been a matter of debate throughout the history of Christianity in India. The early Protestant missionaries while translating the Bible named it as the Veda or Vedāgama (a combination of Veda and Āgama, the two major scriptural corpus in Hinduism). Robert De Nobili had referred to it as the fifth Veda, relating the Bible to the legend that the fifth Veda of the Hindus was lost in antiquity. One of the more creative attempts at relating the Hindu scriptures with the Bible was made by P. Chenchiah, a twentieth-century Christian lay theologian, when he suggested that Indian Christians might accept the Hindu scriptures as their Old Testament instead of the Hebrew Bible. He argued that one could read the Hindu scriptures in light of Christ, in the same way that Jesus' early Jewish disciples read their own Hebrew scriptures (Boyd 1979: 158). Most Christians in India do not accept this view, though many would see the Hindu scriptures as a preparation for the arrival of the Bible in India.

Sacred literature other than the Bible abounds in the history of Christianity in India. Indian Christians have been prolific in the writing of hymns, epic poems, apologetic writings, and theological treatises, both in English and in vernacular languages. These writings were heavily influenced by Hindu ways of thinking, imaging, and articulating. Some of the well-known hymn writers are H. A. Krishna Pillai, Subba Rao, Vedanayagam Sastri, Narayan Vaman Tilak, and Brahmabandhav Upadhyaya. These poets reflected *bhakti* (devotion) sentiments similar to those found in Hindu *bhakti* literature. A significant body of Christian literature, theological and devotional, also exists in the English language. These were produced primarily in the late nineteenth and twentieth centuries. The list of such writers includes Swami Abhisiktananda, A. J. Appasamy, K. M. Banerjea, V. Chakkarai, P. Chenchiah, Raimundo Panikkar, Manilal C. Parekh, M. M. Thomas, and Brahmabandhav Upadhyaya. Similarly, a substantial body of religious, theological, and devotional literature also exists in the Hindi language. Such literature can be traced to the late nineteenth century (an early Hindi-language conversion account comes from 1877) and has grown considerably since the founding in 1954 of the Hindi Theological Literature Committee. Some of the important Hindi-language Christian authors include John Henry Anand, Din Dayal, Benjamin Khan, Sam Bhajan, Pushpa Dongre, Richard Howell, Elizabeth James, Franklin C. Jonathan, Moti Lall, Shivraj K. Mahendra, Komal Masih, Dharamvir Singh, and Winifred Irene Paul. While such treatises are available, the sacred life of Indian Christians, especially in rural settings, is shaped primarily by church worship and home-based religious practices.

• INSTITUTIONS AND PRACTICES

Christianity came to India with its already developed institutional character. The Syrian Orthodox Church inherited the ecclesial structure of the Eastern churches with its patriarch in Syria. The Roman Catholic Church carried with it the Roman and papal structures into Indian church life. Although there were conflicts between the Syrian Christians and Roman Catholics over understandings of ecclesial and institutional governance, Roman Catholics maintained their linkage with the Roman institutional structure. The Protestants, in their denominational multiplicity, also imposed their modes of institutional structure and governance on their own denominational churches in India. While some of the major Protestant churches, such as the Church of South India, the Church of North India, the Methodist Church in India, and most Indian Lutheran churches, operate with the tradition of having bishops as the presiding officers of their churches, others function with the autonomy of congregations over issues of governance. The institutional character of the Christian churches in India has been a contrast and a challenge to the ordering of Hindu religious life, which is independent of clearly defined institutional structure.

The life of the Christian churches in India is also guided by another set of institutions related to the ecclesial structure. These are schools, colleges, hospitals, and social service agencies organized and maintained by Christian churches. The early part of nineteenth century saw the founding of several colleges throughout India due to the work of missionaries, chief of which were Alexander Duff in Calcutta, John Wilson in Bombay whose work led to the establishment of Wilson College, John Anderson in Madras who founded the Madras Christian College, and Stephen Hyslop in Nagpur. While these colleges were admitting only male students, there were separate colleges founded for women as well, notable among them being Women's Christian College in Madras, Isabella Thoburn College in Lucknow, and Lady Doak College in Madurai. Roman Catholic missions were also involved in the founding of several colleges and schools throughout India. Notable among them are Loyola College in Madras, St. Xavier's College in Bombay, and St. Xavier's College in Calcutta. It should be noted that hundreds of elementary, middle, and high schools were founded throughout India by the Christian churches in India. There were varying perceptions about the relationship between these educational institutions and the evangelistic task of the churches. Some missionaries like Alexander Duff saw the educational project as a potential way to convert Hindus to the Christian faith, although in reality Hindus who were educated in Christian schools and colleges did not necessarily abandon the Hindu religion to turn to the Christian faith (Firth 1976: 182–85). Others saw the educational mission simply as a duty of love and care. Even today, the Christian communities in India are heavily invested in this form of educational service. In addition, there is an increasing interest in offering nonformal education to the poor in hopes of raising their sociopolitical consciousness to initiate change and liberation.

Organized medical missions are a phenomenon of the nineteenth- and twentieth-century missionary activity in India. The American Board of Commissioners for Foreign Missions sent John Scudder, the first of many medical missionaries, to Madras in 1836 (Firth 1976: 205). More medical missionaries followed, and hospitals and medical and nursing schools began to appear throughout India. Some of the well-known schools are the Christian Medical College in Vellore and the North India School of Medicine for Christian Women in

Ludhiana, Punjab. The Christian Medical Association of India is currently an organization that functions as a clearinghouse for all Christian medical institutions and medical personnel.

One of the unique features of Indian Christianity is the establishment of Ashram (Sanskrit *āśrama*), patterned after the Hindu ascetic and monastic traditions. Ashrams were places where the residents practiced regular and intense spiritual discipline, followed a simple lifestyle, and adopted Hindu cultural and religious patterns in worship, prayer, and architecture. The twentieth century saw the emergence of several ashrams, both Protestant and Roman Catholic. Two doctors in South India, Savarirayan Jesudason and Ernest Forrester-Paton, founded the Christukula Ashram in Tamil Nadu in 1921. In the same year, Anglican missionary J.C. Winslow established an ashram at Pune that was later renamed as Christa Prema Seva Sangh in 1934 (Neill 1970: 144). There were other ashrams associated with the work of people such as Stanley Jones, an American Methodist missionary, and Bishop Peckenham Walsh of the Anglican Church in India. The Roman Catholics had their own share of ashrams as well. Notable among Roman Catholic ashrams is the Saccidananda Ashram, near Trichy in Tamil Nadu, established by the work of Jules Monchanin in 1950. Bede Griffiths succeeded him. Bold experiments in Hindu-Christian spirituality were attempted and continue to be maintained even today.

• ETHICS AND HUMAN RELATIONS

Indian Christians have needed to discover and negotiate Christian ethical values and understandings of human relations in a context where the ethos and communal values of many religious traditions mingle. Christian life in India has been, for instance, influenced by Hindu ethics and practices, which are dominated by concepts like *dharma*, meaning justice, order, duty, and religion. *Dharma* entails two aspects, namely, *varṇa-dharma* and *āśrama-dharma*. The former is the recognition of one's duty in light of one's position in the caste hierarchy claimed by Brāhmaṇas, and the latter is the discovery of one's duty in relation to one's stage of life. Indian Christians had to negotiate their view of ethics and human relations in interactions with this ethical framework. The Orthodox churches in India adopted themselves the caste structure of Hindu society to an extent.

> Syrian Christians have been for centuries encapsulated within caste society, regarded by Hindus as a caste, occupying a recognized (and high) place within the caste hierarchy . . . and seems to have been quite content to accept and operate the caste system without any egalitarian protest.
>
> (Forrester 1980: 14)

The joining of low-caste groups to the Syrian Church in the nineteenth century jolted this positioning of Syrian Christians within the caste hierarchy. Syrian Christians have since encountered great difficulty in accepting the low-caste Christians as their equals within the church (Forrester 1980: 110–14).

The Roman Catholic Church has its own share in the problem of the practice of caste within the church. A Roman Catholic missionary success was the conversion of fisher-folk on the southern tip of India. The fisher-folk belonged on the lower rungs of the caste ladder, and thus the Roman Catholic Church was a church of the low caste. Missionaries like Robert De Nobili, on the other hand, attempted to win converts from the upper caste by the adoption of Hindu rituals and practices. He believed that one need not renounce caste by becoming a Christian (Forrester 1980: 15). In the midst of all these missionary experiments, the Roman Catholic tradition in India regarded caste as a civil institution and adopted a policy of accommodation. Though the caste system is verbally condemned as contrary to Christian faith, there is an accommodation of it in the organization of the church and in the individual lives of Roman Catholics. Dalit Christians (more on this below) have pointed to Robert de Nobili's toleration of caste in the (Roman Catholic) church on the grounds that (a) caste was primarily a social institution rather than a religious one and (b) the church could gradually remove the caste mindset from society (Fernando and Gispert-Sauch 2004: 187).

Protestant missions did not have a unified view of the role of caste distinctions within the Christian community. For example, the Lutherans were more accommodative than Anglican missionaries were. One success in the Protestant missionary battle against caste is the practice of Eucharistic participation without caste considerations. Ecclesial governance, family relations, and individual Christian behavior are still governed by caste considerations in most Protestant churches. Since many Christians practice endogamy, caste distinctions continue to be perpetuated within the churches. Yet, the changing demographics of churches in India since the early twentieth century have also diminished the toleration of caste within Christian communities in contemporary India. Over the past hundred years, Indian Christian communities have drawn to their fellowship people from a variety of social, religious, and economic backgrounds, most of whom have come from lower castes and discriminated groups (Sahu 1994: 9). The demographics of Indian Christianity have led to greater indigenization, the use of vernaculars, investment in national development, and commitment to social justice among Indian Christian communities.

• MODERN EXPRESSIONS

Five distinct movements/developments are shaping modern expressions of Christianity in India. The first is the movement called inculturation. It attempts to express the Christian faith in and through local cultural and religious idioms and practices. This has been expressed in the use of vernaculars, polytraditional concepts, and the ashrams founded by various Christian leaders and communities. In addition, enculturation is at work in the current intentional liturgical renewal that aims to express Christian worship practices through Indian cultural forms. The Roman Catholic churches in India, for instance, have been on the forefront of this renewal since Vatican II. The National Biblical Catechetical and Liturgical Centre in Bangalore exemplifies such bold attempts.

A renewed interest in Indian classical, folk, and popular music is present in most churches. Since Indian Independence in 1947, Christian communities have been consciously engaging in removing the appearance of "foreignness" in Indian Christianity and creating an Indian Christian existence that is shaped and influenced primarily by Indian cultural and religious ethos.

Due to the processes of globalization, a "glocalized" culture is emerging in India, in which the borderline between Indian and others is blurred. Therefore, churches are adapting themselves to that kind of hybrid culture as well. For example, what is called "Praise-Worship" in the West takes on an Indian form and is gaining popularity in Protestant, Roman Catholic, and Charismatic churches in India.

The second is the Christian Dalit movement. It has grown over the last thirty years. As noted earlier, the majority of Christians belong to the lowest castes in the caste system and are at the lower levels of economic, social, and educational development. Among them, a significantly large proportion of persons belong to the so-called "untouchables," who were named by Mohandas K. Gandhi as *harijan*, meaning "people of God." In the Constitution of India, they are referred to as "Scheduled Castes" for the purposes of affirmative action. In recent times, the scheduled castes have claimed the name Dalit for themselves. The word "Dalit" means "oppressed" or "crushed." Dalit Christians have faced two major challenges.

First, despite converting to Christianity, their status within the Christian churches had not changed significantly. Ecclesial power remained largely in the hands of non-Dalits among Christians. Today, Dalit Christians have made noticeable progress in the sharing of power within the churches' hierarchies. For example, many of the current bishops of the Church of South India belong to the Dalit community. Moreover, theological thinking and ecclesial practice within churches had been historically controlled and shaped by the ethos of Christians other than Dalits. Therefore, a concerted effort has been afoot to develop, and has borne fruits within churches in the development of, Dalit theologies and ecclesial practices. In their theological task, Dalit Christians have discovered an agenda that "includes interacting theologically with the little theological traditions of Dalit Christians, with other theological traditions within the Indian Church, and with Dalits who do not share their Christian convictions" (Webster 1992: 218). Some of the leading figures in the development of Dalit theology are Sathianathan Clarke, V. Devasahayam, James Massey, Arvind Nirmal, and M.E. Prabhakar.

The second challenge for Dalit Christians is the claiming of the compensatory preference available to Dalits within the Constitution of India. The Constitution, while affirming the equality of all citizens before law irrespective of caste, class, race, religion, or place of birth, offers to the states the right to make special provisions for the upliftment of scheduled castes and scheduled tribes. Dalits who became Christian were not included in this provision, on the grounds that Dalits no longer belonged to the caste system once they accepted Christianity as their religion. Currently, the Dalit Christians, with the support of other Christians, are asking the government, via litigation currently under consideration at the

Supreme Court of India, to redress this particular disparity between theory (the claim that conversion to Christianity stops caste-based discrimination) and practice (the reality that Dalit Christians continue to face caste-based discrimination postconversion, in addition to the generational effects of systemic discrimination suffered by Dalits irrespective of their religious affiliations).

In meeting these two challenges, Dalits have made considerable progress. As John C.B. Webster notes,

> the most significant development during this period of Dalit Christian history has not been the emergence of a new Dalit Christian elite. . . . Instead this period has witnessed the emergence of Dalit Christians from the obscurity in both Church and society. . . . Even without political reservations, Dalit Christians have become increasingly active both in the wider Dalit movement and in their own particular movement for equal justice. In this process some of the barriers dividing Christians from other Dalits have been removed and there are signs of the two coming closer together in a shared struggle for equality.
>
> (1992: 176–77)

The third movement within modern Indian Christianity is the rise of indigenous churches in India. Of course, the Orthodox churches are indigenous in that they were dependent right from the beginning on Indian financial resources. The Mar Thoma Church, too, is truly indigenous without any links to traditions outside of India. Protestant churches, however, depended heavily on Western Christian traditions and support. So the founding of indigenous churches began as early as the nineteenth century among Protestants. "One remarkable Hindu believer in Christ at Madras was O. Kandaswamy Chetti, founder of the Fellowship of the Followers of Jesus, who openly confessed his faith in Christ as the only Saviour but declined baptism" (Hedlund 1999: 31). Arumainayagam Sattampillai of south Tamil Nadu founded the Indian Church of the Only Savior (popularly known as the Hindu-Christian community) in 1857 in protest against Western missionary domination (Thangaraj 1971). Roger E. Hedlund (1999: 32) mentions a few others, such as the Indian Pentecostal Church of God, founded by K.E. Abraham around 1930. Some of the contemporary examples of indigenous churches include the Apostolic Christian Assembly, founded by Pastor G. Sundaram, the movement around K. Subba Rao in Andhra Pradesh, the New Life Fellowship in Bombay, Agape Fellowship churches in the state of Punjab, and the Isupanthi movement in North Gujarat (Hedlund 1999: 33–36).

The fourth development is the mushrooming of indigenous missionary organizations. The churches in India have always been committed to the spread of Christianity in India, and individuals and churches have shown great interest in evangelization. Missionary organizations such as the ones that were created in the Western Protestant world during the eighteenth and nineteenth centuries had inspired Indian Christians to come up with their own organizations. In 1903, Bishop Azariah started the Indian Missionary Society of Tinnevelly, which sent its missionaries to work among the tribal people in Andhra Pradesh. Soon after, the National Missionary Society was started in 1905. These were followed by many such organizations in the 1970s, such as the Friends Missionary Prayer Band. Most of these work among Dalits and tribal folks in North India (see Hedlund 2016: 112–14). What is new about the situation today is a "democratization" of such societies in a way that individuals and congregations have started their own "Ministries," which send and support missionaries in various parts of India, especially to the tribal folks in North India.

It is interesting to note that such an increase in organized missionary efforts has paralleled the rising Hindu nationalist movement, which aims at controlling and curtailing religious conversion. There have been clashes and incidents of violence in several parts of India due to this (for a recent account of anti-Christian violence, see Bauman 2015). Here and there, one can see signs in Hindu-dominated villages prohibiting Christian evangelistic visits to their villages.

The fifth development in India Christianity is the explosion of all forms of media—print, Internet, television, and so on. We have already noted the multilanguage body of Christian religious literature in India. Christian Literature Society, Indian Society for Promoting Christian Knowledge (ISPCK), Hindi Theological Literature Committee, Christian World Imprints, and other such publishers continue to bring out religious and theological writings. Churches have always published journals and devotional literature—what is new is the sheer explosion of such activity. Christian homes are flooded with magazines, books, songs, movies, and digital media produced by not only mainline churches, but also by independent preachers, TV evangelists, and others. Churches and individuals have put social media platforms to good use for Christian nurture and for expressions of fellowship.

Most significantly, Christians in India have exploited cable and satellite TV to the fullest extent. Not only are there Christian programs broadcast on local and cable TV channels, but there are Christian channels set up to air 24 hours of the day, 7 days a week. These are in addition to the U.S. TV evangelists who beam their programs to India. Some of the homegrown Protestant-based channels are Angel TV, Bhakti TV, Blessing TV, Jesus the King TV, and so on. The Roman Catholics and Eastern Orthodox have their own TV channels as well, for example, the Roman Catholic channel called Madha TV in Tamil Nadu. These channels aim to both nurture and teach Christians, as well as to share Christian good news to people of other faiths and invite them to join the Christian church. Of course, Christians are not unique in this because of the presence of several Hindu and Muslim channels on TV as well.

• TRANSMISSION OF THE TRADITION OUTSIDE OF INDIA

Indian Christians who immigrated to other nations, especially to the Arabian Peninsula, Europe, and North America, have established Indian Christian congregations in those places. Since Indian Christians speak a wide variety of languages, the diaspora communities have gathered as language-based Christian congregations outside India. Few studies have yet been undertaken to describe and understand the nature of Indian Christianity within the diaspora communities. A major work on this subject is *Christian Pluralism in the United States: The Indian Immigrant Experience* (1996) by Raymond Brady Williams. There are Indian Christian congregations in most of the major cities in the United States, such as Atlanta, Boston, Houston, and New York. These cities have several Indian Christian congregations, and each is organized around either a common language or a common ecclesial tradition. For example,

> An India Catholic Association of America was informally organized in 1979 and then incorporated in 1980. The single organization served Indians of all three rites [Syro-Malabar, Syro-Malankara, and Latin] until 1982, when the Malankara Catholic Church was founded and the other groups began to meet separately.
>
> (Williams 1996: 144)

All the three traditions have established parishes throughout the United States. Protestants from India have their own churches according to their particular ecclesial traditions. The Church of South India bishops authorized extraterritorial parishes in 1975 and have at times supported those parishes with ministerial personnel. Other church groups from India, such as Brethren, Pentecostals, and others, have established their own parishes in the United States. Similar patterns of Indian Christian parishes are occurring in Britain, Canada, and several of the Arab nations, and Eastern Orthodox Christians from India are much more organized in the United States than are Roman Catholics and Protestants from India. In 1979, the Malankara Orthodox Diocese of North America and Europe was established. In 1988, the Mar Thoma Diocese of North America was established. Other Orthodox churches in India have organized missions and dioceses for their members who have immigrated to other countries in the West.

One of the problems that immigrant Indian Christians face outside of India is the practice of their peculiarly Indian Christian faith in a culture other than that which has sustained their own Christian existence. Therefore, Indian Christians face the double challenge of keeping their Christian faith and their Indian cultural ethos together in a foreign land. New immigrants play an important role in maintaining the Indian and Christian sides together in the life of Indian Christians abroad.

• RELATIONS WITH OTHER RELIGIONS

The relations between Indian Christianity and other religious traditions within India take different forms depending on the denomination, region, and caste. As mentioned earlier, the Orthodox traditions in India that accommodated themselves into the prevailing Hindu social ethos for the most part have not experienced any major conflict with the religious communities around. Such friendly relations were extended not only to Hindus and Muslims, but also to a small Jewish community in the state of Kerala. During the precolonial period, the relation between Syrian Christians and Hindus is one of mutual appreciation and help. For example, "At least one Hindu temple regularly lent out its temple elephants to Syrian worshippers for use in their festival processions" (Bayly 1989: 253).

The Roman Catholics and Protestants have maintained overall mutual respect and friendship with people of other religions over the last five centuries. In the field of social reforms and changes, Hindus and Christians have worked together. For example, the work of Hindu reformers like Ram Mohun Roy and Mohandas K. Gandhi has drawn on Christians resources and support. Hindus and Muslims have generally been appreciative of the humanitarian service of Christians throughout India.

After Independence, the provisions of the Constitution of India have guided the relation between Christianity and other religions. The followers of every religion in India are guaranteed the right to practice, profess, and propagate their religion. It is the Indian Christians who have made the most use of the provision given in the Constitution to engage in evangelistic activity. Such an engagement is looked upon with suspicion by a minority of Hindus. It is often represented as Christians' attempt to "proselytize" through fraudulent and coercive means. Recent years have seen a few cases of attacks on individual Christians, their communities, and their churches, especially in the northern part of India. Certain states within the nation have attempted to pass regulations and laws to control the proselytizing activity of Christians. "Freedom of Religion" bills have been passed in several states; the Supreme Court of India has annulled some of them, but the question of "conversion" continues to be a bone of contention in India.

There are also intentional attempts by Indian Christians to promote dialogue between Christianity and other religions in India. The Christian ashrams often function as places of dialogue at the level of mystical religious experience. The Church of South India and the Church of North India have their own programs of dialogue. The Roman Catholic churches in India have promoted friendly and dialogical relations with Hindus through their varied organizations and institutions. The Roman Catholic and Protestant seminaries in India have been pioneers in the promotion of dialogical relations between Christians and others. For example, the Tamilnadu Theological Seminary has an ongoing program of dialogue since 1972. The future of Indian Christians' relationship with Hindus and Muslims in India rests upon how the people of India succeed in maintaining freedom of religion and the possibilities for dialogue and mutual enrichment.

• THE TRADITION IN THE STUDY OF RELIGIONS

Indian Christianity has been the subject of study almost exclusively among church historians and missiologists for a long time in the West. Although Indian Christianity has contributed greatly to the study of religions through the work of several missionary scholars, historians of religion have not paid much attention to the phenomenon of Indian Christianity. For example, Bartholomäus Ziegenbalg, the first Protestant missionary to India, studied the Hindu tradition with care and published an important work titled *The Genealogy of the South Indian Gods*. Other missionary scholars engaged in the translation of Hindu scriptures, and other Indian literature enabled

Western scholars of religion to understand religious traditions of India. G.U. Pope's translation of *Tiruvācakam* (Sacred Utterance), a Tamil Śaiva devotional literature, illustrates this as well.

European missionaries began the tradition of studying Indian Christianity as a separate religious phenomenon in India. C. G. Diehl's *Church and Shrine: Intermingling Patterns of Culture in the Life of Some Christian Groups in South India* (1965), the research on village Christians in Andhra Pradesh conducted by P. Y. Luke and John B. Carman titled *Village Christians and Hindu Culture: Study of a Rural Church in Andhra Pradesh, South India* (1968), and Bror Tiliander's *Christian and Hindu Terminology: A Study in Their Mutual Relations with Special Reference to the Tamil Area* (1974) are supreme examples of such work by missionaries.

In recent times, there is a growing interest among scholars of religion in engaging Indian Christianity as a religious phenomenon in its own right and not just an extension of the Western missionary enterprise. More and more scholars in the West, in India, and elsewhere are turning their attention to Indian Christianity. In the last twenty years, several books have been published in English studying Christianity in India from historical, ethnographic, and sociological angles. These works include, among others, Susan Bayly's *Saints, Goddesses, and Kings: Muslims and Christians in South Indian Society, 1700–1900* (1989); Bent Smidt Hansen's *Dependency and Identity: Problems of Cultural Encounter as a Consequence of the Danish Mission in South India Between the Two World Wars* (1998); Gauri Viswanathan's *Outside the Fold: Conversion, Modernity, and Belief* (1998); Sathianathan Clarke's *Dalits and Christianity: Subaltern Religion and Liberation Theology in India* (1998); Dennis Hudson's *Protestant Origins in India: Tamil Evangelical Christians in India, 1706–1835* (2000); Corinne G. Dempsey's *Kerala Christian Sainthood: Collisions of Culture and Worldview in South India* (2001); Felix Wilfred's *On The Banks of Ganges: Doing Contextual Theology* (2002); Selva J. Raj and Corinne C. Dempsey (eds.), *Popular Christianity in India: Riting Between the Lines* (2002); Robert Eric Frykenberg's *Christianity in India: From Beginnings to the Present* (2008); David Mosse's *The Saint in the Banyan Tree: Christianity and Caste Society in India* (2012); and Chad M. Bauman and Richard Fox Young (eds.), *Constructing Indian Christianities: Culture, Conversion and Caste* (2014).

• DISCUSSION QUESTIONS

1. What are some of the ways in which Indian Christians have incorporated practices from other religious traditions into their own distinctively Christian forms of religious life?
2. What are the major institutional or denominational forms of Christianity that have found a home in India? There are several. Were any of them previously unknown to you, or did any of them become more interesting to you after reading this chapter?

3. Why is it appropriate to title this chapter "Indian Christian Traditions" rather than "Indian Christian Tradition"? There may be a deep unity, but is there also evident diversity among Indian Christians? If so, what are the factors that account for it?

• BIBLIOGRAPHY

Ārādhănā ke Gīt. 2009 [1975]. *Ārādhănā ke Gīt* [Songs of Worship]. Music Edition. Lucknow: Lucknow Publishing House (for Madhya Pradesh Christian Council and Methodist Church of India).

Arya, Sarojini V. 2003. *Kavitā meṃ Śubh Saṃdeś* [Good News in Poetry]. Delhi: Indian Society for Promoting Christian Knowledge.

Bauman, Chad M. 2015. *Pentecostals, Proselytization, and Anti-Christian Violence in Contemporary India*. New York: Oxford University Press.

Bauman, Chad M. and Richard Fox Young, eds. 2014. *Constructing Indian Christianities: Culture, Conversion and Caste*. New Delhi: Routledge.

Bayly, Susan. 1989. *Saints, Goddesses, and Kings: Muslims and Christians in South India, 1700–1900*. Cambridge: Cambridge University Press.

Boyd, Robin H. S. 1979 [1969]. *An Introduction to Indian Christian Theology*. Madras: The Christian Literature Society.

Chadwick, Henry. 1993 [1967]. *The Early Church: The Story of Emergent Christianity From the Apostolic Age to the Dividing of the Ways Between the Greek East and the Latin West*. New York: Penguin Books.

Clarke, Sathianathan. 1998. *Dalits and Christianity: Subaltern Religion and Liberation Theology in India*. New Delhi: Oxford University Press.

Cross, F. L. and E. A. Livingstone, eds. 2005 [1957]. *The Oxford Dictionary of the Christian Church*. New York: Oxford University Press.

Dayal, Din. 2005. *Masīhī Dharmvigyān kā Paricay* [An Introduction to Christian Theology]. Jabalpur: Hindi Theological Literature Committee.

Dempsey, Corinne G. 2001. *Kerala Christian Sainthood: Collisions of Culture and Worldview in South India*. Oxford: Oxford University Press.

Devasahayam, V., ed. 1997. *Frontiers of Dalit Theology*. Madras: Indian Society for Promoting Christian Knowledge.

Diehl, Carl Gustav. 1965. *Church and Shrine: Intermingling Patterns of Culture in the Life of Some Christian Groups in South India*. Uppsala: Hakan Ohlssons Boktryckeri.

Dubois, Abbé J. A. 1977. *Letters on the State of Christianity in India in Which the Conversion of the Hindoos Is Considered as Impracticable to Which is Added a Vindication of the Hindoos Male and Female in Answer to a Severe Attach Made Upon Both by the Reverend* (ed. Sharda Paul). New Delhi: Associated Publishing Press.

Fernando, Leonard and G. Gispert-Sauch. 2004. *Christianity in India: Two Thousand Years of Faith*. New Delhi: Penguin Viking.

Firth, Cyril Bruce. 1976 [1961]. *An Introduction to Indian Church History*. Madras: The Christian Literature Society.

Fisher, Mary Pat. 2014 [1990]. *Living Religions*. Ninth Edition. Boston: Pearson.

Flood, Gavin. 1996. *An Introduction to Hinduism*. Cambridge: Cambridge University Press.

Forrester, Duncan B. 1977. "The Depressed Classes and Conversion to Christianity." *In* G. A. Oddie, ed., *Religion in South Asia: Religious Conversion and Revival Movements in South Asia in Medieval and Modern Time*, 35–66. New Delhi: Manohar.

Forrester, Duncan B. 1980. *Caste and Christianity: Attitudes and Policies on Caste of Anglo-Saxon Protestant Missions in India*. London: Curzon Press.

Frykenberg, Robert Eric. 2008. *Christianity in India: From Beginnings to the Present*. New York: Oxford University Press.

Grafe, Hugald. 1990. *The History of Christianity in Tamilnadu from 1800 to 1975*. Bangalore: Church History Association of India.

Guha, Ramachandra. 2008 [2007]. *India After Gandhi: The History of the World's Largest Democracy*. New York: Harper Perennial.

Hansen, Bent Smidt. 1998. *Dependency and Identity: Problems of Cultural Encounter as a Consequence of the Danish Mission in South India Between the Two World Wars*. St Hyacinthe: World Heritage Press.

Hedlund, Roger E. 1999. "Indian Instituted Churches: Indigenous Christianity Indian Style." *Mission Studies* 16, 1: 26–42.

Hedlund, Roger E. 2016. *Indian Christianity: An Alternate Reading*. New Delhi: Christian World Imprints.

Horsley, Richard A. 2014. "Jesus Movements and the Renewal of Israel." *In* Denis R. Janz, ed., *A People's History of Christianity: One Volume Student Edition*, 11–40. Minneapolis: Fortress Press.

Hudson, D. Dennis. 2000. *Protestant Origins in India: Tamil Evangelical Christians in India, 1706–1835*. Richmond: Curzon.

King, Christopher R. 1994. *One Language, Two Scripts: The Hindi Movement in Nineteenth Century North India*. New Delhi: Oxford University Press.

Lakoff, George. 1987. *Women, Fire, and Dangerous Things: What Categories Reveal About the Mind*. Chicago: Univeristy of Chicago Press.

Luke, P. K. and John B. Carman. 1968. *Village Christians and Hindu Culture: Study of a Rural Church in Andhra Pradesh, South India.* London: Lutterworth.

Mosse, David. 2012. *The Saint in the Banyan Tree: Christianity and Caste Society in India.* Berkeley: University of California Press.

Mundadan, A. Mathias. 1989 [1984]. *History of Christianity in India.* Volume 1: *From the Beginning up to the Middle of the Sixteenth Century (up to 1542).* Bangalore: Church History Association of India.

Narayanan, M. G. S. 1972. *Cultural Symbiosis in Kerala.* Trivandrum: Kerala Historical Society.

Neill, Stephen. 1970. *The Story of the Christian Church in India and Pakistan.* Grand Rapids: William B. Eerdmans Publishing.

Neill, Stephen. 1984. *A History of Christianity in India: The Beginning to AD 1707.* Cambridge: Cambridge University Press.

Neill, Stephen. 1985. *A History of Christianity in India, 1707–1858.* Cambridge: Cambridge University Press.

Omvedt, Gail. 1994. *Dalits and the Democratic Revolution: Dr. Ambedkar and the Dalit Movement in Colonial India.* New Delhi: Sage Publications.

Orsini, Francesca. 2009 [2002]. *The Hindi Public Sphere, 1920–1940: Language and Literature in the Age of Nationalism.* New Delhi: Oxford University Press.

Peter Dass, Rakesh. 2017. "Translating With Care: An Essay on Hindi Protestant Christian Writings." *International Journal of Hindu Studies* 21, 1: 83–98.

Raj, Selva J. and Corinne C. Dempsey. 2002. *Popular Christianity in India: Riting Between the Lines.* Albany: State University of New York Press.

Sahu, Dhirendra Kumar. 1994. *The Church of North India: A Historical and Systematic Theological Inquiry Into an Ecumenical Ecclesiology.* Frankfurt: Peter Lang.

Song, C. S. 1999. *The Believing Heart: An Invitation to Story Theology.* Minneapolis: Fortress Press.

Thangaraj, M. Thomas. 1971. "The History and Teachings of the Hindu Christian Community Commonly Called Nattu Sabai in Tirunelveli." *Indian Church History Review* 5, 1: 43–68.

Thekkedath, Joseph. 1982. *History of Christianity in India: From the Middle of the Sixteenth to the End of the Seventeenth Century (1542–1700).* Bangalore: Theological Publication in India.

Tiliander, Bror. 1974. *Christian and Hindu Terminology: A Study in Their Mutual Relations with Special Reference to the Tamil Area.* Uppsala: Almqvist & Wiksell.

Viswanathan, Gauri. 1998. *Outside the Fold: Conversion, Modernity, and Belief.* Princeton: Princeton University Press.

Webster, John C. B. 1992. *A History of the Dalit Christians in India.* San Francisco: Mellen Research University Press.

Wilfred, Felix. 2002. *On The Banks of Ganges: Doing Contextual Theology.* Delhi: Indian Society for Promoting Christian Knowledge.

Williams, Raymond Brady. 1996. *Christian Pluralism in the United States: The Indian Experience.* Cambridge: Cambridge University Press.

World Christian Encyclopedia: A Comparative Survey of Churches and Religions in the Modern World (eds. David B. Barrett, George T. Kurian, and Todd M. Johnson). 2001 [1983]. Volume 1 of 2: *The World by Countries: Religionists, Churches, Ministries: India*, 359–71. Oxford: Oxford University Press.

FIGURE 8.1 Training in Qur'ān recitation at a *madrasa* in northern India.

Image courtesy of Peter Gottschalk.

8

Indian Muslim Traditions

PETER GOTTSCHALK

THE TRADITIONS DEFINED

Many Muslims speak of "Islam" as a singular phenomenon: a religion, a community, a way of life. For some, this singularity represents a central defining feature of Islam. At times, Muslims appear to describe their religion as an entity, declaring what it "says," "teaches," or "requires." Yet, when we listen to how they describe that phenomenon, we hear divergent portraits of the nature and qualities of "Islam." From the perspective of the empirical study of religion, we need to listen carefully to these different views and simultaneously recognize the importance of singularity for many Muslims and acknowledge the differences among their understandings of it. While not discounting the significance of Islam as a lived reality for Muslims, this chapter will not use the term in its descriptions, in order to avoid the impression that Islamic traditions can be described as a single phenomenon or that they act with their own agency.

Instead, the chapter will focus on Muslims and their communities and how they attempt to live in relation with what they describe as their religion. Hence, when mention of Islam appears in the following pages, it will only signify a particular person's or group's view. Nevertheless, despite the astounding diversity among the myriad Muslims in India and more than one billion Muslims in the world, they all lay claim to a common name for an identity (Muslim) and a way of life (Islam). Hence, the term "Islamic" will be used to describe those traditions, practices, and beliefs that Muslims have associated with what they consider to be Islam.

The religious traditions associated with ideas of Islam are unusual in that they had a term for themselves from the very beginning of their historical origins. In the Qur'ān, the most revered source of understanding for most Muslims about Islam, it is written, "The religion with Allāh is Islam" (3.19).[1] "Islam" means literally "submission" (the word also has a connection—albeit, less direct—to the Arabic for "peace"). The Qur'ān mentions this term repeatedly and uses it in juxtaposition with other religions. Not only does the Qur'ān name this religion but also those who adhere to it. "O Lord!," Qur'ān 2.128 exhorts, "make us Muslims, bowing to Thy (Will)" (Ali 1993). Muslims, then, are those who submit themselves to God. This submission is demonstrated through the utterance of the *shahāda*, "There is no god but God" (*lā ilāha illā'llāh*) and "Muḥammad is the Messenger of God" (*Muḥammadun rasūlu'llāh*). Beyond this, Muslims differ in their understanding of what is necessary to live in submission.

Although many Muslims might disagree, it would be misleading to focus entirely on a fourteen hundred-year-old Arabic text—a focus that would emphasize uniformity and conformity rather than diversity and multiplicity—for an understanding of traditions vibrant among one hundred and forty million Indian Muslims today. Nevertheless, and in spite of the myriad opinions of what constitutes Islam and what defines a Muslim, the overwhelming majority of them will refer to the Qur'ān as an unassailable authority in their answers. Since the first Muslim community, this text has featured prominently in a large variety of Muslim self-perceptions. Not only did Muslims define themselves as such and name their religion as Islam from their earliest days as a community, but the Qur'ān also exhibited what appears as a "self-understanding" of its own role. In the beginning of the book's second chapter, it is written, "This is the Book which cannot be doubted and is a guidance to the God-fearing" (2.2). Most Muslims understand that this book has no rival because it is God's words to humanity as directly revealed to the Prophet Muḥammad and as perfectly preserved by the Muslim community (*umma*).

"Islam" and "Muslim" represent categories of religion and human community, respectively. As such, they are implicitly defined in relation to other religions and human communities. The categories found in the Qur'ān reflect the seventh-century social environment in which the text took form. These include "people of the Book," "believers," and "unbelievers." Before engaging these categories, however, we must clearly distinguish between the terms "Islam" and "Muslim" because, although they are closely associated, they are not interchangeable. "Islam" refers to a specific *dīn* ("way of life") among the many that humans practice. "Muslim" denotes those who identify themselves in some way with this specific *dīn*. In English-language sources, "Islamic" and "Muslim" connote somewhat different meanings. This chapter will use "Islamic" to denote objects and phenomena directly associated with the *dīn* of Islam while "Muslim" will describe any cultural connection to those who identify themselves as such.

It is critical for readers to remember that it is unlikely that religion motivates everything Muslims do, say, or believe. While some Muslims may certainly consider this of themselves, an inherent problem in the study of religion emerges when we confuse those who happen to be religious in *parts* of their lives with those who act religiously in *all parts* of their lives. The same could be said for other groups as well: a study of football fans would err to assume they think of their team all the time, although this may be true for some of them.

Returning to the Qur'ān, the "people of the Book" (*ahl al-kitāb*) are mentioned in the verse (*āya*) following the first Qur'ānic citation above: "Those who were given the Book did not disagree among themselves, except after certain knowledge came to them, out of envy among themselves" (3.19). Although Muslims understand that the Qur'ān has no rival because of the perfection of its preservation, it had predecessors. Most Muslims believe that three revelations in book form preceded the revelation of the Qur'ān: the Psalms, the Torah, and the Gospel. Because Jews and Christians are communities fashioned around these texts—which Muslims consider to have been revealed as the Qur'ān was—Muslims include them among the "people of the Book."[2] However, Jews and Christians differ from Muslims because they failed to maintain their God-entrusted texts and allowed corruptions that misled each community. Therefore, Muslims often define themselves as both among the people of the Book and apart because their careful tending to the Qur'ān has allowed them to lead lives most closely hewing to the way of submission God intended.

More generally, the Qur'ān distinguishes between "believers" and "unbelievers." One Qur'ānic passage reads, "It is He Who has created you. Some of you are unbelievers, and some believers: and Allāh perceives what you do" (64.2). This demonstrates well that Muslims have tended not to define themselves entirely in terms of belief, but in action as well, which their omniscient deity observes. The categories this passage uses of "unbelievers" and "believers" would suggest that what separates Muslims from others is acceptance of a specific belief. Certainly, the *shahāda* mentioned earlier represents, for many Muslims, the essence of their beliefs, and it is for this reason that it is often listed as the first of the "five pillars of Islam." Yet most Muslims expect, as the passage implied, that belief necessarily entails specific behaviors and practices. It comes as no surprise, therefore, that the other four pillars (prayer, alms, fasting, and pilgrimage) involve action. Moreover, each of these actions involves a relationship between the individual and both God and other Muslims. Through these shared practices, each of which has its social dimension, Muslims weave a tapestry of interaction meant to ideally culminate in a single, undivided *umma*. This term can be used for any society, but Muslims primarily use it in reference to the *umma*, their *umma*, and the Muslim *umma*. As a united *umma*, Muslims ideally pray together, share their wealth with the less fortunate, fast at the same time, and join millions of others in Makka (Mecca) for the pilgrimage. Although Muslims practice and believe in a great variety of ways, few use terms like "sect" or "division" to describe these differences, especially because the Qur'ān warns against divisiveness (30.31–32).

For many Muslims, the singularity of the Islamic *umma*, like most other dimensions of Islamic life, was best evidenced in Muḥammad's life. As the messenger who delivered the perfect revelation of the Qur'ān and the leader of the first Islamic society, Muḥammad continues to represent the exemplar of being Muslim and living Islam. Muslims often take the accounts of his interactions with the polytheists, Jews, and Christians who inhabited late sixth- and early seventh-century Arabia as the best demonstration of how Islam defines itself. According to many traditional sources regarding him, Muḥammad—born and bred in Makka—early in his life is understood to have distinguished himself by the integrity of his character. When he shared the revelations that first came to him in 610 CE, the predominantly polytheist Makkans became increasingly incensed with the implications Muḥammad's monotheistic claims would have for their own beliefs and the lucrative visits of the surrounding Arabs, who annually journeyed to the shrines of their gods and goddesses in Makka. Many of the earliest chapters of the Qur'ān sharply condemned the practices of worshiping multiple deities instead of Allāh (literally "the One") who would be understood as an omniscient, omnipotent, and singular deity responsible for creating everything. And so Muḥammad and the earliest Muslims distinguished themselves as monotheists from the polytheists around them.

However, according to the Qur'ān and other early texts, Muslims also soon had to distinguish themselves from the other monotheists in the region: Jews and Christians. Not surprisingly, many in these groups resisted the claims made by Muslims about the priority of their revelation. For instance, Qur'ān 3.65 reflects some of this debate when it asks, "O people of the Book, why do you dispute concerning Abraham, when the Torah and the Gospel were only revealed after him? Do you have no sense?" Qur'ān 3.67 answers the situation, "Abraham was neither a Jew nor a Christian; but a *ḥanīf* [someone who has turned away from paganism] and a Muslim." Along with warnings against the claims made by the first two groups, the Qur'ān contains ample verses promoting the collegiality of Jews, Christians, and Muslims.

Within a few generations after the Prophet's death,[3] certain Muslims began to identify, assess, and compile accounts (*ḥadīth*) of Muḥammad's conversations, perspectives, appearance, and behavior (collectively termed his *sunna*) into collections. These demonstrate the point again that being Muslim ideally connotes more than a set of beliefs but a way of being in relationship with God and humans and that it involves more than a group of ritual practitioners but a way of forming society. Through these core perspectives, Muslims define some of their various cultural traditions as Islamic and, in some (though not necessarily all) spheres of their lives, distinguish themselves from those around them.

Finally, one last caution regarding efforts to describe and define Islamic traditions. For two reasons, what we can conclude about the fourteen hundred-year history of Muslims in South Asia is highly tentative. First, how well can anyone know what premodern Muslims—the historical majority—did, thought, and felt? While a number of texts, images, relics, and architectural specimens survive from before the nineteenth century, they primarily derive from and depict elites. The overwhelming majority of Muslim Indians have left no material attesting to their religious worlds. Hence, unless explicitly stated, the descriptions of Muslim life included here should be read as entirely contemporary ones and should not be considered timeless.

The second reason for a tentativeness regarding our views of the majority of Muslims is that since the twentieth century, a remarkable homogenization of Islamic practice and belief has resulted from the advent of mass communications (pamphlets, books, audio tapes, digital recordings), of rapid transport (trains, airplanes, and automobiles), and of proselytizing that is as well funded as it is centralized. The oil wealth of many Saudi Arabians has allowed some to fund a well-orchestrated effort to convert Muslims around the world so they hew more closely to the highly conservative Wahhābī theology and lifestyle. So not only did none of India's Muslims conform to Wahhābī views or practices before they originated in the eighteenth century, but few Muslims before then were subject to such centralized learning. Instead, highly variable local traditions held sway, perhaps complemented with the occasional influence of visiting teachers or *faqīrs* (devout ascetics). Meanwhile, as a result of contemporary social media and digital diffusion of texts, audios, and videos, Indian Muslims increasingly participate in religious discourse characterized by fragmented authority and personal choice.

• THE TRADITION IN THE STUDY OF RELIGIONS

Among all religions examined in Western studies of religions, it can be argued that the study of Islam has been the most problematic because of social encounters characterized by cultural misunderstandings, religious competition, and political conflict between Europe (and later the United States) and Muslim-majority countries. It must be remembered that nothing like current, nontheistic academic studies of religions has existed in most cultures, or even in Europe before the nineteenth century. As it developed in the West, it derived from a tradition of Christian apologetics and polemics that contrasted Christianity with non-Christian practices and beliefs so as to justify the first against the latter. Only in 1877 did the secular study of religions separate itself from theological studies in European universities. For this reason, this chapter, more necessarily than those dealing with other South Asian traditions, must begin with an exploration of the history and nature of those studies in order to challenge certain understandings deeply embedded among many non-Muslim Western readers. It is important to recognize the roots of Christian and European antagonism to Islamic traditions and Muslims.

Western Antipathy to Islamic traditions and Muslims

Evidence abounds from the *umma*'s origins of a religious competition between Muslims and Christians. In the Qur'ān, a comparison of Muslim belief with that of Christians (as well as Jews and polytheists) serves to differentiate "the straight path" from those who have deviated. Claims that Christians allowed the Bible to be corrupted and to misidentify Jesus as the son of God rather than the prophet he was, serve as a critique warning Muslims to avoid the "mistakes" that characterize Christian belief. Other passages suggest that Christians and Jews responded negatively to these claims. For instance, *āyāt* 6.20 laments, "Those to whom We have given the Book know him [Muḥammad], as they know their own children; but those who have lost their souls will not believe." This competition between some Jews, Christians, and Muslims in parts of Arabia would soon be overshadowed by larger political contests that characterized the first one hundred years that followed the Prophet's death.

Following the death of Muḥammad, an incredible seventh-century expansion of Arab Muslim political control across the Middle East and North Africa and into both the Iberian Peninsula and southern Europe challenged Christian politics and theology. It meant that the Byzantine Empire—ruled from Constantinople (present-day Istanbul) and based on an Eastern Orthodox ideology—lost control over not only the Christian-dominated southern Mediterranean lands but also Jerusalem, cherished site of Christ's resurrection. Worse, although forced conversions occasionally followed these conquests, many residents in these lands voluntarily converted to Islam even though Jews and Christians enjoyed special *dhimmī* status as "people of the Book." (In fact, many Jews and non-Byzantine Christians welcomed Muslim rule because it alleviated them of the occasional persecution they suffered under Constantinople's Orthodox-informed chauvinism.) These losses dealt more than an economic and political blow to Europe's Christian leaders; it also challenged expectations of Christianity's inherent superiority and inevitable expansion. Not surprising then, Christian Europeans (Orthodox and Roman Catholic) portrayed Muslims as a malignant, violent threat whose success must be due to Satan's support for their heretical beliefs. Although this particular image has all but disappeared in the Western study of Islamic traditions, a portrayal remains prevalent of Muslims as intolerant zealots who offer the conquered "infidel" the choice between conversion and death. This depiction may owe more to European Christian self-perceptions than to anything else.

It was, for instance, the papal-approved series of crusades that, from the eleventh to the sixteenth centuries, periodically united Western Europe under a devotedly Christian mission to militarily return Jerusalem to Christian control and resulted in the slaughter of Jewish and Muslim communities in Europe, Anatolia, and the Middle East. Later, Ferdinand and Isabella combined their forces under the banner of a Christian Reconquista that destroyed a centuries-old culture of Jewish-Muslim-Christian interaction and drove most Muslims and Jews off the Iberian Peninsula with the ultimatum of conversion, deportation, or death beginning in 1492. Contemporary conflicts with European nations and the United States regarding political and commercial interests in the Middle East has not offered many avenues for altering Western perceptions. It is emblematic of the persistent focus on militant Muslims and enduring images of violent Islam that much existing scholarship traces the origins of Muslims in South Asia to the conquests of the Turko-Persian rulers of the eleventh century (who, although Muslim, invaded the subcontinent in the cause of looting and political expansion—not Islam). However, Muslims first appeared in India at the time of Muḥammad when Arab traders, long present on the western shores of the subcontinent and on the isle of Sri Lanka, began to convert to the faith.

Contemporary Scholarship on Indian Muslims

Challenges to these assumptions have been retarded by two unfortunate tendencies in much English-language scholarship. First, Muslim studies has generally been equated with Middle Eastern Studies which, reflecting Western geopolitical interests, has often been dominated by political studies. Until the mid-1970s, scholarship paid little attention to Muslim religious traditions even in the Middle East where they were perceived to have little play on the political landscape. This changed drastically in 1979 with twin events. The first was the success of the "Islamic Revolution" that displaced the US-supported Shāh of Iran with a theocratic democracy, and the second was the Soviet Union's invasion of Afghanistan. This brutal incursion would be successfully defeated by the decade-long efforts of Afghans who identified themselves as Islamic warriors (*mujāhidīn*). The second tendency derives from the Arab-centric perspective of English-language scholars (despite the fact that fewer than

20 percent of Muslims are Arab and that Pakistan, India, and Bangladesh have the highest Muslim populations outside Indonesia) that causes Muslim traditions to appear as foreign encroachments on "indigenous" South Asian cultures. Many surveys of "Indian religions" omit Muslim traditions because the subcontinent does not represent their origination point, even though few surveys of European or American religions would omit Christian or Jewish traditions for the same reasons. Moreover, Western biases regarding Muslims' religious zealotry and examples of intolerance toward the non-Muslim (Hindu) majority of India have stirred antipathy among religion scholars of the region, some of whom then view Muslims as primarily a force inimical to the communities they study.

Thus, it has been common to depict Muslim groups as somehow a society apart among other religions in India. Indeed Westerners have long portrayed Muslims throughout the world with the presumption that they practice a deliberate separatism from those among whom they live. This is evident even in the terms utilized by religion scholars. Although Western authors seldom apply the term "Christendom" as a collective epithet for their own Christian-influenced cultures, "the Islamic world" remains a common phrase that implies a world that willfully stands apart. So, for instance, scholarship seldom refers to the British in India as "Christian" (though most were), whereas it by default identifies Indians by religious identity. The implication is that the British primarily act as members of a nation while Indians basically behave as members of a religion.

More recent scholarship has demonstrated, however, how South Asian cultures (like many others, including Western ones) cannot be defined by categories of religion alone and how inter-related faith and practice, let alone daily life, have been. Although some residents in rural and urban areas may differentiate themselves into neighborhoods characterized by religious identity, others live with neighbors based on common caste, class, and regional affiliations. While some such neighborhoods may emerge as conscious endeavors to self-segregate, most likely evolve around shared community lifestyles, religious institutions, and shopping.

So, for instance, in Banaras (Vārāṇasī), some Muslims may gravitate to the predominantly Muslim neighborhood of Dal Mandi, perhaps because of the higher concentration of meat shops there, or the larger number of fellow workers in trades dominated by specific *birādarī*s (kinship groups), or more readily accessible mosques. Their decision partly may stem from their Muslim identity, but it need not be for religious reasons. Even when a resident of a city or village seeks to live in a neighborhood dominated by one religious group, their everyday lives usually require intercommunal relationships. For instance, a Hindu family in Banaras that prepares their daughter's marriage will necessarily have to work with specific Muslim communities: one that will rent the wedding carriage to carry her and another to make the silk *sāṛī*s she will wear. This demonstrates how Muslims dominate some sectors of Indian society, how these sectors are characterized not by religious affiliation alone but by *birādarī* as well, and how daily interactions commonly require mutual interaction among these groups.

Fortunately, in the last few decades a wide-scale reevaluation has been unfolding in scholarship that has recognized that the presumption of a radical separation of Muslims from non-Muslims is simplistic, if not dangerous. Enriching their portrayals of historical and modern Indian Muslim lives, increasing numbers of scholars have turned from a paradigm of incessant conflict toward a more nuanced view of coexistence and interaction. Key to this effort, many now realize, is an attempt to transcend the ready descriptors "Hindu" and "Muslim" that have for too long been the primary means of identifying any specific individual, community, or attribute thereof. In part this has become possible through new historic and ethnographic research that has demonstrated the integrated nature of Indian Muslim communities—no matter whether the royal court of a Muslim sovereign, an artisan group trading with the British empire, or a neighborhood in a contemporary village—that demonstrate that "Indian" and "Muslim" are not mutually exclusive categories nor is "Indian Muslim" an identity that prohibits shared identities with others.

• COSMOS AND HISTORY

The Life of Muḥammad and the Early Umma

For many Muslims, the history of Islam begins with the original humans, Ādam (Adam) and his wife Ḥawwā' (Eve), who first submitted to Allāh (however imperfectly). From an academic standpoint, however, the history of the *umma* began with those who would, historically, first identify themselves as "Muslim" and accept Muḥammad's claim regarding the revelation of the Qur'ān. Because of Muḥammad's role in receiving the revelation and communicating it to humanity, his life has taken on the greatest prominence for most Muslims. The Qur'ān, *sīra* (biographies), and *ḥadīth* (accounts) have represented the most valuable sources about that life for Muslims. However, these sources have often been supplemented by popular legends—often orally maintained and communicated—about Muḥammad that have been developed from interpretations of Qur'ānic passages. The account below draws from all of these sources and reflects a general narrative of the Prophet's life that many Muslims would recognize, even if they might dispute some details.

Muḥammad's early life negotiated a series of pitfalls. Born in perhaps 570 CE, he was soon orphaned. Thereafter, he was raised by, first, his grandfather ʿAbd al-Muṭṭalib and, then, his uncle Abū Ṭālib in Makka and soon found his way, like so many urban Arabs of his time, into the life of a merchant. Islamic legends describe some of his travels with caravans to parts of West Asia. When the wealthy merchant Khadīja proposed marriage to him, he accepted, and they began a twenty-five year life together. Not uncommonly, Muḥammad would climb the rocky hillside of Mount Ḥirā' outside of Makka in order to spend time alone in prayer and meditation. At a time when most Arabs recognized a multitude of deities and worshiped them in iconic form, Muḥammad stood among the few monotheists, known as *ḥanīf*s, who, though not Jewish or Christian, believed in a single god. During one of those prayer sessions, the angel Gabriel (Arabic Jibrīl) appeared to him and commanded "Iqra'!" (Recite!). "I cannot read," Muḥammad replied. The angel persisted, and then, according to a commonly held understanding, he recited *sūra* 96, the first revealed chapter of the Qur'ān (which means "recitation"). When Muḥammad returned to Makka, he shared the revelation with Khadīja, who accepted what he said, thus becoming the first Muslim to embrace what had been given to Muḥammad. ʿAlī ibn Abī Ṭālib, his cousin and son-in-law, and Abū Bakr, his father-in-law, soon followed. Thus, according to Islamic dating, the *jāhiliyya* ("time of ignorance") ended, and a new epoch had begun.

As Muḥammad began to share the revelations publicly, they attracted many Makkans with their message that stressed charity to others as Allāh's will. Accession to this will informs Allāh's ultimate judgment on each individual's life that would condition his or her existence after death. The Arabs of the time would have been largely unfamiliar with these themes of monotheism, judgment, and an afterlife unless they had contact with some of the Jewish and Christian communities that existed on the Arabian Peninsula. For most of the residents of Makka, the message that Muḥammad brought contrasted directly with their polytheistic understandings and their beliefs that death extinguished life entirely without anything to follow. The power of this omniscient, omnipotent, and singular god had no parallel among the many deities worshiped at the time. The notion of a deity's judgment also contrasted with a notion that an inescapable fate ruled one's life and that justice existed solely in the hands of one's tribe. If someone injured a member of the tribe, the tribe exacted a punishment on someone—anyone—from the other tribe. The Qur'ān's concept of individual responsibility clashed with this notion of corporate culpability.

So it should not have come as any surprise that as the nascent Muslim movement attracted numbers, it also attracted resistance due to the divergence in belief and practice. Undoubtedly, this sentiment was only compounded by the threat the growing Muslim community soon posed to Makka's commercial interests. For three months each year, the tribes declared a cessation from the predatory raiding by which many sustained themselves. These months of peace allowed for the unmolested passage of tribes to Makka where images of their three hundred sixty deities were housed in the Kaʿba (Arabic "cube"), an appropriately named building shaped like a towering cube. This pilgrimage provided an important source of income for many of Makka's merchants and other business people. The strength of Islam's monotheism was matched only by its antagonism to worshiped images. Although Abū Ṭālib's support of Muḥammad brought the protection of their tribe, the Quaraysh, as both the numbers of Muslims and the impact of their ideology grew, resistance arose even within the tribe itself. Soon some of Muḥammad's own tribesmen would be plotting to assassinate him. Meanwhile oppression mounted for less prominent Muslims as well. One Makkan tortured his slave, an Abyssinian by the name of Bilāl, while demanding that he renounce his new Islamic faith. Abū Ṭālib eventually ransomed him and released him as a free Muslim. Yet the implications became increasingly threatening for many Makkans. Even the mighty Ḥamza, the renowned and recently converted warrior and another uncle of Muḥammad, could protect Muḥammad for only so long. Vicious oppression drove Muslims from their homes and into desert encampments. The personal toll these attacks brought to Muḥammad is reflected in the many Qur'ānic verses that offer him succor in the face of his travails. For instance, *āyāt* 50.39 cajoles, "Bear up with what they say and proclaim the Praise of your Lord before sunrise and before sunset." The pressure on Muḥammad was soon magnified by the deaths of, first, his beloved and supportive wife Khadīja (about 618) and, then, his protector and kinsman Abū Ṭālib (about 619).

Relief came when a delegation from the neighboring city of Yathrib asked Muḥammad to act as an arbitrator for conflicts between the tribes of the city. He agreed on the conditions that the other Muslims would be allowed to settle there and that all the citizens of Yathrib, except for the four Jewish tribes, agree to convert to Islam. With this agreement in hand, Muḥammad authorized the first gradual emigration of Muslims to Yathrib, which would ever after be known as Madīna ("the city"). Muḥammad left last with Abū Bakr, and they too came safely to Madīna but only through the miracle, according to popular belief, of a spider's quickly spun web that hid their presence in a cave from Makkan pursuers.

That the Islamic calendar begins with the arrival of the emigrants in Madīna (that year is counted as 1 AH or "after hijra") signals the salience of this event in the minds of most Muslims. After all, Madīna represents the first Muslim society in which the followers of Islam no longer existed as a despised outsider group but as a self-supporting society. The revelations shifted in accordance with the new conditions of Muslims. The themes changed from exhortations to monotheism and warnings of judgment to discourse on issues regarding the ordering of society and the compassion of Allāh. The Madinian-revealed verses included general proscriptions and prescriptions about drinking, eating, divorce, and warfare. Primary among those themes were topics of social justice. Perhaps it is for this reason that Islam appealed first to the lower status and less privileged, even before the *hijra* (Denny 1994: 66). Qur'ānic revelation exhorted the maintenance of widows and support of orphans as well as rules for just dealings regarding transactions. In one of its most potent passages, the Qur'ān condemns the practice of female infanticide so common in this patriarchal culture. In this prolonged description of the final judgment day, the juxtaposition with the awesome events of cosmic upheaval underlines the significance of the voice of the forsaken child:

> When the sun shall be coiled up; And when the stars shall be scattered about; And when the mountains shall be set in motion; And when the pregnant camels shall be discarded; And when the beasts shall be corralled; And when the seas shall rise mightily; And when souls shall be paired off; And when the buried infant shall be asked: "For what sin was she killed?"
>
> (81.1–9)

The Arabic for "compassion," *al-Raḥīm*, stands as one of the most prevalent of the ninety-nine names for Allāh, featuring prominently in the *bismillāh* prayer that is commonly recited at the initiation of any new endeavor. Muḥammad frequently manifested this quality in his role of the *umma*'s leader, even in combat.

Muḥammad, previously a prophet heading a small band of followers, became the leader of this society, responsible for coping with problems of law, security, and the economy. Despite the hospitality of the Madinians who became known as the Anṣār (the supporters), life for the displaced Makkans—the Muhājirūn (the emigrants)—did not come easily, as the Madinian economy could not simply expand to accommodate the new population. So some of the Muslims turned to the common Arab tradition of raiding caravans. Their effectiveness excited the concern of Makkan merchants who sent military expeditions to defend their trade routes and attack Madīna itself. Most of these failed, however, and the Muslims' successes seemed to strengthen their resolve that with Allāh's help anything, even the capture of Makka, seemed possible. Meanwhile, through deft diplomacy, which included marrying into a number of tribes following the death of Khadīja, Muḥammad effectively built a remarkable coalition of Bedouin tribes that increased the pressure on Makka. Ultimately, the Makkan leaders capitulated, and the Muslims reentered Makka with little bloodshed. Muḥammad led Muslims into the Kaʿba that was cleansed immediately of the images it contained and rededicated to the One God.

Muḥammad returned to Madīna for his final two years of life. The revelations continued and were recorded conscientiously, even as more Arabian tribes joined his coalition and became Muslim. In 632 CE, he died having completed a final pilgrimage to Makka. His close companion ʿUmar ibn al-Khaṭṭāb, approaching a crowd gathered to hear about their leader, declared: "O men, if anyone worships Muḥammad, Muḥammad is dead: if anyone worships God, God is alive, immortal" (Isḥāq 1987: 683). In this way, Muḥammad's final act in life served as yet another testament to the beliefs he promoted.

This story of Muḥammad, from the perspective of most Muslims, represents a central narrative of understanding what Islam is and how to be a Muslim. Muḥammad, indeed, was never anything more than a man, and the narrative provides its own warning about what happens when the shape of humans becomes mistaken for the presence of Allāh. Nevertheless, Allāh chose Muḥammad as the final prophet who would both communicate the most perfect text and, as the person most intimate with it, act as its most important interpreter. For this reason, many Muslims, informed about the Prophet's personal perspectives, behavior, and appearance through the *ḥadīth*, model themselves on his example physically and in their mannerisms. They demonstrate their respect for him when they say or write the equivalent of "peace be upon him" (P.B.U.H.) when they pronounce or write his name. Yet, most Muslims would take the mistaken Western term for them as "Muhammadans" with chagrin because their commitment is to Allāh, as the proclamation of faith makes clear, "There is no god but God, and Muḥammad is the Messenger of God."

Although only a man, Muḥammad was witness to miracles beyond the revelation of the Qur'ān. Perhaps one of the most famous involved his Night Journey (*isrā'*) and Ascension (*miʿraj*). As implied in the Qur'ān (17.1) and reported in the *ḥadīth* literature, a winged horse summoned Muḥammad one night for a journey from Makka to "the far mosque" which later traditions would understand as Jerusalem. Astride this creature, known as Burāq, Muḥammad flew to the top of what is now known as the Temple Mount, the then-abandoned plateau on which the Jewish temple had stood centuries earlier. From there, after leading the preceding prophets in prayer, he ascended a ladder to Paradise in the company of Jibrīl. At each level of this multilayered Paradise, he met earlier prophets until, on the penultimate level, he encountered Mūsā (Moses), the first of Allāh's *rasūl* (literally "messenger"), who prepared him for his meeting with the One God and had him petition Allāh to decrease to five daily prayers, instead of the originally commanded fifty. Upon his return from Paradise and return flight on Burāq, the regular practice of daily prayers is understood to have begun.

Cosmic History

Despite the significant historical and cultural diversity in their understandings, most Muslims believe that it is this Paradise that the righteous will encounter on the Day of Judgment (*Yawn ad-Dīn*). Preceding this event, according to Shīʿa and some Sunnī theology, a *mahdī* ("divinely guided leader") will return to guide the faithful after all moral order in the world has decayed entirely. Then a *dajjāl* ("deceiver") will arise in an attempt to lead believers astray, only to be destroyed by the *mahdī* and a returned Jesus (Smith and Haddad 1981: 66–70). Final judgment follows. As part of the Islamic emphasis on individual responsibility and culpability, the Qur'ān warns of this Reckoning—a day when all humans will be resurrected and face Allāh, one at a time, to have their deeds judged. Those whose good deeds outweigh their bad enjoy an eternal Paradise; those whose do not, face one of the seven levels of the inferno. (Dante would later fashion the topography of his Divine Comedy after this model.) So history culminates (and ends) with this event—a history that involves the consistent effort on the part of Allāh to mercifully guide humanity despite their repetitive failures to accede to his guidelines. The repeated revelation of Allāh's Book, despite earlier failures to keep it free of corruption, provides one example of that mercy, while the finality of the Qur'ānic revelation and Muḥammad's prophethood reflects Allāh's expectations, reinforced by the inevitability of judgment, that Muslims will maintain Islam.

Muḥammad represents the end of a succession of prophets (*anbiyā'*) who testified to Allāh's "signs." These prophets did not act as predictors of the future as the common English usage would suggest, but rather as individuals who warned about the mistakes the society around them were making. Ādam represented the first prophet and others are Nūḥ (Noah), Sulaymān (Solomon), and Ayyūb (Job). Often, four prophets are understood to be ranked on a level of higher regard because they brought books that Allāh intended to help humanity live in the way Allāh prescribed. These four, known as *rusul* (plural of *rasūl*), are Mūsā (Moses) who brought the Torah, Dāwd (David) who brought the Psalms, ʿĪsā (Jesus) with the Gospel, and Muḥammad with the Qur'ān. This list makes clear that Muslims understand Judaic and Christian traditions to be the predecessors mentioned in the previous section—the "people of the Book." No prophets, however, would follow Muḥammad—another mark of his uniqueness. So when the early *umma* lost Muḥammad, they lost their religious leader as well as their social and military leader.

After Muḥammad

The inertia behind the expansion of Islamic traditions, however, could not be stopped by Muḥammad's death. After an initial period of uncertainty regarding the leadership of the *umma* and the fidelity of previously converted tribes, Muslim Arabs exploded out of Arabia, certainly inspired by their ideology and likely propelled by population pressures. Within a hundred years, Muslim armies conquered lands from the Iberian Peninsula to the periphery of South Asia, which they knew as al-Hind. Just as the unity of this empire would soon be rent by divergent interests and regional forces, so the singularity of the *umma* that has remained an important ideal of Muslims today began to be threatened by differences in groups with the death of the charismatic Muḥammad, who had previously provided uncontested leadership.

Upon his death, dissent arose as to who would succeed Muḥammad as leader of the *umma*. Since Muslims understood that no one could replace Muḥammad, a deputy (caliph) would be appointed. But how would that person be chosen? Most believed that the Arab tradition of choosing the first among equals from the tribal heads would suffice. One group, however, argued that the leadership should be a matter of familial descent and looked to ʿAlī, his cousin and son-in-law and father of Muḥammad two grandsons. In contrast with the majority, who came to be known as Sunnī ("of the custom"), this protesting group came to be known as Shīʿa ("the party [of ʿAlī]"). The Shīʿa represent the largest non-Sunnī community among Muslims. Although the *umma* overruled the Shīʿa in its first three choices of caliphs (Abū Bakr, ʿUmar ibn al-Khaṭṭāb, and Uthmān ibn ʿAffān), ʿAlī became the fourth caliph. In the power struggle that followed ʿAlī's death in 660, his first son, Ḥasan, soon withdrew his bid for leadership, while his second son, Ḥusayn, was slain in a tragic battle by his political contenders while on his way to meet partisans who encouraged him to seek the leadership. This battle, which occurred at Karbalā' in what is today Iraq, followed a heroic stand by Ḥusayn and his entourage (including family members) as they faced starvation, dehydration, and overwhelming military force. Ḥusayn's death continues to be commemorated today by Shīʿa and some Sunnī on Muḥarram (the "sacred month"). But the Shīʿa did not alone challenge the direction that many of the *umma* sought to take, although no other group would remain such an identifiably discernible community.

Islamic traditions in Premodern South Asia

Islamic traditions arrived on the subcontinent long before any Muslim armies did. Some of the Arab traders who had established homes on the coasts of Sri Lanka and southern India converted to Islam in the course of their commerce with the residents of the Arabian Peninsula. In 711 CE, a Muslim-led Arab army reached Baluchistan and Sindh in the south of today's Pakistan. This represented the last gasp and easternmost extent of the century-long military expansion that followed Muḥammad's death. The wealth and strength of regional rulers blunted the edge of the incursion and brought it to a halt. For the next three hundred years, the states ruled by Muslims from Spain to Sindh demonstrated increasing cultural divergence from the Arab patterns that informed the early *umma* as regional cultures influenced the émigré Arabs, and their newborn religion, through a process of gradual inculturation. When Muslim-dominated states began to pressure Indian territories in the eleventh century, they did so as part of neither a singular social body, nor unified political system, nor continuous religious expansion, but rather as something quite different.

Ethnically Turkish and Persian groups in Central Asia vied with one another for control over territory and wealth. As some of these succeeded in consolidating their powerbases and could afford to look beyond the regions of their direct control, South Asia became a tempting opportunity. Contrary to the frequent perception today of the subcontinent as an economically impoverished place, al-Hind had long held the reputation as a fabulously wealthy land. And so Maḥmūd of Ghazna (a city in Afghanistan) began a series of raids into the upper plains of the Indus and Ganges valleys in quest of loot at the turn of the eleventh century. His soldiers targeted whatever sites promised the most treasure, and these were royal palaces, Hindu temples, and Hindu and Buddhist monasteries. That these men identified themselves as Muslim seems incidental because Islamic ideologies no more justified their attacks than Hindu or Buddhist ideologies motivated their opponents' defense. Maḥmūd's raids were followed by the efforts of some Turko-Persians to expand the extent of their rule beyond the Hindu Kush mountains that separate Afghanistan from South Asia. Ultimately, a series of dynasties established themselves in the northern Indus Valley in the city of Lahore and in the northern Gangetic Valley in and around the city of Delhi.

These courts more obviously relied on forms of Islamic state ideologies, including the justification of rule. They therefore destroyed temples associated with the political entities that preceded them and founded mosques, sometimes atop the temple ruins, as expressions of their new rule. This has long been contrived as a wholesale assault on Hindu traditions: the natural result of an endemic fanatical religious bigotry. But such was seldom the case, and in fact many Hindu leaders acted similarly against the symbolic centers of vanquished Hindu rulers. The influence of a particularly prevalent Indic mode of rule on Muslim courts became most apparent with the arrival of the Mughals.

A displaced Turko-Mongolian family, they claimed descent from the Mongols Jenghiz Khān and Tīmūr—hence the name bequeathed to them by others: Mughal (their name for themselves was Gūrkānī) (Thackston 2002: xlvi). Each capital city that the Mughals at one time or another used eventually developed a large mosque opposite a massive fortress that housed the royal residence. Although few of the Mughal emperors followed a particularly strict Islamic lifestyle or aggressively promoted Islamic traditions, the Mughal state premised its authority to rule on the claim that it manifested the sovereignty of Allāh. This legitimation via a deity paralleled earlier, non-Muslim forms in India so that non-Muslims recognized the form and accommodated themselves in such a way as to be able to serve the state. Inversely, many Muslims accommodated themselves to serve states based on Hindu-legitimation schemes, as demonstrated through the life of one member of the contemporary military elite.

In sixteenth-century South India, ʿAin al-Mulk Gīlāni, a Muslim by name, served the Muslim Bahmanī sulṭān, the Hindu Vijayanagara king, and the Muslim Bījāpūr sulṭān without exercising any apparent preference or experiencing any obvious discrimination. Rather, like other members of a military elite whose services royal courts sought enthusiastically, ʿAin al-Mulk adapted himself to the ritual language and procedures of each newly adopted employer. ʿAin al-Mulk's service to Vijayanagara would have required some fluency in the Telegu, Kannada, and/or Sanskrit languages, and while in Bījāpūr he would have relied on Dakhni, Persian, and/or Arabic. Premodern rulers defined their courtiers primarily according to their loyalty, not religious identity (Wagoner 2003).

Just as Muslim Arab culture transformed as it moved into new social environments, so did the Turkish and Persianate Muslim cultures that Central Asians introduced, including its forms of Islam. The three most prominent agents in this transformation were the royal court, the army camp, and "Ṣūfīs."

As just mentioned, Islamic political ideologies played a legitimating role in the rule of many Muslims before Independence, and so those who participated in the court required familiarity with an Islamic vocabulary used in the language and ritual of rule. This no more required the adoption of personal Islamic practices and beliefs than did participation in Hindu-defined courts with their reliance on Sanskrit and particular forms of patronage. However, depending on any particular ruler's proclivities, becoming a Muslim may have been perceived to offer enough advantage to warrant formal conversion. Besides these courtiers who circulated through Hindu and Muslim court life, rulers too typically negotiated a variety of religious traditions in the efforts to maintain their position. Because rulers had domain over territories that included people with a range of religious affiliations, most patronized a variety of religious institutions and specialists. Although their non-Muslim subjects may have recognized the form of Islamic ritual as legitimating the rule, they did so with the expectation that the ruler would protect all the various forms of religious order among the population under his dominion. Thus the same Muslim rulers who had destroyed temples that manifested the legitimation of their political rivals patronized yet other temples (as well as Brāhmaṇas) in their effort to demonstrate their role of protecting the *dharma* (that is, the Hindu moral order), as Hindus expected of whomever ruled them. This required familiarity by the sulṭāns and emperors with the cultures of their subjects. Mughal emperors famously sponsored translations of Sanskrit epics, such as the *Rāmāyaṇa* and the *Mahābhārata*, in Persian texts adorned with meticulously painted miniatures that drew on a wealth of ethnographic details regarding contemporary non-Muslim dress, practices, and food.

The Turkish-speaking soldiers who served these courts lived a life quite apart from their superiors. Their encampments involved intimate interaction with local residents in *bāẓār*s, and the like. As a measure of these interactions, a new language arose called Urdu that literally means "the camp." This language merged Persian and Arabic with the local vernacular to provide a means of everyday communication. Although Urdu would develop over the next several centuries as a means of both crafting refined poetry and being eloquent in a status-conscious society, it undoubtedly served as an interlinguistic bridge, a vehicle of mutual experience that facilitated the increased familiarity of the general population with Islamic practices and ideals.

Finally, Ṣūfīs—or at least those later identified as such—served to transmit Islamic paradigms to the broader population and to translate them into local understandings. Many of these individuals (mostly men, but including some women) associated with *ṭarīqa*s ("brotherhoods"), which defined themselves according to the spiritual lineage of teachers. However others did not. Although the *ṭarīqa*s would commonly claim Muḥammad as the originator of a chain (*silsila*) of spiritual teaching, the actual origins of these traditions cannot be easily discerned. The famous eleventh-century Ṣūfī of Lahore, Abu 'l-Ḥasan

ʿAlī al-Hujwīrī, quotes a much earlier Ṣūfī when he wrote, "Today Sufism is a name without a reality, but formerly it was a reality without a name" (1990: 14). Hujwīrī's sanguine statement reflects both the ill-defined origins of Ṣūfī practices and beliefs and the contempt that many Muslims have for those who claim to be contemporary mystics. This continues today as many Muslims look suspiciously at some of the *faqir*s who wander from village to village, town to town seeking alms and perhaps offering special services such as healing.

Nevertheless, currently in Bihar, Jharkand, and West Bengal, Ṣūfīs hold a revered place in the social memory of many communities, associated both with the foundation of many villages and towns and with the peaceful impulse to conversion for residents. Local residents explain that Ṣūfīs settled deliberately in less developed rural areas so as to develop "junglī" areas and teach Islamic lessons to locals. Richard Eaton (1993) has critically challenged the literal truth of these narratives, arguing persuasively that these stories derive from sixteenth- and seventeenth-century hagiographic traditions that have been reinforced by the Protestant-informed worldview of Western scholars. Whoever these land developers were, they apparently learned the vernacular languages of the region and translated Islamic perspectives into linguistic and conceptual idioms that were locally understandable and to which some indigenous perspectives slowly conformed. Whether they understood themselves as such, those popularly identified today as Ṣūfīs played a critical role in the expansion of the *umma* in South Asia, as demonstrated in the popular narrative of one Ṣūfī enshrined in rural India.

In Chainpur, a village in the North Indian state of Bihar, a Ṣūfī tomb stands at the edge of the dried-mud-covered brick houses that crowd away from the precious, dark-colored farmland. A gathering assembles during the annual celebration of the entombed Aṣṭa Awliyā'. A few men who join the festivities answer the questions of someone new to the area about the Ṣūfī. "He was a *walī* ('a favorite of God')," Ahmed Khan explains. "Seven hundred years ago . . . when he came here, people were uncivilized. They did not know about *dharma*, *mazhab* ['religion']. . . . He was born in Makka." When asked why Aṣṭa Awliyā' came to this area, another man replies, "To spread Islam," to which Ahmed adds, "It was jungle then. There was only jungle." Asked to explain the changes the Ṣūfī brought, Ahmed explains that the local people believed in him strongly and so they built his tomb. A third person adds, "For the people of [the village], Aṣṭa Awliyā' is a special *guru*." Although all three men identified themselves as Muslim, their answers reflect the composite culture of many parts of India as they use terms (*dharma* and *guru*) that derive from Sanskrit-based religious cultures.

Complex cultural contexts such as this prove difficult to describe, reliant as we are on the concept of "religions" which includes the mutually exclusive categories of "Islam," "Hinduism," and "Buddhism." Although it may be true that on the level of certain elites (such as the *ʿulamā'*, Brāhmaṇa scholars, and monks) that a rigid orthopraxy ("proper practice") or orthodoxy ("proper thought") could be imagined and maintained, among most Indians no such jealous allegiance led to a firm refusal to engage in practices or beliefs defined as non-Islamic or non-Hindu. Such expectations reflect the Protestant origins of the Western study of religions with defined confessions of belief that prompted inclusion or exclusion based on a strict set of beliefs. Although some Muslims assiduously distinguished Muslims from *kāfir*s (nonbelievers), for many during the era of the Delhi Sultanate and Mughal rule, religion did not provide an exclusive community of belief so much as a range of options for devotion to a deity or saints, for remedy from malaise, and for discernment of the future. Non-Muslims frequented Ṣūfī shrines, and Muslims the *samādhi* of non-Muslim *sant*s (saints). Meanwhile, elites often patronized temples, tombs, mosques, and other religious institutions without regard to their own religious identity. As a result, many ideas and practices that we may be tempted to describe as "Islamic" could be found practiced by non-Muslims, while styles of poetry, fashions of literature, and styles of artistic representation derived from non-Muslim sources influenced developing expressions of regional Muslim religiosity.

One of the best demonstrations of this is the *bhakti* movement. Undoubtedly influenced by Islamic monotheism and mysticism, *bhakti* poets wrote and sang their devotion to a god or goddess, portraying themselves as the friend, child, or even lover of the deity. The fifteenth-century poet Kabīr represents an unusual *bhakti* because of his unrelenting criticism of orthoprax practices among both Hindus and Muslims. However, this unique approach also demonstrates the fusion of devotional elements from both traditions into a vision very difficult to categorize. The blunt blandishments he administers to members of various traditions demonstrates both the existence of Hindu and Muslim identities in his day and a popular movement's willingness to deride the significance of such identities relative to devotion to God. So writes Kabīr (1986: 50–51; *śabda* 30):

> Brother, where did your two gods come from?
> Tell me, who made you mad?
> Ram, Allah, Keshav, Karim, Hari, Hazrat—
> so many names.
> So many ornaments, all one gold,
> it has no double nature.
> For conversation we make two—
> this *namāz*, that *pujā*,
> this Mahadev, that Muhammed,
> this Brahma, that Adam,
> this a Hindu, that a Turk,
> but all belong to earth.
> Vedas, Korans, all those books,
> those Mullas and those Brahmins—
> so many names, so many names,
> but the pots are all one clay.
> Kabir says, nobody can find Ram,
> both sides are lost in schisms.
> One slaughters goats, one slaughters cows,
> they squander their birth in isms.

Kabīr's carefully calibrated and balanced poetry uniformly criticizes Hindu and "Turk" (a common description of Muslims harkening to the Turkish cultural and linguistic identity of much of the invading Central Asian armies). His sing-song litany of practices (*namāz* and *pūjā*), figures (Mahādeva and Muḥammad), texts (Vedas and Qur'āns), and specialists (mullās and Brāhmaṇas) rattle the sanctity they might hold for the audience in provocative challenge to focus on Rām (Kabīr's ubiquitous and nonsectarian name for the One God) instead of trappings of devotion external to the relationship with God.

"Islam," therefore, represents a set of practices and beliefs that, considered together, represent a sort of ideal. Muslims may have, at times, recourse to this ideal but more often negotiated a complex landscape of religious opportunity and commitments that varied tremendously among India's myriad cultures. Some practices, such as the formal prayer or *namāz*, were likely to have been exclusive to Muslims. Shrine visitation would not have been, though, and neither would Muslim participation in holidays such as Holī and Dīvālī. Much of this changed, however, in the modern period.

Islamic Traditions in Modern India

Since the beginning of the period of British rule, a set of impulses for far more exclusive notions of Islam and Muslim identity has arisen. The causes of this are multiple, and since a later section will provide more details on specific movements, only a few prominent historical influences will be briefly considered here.

British Imperialism

Although they competed for business with several other European companies, the British East India Company would achieve goals unimaginable in 1600 when it received a royal charter to trade in South Asia. By 1757, the Company had taken the place of a regional ruler as Bengal's tax collector in the service of the Mughal emperor. A century later, they had effectively executed such successful political and military strategies that they held a great many more territories by direct or indirect rule. But in 1857, a rebellion (described by the British as the mutiny and by Indian nationalists as the First War of Independence) swept across North India. In their effort to find a cause to explain this bloody uprising against the supposedly munificent rule of the "British Rāj," the British fell back on long-held European images of fanatical Muslim men inspired by Islamic rage. Although those who had rebelled had been encouraged by some Muslim leaders and enlisted the support of the powerless Mughal heir, more Hindus than Muslims participated in the violence. Nevertheless, the British apportioned blame overwhelmingly to Muslims (associated as they were with the previous political order) and convinced themselves that Muslims could no longer be trusted (Robb 2002: 146–47).

The British government gave increasing preference to Hindus and Sikhs in a political system that severed the inter-religious patronage exchanges existing in the pre-British period while polarizing indigenous identities overwhelmingly along religious lines. Hindus and Muslims increasingly identified themselves primarily as such in part to fit within imperial systems (such as the law courts) that provided segregated systems for different "religious communities." As observed earlier, many premodern South Asians certainly identified themselves and one another according to religious association, but governmental and legal systems did not systematically and universally define them as such. In response to their declining fortunes, many Muslims pined nostalgically for the Mughal past, while others promoted Islamic revival and reform that often relied on sharp differentiation between Muslims and their Hindu and Sikh neighbors and (predominantly) Christian overlords.

Representational Democracy

The British often justified their rule and exploitation of India because Indians had yet to learn the art of what the British envisioned as enlightened self-government. Many Indians rose to the challenge motivated by the tantalizing goal of self-rule, the attractive ideals of democracy, and/or political ambition and adapted themselves to the evolving form of government. In this new system, political parties economized their effort to attract votes by identifying and appealing to blocs of voters. Influenced by British classifications of the population (especially informed by the decadal censuses), Indian politicians often appealed to the supposed (and supposedly shared) interests of religious groups. The success of the Indian National Congress party in the 1930s, for instance, to stump for restrictions on the slaughter of cows (bovine being revered by most Hindus and consumed by many Muslims) was an attempt to define an issue attractive to Hindus at the expense of Muslims who felt increasingly targeted and alienated.

Communication and Transportation Technology

The tremendous technological advances that brought increasingly rapid improvements in the efficiency of communication and transportation and an accompanying decline in costs meant that far-flung members of the *umma* could communicate with and encounter one another far more easily than ever before. These technologies existed in a symbiotic relationship with European imperialism that both succeeded because of its technical superiority and expanded its reach through a worldwide infrastructure made possible through that same success. For instance, each foreign harbor secured by European coal-fired warships (superior technology in the nineteenth century) meant the possibility of a new coaling station from which naval power, and commercial shipping, could be projected yet further. But not only Europeans enjoyed the faster, cheaper, and safer passage steamships provided. Whereas less than three hundred thousand Muslims performed the *ḥajj* in 1965 (Bukhari 2002), today, benefiting from consumer air travel, more than two million participate. Among Indians, at least ten thousand participated in the *ḥajj* annually in the 1880s (Pearson 1996: 54) while more than one hundred thousand travel today. This means that more Indian

Muslims encounter increasing numbers of Muslims from around the world, accelerating the spread of perspectives and ideologies. Even as more Muslims increasingly encounter the diversity among Muslims, movements seeking to unify Muslims become increasingly successful. This has particularly been true in South Asia with, for instance, Mawlānā Mawdūdī, whose works find interested audiences worldwide.

The culmination of these dynamics crested fatefully with Partition. Faced with the imminent departure of the British and the successful rise of Hindu-themed politics of the Indian National Congress, a group of Muslim politicians in the Muslim League gradually decided that only the threat of Muslims demanding a separate Muslim-majority nation would safeguard the interests of Muslims. When this strategy failed, they considered the actual creation of such a state their best option. They intended Pakistan, as they called the state, to be a haven for Muslims and Muslim culture with a secular government, not a theocratically Islamic one. Although many South Asian Muslims disagreed that there was any need for the creation of this state, the Muslim League successfully brokered a deal with the British and used both the threat and action of violence to finally gain the agreement of the Indian National Congress.

Waves of violence rolled across the northern parts of South Asia preceding and following the celebration of India's and Pakistan's Independence at midnight on August 14/15, 1947, as whole populations of Hindus, Muslims, and Sikhs moved toward their adopted homelands. Although most Muslims preferred to remain where they lived already, the severity of the violence caused more violence, and so many moved to avoid the worsening local situation. Hindu and Sikh emigrants to India shared horrific stories of slaughter, assault, and plunder, reaffirming depictions common in the minds of many British of Muslims as intolerant barbarians even as non-Muslims visited these same horrors on Muslims. The perpetual conflict between India and Pakistan—usually characterized by political tension and low-scale military exchanges but erupting in full-scale war three times since Independence—has made Muslims in India self-conscious of their patriotism. Not infrequently, their allegiance to India has been challenged with a suspicion that their sympathies—whether during open combat or cricket matches—lies with Pakistan. This contributes to a sense among many that to be Muslim is to be a marginalized Indian.

Contributing to a rise in this suspicion about Muslims has been the ascent of the Hindutva movement. Drawing on the worldview of various nineteenth-century thinkers and using specific premodern heroes as symbols, Hindutva proponents consider India to be essentially a Hindu nation. Hindu, for them, represents less a religious identity and more a cultural identity that anyone who considers himself or herself Indian must embrace. The movement, most forcefully manifest in the Saṅgh Parivār (Family of Organizations) led by the Rāṣṭriya Svayamsevak Saṅgh (RSS, or Society of National Volunteers), depicts Muslims as perpetual foreigners (since they descend from outside invaders) or lost brethren forcibly converted from Hindu traditions. The destruction of the then-unused Bābrī masjid in 1992 most poignantly illustrated this perspective. Charging that the first Mughal emperor, Bābur, had demolished a temple commemorating the site of the god Rāma's birthplace and erected a mosque in its stead, members of the Rāṣṭriya Svayamsevak Saṅgh as well as a large number of other angry activists stormed the controversial site and demolished the four hundred-year-old unused mosque. When Muslims protested, riots ensued in which thousands died. Another round of violence was sparked in Gujarat in 2002 when a group of Muslims burned Hindus alive in a train carriage. In reaction, Hindu mobs used their superior numbers to overwhelm the aggressors, but then went on to attack other Muslims across the state.

Among the outcomes of these events, individual Muslims have had their identity more poignantly defined as "Muslim" despite the multiple social worlds most engage. Every individual person lives in communion with a number of different groups (for example, family, neighborhood, work-related, nation, sports teams), and so encounters the world with multiple identities. The identity that comes to the fore depends on the social context in which the individual finds himself or herself. However, whenever there is communal politics in India, it decreases the identities shared between Hindus and Muslims. Although many Muslims remember playing Holī or celebrating Dīvālī with their neighbors or fellow workers, today more consider these to be "Hindu activities" that Muslims must exclude themselves from in accordance with a more rigidly defined identity of "Muslim." Nevertheless, many Muslims share overlapping lives with their neighbors and other Indians.

• RELIGIOUS LIFE AND LITERATURES

Many Muslims describe their Islamic traditions as involving not only a relationship between the individual and Allāh, but relationships with other humans as well. Social justice features prominently in those relationships and shall be considered in the section "Ethics and Human Relations." Moreover, the social dimensions of Islamic prescriptions for life are prominent in the practices that compose the various ideals for living. Once again, most Muslims first turn to the Qur'ān (or to traditions that claim to do so) and then to the *ḥadīth* for the basis of this ideal and the practices the Qur'ān suggests. But in doing so, they unconsciously or not are drawing first on the traditions of embodied practice, emotional sentiment, textual hermeneutics, and oral tradition instilled in them since childhood by family and immediate community. They, like all of us, are born into interpretative and performative worlds that shape and saturate their somatic, affective, and—perhaps last of all—intellectual reflexes until various premises and conclusions are simply and unreflexively "common sense."

The Qur'ān

The angel Jibrīl first commanded Muḥammad, "Iqra'!" (Recite!), and the culmination of the recitations that Muḥammad communicated over the next twenty-two years became the Qur'ān (literally "recitation"). The complete text includes 114 chapters, or *sūrāh*. This text has a number of significant features.

Revelation

Most Muslims understand the Qur'ān to be the revealed word of Allāh communicated to Muḥammad by Jibrīl and related by Muḥammad to Muslims who recorded it in writing. Arabs in seventh-century Arabia had scant access to paper, and so Muslims recorded the revelations on whatever they had available which might be paper, leather, or even bone. Most Muslims understand the revelation as deriving from a heavenly book written in Arabic. The elegance and sophistication of its poetry demonstrates for many that this text could not have originated from the illiterate Muḥammad. Many understand the inimitability of the Qur'ān as demonstrative of its unique nature and authorship. The Qur'ān appears to understand itself in this way as well when it challenges its detractors: "If you are in doubt of what We have revealed to Our votary, then bring a *sūra* like this and call any witness, apart from God, you like, if you are truthful" (2.23). This notion of the inability to produce any text equal to the Qur'ān has also informed the long-standing injunction against declaring a rendering of the Qur'ān into another language as a translation. The conceit of a translation is that it places into another language the meaning and form of a text. Many Muslims argue that this is not possible with the Qur'ān because its Arabic, composition, and meaning are inexorably interlinked. While most Indian Muslims rely on an Urdu interpretation of the text because they cannot understand the Arabic original, many will describe it as only an interpretation, not a translation. Booksellers make available Qur'āns with alternating lines of Arabic and Urdu—among other languages.

Most Muslims understand that, as revelation, the Qur'ān must be safeguarded against any corruption that might affect the text. The history of the three previously revealed books, their careless treatment, and the distortions that ultimately misled their communities required Muslims to go to great lengths to protect this final revelation. And so the third caliph, Uthmān, oversaw the final arrangement of the Qur'ān and the destruction of alternative editions so that the Qur'ān appears the same in any house or mosque in India, Asia, or any other continent. Although print technology makes the publication of the Qur'ān a relatively inexpensive proposition today, the practice continues that some Muslims memorize the entire text. They obtain the title *ḥāfiẓ* ("protector").

Themes

The Qur'ān arrived in portions over two decades, often directly addressing the current social or military conditions that the *umma* was confronting at a specific time. This is most clearly evident in the contrast between the Makkan and the Madinian verses. The verses revealed in Makka to a nascent community underscored themes of warning and exhortation. Specifically, these verses alerted all to the Day of Judgment and the individual accountability each person would undergo. This contrasted pointedly with Arab traditions that eschewed an afterlife and focused on the individual's accountability to the tribe and the tribe's accountability for each of its member's actions. The Qur'ān's original verses appeared to advise nonbelievers of the need for change, using dire warnings that they otherwise would suffer the consequences that Allāh, the Judge, would levy.

The verses revealed to Muḥammad in Madīna addressed the very different situation the *umma* experienced once it transformed from a movement into a society in its adopted home. These focus on the ordering of society on domestic and social levels while also exhorting Muslims to be brave in the face of violent oppression. These verses also stress the notion of "signs" provided by Allāh that demonstrate Allāh's presence and involvement in history for the benefit of believers. Nature represents the first sign Allāh provided humanity. The balance, regularity, and intricacy of nature all demonstrate the involvement of a creator.

Referentiality

"This is the Book which cannot be doubted and is a guidance to the God-fearing," *āyāt* 2.2 explains. It is almost as though, as revelation, the Qur'ān demonstrates an awareness of the book that it is, the audience it addresses, and the sense of purpose that informs it. Much of the Qur'ān appeals to Muslims who are variously exhorted and encouraged to various efforts. In some places, the Qur'ān appears to address non-Muslims with its warnings of imminent and long-term dangers caused by either their lack of belief and obstruction (in the case of polytheists) or their corrupt beliefs and resistance (in the case of Jews and Christians). Overall, although the revelations continued for more than two decades, various verses reflected an assumption that they cohered together.

Arrangement

Although the Qur'ān includes many narratives of events understood to have occurred in a specific order, its redactor(s) arranged it after Muḥammad's death neither as a narrative nor in chronological order of its revelation. Instead, after the first *sūra*, the remaining *sūrāh* were organized from longest first to shortest last. Each *sūra* is known by a name that derives from some unique feature of the chapter, undoubtedly to act as a mnemonic device for those who memorized the text in its entirety.

The first chapter of the Qur'ān is known as the *ṣura al-Fātiḥa* (Chapter of the Opening). Neither the first revealed (that was *sūra* 96) nor the longest (*sūra* 2), it acts as a distillation of the entire book.

> In the name of Allāh, the Compassionate, the Merciful
> Praise be to Allāh, the Lord of the Worlds,
> The Compassionate, the Merciful,
> Master of the Day of Judgment.
> Only You do we worship, and only You do we implore for help.
> Lead us to the right path,
> The path of those You have favored,
> Not those who have incurred your wrath,
> or who have gone astray.

The first verse, known as the *bismillāh*, represents a prayer unto itself. Just as most *sūrāh* begin with this verse, so new endeavors too are often initiated with its recitation. It dedicates the text or act "in the name of Allāh." The next four verses describe Allāh in praise, explicating the basic characteristics of the singular God who Muslims worship, the final yet compassionate judge. The exhortation of the concluding four verses expresses the Muslim faith that their God is involved in their lives and has a way that has been sanctioned but that not all follow. The Fātiḥah expresses the essence of the Qur'ān through its orientation to Allāh in the voice of the faithful who recognizes a path made apparent by the One God's direct guidance.

Demonstrating how many Muslims incorporate Qur'ānic elements directly into their lives, the Fātiḥa often acts as a prayer in its entirety. For instance in many communities, after a Muslim's death, he or she is buried with it read over the grave. Then, each month for the first year, close relatives will visit the gravesite and recite the Fātiḥa again. Not uncommonly, children continue this annually at their parents' graves.

If the first *sūra* reflects the entirety of the Qur'ān in its most reduced form, the second *sūra* demonstrates the general features of the Qur'ān. Generally, it can be divided into three components. In the first, the text refers to itself and its audience, as has been quoted earlier. Like the Fātiḥa, it also refers to those who have failed to listen to Allāh's message. In the second, examples from the lives of the prophets and others illustrate humanity's repetitive failures to abide by their God's will despite the multiple demonstrations of divine power. It advances this theme with a reflection on the individual's journey from prenatal nonexistence to birth to death to resurrection: "Then how can you disbelieve in Allāh? You were dead and He brought you back to life, then He will cause you to die and then bring you back to life again; then unto Him you will return" (2.28). The chapter then continues with examples of humanity's failures using the examples of Iblīs (a satanic being), Ādam and his wife, Mūsā (Moses) and the children of Israel, and ʿĪsā (Jesus) and the people of the Book. Although this list follows a generally recognized chronology of the lives of these prophets, the text's compilers clearly do not intend to provide an overall narrative of these lives. Rather, the text appears to assume its audience's familiarity with the various stories, as indeed seventh-century Arabs apparently were. In fact, Arabs understood their lineage as deriving from Ibrāhīm (Abraham) just as Jews did. However, the two groups differed as Arabs traced their genealogy through Ibrāhīm's son Ismāʿīl (Ishmael) and Jews through Isḥāq (Isaac). More generally, the stories of the prophets apparently required, and received, little elaboration for the Qur'ān's initial audience. Therefore, the prophets served as familiar examples and illustrations for the novel themes expressed in the *sūrāh*. The final section of the *sūra* concludes with a consideration of a range of prescribed and proscribed behaviors in the realms of diet, justice, fasting, pilgrimage, wine, marriage, and money.

Of course, despite the centrality of the Qur'ān, or rather because of it, the Qur'ān required interpretation. Although the text is ideally understood by many to be as transparent in meaning as it is sophisticated in its poetry, it—like all verbal expressions—requires interpretation because it cannot of itself speak. Traditions of interpretation (*tafsīr*) evolved over time and commonly drew first on the *sunna* of the Prophet as the baseline of interpretation. That the

Prophet had been the original interpreter of the text to Muslims only stood to reason considering his intimacy with the revealed word. Upon his death, his *sunna* became important not only to describe as many details as possible of this exemplary figure's life, but also to better understand the book he helped bring to humanity.

Ḥadīth

Toward this aim, various individuals began to collect *ḥadīth* ("reports") about Muḥammad as remembered by those who knew or encountered him. Two centuries after Muḥammad's death, the effort to collect *ḥadīth* culminated with compilers such as Abū-l-Ḥusayn Muslim (*died* 875) and Muḥammad Ibn Ismāʿīl Bukhārī (*died* 870) who traveled throughout Mediterranean and West Asian regions to record as many as possible. Gradually a system of collecting *ḥadīth* coalesced that took into account the volatile nature of memory and assessed not only the individual *ḥadīth* and its reporter, but also all the individuals who served as links in the chain of its transmission. A "science of humans" developed that maintained written biographies of the reporters with details including their family origins, general character, access to and closeness with Muḥammad, and, most importantly, the trustworthiness of their memory.

Two parts, therefore, compose each *ḥadīth*: the *isnād* (chain of transmitters) and *matn* (main text). So, for example, the following *ḥadīth*—regarding Muḥammad's practice of reciting the Fātiḥa *sūra* of the Qur'ān in each part of *namāz*, or the formal prayer—states:

> ʿAṭā reported it on the authority of Abū Huraira who said: Recitation Sūraṭ al-Fātiḥa in every (rakʿah) [part] of prayer is essential. (The recitation) that we listened to from the Apostle of Allah (may peace be upon him) we made you listen to it. And that which he recited inwardly to us, we recited it inwardly for you.
>
> (Muslim 1990, 1: 218)

The *isnād* in this case would link Imām Muslim (who compiled the collection in which this report appears) to ʿAṭā who communicates what Abū Hurayra has heard from Muḥammad himself. The *matn* includes the discussion that follows. Should someone question the authenticity of this claim based on the quality of the *isnād*, they only have to check one of the biographical volumes that qualify each link in the chain of transmission. This genre of literature would inform the skeptic that Abū Hurayra's real name was ʿAbd al-Raḥmān ad-Dawsī, although he went by 'Abd Shams before his conversion to Islam at which point he took the name of either 'Abd Allāh or ʿAbd al-Raḥmān. The biography includes such minutiae about individual transmitters that one learns that Abū Hurayra received that name because he played with a kitten while goat herding! More importantly, the biographies record that when he arrived in Madīna in 629 CE, Abū Hurayra had no responsibilities to distract him away from his rapt attention to Muḥammad. Because of his excellent memory (an obviously critical characteristic for a transmitter), about thirty-five hundred *ḥadīth*s have been narrated on his authority (Muslim 1990, 1: 3fn7). With this attention to the details of Muḥammad's *sunna*, those who observed his life, and those who communicated those observations, it comes as no surprise that a host of ancillary literatures developed to support knowledge about Muḥammad. Besides the *ḥadīth* collections and transmitter biographies, these included histories and "divine sayings" (*ḥadīth qudsī*) of Muḥammad.

The compilers arranged the *ḥadīth* according to themes, such as faith, purification, prayer, and warfare. In this form, the *ḥadīth* literature offered a compendium of reports on specific topics that could be compared in the search for an answer to a particular question regarding proper conduct or belief. Muslim communities have differed in their assessment of the various reporters and the collections themselves. Most Sunnīs rely heavily on the reports of Ā'isha who, as Muḥammad's youngest and favorite wife after Khadīja's death, is understood to offer a favored eyewitness to the life of Muḥammad. However, Shī'a tend to ignore her reports as her opposition to 'Alī's claim to the caliphate mars her reputation in the eyes of many. Regardless of which collections have been used, the *ḥadīth* tradition has featured prominently in Muslim efforts to discern the best way to live according to the will of Allāh.

One report, in particular, demonstrates the balance between Allāh's command and compassion, as well as the role of the *ḥadīth* literature to supplement the Qur'ān. It reports that, after his ascension, as Muḥammad returned from visiting Allāh, Mūsā asked him how many prayers Allāh had commanded Muslims to make daily. "Fifty" was Muḥammad's reply. Mūsā explained that Muḥammad needed to return and ask for a lower number because fifty prayers a day would be too onerous. Muḥammad did so and, upon his return, was questioned by Mūsā once again. Muḥammad explained that Allāh had reduced the original fifty daily prayers to forty but, at Muḥammad's urging, then to ten fewer. Muḥammad persisted until Allāh required five. Mūsā exclaimed that this would still be too difficult, but Muḥammad replied that he did not dare ask for anything less. This *ḥadīth* demonstrates a number of important dimensions of Muslim practice and literature. First, the *ḥadīth*'s importance derives at least in part from the lack of specificity regarding prayer in the Qur'ān. Although the text exhorts Muslims to pray as part of the "five pillars," it provides no details about the prayer such as its frequency. The *ḥadīth* literature complements the Qur'ān by detailing the number of times Muḥammad prayed and the manner of the action. Second, the *ḥadīth* reflects an understanding of Allāh as compassionate and unwilling to set requirements that would be too burdensome for the believers. Muslims should wait until they are capable to perform a prescribed duty before doing so. The young, the ill, the elderly, and travelers are all exempt from requirements that cause duress until the time, if possible, for them to do so.

The Five Pillars

The Qur'ān emphasizes a variety of beliefs and practices:

> Righteousness is not to turn your faces towards the East and the West; the righteous is he who believes in Allāh, the Last Day, the angels, the Book and the Prophets; who

> gives of his money, in spite of loving it, to the near of kin, the orphans, the needy, the wayfarers and the beggars, and for the freeing of slaves; who performs the prayers and pays the alms-tax. Such are also those who keep their pledges once they have made them, and endure patiently privation, affliction and in times of fighting. Those are the truthful and the God-fearing.
>
> (2.177)

However, no uniformity characterizes such lists as they appear in the Qur'ān. This underlines the fact that for all the Qur'ān provides for Muslims, it offers neither a detailed nor systematic outline for devotional or community life. This demonstrates why the early *umma* considered the development of supplemental literature a necessity.

Compensating for the Qur'ān's lack of specificity in many topics, certain *ḥadīth* clearly delineate the five central components of Muslim life central to "the straight path" which have come to be known as the "five pillars of Islam." Indeed, the very first *ḥadīth* in the collection Ṣaḥīḥ, Imām Muslim relates how ʿUmar ibn al-Khaṭṭāb remembered that a man (whom Muḥammad recognized as Jibrīl) asked the Prophet to tell him about Islam.

> The Messenger of Allāh (may peace be upon him) said: Al-Islam implies that you testify that there is no god but Allāh and the Muḥammad is the messenger of Allāh, and you establish prayer, pay Zakāt, observe the fast of Ramaḍān, and perform pilgrimage to the (House) if you are solvent enough (to bear the expense of) journey.
>
> (Muslim 1990, 1: 2)

These have come to be known as the five pillars of Islam, or the *arkān*. These should not be construed as the complete list of—or even the most important—Islamic practices for Muslims universally, since these would vary significantly among communities and individuals. Nevertheless, given their prominence among many Muslims, we shall examine each in turn.

Shahāda

The declaration of faith exactly states the central tenets of belief for almost all Muslims: *lā ilāha illā'llāh, Muḥammadun rāsūlu'llāh* (There is no god but God, and Muḥammad is the Messenger of God). In keeping with the revelation itself, the Muslim's religious emphasis begins with Allāh who, as Allāh's name implies, is "the One" (and only One). Yet the special prophethood of Muḥammad (whose *rasūl* status elevates him in status above all but the three other prophets who delivered books to humanity) must be mentioned because of his role in communicating the perfect revelation, but whose importance entirely derives from God. Many Muslims accept the recitation of the *shahāda* as a proclamation of one's embracing of Islam.

Ṣalāt/Namāz

As mentioned earlier, this formal prayer is ideally performed five times daily, although many who identify themselves as Muslims do so with far less regularity, if at all. Almost all Muslim women in India pray at home if they do not work outside the house, while men have the option of praying at home, at work, or in a mosque. Many Muslims consider social interactions between unrelated men and women as potentially dangerous—morally and physically—and so mosques that accommodate both genders must have some form of separation. Although in some parts of India, Ladakh for instance, men and women may pray together (perhaps in separate rooms, perhaps in one room divided by a sheet), most mosques exclude women for lack of an appropriate space for them. That is to say that because almost all Muslims in India live in patriarchal communities that define the public sphere as a primarily masculine realm and the domestic as principally feminine, Muslims have constructed mosques as public spaces mostly reserved for men. Those who do not practice *namāz* (the Persian-derived term more commonly used than the Arabic *ṣalāt*) daily may be more likely to do so on Friday when many, if not most, of the men assemble for the noonday prayer. The majority of Muslims understand this time to be the most important one to perform *namāz* together because Friday, according to the term used in the Islamic calendar, is "the day of the congregation." Cities and villages often have a designated *jumā masjid* (congregational mosque) in which Muslim men assemble for these prayers. At the end of the Friday prayers, the assembled listen to a sermon given by the prayer leader (*imām*) for that day.

Whenever and wherever it is performed, the ritual remains basically the same (Sunnī and Shīʿa practices differ slightly). A muezzin performs the call to prayer (Urdu *azān*; Arabic *a<u>dh</u>ān*) from the *mīnār* (English minaret) attached to the mosque. Previously, Muslims built *mīnār*s large enough to accommodate a staircase by which the muezzins ascended to ensure that their call would be heard at a distance. Today, loudspeakers commonly replace the muezzin's labored climb five times a day. Many smaller mosques include a *mīnār* big enough for nothing more than loudspeakers. The calls announce the five prayer times: sunrise, midday, afternoon, sunset, and evening. Whether in a mosque or at home, hearing the call or watching the time, a praying Muslim proceeds to perform a series of ablutions (Urdu *wuzū*; Arabic *wuḍū*') in which he or she cleans hands, mouth, forearms, and feet. This purifies the Muslim in preparation for prayer to Allāh. No matter where they pray, Muslims stand side-by-side where room allows it. In a mosque, the congregation follows the lead of the *imām* (leader) who stands in front and begins the prayer by methodically moving through its different components. These involve the specific bodily postures of standing, bowing, kneeling, and prostrating with head to ground. Prayer ends with a ritual greeting to those on either side of the Muslim who may take this time to supplicate or praise Allāh using the more informal *duʿā'* style of prayer.

Ṣawm

The month of Ramaḍān (many Indian Muslims refer to it as Ramẓān) represents the celebration of the revelation of the Qur'ān because in this month, in 610 CE, Allāh revealed the first verse to Muḥammad. Many Muslims celebrate this dimension by reading the Qur'ān regularly throughout the month. Some publications of the Qur'ān are specially printed—divided into thirty portions to facilitate this. At least equally prominent in this month, fasting occupies most Muslims' efforts. From before sunrise to just after sunset, Muslims forego any drink or food, using this opportunity to call to mind the suffering of the poor. This sacrifice becomes more acute in the years when this month on the Islamic calendar occurs in the summer, as the days are longer and the weather warmer (the Islamic calendar operates on a lunar system, and so its months annually shift relative to the seasons). Although some will even avoid swallowing their own saliva, many describe the experience as liberating and that it brings them so close to Allāh that they do not feel any discomfort.

As with most of the other pillars of Islam, *ṣawm* includes an important social dimension. At the conclusion of every day, everyone gathers for *ifṭār*, a special meal marking the breaking of the fast. Generally, the family gathers and eats together (whereas often men would be served by the women who prepare the meal first and eat last) around a large spread of different foods. Customarily, the meal begins with dates because Muḥammad enjoyed them especially. Non-Muslim friends may be invited as well. For obvious reasons, the final day of Ramaḍān means a particularly special celebration. Whatever benefits may be claimed from the fasting, the return to the rest of the year's routine is welcome. Even before the first sliver of the moon is seen following the new moon ending the month, families make preparations for *ʿīd al-fiṭr* so that on the day after the sighting, everyone who can afford it dons new clothes. The men proceed to the *ʿīdgāh*—an enclosed field reserved specifically for the communal prayer of the two annual *ʿīds* (*ʿīd al-fiṭr*, "feast of breaking fast," and *ʿīd al-aḍḥā*, "feast of sacrifice"). This *namāz* ends with everyone hugging one another and saying "ʿīd mubārak" (congratulations on the ʿīd). Children enjoy special treats, and family members visit one another and friends.

Zakāt

The Qur'ān and the *ḥadīth* include many passages exhorting social justice, especially care for the orphans and the impoverished, and many communities reinforce these messages through their own traditions, practices, and sentiments. *Zakāt* works to provide for the distribution of wealth and for the protection of the less well off in society. It ideally amounts to a 2.5 percent annual levy on the total wealth of individuals comfortable enough to afford it. Muḥammad institutionalized the practice (mentioned in the Qur'ān, later detailed in the *ḥadīth*) a few years after arriving in Madīna. Premodern governments operating under an Islamic ideology commonly collected the *zakāt*, but the introduction of secular states led to a decline in its collection. It no longer exists as an operation of government in India, so—as in much of the world—individual Muslims determine for themselves to what degree they practice *zakāt*.

Ḥajj

Pilgrimage to Makka composed part of the religious lives of the Arabs in pre-Islamic Arabia who traveled to worship images of their tribal deities housed in and around the Kaʿba. Muḥammad's cleansing and rededication of the Kaʿba reoriented it solely toward Islamic practices. Even before this event, its centrality for Muslims was encouraged when Muḥammad, as directed by a Qur'ānic verse, shifted the direction of prayer away from Jerusalem (an orientation they shared with the Jewish tribes of Madīna) toward Makka.

Historically, the *ḥajj* has served to bring Muslims from throughout the world into contact with one another annually and communicate this experience to the people of their homelands upon their return. The *ḥajj* unites Muslim social memories of the lives of the prophets with the landscape on which they purportedly lived. With the increased communications and transportation systems of today, more than two million Muslims arrive every year (more than one hundred thousand from India) at the beginning of the month on the Islamic calendar specifically designated for the *ḥajj* (pilgrimage to Makka during any other month is designated *ʿumra*). During the ten or so days of the *ḥajj*, pilgrims will circumambulate the Kaʿba, the reconstruction Ibrāhīm and Ismāʿīl accomplished on the spot where Ādam built the first mosque; run between the two hills where Hājar (English Hagar) once desperately sought water for her dying son Ismāʿīl; stand on Mount Arafāt where Ādam and his wife Ḥawwā' reunited following their dispatch from Paradise; and walk in the city where the final prophet, Muḥammad, lived most of his life.

The incorporation of the individual Muslim into the larger *umma* occurs through not only ritual reenactment but also dress. As though in recognition of the dual ideal nature of the *umma*, male pilgrims dress themselves in two lengths of plain white cloth that signals the equality of all humans before Allāh, while women may wear their native clothes (so long as they are appropriately austere) in recognition of the diversity of cultures in which Muslims live. Upon their return home, pilgrims often accept the honorific title *ḥajjī* or *ḥajjā* ("one who has performed the *ḥajj*") as a marker of their accomplishment.

Muḥarram

The commemoration of the martyrdom of Ḥusayn and his companions plays an important, annual part in the lives of many Indian Muslims. Although some Muslims object to the celebration of individuals—whether it be a Ṣūfī on his *ʿurs* (death day) or even Muḥammad on his birthday, Mawlid *al-Nabī*—Shīʿas consider Muḥarram a crucial commemoration. The death of the Prophet's grandson at the hands of a Muslim army summons waves of lament for a terrible tragedy experienced anew through the symbols and rituals of participants focused in a procession fueled by pathos. Despite the particularly special meaning Ḥusayn has for Shīʿa as the rightful successor to the Prophet and one of the infallible *imāms* (of which there were only seven or twelve depending on the specific tradition), some Sunnīs too participate in the commemorations. In places without any Shīʿa, sometimes Sunnīs take responsibility for the procession. It is not surprising that this emotionally charged atmosphere has been one of the most frequent environments for Hindu-Muslim conflict, as the processions move through shared public space in cities and villages, past temples, shrines, and sacred trees that if treated in a manner considered inappropriate may incite a defensive response. Such is not, however, usually the case, as demonstrated in the example of one contemporary Muḥarram procession.

In Dehradun, at the edge of the foothills of the Himālayas, tens of thousands of Muslims line the annual Muḥarram procession's anticipated route. As it arrives, the audience watches very tall poles bearing black standards precede the slowly moving procession that gently parts the swelling crowd along the roadside. Atop each standard is a symbolic outstretched hand, each finger representing one member of the cherished family: Muḥammad, his daughter Fāṭimah, her husband ʿAlī, and their sons Ḥasan and Ḥusayn. Behind them a horse draped in a blood-stained cloth suggests Ḥusayn's horse dappled by his blood. Finally, a *taʿziya* (replica of Ḥusayn's tomb in Karbalā') is carried aloft by a group of men. Occasionally the procession halts, and a small circle of primarily young men forms. They whip themselves with chains or slap their chests in an attempt to draw blood in order to feel an empathetic connection to their slain *imām*. From the balconies above, women and girls watch, drawn by its passion and spectacle, before it moves off down the building-lined street.

Ṣūfī Poetry

Among religious literature significant to Indian Muslims, Ṣūfī poetry deserves particular attention. As described in the previous section, Ṣūfīs have molded the shape of many South Asians' religious lives by providing a language of devotion, an avenue to Islam, and a model for the devotee. Some of these Ṣūfīs have written important treatises on their mystical relationship with Allāh, but their most enduring and widespread impact has been through the devotional poems that they have crafted, which have inspired Muslims and others for centuries. The first significant Ṣūfī treatise crafted in South Asia, Abu-l-Ḥasan ʿAlī al-Hujwīrī's *Kashf al-Mahjūb li-Arbāb al-Qulūb* (The Unveiling of the Hidden for the Lords of the Heart), may still be studied a thousand years after its formulation, but a small proportion of Indian Muslims know of this Persian language text. However, the vernacular poems performed in the *dargāh*s of Ṣūfī saints remain the most celebrated because of the significance of these shrines for the lives of so many Muslims and others. Rich in metaphor and imagery, these poems compel many of their readers, reciters, and audience members to engage in a religious reality distinct from the everyday world. The best-known form of Ṣūfī devotional performance is *qawwālī*. Every Thursday night at *dargāh*s large enough to attract them, *qawwāl*s perform for devotees. Some become entranced because of the presence of the *pīr*'s ("respected leader") tomb and the power of the music. A few may begin to clap and dance to the *qawwālī* and perhaps are even taken into momentary ecstasy by the experience.

• INSTITUTIONS AND PRACTICES

The arrival in the Middle period of rulers who happened to be Muslim introduced the wide-scale support of Islamic institutions and practices as never before. Just as earlier kingdoms might support Jaina or Buddhist institutions even as they defined themselves as supportive of a Brāhmaṇa-derived order with legitimacy expressed through the financial support of

Brāhmaṇas, patronage of temples, and ritual confirmation of the king using Brāhmaṇic rituals, so Muslim rulership did not automatically negate or erase Hindu establishments. While Muslim courts did displace many of these institutions with systems of rule that made claims to legitimacy based on an Islamic—not Brāhmaṇic—order, nevertheless, many Brāhmaṇic institutions continued to receive state support as Muslim rulers sought to demonstrate the worth of their rule to their non-Muslim subjects.

No central institutions characterize Islam or organize the *umma*: the earlier ideal of a politically and religiously united caliphate faded before Muslims came to be a large population in South Asia. Although Muslim Indian rulers often characterized themselves as the leaders of a united Muslim community, they did not attempt to centralize the diverse practices of Islam. Instead, a variety of elements exist that provide Muslims with a collection of organizing and authoritative bodies, specifically the mosque, the *ʿulamā'*, the Islamic education system, *dargāh*s, and *ṭarīqa*s.

The Family

But before considering any of these formal institutions, perhaps the most important organizing body needs to be considered: the family. Throughout the Qur'ān, the *ḥadīth*, and most Muslim traditions in India, the family stands as the bulwark for the *umma*. Such a notion appears at odds with modern Western assumptions that the preservation of individual rights and expressions outweigh group concerns. Nevertheless, their place in the family for most Indian Muslims—and most Indians—greatly defines who they are and how they behave. This perspective can be understood as one of the most influential dynamics in the definition of Muslim gender roles. As both the portals for the next generation and the primary caregivers for children, women have commonly borne a weighty responsibility by embodying the honor (Urdu *izzat*) of the family. Such perspectives are less endemic to Islamic ideologies imported into South Asia than in the cultures that have adopted and adapted Islamic traditions and justified their practices in the context of their religious interpretations. Perhaps the most prominent issue regarding *izzat* debated in Indian Muslim circles pertains to the importance and rationale for *purdah*, the withdrawal of women from public view. Because the life of the Prophet, and his family, provides such an exemplar for most Muslims, it is not a surprise that the controversy regarding *purdah* often gravitates toward a discussion of the conditions in the early *umma*.

No consensus has been reached by Muslim reformers and secular scholars who have questioned whether life in the original *umma* brought greater liberties or restrictions to Arab women.[4] However, much of the ensuing debate has wrestled with the Qur'ānic meaning of the term "*ḥijāb*" (commonly rendered into English as the misleading "veil" but which can also mean "curtain," "screen," "concealment," "headscarf," and "modesty") and its import to Muslim life. It does appear that however they have been interpreted later, the relevant Qur'ānic verses generally do not specifically pertain to women except one, which is narrowly in regard to Muḥammad's family:

> O believers, do not enter the houses of the Prophet, unless you are invited to a meal, without awaiting the hour; but if you are invited, then enter; when you have eaten, disperse, without lingering for idle talk. That is vexing to the Prophet who might be wary of you, but Allāh is not wary of the truth. If you ask them for an object, ask them from behind a curtain.
>
> (33.53; Altorki 1995: 324)

What appears to many Muslims as a cautionary injunction to protect the household privacy of the publicly high-profile Muḥammad was taken by other Muslims as another of the Prophet's examples to be followed universally. However, *āyāt* 24.31 demonstrates well the greater expectations of modesty placed on women than men and that should be practiced in front of nonrelated men, perhaps because of an understood need to control women as the embodiment of the family's honor. Various *ḥadīth* would elaborate on the issues of a woman's concealment, and many propound more restrictive perspectives.

Mirroring the academic situation regarding women in the early *umma*, scholarly debate has ensued in the effort to determine whether South Asian women lost public freedoms with the advent of Muslim-dominated states after the eleventh century. The prevalence of similar *purdah* restrictions among many Muslim and Hindu women today has been considered evidence of pre-Muslim patriarchal limits (which would suggest that these are endemic to many South Asian cultures) and—alternatively—as the result of Muslim political dominance (suggesting an inequality introduced through Islamic traditions). Whatever its cultural origins, Muslim reformers began to mount wide-scale challenges to *purdah* beginning in the nineteenth century. Nevertheless, these ideologies of reform often promoted change in the interest of the family and for the greater fulfillment of women as mothers and wives, not in reference to greater individual freedom. For a great number of families, *purdah* represents the luxury of the economically well off. Women whose families rely on them to work in fields and factories cannot afford to remain secluded from nonfamily members. Meanwhile, men—although allowed a variety of public roles outside the family-dominated domestic sphere—are also commonly defined according to their place in the family.

The Mosque

As mentioned above, the mosque in India provides a central location for Muslim men (and, in a very few places, women) to pray together. However, this space often serves as a gathering place for celebrations, as a place of reverie, and as a place of study. Mosque designs vary tremendously according to the local space limitations, community financial resources, and regional architectural styles. Yet they often include a walled courtyard, a central structure at one end, and a *mīnār* (minaret). The courtyard serves as an open space in which the faithful gather for prayers without chairs or benches. Its walls shield the individual from whatever commotion may occur in the neighborhood outside. Commonly white with bare walls and perhaps a clock for knowing the prayer times, the mosque provides a place usually with few distractions. At the west end of the courtyard stands a prayer hall of varying size that allows prayers to be said indoors to avoid the monsoon rain, winter cold, or summer sun. A niche (*miḥrāb*) in the west wall of this enclosure indicates the direction of Makka (*qiblah*). Like a gravitational pole, Makka serves to orientate all Muslims who pray facing it.

Even after the decline of Muslim monarchs who built mosques as emblems of their legitimation to rule, mosques today can play a central role in political mobilization. For instance, in Delhi the Mughal-built *jamaʿ masjid*—meaningfully positioned across from the Red Fort with its imperial residence and at the edge of the Muslim-dominated Old City—has served as a forum for political activity. In an unexpected moment in 1920, for instance, Muslims and Hindus gathered there to mourn activists shot dead by police during a general strike against British rule organized by Mohandas K. Gandhi and leaders of the Khilāfat Movement (see below). Reflecting the intercommunal nature of that movement, a Hindu was among those prompted to address the gathered assembly (Minault 1982: 70). However, mosques, even those once built as the concrete expression of a state's Islamic polity, on a day-to-day basis usually serve far less politically charged purposes, as could be seen one day recently in the South Indian city of Bijapur.

> A group of men sit with their back against one of the four dozen towering pillars from which arches spring on each side. As they talk over the large Qur'ān open on a winged, wooden bookstand, their voices dwindle in the vastness of the cavernous prayer hall. Above them, a dome caps the center of the hall, double in height from the already distant ceiling. The comforting cooling shade contrasts with the sharp sunlight of the Deccan sky that ̣Loods the courtyard outside the prayer hall. Sulṭān ʿAlī ʿĀdil Shāh I built this mosque in 1565 as the *masjid al-jāmi* of the capital city, Bījāpūr, of his sprawling kingdom. More than two thousand can gather inside for *namāz*. Although most of India's myriad mosques do not approximate the grandeur of this building, the care and commitment required to design, construct, and maintain such a sophisticated and graceful piece of architecture demonstrates the signiẉcance of mosques as emblems of rulership legitimated using Islamic symbols.

The ʿUlamā'

Because of the importance of living according to Allāh's guidelines provided by the Qur'ān, elaborated upon in the *ḥadīth*, and developed through the *s̲h̲arīʿa*, experts in the law have long had a prominent role among many Muslim communities. These juridical specialists, termed *ʿulamā'* ("learned"), have trained in one of the schools of law. However, the definition of *ʿulamā'* as jurists reflects the changes wrought by global European imperialism in the nineteenth and twentieth centuries, which established a hegemony that radically altered the understanding of what learning the *ʿulamā'* represented. For the millennium that preceded this period, the *ʿulamā'* specialized not only in *s̲h̲arīʿa* and its supporting studies (for example, Qur'ān and *tafsīr*) but also in geometry, astronomy, logic, and medicine. The ascent of Western forms of knowledge eclipsed these studies just as English and French replaced many indigenous languages as the languages of learning. A decline in the number of states instituting <u>sh</u>*arīʿa* followed the expansion of British rule and the ascent of English law (Zaman 1995: 259–60). Many among the *ʿulamā'*, therefore, became less cosmopolitan and more isolated, especially in schools of its instruction. This accelerated following the 1857 rebellion, when the British state curtailed funding for *madrasa*s ("schools") for fear that the more educated an Indian might become, the more prone he or she was to nationalism (Reid 1995: 413–14). Today, some of the *madrasa*s run by *ʿulamā'* provide only the basics of Qur'ānic recitation (that is, proper pronunciation of Qur'ānic Arabic but not interpretation into vernacular languages) for very young children, while others include a range of subjects that might be pursued at higher levels of education.

The Ṣūfī Dargāh

The final institution we will consider will be the Ṣūfī *dargāh*. Ubiquitous across much of South Asia, *dargāh*s represent nodes of popular religiosity and perceived conduits of superhuman power. Individual living Ṣūfīs, when a community recognizes them as spiritually powerful, can serve a variety of roles. Parents may bring sick children, the despondent may seek insightful advice, and legal adversaries may request arbitration from a living Ṣūfī. When one dies, if he or she is particularly revered, the community may build a shrine to house their grave, patrons adding features as an indication of their devoted respect for or specific request of the dead saint or *pīr* ("respected leader"). The *dargāh* becomes a place for venerating the dead Ṣūfī and a site of superhuman power (*baraka*). Infertile women may kneel before the tomb vowing a gift to the Ṣūfī should she become pregnant, or a young person may touch their hand to the tomb's wall and then their head in veneration while praying for better school exam results. Some leave bottles of water on the tomb overnight and then, collecting them the next day, administer the liquid to the infirm as though the proximity to the tomb charged the liquid with an energy that can be consumed. Hindus, Christians, Sikhs, and others may join Muslims at the tomb because of their recognition of the power available for those who know how to access it through their devotions. Just as shrines offer a place of connection between Muslims and non-Muslims, most also provide a rare place of public worship for Muslim women. The shrines often, but not always, offer separate entrances and/or prayer spaces for women and men to minimize sexual distraction. However, many Muslims dismiss the practices surrounding Ṣūfīs as, at best, superstition and, at worst, idolatry. Nevertheless, many defenders of these graveside devotions argue that the Ṣūfī only provides an example of true submission and performs no miracles himself or herself.

The political involvement of Ṣūfīs reflects the reverence they can command in life and death. Many of the premodern Muslim rulers sought affirmation of their mandate from Ṣūfīs and offered patronage to those who gave it. For instance, the Mughal emperor Akbar received the blessing for a son from the revered Salīm Chi<u>sh</u>tī. When his prayer appeared answered, he not only named his son Salīm in appreciation and built a dazzling white marble shrine around the now-dead saint's tomb, he also removed his entire court from the competing imperial centers of Delhi and Agra (Ernst and Lawrence 2002: 98–9) and settled them in Fatehpur Sikri, a new city the emperor built near Chishtī's *dargāh*.

Not all Ṣūfīs have willingly involved themselves in politics, however. According to one popular story, when Niẓām ad-Dīn Awliyā' (*died* 1325), another member of the Chishtiyya *ṭarīqa* (branch), was summoned by the sulṭān to his encampment quite far away, the Ṣūfī refused to leave Delhi and attend to him. When the sulṭān's camp was but one day's march away from its return to Delhi, the Ṣūfī was warned of the threat of the sulṭān's punishment. Niẓām ad-Dīn famously replied, "Delhi is still far." His devotees have understood this as an expression of his preternatural knowledge that in the following night one of the elephants of the sulṭān's retinue would accidentally back into his tent, felling a pole that crushed the sulṭān. Narratives demonstrating the divine punishment for political leaders who presume superiority over Ṣūfīs are familiar among devotees in many parts of the world.

The death anniversary provides an occasion for special celebration at the *dargāh*. During the *ʿurs* ("wedding"), devotees of a *pīr* may arrive from other states or—if the *pīr* is of high enough stature—from other countries to celebrate this day. Why celebrate a death day? Most Ṣūfīs have understood that the final communion with Allāh (*fanā'*) is impossible before death when the "final veil" (to borrow one of myriad metaphors) falls. The *pīr* walks through the door to Paradise. During the *ʿurs*, groups of devotees carry funeral shrouds, some decorated with Qur'ānic verse or geometric designs outlined in glitter, through the streets of the *pīr*'s village or city and then place it on the tomb's barrow along with garlands of flowers and incense. Group prayer around the tomb may offer a brief interlude for the day- and night-long commotion as attendees enjoy children's games, shopping from peddlers, and socializing. Throughout, *qawwāl*s (performers of the Ṣūfī devotional music *qawwālī*) sing their songs, at times competing among one another for the crowds' attention. But devotees and others need not wait until a Ṣūfī's *ʿurs* to demonstrate their devotion or petition for help as can be seen most days at the famous *dargāh* of Niẓām ad-Dīn in Delhi.

The significance of Niẓām ad-Dīn's *dargāh* becomes apparent long before one reaches its actual grounds. The police barriers that protect the long alley leading to the *dargāh* announce that the local police station and entire neighborhood is named after him. Walking down the alley often means following a busy stream of people as they make their way through the various shops that line the route offering Qur'āns and bangles, incense and toys, and Islamic calendars and sports shoes. The way leads into a large stone-paved area surrounded by religious buildings and homes in this densely populated part of Delhi. A sign announces the offices of the descendants of Niẓām ad-Dīn's family, recognized as the custodians of his tomb and guardians of his legacy. The devotee passes a low wall enclosing a dozen or so tombs of prominent family members before arriving at the shrine itself. However grand this is, composed of a one-story building with red sandstone walls, it seems diminutive compared to the long, domed mosque that extends the length of the *dargāh* grounds. Some men sleep in the shelter it provides from the mild rain that falls. Nevertheless, the shrine itself draws most of the attention of visitors who approach it with evident veneration and respect. Removing their shoes and covering their heads, men enter the inner sanctum and pray while women do their devotions from an area separated from the men by a screen intricately carved from the red sandstone. Many leave behind ribbons and tufts of hair tied to the screen as evidence of some vow they have made there. Meanwhile two middle-aged men sit themselves in front of the *dargāh* entrance and begin to sing *qawwālī*, one pumping his accordion-like harmonium and the other playing a small set of drums, while a crowd slowly coalesces, sitting and listening to the sonorous music.

• ETHICS AND HUMAN RELATIONS

Overall, most Muslims view Islamic practices as involving relationships with other humans as surely as they do with Allāh. For instance, social reformers have often drawn on Islamic concepts to correct inequalities existing in their societies. In doing so, they frequently point to the example of Muḥammad and various Qur'ānic prescriptions and proscriptions regulating behavior as evidence of the original impulse to create an equitable *umma* and as a source for more contemporary efforts.

The Qur'ān makes explicit that submission to Allāh requires appropriate individual and community behavior: "Say: 'My Lord commands justice. Set your faces straight at every place of prayer and call on Him in true devotion'" (7.29). It balances reflections on the persecution of the early *umma* (which followed their condemnation of the injustices of contemporary Makkan society) with requirements for behavior. Meanwhile, the Qur'ān emphasizes the responsibility of the *umma* to "enjoin the right and forbid the wrong" in all facets of society (such as the political, economic, and legal). Some verses condemn outright contemporary practices such as female infanticide, mentioned earlier. Other *āyāt* seemingly attempt to moderate behaviors that perhaps were considered not as easily halted because of social intractability. For instance, a passage (4.3) dealing with polygyny explains that Muslim men may marry "two, three, or four" wives, and then warns that if each cannot be treated equitably, then they should marry only one. However, a later verse implies the impossibility of treating multiple wives, the same. According to the interpretation of some, these verses implicitly prohibit polygyny. They view these verses as evidence that the early *umma* sought to curtail a pre-Islamic Arab practice that could not be prohibited outright at a time when many widows were left economically helpless after their husbands died in battles against the Makkans. Others have suggested that the Qur'ān endorses a change from pre-Islamic monogyny. Whatever the case may have been, what is clear is that the Qur'ān does not represent a legal code. In fact, less than one hundred verses deal with legal matters. Instead, it acts as the guidance it describes itself at the beginning of "The Cow" *sūra* (see 2.2).

Meanwhile, the centrality of just human relations became ritualized through some of the most common practices. For instance, the institution of *zakāt* seeks to redistribute wealth to those with fewer resources, a perennial concern in the Qur'ān and the *ḥadīth*. It ideally offers both support for the impoverished and a check on the wealth accumulation of the wealthy, as well as a bond between these two groups. As such, it should not be considered "charity" because it is neither voluntary, nor an act of pity, but rather an act of devotion and justice.

Ṣawm, or the Ramaḍān fasting, represents another common practice with an implicit focus on human relations. Although Ramaḍān celebrates Allāh's revelation of the Qur'ān to humanity (and prompts Muslims to focus on this connection with God), it also involves a fast understood by many Muslims as allowing for empathy with the poor. The *ʿīd al-fiṭr* celebration that concludes the month further manifests the connections and responsibilities of Muslims to others through the distribution of alms before the morning feast.

Finally, the conclusion of the *ḥajj* also includes a ritualized expression of concern for others. In memory of Ibrāhīm's willingness to sacrifice his son Ismāʿīl (notice the difference from the Jewish and Christian narratives, which put Isḥāq in the son's place) to Allāh and Allāh's merciful exchange of a heaven-sent ram for the boy, Muslims conclude the ten-day period of the pilgrimage with *baqr ʿīd*. This feast centrally features the meat of an animal especially slaughtered on *ʿīd* itself. Many families keep the animal (by tradition a goat) intended for the next *ʿīd* near their home so that the emotional impact of the sacrifice can be experienced fully. The butcher follows the rules of *ḥalāl*, which prescribe the proper manner of slaughtering and bleeding the animal. After the sacrifice, in which a prayer recited over the animal precedes its slaughter, the meat is divided into three portions equally: one-third to the immediate family, one-third to other family and friends, and one-third to the poor. In many places, the impoverished arrive at the gates of homes engaged in their butchering and wait for the householders to offer them part of the sacrifice. Family members dispatch other pieces to homes in the area.

Mosques and *dargāh*s offer another form of giving: that of hospitality. It is generally understood that travelers can find shelter in a mosque or a *dargāh* for up to three nights. Moreover, *dargāh*s commonly operate as sites for the distribution of charity to the needy. Most *dargāh*s with sufficient resources offer a free meal daily that anyone can accept. At Niẓām ad-Dīn's shrine in Delhi, for example, a long line assembles as the distribution time arrives, stretching in front of the large mosque that stands at one side of the expansive courtyard. Meanwhile, the poor commonly line the entrances to *dargāh*s at any time of day in the hope that a generous devotee might offer them some money as they pass. These often include those unemployed due to physical disfigurement caused by accident, debilitating illness, or birth deformation.

However, the primary means by which Muslims have historically expressed their concerns for ethical behavior and human relations has been through *sharīʿa*, Islamic law as established by Allāh. Even though it does not represent the primary law code for Muslims in today's secular India, *sharīʿa* nevertheless plays a role in the lives of many. Reflecting, like most other Islamic institutions, the primacy of the Qur'ān and then the Prophet's *sunna*, *sharīʿa* attempts to provide what neither of these sources offers: a complete law code for the regulation of society and structures for legislation and adjudication. Therefore, *sharīʿa* developed a reliance on other sources and specific traditions of interpreting them. The human effort to discern the details, extent, and application of *sharīʿa* is called *fiqh*. If *sharīʿa* is the law God intends, then *fiqh* is the human effort to understand and apply that law.

The various traditions of *sharīʿa* that developed globally among Muslims differ in two ways: the supplementary sources on which they define *sharīʿa* and the specific intellectual tools used in *fiqh*. The *ʿulamāʾ*, as scholars of law, mediated the interpretation of *sharīʿa* and the operations of *fiqh*. Among Sunnīs worldwide, four legal traditions developed, and two of these dominated India: Mālikī in the south and Ḥanafī in the north. They differ only in the emphasis they put on various elements of legal reasoning, since they draw from the same sources and use similar legal techniques. The Mālikī school, which developed in eighth-century Arabia, relies heavily on the *ḥadīth* and the practices of Muḥammad's contemporaries in Makka. The Ḥanafī school, originating in eighth-century Iraq, relies less on these traditions and more on opinion derived from reason and analogy. This has allowed Ḥanafī decisions to demonstrate more liberal judgments in law than the Mālikī. Ultimately, Mālikī would become eclipsed in importance in India, even in the south. Generally, the Shīʿa have their own traditions of *sharīʿa* that place special emphasis on *ijtihād* (interpretation), but because of the rarity of Shīʿa rule on the subcontinent, they have seldom been instituted.

In the period when Muslims ruled as Islamicly legitimated leaders, they claimed legitimacy for their rule by speaking, at least in part, to the expectations of the *ʿulamāʾ*. These included the promotion of *sharīʿa* and the protection of what they considered Islam that together defined *dār al-Islām* (the "abode of Islam"). However, the actual implementation of *sharīʿa* varied from ruler to ruler so that, for instance, the Mughal emperor Akbar routinely frustrated the *ʿulamāʾ* in pursuit of his own eclectic religious pursuits (which may have only been his effort to appeal to the diverse religious population he ruled), while his great-grandson Awrangzeb tended to cater to the *ʿulamāʾ* while disparaging Ṣūfīs and other forms of "unorthodoxy."

The decline of Islamic political ideologies on the subcontinent followed the ascent of British imperialism that introduced its own forms of law and legal reasoning based on secular, "rationalist" models. Complementing their universal criminal law, however, the British communalized "personal law" by establishing separate law codes governing individual affairs as defined by the religion to which the individual belongs. One British court explained this system in an 1871 legal decision:

> While Brahmin, Buddhist, Christian, Mahomedan, Parsee, and Sikh are one nation, enjoying equal political rights and having perfect equality before the Tribunals, they co-exist as separate and very distinct communities, having distinct laws affecting every relation in life.
>
> (Derrett 1999: 39)

The legal situation remains largely unchanged today, although cases such as the Shah Bano trial (in 1985) have prompted calls for a uniform civil code that would apply to all regardless of religious community. Shah Bano sought maintenance from the husband divorcing her, not according to the Muslim Personal Law that applied by precedent to her as a Muslim, but according to the civil law governing all who do not claim minority status. Although the central government at first supported the decision for her to do so, it flipped its decision once it recognized the depth of Muslim anger regarding the situation. Many Muslims feared that such a code would subject India's Muslim minority to the legal traditions of the Hindu majority, and thereby further increase their social subordination. Other Muslims call for reform of Muslim Personal Law and/or the implementation of the uniform code.

• MODERN EXPRESSIONS

Many Muslims describe "Islam" as a singular collection of practices and beliefs which, like the Qur'ān, Allāh created. Putting aside questions of the truth of this theology, we recognize that because all people live in cultures, the Muslim expressions associated with "Islam" reflect the experiences, attitudes, ideals, and concerns of the myriad cultures of which Muslims are a part. Like the societies that influence them, these expressions differ among one another and have changed over time, even as many lay claim to being the "true" expression of the Qur'ān's injunctions and Muḥammad's example. In fact, modern Islamic expressions, even in India alone, cannot be numbered because of the amazing diversity of rituals, ideas, and communities among Muslims. However, what non-Muslims may perceive from a distance as a uniformity in Islamic practices, beliefs, and sentiments becomes more apparently nonuniform the greater the familiarity one has with Muslim communities and individuals. Although we can certainly claim that most Muslims recognize the supremacy of the Qur'ān and appreciate the example of the Prophet, universal claims can only be made at one's peril. Described below are some of the more significant organized Islamic expressions among modern Muslims. Although many of the organizations mentioned were established and later run by men, many developed important women's wings, such as did the Tablīg̱ẖī Jamāʿat considered in the last section.

First, however, a note of caution is needed. Throughout history there have consistently been those who would critique, reinterpret, or reform contemporary forms of Islam in response to various internal social changes or external geopolitical conditions. Notably, most modern Muslims, and certainly those in India, have found themselves in a context of Western hegemony since the eighteenth century. Although the direct political and military control of the subcontinent that existed during the era of British imperial rule ended in 1947, Western hegemony in economic and cultural (if not political) spheres remains and has often influenced, if not inspired, some of the more recent expressions of Islam. We must beware caricaturing these expressions as only a reaction to the West—and thereby affirm a Eurocentric image of Westerners as the agents of historical change and Muslims as reactive, never innovative—yet recognize the unprecedented marriage of political and economic control with cultural persuasion that imperial Western powers have practiced. The imperially dominated necessarily responded to this pervasive situation even as they creatively promoted their own visions of Islam and Muslim life.

Muhammad Iqbal

Muhammad Iqbal's life clearly demonstrates this situation. Iqbal (about 1877–1938) pursued advanced studies in Lahore, Cambridge, and Munich. Although originally an Indian nationalist, he came to disparage nationalism through critical reflection on the imperialism and chauvinism he believed it fostered in Europe. Instead, he promoted a reformed Muslim society that would rely on *ijtihād* both to modernize Islam and to revive past ideals in contemporary Muslim societies. He understood that in this way democracy should become a fixture among Muslims. Ultimately, his support for an independent Muslim state in South Asia became instrumental in the campaign to create Pakistan, in part because of his fame as a Persian and Urdu poet—and he remains today the most renowned of all Urdu poets. Iqbal's influential vision, therefore, cannot be explained simply as the absorption of Western ideals or as a reaction against them. Instead, it involves the incorporation of many divergent trains of thought into his own creative concept. However, Islamic reform predated Iqbal, and the nineteenth century was a particularly busy time for Muslims who questioned the status quo and advocated changes.

The impulse to reform quickened after the failure of the 1857 rebellion that led to the exile of the last Mughal descendent and the political disenfranchisement of many Muslim elites. In their effort to understand their collective decline, some Muslims blamed a failure in Muslim morality. Various movements sought to address this perceived condition at a time when pervasive social change challenged existing traditions and the leadership of the North Indian *ʿulamā'* remained deeply disrupted by the violence of 1857–58.

Ahl-e Sunnat wa'l-Jama'āh

In response to this situation, some Indian Muslims sought to reform society by reforming individuals. That is, they sought to reaffirm a personal Muslim responsibility for living an ethical and orthoprax life. One group that attempted such reforms is commonly referred to as "Barēlwī" in India, a term members reject. The word derives from Bareilly (Uttar Pradesh), the town in which the initiator of this movement resided. Ahmad Riza Khan (*died* 1921), a member of the *ʿulamā'*, sought to renew Islam by prompting Muslims to remember the message Muḥammad delivered regarding the path prescribed by Allāh. Hence, the movement's preferred name means literally "People of the Way and the Community" (Sanyal 1996: 8–11). In part, the Ahl-e Sunnat attempts to do this through a focus on the Prophet as the exemplary Muslim who models individual responsibility, while it also promotes the veneration of Ṣūfī *pīr*s (Sanyal 1996: 328). Though the movement originally expanded in a rural environment, it has become popular in urban areas of India, Pakistan, Bangladesh, the United Kingdom, and North America.

Deoband School

Another group of reformers influenced by Ahmad Riza Khan's emphasis on individual responsibility established the university Dār al-ʿUlūm in Deoband, northeast of Delhi, in 1867. They formulated a curriculum that featured traditional Islamic Studies (such as Arabic, rhetoric, logic, *fiqh*, and medicine) to be taught in Urdu. Neither English nor Western science would be included, as some Deobandis critically rejected Sayyid Ahmad Khan's perspectives (see following), although they borrowed various education institutional features from British models. In the course of offering opinions on a wide range of issues in everyday life, Deobandis also eschewed many Muslim practices associated with Ṣūfī traditions (such as veneration and festivals at shrines) as dangerous accretions that misdirected the attention of Muslims (Hardy 1972: 170–72).

One of the most famous members of the Deoband *ʿulamā'*, Mawlana Ashraf Ali Thanawi (*died* 1943), exemplified the Deobandi goal of educating preachers, authors, and *madrasa* educators who would encourage personal reform. His *Bihishtī Zewar* (Heavenly Ornaments) sought to reform society through an education that inculcates a renewed ethical sense among individual Muslim women. The book has become so popular that it continues to be published not only in multiple languages throughout the subcontinent, but also in English in the West. Thanawi's book has been especially promoted by the Tablīghī-Islām, an outgrowth of the Deoband *ʿulamā'*, and perhaps the most influential Islamic movement in the world today (Metcalf 1990: 3–5). Because of its international profile—some Islamist movements such as the Ṭālibān in Afghanistan have been inspired by Deobandi ideals—it will be considered in the next section.

At the same time as these movements developed, other Muslims promoted an acceptance of Western intellectual paradigms in the effort to maintain a place in the new social order as they found themselves overshadowed by the growing political power of the British, persuaded of their superior technological capabilities, and convinced of the need to adapt to the sociopolitical order the British were engineering.

Muhammadan Anglo-Oriental College

Sayyid Ahmad Khan (*died* 1898) represents yet another social reformer struggling to adapt Islamic thought and Muslim culture to the new sociopolitical realities of British rule. Knighted for his contribution to the British Empire, Sayyid Ahmad established the Muhammadan Anglo-Oriental College in 1875 with the intention of providing Indian Muslim students an alternative to both British schools and Islamic *madrasa*s. Compelled to both critique faults in Indian culture and correct English misunderstandings about India, Sayyid Ahmad became dedicated to widening access to quality education in an attempt to correct what he saw as a lacuna in the British rule that he embraced. This education, he believed, would need to include the technological and scientific dimensions fundamental to the innovative successes of Western societies that made British domination possible. Sayyid Ahmad realized his ambitions with the college he founded (as well as the Aligarh Scientific Society he helped establish a decade earlier). Although he rejected many of the traditional subjects of *madrasa* education as antiquated and earned rebukes by some *ʿulamā'*, the Islamic orientation of the education remained central. However, this religious quality, like every aspect of the curriculum, had to comply with the rationalism foundational to both Western learning and the reformed Islamic theology that he pioneered. Sayyid Ahmad believed in the inherent compatibility of the

Qur'ān and Western science (Lelyveld 1978: 104–31). Reconstituted as Aligarh Muslim University, the institution Sayyid Ahmad helped found joined the ranks of national universities following Partition.

The Khilāfat Movement

The First World War ended with the defeat and disassembly of the Ottoman Empire—the largest and longest surviving of the three major Islamicate empires of the Middle period (which included the Mughals in South Asia and the Ṣafawids in Persia). The Allied forces hungrily claimed the former territories for their own empires while the Ottoman heartland became the modern nation of Turkey. Yet one component of the Ottomans remained—the *khalīfa* (caliph or "deputy"), an institution dating back to the generation immediately following Muḥammad's death to provide a political and spiritual leader for the *umma*. Muslims throughout the world rallied to protest Allied plans to dissolve this significantly symbolic, but politically powerless, position because it represented the very last vestige of Muslim geopolitical rule under an Islamic ideology. In British India in 1919, the Khilāfat movement sought to preserve not only the position of the *khalīfa* but also the territories of the erstwhile empire. Although often understood as a pan-Islamic effort, the movement in India, according to historian Gail Minault (1982: 1–3), only ever sought to create a domestic political constituency with the hope of this as a unifying issue. The Ali Brothers (Muhammad and Shaukat), graduates of Aligarh College, became the most prominent leaders of the Khilāfat Movement and successfully enlisted the aid of M.K. Gandhi and his Indian National Congress. The two groups equally saw the opportunity to build mass movements by defining themselves as nationalists willing and able to stand up to the British (Minault 1982: 11). The issue collapsed when the secularist Turkish leader, Kamal Attatürk, abolished the Khilāfat himself in 1924. However, the movement in British India, despite its subsequent evaporation, set the stage for future, more nationalist Muslim involvement in mass political movements (Minault 1982: 211–12).

Muslim Secularism and Nationalism

Forms of Muslim nationalism represent yet another modern Islamic expression. Indeed, the concept of the nation-state—a union of individual citizens who identify as a unified people associated with a specific, bounded territory—results from modern forces, first in Europe and then in most of the rest of the world. As people colonized or otherwise subjugated by Europeans began to develop resistance to their dominated condition, many drew (ironically) on the ideologies of nationalism that the Europeans had introduced. Although the form may have been borrowed, the content of the nascent nationalist identities by necessity had to be indigenous if a critical mass of supporters would be attracted. As a democratic political system slowly coalesced under the conservative aegis of the British government, politicians sought to identify potential voting blocs to which they could appeal and gain votes. Not unexpectedly, considering the emphasis the British put on defining Indians according to religion, some

Muslims identified their coreligionists as a potentially substantial voting bloc if only they could be convinced that their "natural" interests defined them as a united constituency. However, this cultivated unity did not necessarily include a sense of separatism. Many Muslims, particularly those in Muslim majority parts of the country who felt little threat from their Hindu and Sikh neighbors and/or a strong sense of identification with what they projected as a historically united India, supported a united independent India as a matter of course. Mawlana Abu'l-Kalam Azad became one of the most prominent of these Indian nationalists.

Abu'l-Kalam (*died* 1958) worked with Gandhi in the Khilāfat movement before joining the Indian National Congress in the 1920s. By 1940, he was president of the Congress, and after Independence and until his death he served as India's Minister of Education. Throughout his career, he resisted the call for a separate Muslim state even as he affirmed his Muslim identity, for reasons evident in his presidential address of 1940:

> I am a Musalman and am proud of that fact. Islam's splendid traditions of thirteen hundred years are my inheritance. I am unwilling to lose even the smallest part of this inheritance. The teaching and history of Islam, its arts and letters and civilization are my wealth and my fortune. It is my duty to protect them. . . .
>
> I am proud of being an Indian. I am part of the indivisible unity that is Indian nationality. I am indispensable to this noble edifice and without me this splendid structure of India is incomplete. I am an essential element which has gone to build India. I can never surrender this claim. . . .
>
> Whether we like it or not, we have now become an Indian nation, united and indivisible. No fantasy or artificial scheming to separate and divide can break this unity. We must accept the logic of fact and history and engage ourselves in the fashioning of our future destiny.
>
> (Hasan 1993: 66–68)

Despite such assurances from Abu'l-Kalam, some Muslim leaders perceived that an alarming number of campaign issues promoted by the Congress Party seemed tailored to suit the subcontinent's Hindu majority at the expense of Muslims.

These Muslim leaders began to express doubts that Muslims and their cultural traditions and values would be respected in an independent, majority-rule India and sought to rally them as a cohesive political voice. However, as the Khilāfat issue in British India had already demonstrated, the unity of Muslims could not be taken for granted due to the tremendous regional, linguistic, social, class, *zāt*, and *birādarī* (caste- or clan-like Muslim groups) differences. This culminated in 1940 with the decision by leaders of the All-India Muslim League like Muhammad Ali Jinnah (*died* 1948) to call for a state in which Muslims would be the majority. This idea would eventually coalesce into the Pakistan movement that led to the establishment of a Muslim homeland (with Jinnah as its first Governor-General) at the same time that India won its Independence. However, it is again critical to differentiate between a Muslim state and an Islamic one. Jinnah, celebrated as the Qāid-i Aẓam (the Great Leader) in Pakistan to this day, helped create a secular state that ensured tolerance for all religions and was governed by civil law, not *s͟harīʿa*. However, many others in the 1930s and 1940s supported the establishment of an Islamic state and distrusted the Western-educated leaders of the Muslim League, a sentiment that culminated when President Zia al-Haq, courting the *ʿulamā'* to support his military dictatorship, worked to implement *s͟harīʿa* in Pakistan in 1980s.

Jamāʿat-i Islāmī

One of those who rejected the call for Pakistan was Mawlana Sayyid Abul-Ala Mawdudi (*died* 1979). In 1941, he established the Jamāʿat-i Islāmī (Islamic Party) as part of his effort to revive Islam, which he viewed as in decline. Having refused membership in both the Indian National Congress and Muslim League, Mawdudi promoted a communalist agenda in his attempt to supplant Jinnah as the "sole spokesman" of India's Muslims. Before Partition, he rejected nationalism and secularism. However, with the actualization of Pakistan in 1947, he moved there and shifted his platform to support an Islamic, *s͟harīʿa*-bound state. For the elder Mawdudi, politics was inherent to Islam and Indian Muslims needed a nation defined by an Islamic polity (Nasr 1994: 3–16). Mawdudi's thought, especially as it developed during his years in Pakistan, has found a global audience, and he remains one of the most influential Islamic ideologues to this day. His works, translated into multiple languages, have been circulated internationally, supporters distributing them for free as far away from the subcontinent as the streets of Toronto.

Muslim Women's Groups

As Sylvia Vatuk and other scholars have described, important women's organizations have arisen that assert the necessity for changes in Muslim women's rights and roles. Many participants, spurred by the Shah Bano case described earlier, seek adjustments to Muslim Personal Law. While they may or may not associate with the term "feminist" (which many Muslims—women and men—view as entailing an agenda advocating Western gender norms), the loose network of women involved share a sense that a patriarchal *ʿulamā'* have deprived them of their Islamically endowed rights. These groups are determined to advocate change not based on the Indian constitution or international human rights declarations, but rather on Qur'ānic justifications. The participating women challenge male interpretations of traditions and embrace the notion of *ijtihād* (ongoing juridical interpretation) that most Sunnī Indian *ʿulamā'* abjure (Vatuk 2008).

One outcome of these efforts emerged in Mumbai as the Awaaz-e-Niswaan ("Women's Voice"), a nongovernment organization founded in 1987. Besides offering training classes for women, the group provides marital resolutions for complaints raised by wives. Their solutions may rely on Islamic or secular law, depending on the situation. A more recent example of these groups coalesced in Lucknow in 2005 as the All-India Muslim Women's Personal Law Board, which seeks to challenge the male-dominated All India Muslim Personal Law Board, an influential, self-appointed body that publicly opines on Muslim

Personal Law. Because this law allows Muslims to settle personal and familial matters using Islamic principles, the women have at least sought to push their rivals to consider women's issues more thoughtfully while demonstrating their fidelity to Islamic sources. Central to their effort is a concern that the Muslim Personal Law in its current form does not reflect the Qur'ān's intention and that the text requires all Muslims to individually read and understand it, thus eliminating the need for interpretative intermediaries such as the *ʿulamā'*. By challenging and even sidestepping patriarchal authorities, this and other groups seek to empower Muslim women together and individually (Vatuk 2008).

• TRANSMISSION OF THE TRADITION OUTSIDE OF INDIA

Just as surely as various Islamic traditions arrived from outside South Asia through the movements of Arabs, Turks, Persians, and others, Indic Islamic traditions have traveled beyond the subcontinent in the company of locals and foreign visitors. India has often been described as a vast sponge that absorbs those who enter it from beyond the isolating mountain ranges of the Himālayas and Hindu Kush. However, this metaphor fails to communicate the fluid, mobile nature of Islamic and Muslim migrations that have repeatedly moved into and beyond the regions, becoming inculturated in some ways yet distinct in others. These transregional flows become more apparent when we focus less on land masses and more on the large bodies of water that surround the peninsula. The Indian Ocean and Arabian Sea make readily accessible to deep water and coastal sailors the shorelines of Africa, Southeast Asia, Malaysia, and Indonesia. Of course, with the advent of air travel, these flows have expanded in their direction and distance.

The Indian Diaspora

The earliest large-scale movement of South Asian Muslims beyond the subcontinent occurred through the migrations of labor precipitated and organized by the British Empire. Various British projects recruited Indians as indentured laborers and sponsored their relocation to the diverse corners of the empire, particularly South Africa, Nigeria, Uganda, and around the Caribbean. Additionally, Indians recruited for various armed forces also found themselves throughout the empire, although they seldom settled permanently outside the subcontinent. These populations represent the first wave of what would become a swelling global South Asian Muslim diaspora.

A second diasporic wave occurred following India's Independence with the migration of Indians to the imperial heartland, taking advantage of commonwealth status and relaxed immigration laws. Although South Asians had gone to Britain during the period of direct rule to participate in educational opportunities (such as M.A. Jinnah and M.K. Gandhi, both of whom received their law training in London), most returned without settling. The immigration movements following the Second World War differed, as many took permanent settlement in the British Isles having been recruited to address a domestic labor shortage. Although curtailed in the late 1960s and 1970s, the migrations, some of which entailed previously established communities in British settlements in Africa and elsewhere relocating once again, resulted in significant Indian Muslim populations throughout Great Britain (Nielsen 1995). Canada, Australia, and other parts of the Commonwealth that succeeded the dismembered British Empire also became popular destinations for Indian Muslim émigrés. Meanwhile, migration from the subcontinent to the United States began in significant numbers only following the relaxation of racist immigration and naturalization laws in 1965, although Punjabis had already begun arriving on the West Coast by 1895 (Smith 1999: 58). In locales where a critical mass had settled, ethnic-specific mosques have formed, while in more heterogeneous communities, Muslims from diverse backgrounds share mosques.

The Bradford community of Indian Muslims in Britain gained international visibility when some members burned copies of Salman Rushdie's *The Satanic Verses* after its release in 1989. Although protest of Rushdie's novel culminated in fatal riots in Pakistan and the Ayatollah Khomeini's largely ignored *fatwā* (legal ruling) demanding Rushdie's death as an apostate, the Bradford burning caught many British particularly off guard. The event revealed a long-simmering frustration among many British South Asians that the ideals of multiculturalism had failed to protect them from discrimination and exclusion. Paradoxically, Rushdie (a London-resident immigrant from an Indian Muslim family) had sought to portray exactly this simmering dissatisfaction in his novel. However, his highly controversial use of both Western scholarship to analyze the Qur'ān and what seemed to be a satirical depiction of the Prophet Muḥammad transformed the author in the minds of many British Muslims into a symbol of the very depreciative elements in British culture that he thought he was exposing.

Among the diasporic communities of Indian Muslims, various movements have had varying degrees of success establishing networks. The most prominent among these are the Deobandis, Ahl-e Sunnat wa'l-Jama'āh, Ṣūfī orders (especially Chishtiyya and Naqshbandiyya), and, perhaps most importantly, Tablīghī Jamā'at. Because the others have been considered above, we will examine only the latter as well as the thought of Mawlana Mawdudi.

Before outlining these, however, it is crucial to mention the important role that South Asian heritage Muslims play in many diasporic communities. In the United States, for instance, a significant percentage of Muslims are of South Asian origin or heritage; many participate in organizations such as the Islamic Society of North America (ISNA) and Muslim Student Association (MSA). Among other important roles played by such groups, they serve as significant arenas of exchange and mixture regarding different Islamic traditions for Muslims informed by Arab, African, Black American, South Asian, and other customs and perspectives. These and other organizations have also provided places of solidarity and protest in the face of rising American Islamophobia and anti-Muslim sentiment in the twenty-first century that has threatened to marginalize Muslim Americans. Similar dynamics exist in Britain, where a far higher percentage of Muslims (more than 60 percent) claim a South Asian ethnicity in whole or in part (Muslim Council of Britain 2015: 24).

Tablīghī Jamāʿat

Mawlana Muhammad Ilyas (*died* 1944) founded the Tablīghī Jamāʿat in 1926 as a reformist movement that would foster imitation of the Prophet's companions. Specifically, this program entailed a personal commitment to practicing the five pillars, encouraging other Muslims to participate in mosque prayer, and rejecting the worship of Ṣūfī *pīr*s. Their dedication to a missionary sense of *daʿwa* ("call") has led them to promote their Islamic vision in India, in neighboring countries, and to those at a distance. This vision includes a promotion of a transnational, pan-Islamic, and united *umma* that sets itself apart from other communities in protective isolation. However, the Tablīghī Jamāʿat eschews political change in favor of gradual personal transformation (Munck 2001: 561–63). In 1952, Tablīghīs began their mission in the United States and represent perhaps the most influential reform group in the world.

Mawlana Sayyid Abul-Ala Mawdudi

The widely influential thought of Mawlana Mawdudi, on the other hand, has an implicit political agenda. Mawdudi joins Iran's Ayatollah Khomeini and Egypt's Sayyid Qutb as the three most influential Islamic political thinkers to propose definite programs of social change through Islamic revival. Mawdudi's works greatly influenced Qutb's thinking. Far beyond the Jamāʿat-i Islāmī movement he helped found, his ideas have inspired revivalism in North Africa, Central Asia, and Southeast Asia in part because they provide a non-Western alternative for imagining nationhood in areas profoundly challenged by Western imperialism and hegemony. Of course, the notion of the nation is itself a European concept, and it is a measure of the degree to which the West has defined a global order that the nation has become the universally accepted unit by which a sovereign state is defined. So although Mawdudi necessarily acquiesced to the concept of nation, he did so only within an Islamic framework that rejected Western secularism and promoted a united *umma*. He deftly crafted the use of Islamic symbols and ideology as tools for political mobilization to Indian Muslims, then Pakistanis, and finally Muslims around the globe (Nasr 1996: 3–5).

• RELATIONS WITH OTHER RELIGIOUS TRADITIONS

A number of staid perceptions for centuries have framed Western understandings of Islamic traditions, especially in India. Although these have been explored in detail in the second section, they must be addressed in this final section because they have most centrally had to do with relations with other religious groups. These relations have commonly been depicted as inherently antagonistic, fueled by a severe chauvinism regarding proper practice and belief. Although specific moments of confrontation have erupted between particular Muslim and non-Muslim groups—often driven by political, economic, and social factors—these occasions have been relatively few relative to the millennium-long history of Muslim presence. Despite the common conquer-and-convert narrative too often used to describe this history, Richard Eaton's work on Ṣūfī traditions demonstrates that no scenario of forced conversion could entirely account for the vast distribution, particular concentrations, and continued adherence of Muslims in South Asia—especially in areas most removed from Muslim political power, like contemporary Bangladesh. These tired yet persistent images owe far more to European Christian self-perceptions and historical competition with Mediterranean Muslims as well as current Hindu nationalist antipathy towards Muslim Indians than empirical information about India. Unfortunately, the establishment of British educational systems and historiographical projects during the centuries of British rule inculcated among many Indians the same image of aggressive and intolerant Muslims discriminating against their non-Muslim political subjects and domestic neighbors.

Histories of religion in India commonly trace Islam's entrance into the subcontinent to the military incursion of "Muslim armies" in the eleventh century. This belies the four centuries in which Muslims lived as integrated members of coastal communities in South India. It also suggests that because mostly Muslims comprised these armies that their religious identity somehow informed their military participation. Because these histories prefer to depict more dramatic conflicts than peaceful coexistence and ascribe the motivations of any who happen to be Muslim to Islamic ideologies, they describe the first interactions between Muslims and other religious communities as inevitably destructive and religiously compelled.

As evidence, two events have become salient among both scholars and religious nationalists. The first pertains to the collapse of Buddhism in South Asia. Attempting to explain the paradoxical disappearance of Buddhist communities in the region of Buddhist origin, many historians have blamed Muslim persecution for this decline. However, evidence strongly suggests that by the eleventh century, Buddhist Indian traditions had contracted significantly from the widespread, popular movements they had once been into only a series of monasteries dependent entirely on court patronage for survival. When the Turko-Persians destroyed these courts and looted the monasteries for their wealth, it doomed the remains of Buddhist Indian customs. The second event taken to prove the inherent antipathy of Muslims to non-Muslim religions was the desecration of the Somnātha Temple in Gujarat by Maḥmūd of Ghazna. Modern Hindu nationalists have used this act in particular to perpetuate images of Muslims as inherently violent and anti-Hindu. Yet, as discussed in the third section, such destruction was more a political act than a sectarian one.

When discussing "Hinduism" and "Islam," it might appear they could not be more ill-suited for one another. Hindus are commonly understood to accept multiple deities, use icons for prayer, and venerate cows, while most Muslims believe in one god, have an aversion to iconic worship, and enjoy beef. Yet to settle for this juxtaposition is to make two mistakes. The first is that such a formulation depends on a fallacious formulation of Hindu and Islamic traditions as cumulatively forming two monolithic entities at odds with one another. In contrast, neither exists in any kind of centralized, institutional form that would allow for this possibility. Second, this comparison reduces all Hindus and Muslims to a singular, mutually exclusive religious identity that disallows even the possibility of any common interest, activity, concern, or experience. In fact, during the sixteen centuries in which Muslims have lived in South Asia, they have lived in a great diversity of communities. Some, such as the large Muslim neighborhoods (sometimes referred to as *qaṣba*) of some cities, towns, and even villages, appear exclusive of non-Muslims. Yet even these do not make it possible for most Muslims to live in isolation from non-Muslims with whom they may share business interests, school classrooms, or team sports. A great many Muslims, however, live in mixed neighborhoods of villages and towns or, even if separated by neighborhood, exist in such intimate everyday interactions that isolation would be nearly impossible. In this way they not only encounter one another in tea stalls and restaurants, *bāẓār* shops and theaters, buses and public parks, but they also often share certain identities that cut across religious groupings. For instance, the devotees of a particular Ṣūfī may identify themselves as Muslim, Hindu, Sikh, or Christian as they share a common devotion to the Ṣūfī whose efficacy they rely on. This dynamic is particularly obvious during the *ʿurs* celebrations of one Ṣūfī at his tomb in a Bihar village.

> The courtyard of G͟hulām Ṣāḥib's shrine buzzes with commotion as devotees and visitors pass in and out of the gates, some approaching the tomb to do obeisance, and others sitting under the canvas sheets stretched above parts of the courtyard to offer shade on this, the *ʿurs* ("marriage") of the Ṣūfī, the busiest day of the *dargāh*'s life. Recognizing the special auspiciousness of the saint's death day, many have arrived in this North Indian village seeking help from the power that emanates from the green-domed tomb. Various *qawwāl*s take their position in the entrance to the tomb and take turns singing their sonorous music that celebrates the Ṣūfī, Allāh, and the Prophet. While strung plastic Ḷags Ḷutter in the slight breeze, one Hindu woman begins to moan and sway as she sits with her family in the courtyard. Soon her arms begin to Ḷail alarmingly and her hands to shake rapidly. Those around her watch impassively, allowing the *dargāh*'s power to confront the ghost or other noncorporeal entity they know possesses her. They have brought the young woman here in the effort to relieve her of the suffering the intruder is causing. Perhaps they understand that the dead Ṣūfī empowers the exorcism. Some Muslim devotees would argue that only Allāh can perform such feats. Other Muslims disparage the *ʿurs* celebration and saint worship altogether. But for the possessed woman and her family, the only thing that matters is that her proximity to Ghulām Sāhib is working. They escort her into the tomb itself—now that they have the attention of the malevolent entity—so that they can identify it, discover its demands, and negotiate its departure while within the effective inḶuence of the dead Ṣūfī who serves the Hindus, Muslims, Sikhs, and Christians gathered in his *dargāh* without discrimination.

History proves the presence of the multiple identities and social complexities, such as those apparent at this *dargāh*, that defy simple formulations of identity defined entirely by religion. From its origins, the Islamic *umma* has differentiated itself from other *umma*s. As described in previous sections, the people of the Book (Jews, Christians, and "Sabians") enjoyed *dhimmī* status by which governing Muslims allowed them the protection of the state, control over their community affairs, and freedom of religion but at the cost of fewer freedoms and a special tax. The *jizya* (compensation) tax, alluded to in the Qur'ān, relieved all non-Muslim men from military service. However, those who did not belong to the people of the Book, often described as *kāfir* (unbelievers), faced far more severe restrictions, which might include prohibitions on the construction of new places of worship or repair of existing ones.

In India, during the period of states legitimated by Islamic ideologies, political attitudes toward non-Muslims wavered. Some members of the *'ulamā'* who advised rulers how to govern according to their vision of Islam recommended harsh treatment of non-Muslim subjects. However, the realities of rule and the experiences of individuals mitigated such purely ideological policies. For example, early during Mughal rule, the emperor Akbar granted Hindus *dhimmī* status on the basis of their adherence to "the Book" (that is, the Vedas—considered by few *'ulamā'* to be on par with the Qur'ān or its three preceding revelations). Even Awrangzeb, depicted as the most orthodox Mughal emperor and infamous for temple destruction and collecting *jizya*, soon found himself financing temples and abolishing *jizya* for the sake of both ruling the polyglot, multireligious people under his extensive political sway and encouraging Hindu and Sikh elites to help him maintain the empire as integral members of his court. The decline of the Mughals and ascent of Western legal forms ended any efforts of *jizya* collection. Meanwhile, the coalescing of nationalist ideologies made *dhimmī* status irrelevant in the face of ideals of equality based on citizenship for all members of the nation rather than divergent responsibilities as members or not of the *umma*.

As Abu'l-Kalam Azad's quote in the previous section demonstrates, most Muslims increasingly envisioned themselves to be as equal a part of the Indian nation as any other religious community. Although the British did not invent the notion of religious difference in India, their policies and practices went far toward engraining the notion of exclusive communalism among South Asians. While the effects of these endeavors varied among the population and certainly prompted some Hindus and Muslims to campaign for an exclusively Hindu or Muslim nationalism, most understood that Indian nationalism required a unity in the face of diversity, including religious diversity. For many, unity across lines of supposed "religious communities" did not require much effort because their everyday lives involved it. The Pakistan movement appealed to many Muslims enough to severe these ties, especially among those suspicious of the future secularity of Indian politics. Today, ascendant Hindu nationalism threatens to imbue increasing numbers of Hindus with an exclusionary vision of their communities and nation as necessarily Hindu. Bigoted and at times volatile leaders among both Hindus and Muslims at times exacerbate cultural and political tensions. Although the fabric of Indian societies demonstrates a complex and interwoven character, it is yet to be seen whether the political polarization of neighbors, classmates, customers, and competitors will succeed in sundering the everyday connections among the residents of India's cities, towns, and villages.

• DISCUSSION QUESTIONS

1. If you were asked to give a brief definition of the religion of Indian Muslims, one that would include only the most central elements that distinguished Muslims from non-Muslims, what would it be? Is there anything difficult about arriving at a definition of this kind, or is it a straightforward matter?
2. What is indicated by the phrase "people of the Book" as it is applied by and to Muslims? Does the phrase indicate a connection with followers of other faiths, or a disconnection from them, or both?
3. Is there more than one source authority in matters of religious practice and ordinary life for Indian Muslims, perhaps an ultimate authority that is mediated through a number of other authorities? If so, how would you describe the pattern of religious authority or authorities?

• NOTES

1 All quotes from the Qur'ān, unless otherwise noted, derive from Fakhry 2004.

2 The Qur'ān also names "Sabians" as people of the Book, although contemporary scholars remain unclear who is intended by the term. Most commentators identify them as Zoroastrians.

3 Throughout this chapter, whenever the word "Prophet" is used in a capitalized form, it is in reference to the Prophet of Islam.

4 For an example of the view that Arab women lost freedoms under Islam, see Ahmed (1992). On the other hand, an argument for the improvement of women's social conditions can be seen in Altorki (1995).

• BIBLIOGRAPHY

Ahmad, Imtiaz and Helmut Reifeld, eds. 2004. *Lived Islam in South Asia: Adaptation, Accommodation and Conflict*. New Delhi: Social Science Press.

Ahmed, Leila. 1992. *Women and Gender in Islam: Historical Roots of a Modern Debate*. New Haven: Yale University Press.

Ali, Ahmed, trans. 1993 [1984]. *Al-Qur'ān: A Contemporary Translation*. Princeton: Princeton University Press.

Altorki, Soraya. 1995. "Women and Islam: Role and Status of Women." *In* John L. Esposito, ed., *The Oxford Encyclopedia of the Modern Islamic World*. volume 4, 323–27. New York: Oxford University Press.

Bellamy, Carla. 2011. *The Powerful Ephemeral: Everyday Healing in an Ambiguously Islamic Place*. Berkeley: University of California Press.

Bigelow, Anna. 2010. *Sharing the Sacred: Practicing Pluralism in Muslim North India*. New York: Oxford University Press.

Bukhari, Saleem. 2002. "Hajj by the Numbers." *Saudi Aramco World* 53, 3: 27.

Denny, Frederick Mathewson. 1994 [1985]. *An Introduction to Islam.* New York: Macmillan.

Derrett, John and Martin Duncan. 1999 [1968]. *Religion, Law, and the State in India.* New Delhi: Oxford University Press.

Eaton, Richard. 1993. *The Rise of Islam and the Bengal Frontier, 1204–1760.* Berkeley: University of California Press.

Eaton, Richard, ed. 2003. *India's Islamic Traditions, 711–1750.* New Delhi: Oxford University Press.

Ernst, Carl W. and Bruce B. Lawrence. 2002. *Sufi Martyrs of Love: The Chishti Order in South Asia and Beyond.* New York: Palgrave Macmillan.

Ernst, Carl W. and Richard C. Martin, eds. 2010. *Rethinking Islamic Studies: From Orientalism to Cosmopolitanism.* Columbia: University of South Carolina Press.

Esposito, John L., ed. 1995. *The Oxford Encyclopedia of the Modern Islamic World.* 4 volumes. New York: Oxford University Press.

Esposito, John L., ed. 2003. *The Oxford Dictionary of Islam.* New York: Oxford University Press.

Fakhry, Majid, trans. 2004 [2000]. *An Interpretation of the Qur'an: English Translation of the Meanings.* A Bilingual Edition. New York: New York University Press.

Gilmartin, David and Bruce Lawrence, eds. 2000. *Beyond Turk and Hindu: Rethinking Religious Identities in Islamicate South Asia.* Gainesville: University of Florida Press.

Gottschalk, Peter. 2000. *Beyond Hindu and Muslim: Multiple Identity in Narratives From Village India.* New York: Oxford University Press.

Gottschalk, Peter. 2013. *Religion, Science, and Empire: Classifying Hinduism and Islam in British India.* New York: Oxford University Press.

Haddad, Yvonne Yazbeck, ed. 1991. *The Muslims of America.* New York: Oxford University Press.

Hardy, Peter. 1972. *The Muslims of British India.* Cambridge: Cambridge University Press.

Hasan, Mushirul, ed. 1993. *India's Partition: Process, Strategy and Mobilization.* New Delhi: Oxford University Press.

Hodgson, Marshall. 1974. *The Venture of Islam: Conscience and History in a World Civilization.* 3 volumes. Chicago: University of Chicago Press.

Al-Hujwīrī, ʿAlī ibn ʻUthman al-Jullabi. 1990 [1911]. *The Kashf al-Majhub* (trans. Reynold A. Nicholson). Karachi: Darul-Ishaat Urdu Bazar.

Isḥāq. 1987 [1955]. *The Life of Muhammad: A Translation of Isḥāq's Sīrat Rasūl Allāh* (trans. A. Guillaume). Karachi: Oxford University Press.

Jalal, Ayesha. 1994 [1985]. *The Sole Spokesman: Jinnah, the Muslim League and the Demand for Pakistan*. Cambridge: Cambridge University Press.

Kabīr. 1986 [1983]. *The Bījak of Kabir* (trans. Linda Hess and Shukdev Singh; Essays and Notes by Linda Hess). New Delhi: Motilal Banarsidass.

Lelyveld, David. 1978. *Aligarh's First Generation: Muslim Solidarity in British India*. Princeton: Princeton University Press.

Lewis, Bernard. 1993. *Islam and the West*. New York: Oxford University Press.

Madan, T. N., ed. 2001 [1976]. *Muslim Communities of South Asia: Culture, Society and Power*. New Delhi: Manohar.

Martin, Richard, ed. 1985. *Approaches to Islam in Religious Studies*. Tucson: University of Arizona Press.

Metcalf, Barbara Daly. 1990. *Perfecting Women: Maulana Ashraf ʿAli Thanawi's Bihishti Zewar: A Partial Translation with Commentary*. Berkeley: University of California Press.

Metcalf, Barbara Daly, ed. 1996. *Making Muslim Space in North America and Europe*. Berkeley: University of California Press.

Minault, Gail. 1982. *The Khilāfat Movement: Religious Symbolism and Political Mobilization in India*. New York: Columbia University Press.

Mittal, Sushil, ed. 2003. *Surprising Bedfellows: Hindus and Muslims in Medieval and Early Modern India*. Lanham: Lexington Books.

Munck, Victor C. de. 2001 [1975]. "Sufi, Reformist and National Models of Identity: The History of a Muslim Village Festival in Sri Lanka." *In* T. N. Madan, ed., *Muslim Communities of South Asia: Culture, Society and Power*, 493–521. New Delhi: Manohar.

Muslim, Imām. 1990 [1971]. *Ṣaḥīḥ Muslim: Being Traditions of the Sayings and Doings of the Prophet Muḥammad as Narrative by His Companions and Compiled Under the Title Al-Jāmiʿ-Uṣ-Ṣaḥīh*. 4 volumes. Lahore: Shaikh Muhammad Ashraf.

Muslim Council of Britain. 2015. *British Muslims in Numbers: A Demographic, Socio-Economic and Health Profile of Muslims in Britain Drawing on the 2011 Census*. London: The Muslim Council of Britain.

Nasr, Seyyed Vali Reza. 1994. *The Vanguard of the Islamic Revolution: The Jamaʿat-i Islami of Pakistan*. Berkeley: University of California Press.

Nasr, Seyyed Vali Reza. 1996. *Mawdudi and the Making of Islamic Revivalism*. New York: Oxford University Press.

Nielsen, Jṁrgen S. 1995. "Great Britain." *In* John L. Esposito, ed., *The Oxford Encyclopedia of the Modern Islamic World*. volume 2, 69–72. New York: Oxford University Press.

Pearson, Michael N. 1996. *Pilgrimage to Mecca: The Indian Experience, 1500–1800.* Princeton: Markus Wiener.

Reid, Donald Malcolm. 1995. "Educational Institutions." *In* John L. Esposito, ed., *The Oxford Encyclopedia of the Modern Islamic World.* volume 1, 412–16. New York: Oxford University Press.

Robb, Peter. 2002. *A History of India.* New York: Palgrave.

Sanyal, Usha. 1996. *Devotional Islam and Politics in British India: Ahmad Riza Khan Barelwi and His Movement, 1870–1920.* New Delhi: Oxford University Press.

Smith, Jane Idleman. 1999. *Islam in America.* New York: Columbia University Press.

Smith, Jane Idleman and Yvonne Yazbeck Haddad. 1981. *The Islamic Understanding of Death and Resurrection.* Albany: State University of New York.

Tadgell, Christopher. 1990. *The History of Architecture in India: From the Dawn of Civilization to the End of the Raj.* New Delhi: Viking.

Thackston, Wheeler M., ed., trans. and annotated. 2002. *The Baburnama: Memoirs of Babur, Prince and Emperor.* New York: The Modern Library.

Vatuk, Sylvia. 2008. "Islamic Feminism in India: Indian Muslim Women Activists and the Reform of Muslim Personal Law." *Modern Asian Studies* 42, 2–3 (Islam in South Asia): 489–518.

Wagoner, Philip. 2003. "Fortuitous Convergences and Essential Ambiguities: Transcultural Political Elites in the Medieval Deccan." *In* Sushil Mittal, ed., *Surprising Bedfellows: Hindus and Muslims in Medieval and Early Modern India*, 31–54. Lanham: Lexington Books.

Zaman, Iftikhar. 1995. "ʿUlamāʾ: Sunnī ʿulamāʾ." *In* John L. Esposito, ed., *The Oxford Encyclopedia of the Modern Islamic World.* volume 4, 258–61. New York: Oxford University Press.

Part III

Beyond the Introductory Study of Religions

FIGURE 9.1 A woman, her religion not apparent, seated in prayer at the tomb of a Ṣūfī saint in a village in Bihar.

Image courtesy of Peter Gottschalk.

9

Beyond the Introduction—Alternative Perspectives

PETER GOTTSCHALK

Congratulations. You've just finished all or part of this volume and might feel like you've got a much greater handle on the religious traditions about which you read than you did when you began. As scholars are wont to do, it's now my job to say "Yes, but . . . ". Yes, these chapters offer important insights, but they are structured in a "world religions" model that we now need to unpack, so you can understand and appreciate the delicious complexities that undergird what you've read and inflect these traditions with the tantalizing humanity that makes them each particularly rich and, often, overlapping if not interwoven. This may seem like a mean trick but it's one with which students of religions—or rather, careful students of religion—have wrestled for a long while.

Most of the chapters have cautioned you about simplistic assumptions regarding "Hinduism," "Buddhism," and the like. But we need to unpack this and explore it more deeply in order to better gauge the dynamics at play in the religious lives of individuals and communities. The problem arises because—paradoxically enough—the study of religion commonly focuses on religions. In my personal encounters with Indian Hindus, Muslims, Christians, Sikhs, Jainas, and Buddhists, when they speak about their religious lives, most spend much more time talking about what they practice than about "Hinduism," "Islam," "Christianity," "Sikhism," "Jainism," and "Buddhism"; and they spend much more doing those practices than talking about them. Most readers of this volume have had their expectations about what religions "are" and "do" shaped by a model of "religion" formed largely in the crucible of the Protestant Reformation and in the interactions of Christian Europeans with Jews locally and other religious groups abroad. This resulted in a "world religions" model based on the notion of mutually exclusive sets of traditions with essentially different beliefs, rituals, origination narratives, and religious identities. Yet, this does not reflect well the reality on the ground throughout much of the subcontinent.

This is akin to initially thinking that everyone belongs to one and only one nation. However, one begins to realize that some folks may have grown up in one nation, but have family, ethnic, cultural, or religious roots in another (or two or more), such as many refugees and other immigrants experience. Then one understands that yet other people live transnational lives, repeatedly moving across borders and maintaining multiple national identities even as they generate and participate in cross-cultural, inter-cultural, and trans-cultural communities. Such are the experiences of many Indian Americans who may work in the United States yet maintain family connections in India, visiting family frequently and perhaps intending to permanently return there after retirement. Finally, there are those who either have eschewed any national identity or have had it stripped from them and exist in a nationless context. Given these complexities, the study of "nations" appears like only one component—albeit an important one—of national identity. Moreover, we realize that in premodern times—before the advent of nation-states—many if not most people in the world may have lived in countries defined by particular political states, yet may not have held any identification with that country or state. No convincing evidence suggests that most people living under the Vijayanagara *rājā* or the Mughal *pād<u>sh</u>āh* (other than the elites who served them) affiliated with either their rulers, their states, or their domains, let alone with "India." Instead, their identities probably were more locally centered. Returning to the issue of religion, examples of these more complex situations are easy to find throughout South Asia.

At a Roman Catholic church in India, as the mass turns toward the liturgy of the Eucharist, a line of attendees solemnly approach the altar, each holding a plate of offerings. On one, piles of tangerines and grapes. On another, some bread. On yet another, a clump of flowers from which burning incense leaves a corkscrew trail as the person holding it processes up through the center of the congregation. The white-clad Catholic priest accepts each in turn, much as a Brāhmaṇa might at a temple where the offerings would be presented to the deity as *prasāda*, a practice far more familiar to Hindus around the world than to Catholics.

Elsewhere, at a Muslim's tomb, Hindus, Christians, and others visit to request help in their own or their loved ones' lives. Positioned in a field outside a village, the *dargāh* attracts local devotees who pray here weekly and those who may travel an hour or more just to make their devotions. Some kneel in still, earnest prayer atop the large brick platform, some rock back and forth making barely voiced petitions, others leave at the tomb's entrance bottles of water or oil that will absorb the saint's *baraka* (miraculous energy) and might be used to heal the ill, make fertile the infertile, or assure better test scores.

These examples demonstrate how constraining our notion of "religions" can be if that term assumes mutually exclusive traditions defined by essential beliefs, practices, texts, and institutions. A vast number of people in India—without regard for their personal religious identity (if they have one)—engage living *sant*s (saints), the animate dead, demons, and deities in an effort to solve problems, address infertility, heal illnesses, reverse misfortune, and obtain boons. For many Indians (though not for all), this is comparable to someone trying to recharge her cellphone who finds herself in a home that uses a different brand of phone. Her home and this home have different rechargers, but if she can find some sort of adapter, she will tap into the electricity that will resuscitate her dying phone. Drawing attention to these processes may offend some members of the traditions we describe, especially if claims of authenticity and authority draw from presumptions of exclusive truth or unchanging tradition. Moreover, some view their religious traditions as demanding a jealously exclusive membership, foreclosing the possibility of participation in other communities. Yet our observations make clear that these processes occur and may significantly influence the historical changes inevitable to any religious tradition.

THE CHALLENGES OF COMPARISON

"Religions" are commonly imagined as uniformly built from the same materials, like so many houses that may have different layouts, entrances, exteriors, and roof designs, but share fundamentally similar features like foundations, windows, and walls. In their endeavor to understand and compare the myriad religious traditions encountered as their burgeoning empires expanded, European intellectuals from the seventeenth to the nineteenth centuries frequently used an analytic shorthand. In the case of the most populous "religions"—and in comparison with an idealized form of the Catholic or Protestant Christianity with which the author usually associated—their schemes of comparison often looked like this:

	Christianity	**Hinduism**	**Islam**
Central Scripture	Bible	Vedas	Qur'ān
Founder	Jesus	none	Muḥammad
Deities	one	many	one
Leaders	ministers/priests	Brāhmaṇa	*ʿulamā'*
Place of Worship	church	temple	mosque

One can appreciate the seductive simplicity of this model, in which—at a glance—the purportedly fundamental characteristics of these traditions can be grasped and the differences between them understood, all via a straightforward outline of essential features.

But, of course, this volume's earlier chapters about these specific traditions has already demonstrated how fundamentally flawed such an overly simplistic formulation must be. This is so for four reasons. First, these one-word characterizations cannot hope to capture the complexities and diversities involved. Yes, most Muslims believe in one god. But what about the role of angels and *jinn*—superhuman agents—who also figure into the worldview of many Muslims? Yes, monotheism is central to most Christian theologies, but how well does "one god" reflect the intricacies and nuances of Trinitarian claims that Christ and the Spirit represent components of the Godhead, which is equally central to those theologies?

Meanwhile, the "polytheism" supposedly characteristic of Hinduism hardly describes the polymorphic monotheism that many Hindus evince when they describe Deva or Bhagavān as the ultimate root of various other divine manifestations (Lipner 2006).

A second issue arises from the schema's suggestion of consistency *within* Christian, Hindu, and Muslim traditions. Yes, for many Hindus, some Brāhmaṇas serve as crucial ritual leaders and textual authorities. But many others, especially among Dalits (low-caste-status Hindus), have rejected this leadership, if they ever had acknowledged it. Meanwhile, charismatic Catholics occasionally recognize the leadership of individuals viewed as specially imbued with spiritual power due to their direct access to God outside of—and sometimes in challenge to—official church hierarchies (Schmalz 2011).

The third problem with this kind of thumbnail sketch derives from the misleading character of the comparison itself. Placing these elements like this implies that the answers are roughly parallel to one another. For instance, the importance of identifying a central scripture assumes that these play commensurate roles in each tradition. In the age of imperialism (and even among some today), European Christians assumed that the Vedas and the Qur'ān played the same role in Hinduism and Islam as the Bible does for Christianity. Yet, whereas most Christians only engage the Bible in their native language, most Muslims engage the Qur'ān in both vernacular and Arabic languages, especially during rituals. Meanwhile, most Hindus do not read the Vedas at all, though recitations from the original Sanskrit texts play important roles in many Hindu practices. Hence, the category of "scripture" (which itself borrows from a term rooted in Christian contexts) reinforces Christian presumptions about texts, how they are read and when they are used.

Perhaps more critically, the suggestion that Jesus and Muḥammad were commensurate "founders" of religions inherently skews our understanding of them. While Jesus as described by the Gospels acted as an itinerant preacher among disparate communities who seemingly embraced an ascetic lifestyle for three years before his demise, Muḥammad as described in the *ḥadīth*s and other literature served as a religious, social, political, and military leader of a single community for at least a decade. Whereas neither the Gospels—nor any other part of the New Testament—ever make mention of "Christianity," Muḥammad engaged the term *islām* through the divine words purportedly revealed to him. However, it remains debatable if his understanding of the word approximated the meanings of "religion" associated with it as understood today. So, although the Gospels depict Jesus as engaging various religious authorities, they do not describe him creating an alternative religious structure or social system in the manner that early Islamic materials describe Muḥammad's mission. What then does "founding a religion" mean?

In fact, the entire matrix of this form of comparison projects common Christian views regarding their "house"—that is, the structure of their traditions—leading to the conclusion that traditions that do not fit appear deficient as religions. Take for example the religious practices among many communities that self-describe as Ādivāsīs ("original inhabitants"), and that the Constitution of India labels as "Scheduled Tribes" (meaning that their tribe appears on a list of state-recognized tribes). Portraying Ādivāsī worship and belief proves exceedingly challenging given the vast variety among these groups and the prevalence of Hindu, Muslim, and Christian forms among them, as well as other religious practices often simply—and overly simply—described as "animist" or "tribal religion." While the 2011 Census of India counted one hundred and four million citizens belonging to "Scheduled Tribes,"[1] it provided no similar category for Ādivāsīs who did not count themselves among Hindus, Muslims, Christians, Sikhs, Buddhists, Jainas, and "religion not stated." Instead, the census swept them into the classic category for the uncategorized, "Other religions and persuasions (including Unclassified Sect)."[2] It might be noted that the structure of even this volume, with its sensitivity to these issues, demonstrates the dominance of the Christian-informed world religions model by omitting almost any mention of Ādivāsīs traditions. Hence, this model promotes the invisibility of certain communities whose identities are not considered legible based on the model's inherent schema.

The fourth problem with this sort of comparison arises because the categories may also elide important similarities between the traditions. In its endeavor to demonstrate the distinctiveness of each religion, this schema employs comparative categories premised on difference. Take, for example, the category of "place of worship." In fact, the home proves a crucial context for religiosity for innumerable Christians, Hindus, and Muslims. Yet listing that in each category seems counterintuitive given our implicit expectation that such comparative tables are premised on illuminating difference (even as they are based on categorical similarities). While orthodox and orthoprax authorities (usually men) frequently promote distinctive beliefs and practices to distinguish members from nonmembers, common folk often think and act in ways less distinct (or at least less concerned with being distinct) from those of other religious communities. In this way, the focus on elite-defined "religions" has often led to the overlooking of women and nonelites in general.

The chapters in this volume all avoid such a simplistic model for comparing the religious traditions that they describe, reflecting the developing awareness of these issues among scholars of religions. However, the reliance on the term "religion" to describe these traditions and their conceptualization as contained phenomena that fall under a single label and that are given committed chapters remains a salient model not only in this volume, but in the empirical study of religions in general. This is particularly remarkable given that little evidence exists that any religious community besides Christians imagined themselves as belonging to anything described as a "religion" before the nineteenth century (although many Muslims may have had an analogous notion). So how did the notion of the metacategory "religion" with its various subcategories of "religions" become so central to so many people's views around the globe? The narrative of this development helps us unpack the assumptions many of us have about "religions" and how to consider their possible interactions.

In the Middle Ages, western European Christians—primarily informed by the authority of and learning in the Roman Catholic hierarchy—viewed all known humans as divisible into one of four categories: Christian, Jew, pagan/idolater, and heretic. However, these were seldom considered equally valid: most Christians viewed these categories as differently valued. This generated a hierarchy based on the propriety of the different groups' actions, especially their worship to God.

(+) Christians			
	Jews		
		pagans/idolaters	
			heretics (–)

Jews bore the stain of Jesus' death because of the collective guilt and generational blame assigned to them in the Gospel of Matthew (27:25). Pagans and idolaters worshiped objects, if not devils. Heretics—worst of all—had known the truth of Christian worship and belief but turned away. Quite notably, medieval Christians tended to reference people, not religions, in their written references. This suggested that they were less entranced by reifications of abstractions like "Judaism"—a term not used by Jews until the nineteenth century—than modern Europeans would be.

In the centuries since then, a different paradigm emerged premised on the notion of "world religions." This identified various sorts of traditions, all subsets of the metacategory of "religion." This seemingly allowed for a more value-neutral comparison, given that it was not premised on a Christian-defined notion of proper worship, as was the medieval model. Nevertheless, it could not wholly escape certain Christian norms, as was evident by its implicit reliance on a notion of "religion" that stemmed from the Christian abstraction "Christianity."

Religions					
Hinduism	Jainism	Sikhism	Christianity	Islam	Judaism

Scholar of religion Tomoko Masuzawa (2005) has detailed the emergence and consequences of this "world religions" model. The assumption in this model holds each category as essentially defined by authorities who helped shape a system of beliefs (from which practices were assumed to follow) so definitively specific and rigorously followed as to establish an exclusive sense of belonging. In other words, "Hinduism" did not "allow" Hindus to be Christian, Muslim, or any other identity. The Protestant Reformation (sixteenth century) and the accompanying Catholic Counter Reformation (sixteenth to seventeenth centuries) redirected medieval Christian emphasis on worship as definitive of religion to a focus on belief. Hence, belief proved essential to the definition of each religion, as it did in European understandings of Christianity. This led to a conclusion about the mutual exclusivity of belief. For example, the monotheism of Judaism inherently prohibits Jews from believing in Buddhism that characterizes all deities as merely impermanent and far less significant than the eternal condition of *nirvāṇa*. Nevertheless, many embrace this duality and identify themselves as "Ju-Bus" even as others define themselves as "Hin-Jus" (Kamenetz 2007).

Yet another consequence flowed from the world religions model of comparison founded on European idealized views of Christianity. Inevitably, the other "religions" had some difference with this Christian normative notion of religion—such as Hinduism's supposed slavishness to Brāhmaṇas or Islam's purported political nature—that appeared to make them deficient as religions relative to "true" Christianity's reputed emphasis on individual faith and political neutrality.

From this archaeology of the medieval and modern models of religious difference, we learn a great deal about many of our assumptions regarding religion and religions. The change from one to the other meant that the overall metacategory was no longer "humanity" but "religion," a term with ancient roots in Europe and no historical equivalent nearly anywhere else on the planet. The second important difference was that the categories of comparison shifted from groups of people to religions. The fact that no other set of traditions projected anything similar is reflected in the English names of most religions: "Hindu*ism*," "Buddh*ism*," "Jain*ism*," "Juda*ism*." As opposed to "Christianity" and "Islam"—terms that emerged from Christian and Muslim communities—these names marry an indigenous root to an English suffix. English speakers commonly use the suffix *ism* for certain ideologies such as capitalism, Marxism, or socialism. So the inclusion of this suffix in the names of so many current religions reveals that most of these terms did not originate in their present form from among those who identify with them today. Moreover, it demonstrates an assumption that the foundations of religions rest on ideologies, and are therefore primarily defined by belief: a very Protestant perspective. And, finally, the fact that currently so many Hindus, Jainas, Sikhs, and Jews use these names reflects the widespread (but by no means universal) acceptance of their traditions as religions in ways that fit this model. The arrival of European empires on the subcontinent proved catalytic for this change, as Westerners adapted their systems of classification to the situation on the ground and increasing numbers of Indians appropriated components of these for themselves.

THE BRITISH EMPIRE AND THE INSTANTIATION OF "COMPARATIVE RELIGIOUS STUDIES"

It proves difficult to overestimate the impact of European imperialism on the ways in which people around the globe have come to perceive "religion." Despite the significant differences among them, the European powers projecting their commercial, political, and military interests helped create an epistemic regime—a remarkably standardized constellation of new disciplines of knowledge—that they utilized and promoted in their various corners of empire. From the prosaic agreement on a common system of latitude and longitude to the standardization of scientific names for animals to the formation of empirical studies of religion, Europeans exported their developing forms of knowledge for use and education to their foreign domains. Given the remarkable success of the Western powers to militarily conquer, economically outpace, and politically subject so many non-Western powers, many colonized and imperially dominated peoples willingly embraced this epistemic regime—sometimes alongside preexisting forms, sometimes in lieu of them, and sometimes merging them. Others had to accept it in order to participate in public discourse that increasingly viewed these disciplines as authoritative. Non-Westerners contributed significantly to the development of what has been called "empirical science" (as well as other disciplines), although their work has largely been overlooked in histories of "Western science." The data collected and information formulated by Europeans and their indigenous collaborators proved crucial for nascent secular studies of religion as they developed in the eighteenth and nineteenth centuries. The comparative approach it promoted relied heavily on the categories and assumptions devised in the colonies and imperial domains, as demonstrated in the history of India.

The initial presence of Europeans on the subcontinent had little impact on Indian notions. The first groups of Portuguese, Dutch, French, and Britons—arriving in the sixteenth century—were intended to promote commercial relations. The few Christian missionaries who arrived at this time made little meaningful impact. European visitors to Indian royal courts, like those of the Mughals, were immediately humbled by the incredible wealth, political power, and religious pluralism evident in most of them. The handful of European merchants initially seemed like curiosities offering potential commercial opportunities (although European cultural productions—such as the paintings gifted to Mughal royalty who relished new artistic techniques—initiated the first of many significant cultural influences that would affect India, as well as Europe). European reports about Indian religions remained limited to occasional mentions in merchant travel accounts and reports from the scattered, mainly Catholic, missionaries.

However, in 1757 conflict between the East India Company in Calcutta and the local Mughal governor for the first time left the British in political control of Indian territory. Merchant officials now had to learn how to collect taxes, administer justice, and adjudicate disputes, all of which required knowing much more about Indians than they did at the time. And so the company initiated systematic ethnographic, topographical, economic, and social surveys. Initially, each surveyor might be tasked with surveying on foot an area the size of New Jersey in the course of a few months and compiling an exhaustive account of everything he saw. He reported on the immense variety of cultural, artistic, economic, and religious practices they encountered, but their superiors distilled a far less nuanced social picture for their own purposes. Given their workload and the need to briefly sum up their experiences, both surveyors and administrators sought to distinguish Indians into identifiable categories that could be characterized by interests and propensities. Many, if not most, relied upon religious categorization (Hindu, Muslim, Sikh, and so on) as the primary, most definitive classificatory tool in their surveys. The historical luggage these men carried with them from home predisposed them to this.

When Britons (like their European competitors) arrived on the subcontinent, their nation's history following the Protestant Reformation and the succeeding Wars of Religion (sixteenth and seventeenth centuries) decisively shaped their understandings of religion in two ways. First, religious enthusiasm appeared threatening to social and political stability unless properly contained by appropriate government policing. Second, the division of nearly all European royal courts into Protestant or Catholic—with the common, accompanying expectation that the country's populace would identify with the monarch—established an assumption that religiously defined populations and polities do not and cannot mix without the near constant threat of combustion. India, therefore, was viewed by Europeans as inherently bifurcated into Hindu and Muslim communities whose presumed inherent antagonism (for example, "polytheism" versus "monotheism," "idolatry" verses "iconoclasm") seemed to make peace a fragile business and business a vulnerable enterprise. Early surveyors like Colin Mackenzie (*died* 1821) and Francis Buchanan[3] (*died* 1829) helped establish the templates for how Britons viewed Indians, and religion proved most salient. The emphasis on religious antagonism and fear of social instability were overstated, but the secular ideals emerging in parts of Europe during the Enlightenment appeared to bring greater tolerance for religious minorities while settling political upheavals associated with them. Ideologies of tolerance, if not pluralism, proved necessary as medieval royal states gave way to modern nation states and a notion of political sovereignty based no longer on the divine right of kings but on the collective citizenry of the nation. The emphasis on galvanizing society through feelings of nationalist belonging made religious sentiments potentially competitive (if not divisive), and therefore in need of constraint. Ultimately, many Europeans viewed their "civilization" as having progressed to a point that tamed the religious furies. Hence, British and other European observers overemphasized the severity of religious difference among Indians in part because of both the terrors from their own national histories and a sense of secular superiority over Indians.

Over the next century and a half, as the British expanded their empire to control, directly or indirectly, nearly all Indian territory, they similarly expanded their production of knowledge about Indians. Through images, reports, statistics, travelogues, histories, and gazetteers, the British government (and private individuals whom it often sponsored) published myriad pamphlets and books about South Asia that emphasized and reemphasized the seemingly primordial difference between Hindus and Muslims, Hinduism and Islam. Frequently, the British officials who collected this information and wrote reports and publications had long experience on the ground. They often noted how impossible it was to fit everyone into strict categories—especially "Hindu" and "Muslim"—given the inestimable variety of practices and beliefs observed. Nevertheless, they almost always defaulted to the given categories in order to abstract a larger picture about India writ large.

In 1878, Major P.W. Powlett illustrated this dynamic when he described the Meo of the northwest as

> Musalmans in name; but their village deities . . . are the same as those of Hindú Zamindars. They keep, too, several Hindú festivals. Thus, the Holí is with Meos a season of rough play, and is considered as important a festival as the *Muharram, Id*, and *Shabíbarát*; and they likewise observe the *Janam ashtmí, Dasehra*, and *Diwálí*. They often keep Brahmin priests to write the *pílí chitthí*, or note fixing the date of a marriage. They call themselves by Hindú names, with the exception of "Rám"; and "Singh" is a frequent affix, though not so common as "Khán."
>
> (1878: 38)

Despite his energetic and detailed description of the diverse components of their religious lives, Powlett retreats to an essentialized understanding—or rather judgement—of their "Islam" relative to his own definition thereof: "As regards their own religion, Meos are very ignorant. Few know the Kalima, and fewer still the regular prayers, the seasons of which they entirely neglect" (1878: 38).

Perhaps the decennial census provides the most illustrative example of this dynamic of British categorization, and the influence it ultimately had on Indians. In 1871, the British government initiated an effort that every decade sought to count each individual Indian under British administration on the same night throughout British-controlled India—nearly two hundred million people. This proved the culmination of the British endeavor to have a totalizing view of the entirety of the subcontinent. But no government can operate with an individual focus on that many people, so they had to be sorted into social categories. The enumerators who visited each home on that one night asked the occupants for the names of those living there, their sex, age, occupation, and religion (more questions were added to subsequent censuses). Occupants could give whatever answers they wanted and the enumerators dutifully recorded them. In 1911, two hundred thousand respondents in Gujarat declared themselves "Mohammedan Hindus" (Nandy 1990: 70). However, when the census-takers went to their offices to tabulate these returns, each individual's form had to be slotted into one of the limited number of boxes labeled with a category, and none existed for overlapping identities. Instead, "Hindu," "Muslim," "Sikh," and "Jaina" provided the strictly singular boxes, reflecting the official pigeonholing of each individual. The government then published several reports for each census year, distributing them not only throughout India, but also across the English-speaking world to libraries, universities, government offices, and private institutions throughout their empire, as well as to the United States. These became important source materials for individual authors and government officials around the world who wrote about India and Indians, but more importantly these became authoritative sources for Indians themselves who had no other avenue for gathering information about the subcontinent's entire population and often trusted British reports because of their purportedly scientific character.

The emerging authority of "science"—in this case, conceived as European-originated disciplines of empirical investigation—ironically strengthened the taxonomic scheme of "religions" developed from Christian sources. The key precept of scientific classification establishes sets of mutually exclusive categories (species) into which every individual specimen can be sorted. Species are then gathered into higher related groups at various levels (genus, family, order). In this way, every individual can be characterized according to the defining features belonging to its species that, in turn, differentiate the species from other species. The census reports reinforced notions that religious identities—and the religions from which they stemmed—similarly were concrete, mutually exclusive categories that allowed no overlap, although genetic relation might be possible. The first census commissioner made space in his report to describe "the sect of Jains, a comparatively late offshoot from Hindooism which shares several of the tenets of the Buddhists" (Waterfield 1875: 18). This demonstrates well how the census not only counted Indians and enumerated their religions, but also helped define their character and the quality of their interactions. As Indians increasingly granted European-defined science authority to explain the natural and human worlds, similar views of mutually exclusive religious identities became increasingly popular, especially among the more educated who often trusted Western forms of knowledge even as nationalist feelings began to stir among them by the turn of the twentieth century.

Indeed, as the British buckled to Indian nationalist pressure and grudgingly allowed increasing levels of democratic self-representation, Indian elites sought to identify and/or construct electoral constituencies whose presumed interests they could address, serve, and represent in the hopes of gaining their votes. Political groups identified a variety of constituencies, but given the prominence of religious identity for British (and increasingly Indian) portrayals of Indian societies, it cannot surprise us that some would seek to speak to distinctly "Hindu concerns," given that Hindus represented the single-largest demographic group identified by the census. The Indian National Congress—the party of Mohandas K. Gandhi and the most prominent Indian political organization—promoted issues like cow protection as an appeal to Hindu voters, despite the clear consequences for Muslims who butchered cows and ate beef. Hindu nationalist organizations like the Hindu Mahāsabhā took such strategies yet further, more actively portraying Muslims as a threat to Hindus and alien to India. In order to gain political advantage, they sought to use the census to expand the totals of Hindus by demanding that Sikhs, Buddhists, Jainas, and tribal groups be counted as Hindus. Organizations from these groups resisted these claims, and the census office refused the amalgamation. Meanwhile, sensing the threat of a Hindu-defined Congress Party, the Muslim League formed in order to protect what they defined as Muslim interests. Both parties relied heavily on census materials as they mounted their arguments against one another. Eventually, because these two heavyweights among Indian nationalist parties could not reconcile, the British partitioned most of the subcontinent into separate Pakistani and Indian nations. The British official who was burdened with the unenviable task of creating a border relied largely on census data counting the population according to religion to determine where to divide Muslim-majority areas from Hindu and Sikh-majority areas. Although both Pakistan and India were established as secular states, Pakistan eventually declared itself an Islamic state and various Hindutva (Hindu nationalist) groups have sought to define independent India as culturally and religiously Hindu. Such declarations demonstrate how the exclusive qualification of religious identities and national identities parallel and intersect in a manner unseen in the premodern era.

A final ingredient to the quickening certainty of exclusive categories among both Indians and Europeans arose among Christian missionaries. Although the East India Company sought to exclude them from India for fear they might cause social disruptions that could imperil profits, missionary groups successfully pressured the British government to allow them admittance in 1813. While they varied greatly in their methods and tenor, many Christian missionaries wrote and preached excoriations of Hindu and Islamic "religions." For instance, one proponent of proselytizing in India wrote to hesitant company officials that "the Bible is the only Book which contains the revealed will of God; that the sooner it supersedes the Shaster [the *śāstra*s] and the Koran, the sooner will the happiness of India be consummated" (Owen 1807: 29). Both by touring through cities and the countryside attesting to the truth of Christianity and the faults of "Hinduism" and "Islam" and by dispatching their ideas through books published on numerous missionary presses, these missionaries not only promoted their own views of strictly delineated religious categorization (often echoing medieval models), but also helped to promote the same among Indians.

Stung by the criticisms they heard or read, many Indians defensively responded by countering missionary arguments using similarly reified portrayals of their own "religion." This was so for Svāmī Vivekānanda, the Bengali *sannyāsī* (ascetic) who did more than perhaps any Hindu in establishing a singular vision for Hinduism in both India and the West, where he toured and spoke. He expressed how completely he accepted the "religion" paradigm when he joined representatives from religions from across the globe and in 1893 famously addressed the World's Parliament of Religions in Chicago (itself a manifestation of the coalescing acceptance of the paradigm) and stated, "The relation between Hinduism (by Hinduism, I mean the religion of the Vedas) and what is called Buddhism at the present day is nearly the same as between Judaism and Christianity" (Paranjape 2015: 17). In another example, a 1904 editorial in the *Khalsa Advocate* reflected the dual concerns among many Sikhs of missionary pressure and decline of Sikh traditions, "Properly speaking, there was no Sikhism. Belief in the Gurus was gone" (cited in Fazal 2015: 107). Just as Hindu and Muslim nationalists—as well as self-protective Sikh, Jaina, and tribal organizations—inveighed their community members to identify as "Hindu," "Muslim, "Sikh," "Jaina," and "animist" to the census enumerators so as to increase the visibility and political power of their group, defenders and reformers sought to portray "Hinduism," "Islam," "Sikhism," and others as reputable religions comprised of the same ideal components (scripture, theology, founders, ethics) that missionaries had used to valorize "Christianity."

Since India's Independence in 1947, social and political pressures have mounted in some circles to adhere to new formulations of religious identity and to purify religions from the accretions and excesses that purportedly deform them from their ideal (Protestant-informed) form that have become authoritative for many, though certainly not all. Wahhābī and other Salafī influences absorbed by migrant laborers working in the Middle East and reformist organizations like the Ahl-i Ḥadīth, Deoband movement, and Jamāʿat-i Islām attempt to dissuade or prohibit Muslims from attending non-Muslim rituals or worshiping at non-Muslim worship sites. Among Hindus, the Rāṣṭriya Svayamsevak Saṅgh (RSS, or Society of National Volunteers) proposes that all Indians must identify themselves as "culturally" Hindu or should leave the country, daring Muslims and Christians to abjure their singular religious identities by accepting the additional label of "Hindu" or risk the denouncing of their Indian citizenship. These efforts to purify religious communities by essentializing them as mutually exclusive categories of belonging, belief, and practice might compel some students of religion to advocate against classification by "religions" or even oppose the act of religious comparison itself.

YET COMPARE WE MUST: RELIGIONS AND TRADITIONS

If "religion" proves such an imperfect metacategory and few Indians associated with "religions" before the arrival of European imperialism, why use the term? The scholar of religion Jonathan Z. Smith has written that "'Religion' is not a native term; it is a term created by scholars for their intellectual purposes and therefore is theirs to define" (Smith 1998: 281).

Some scholars argue against its use at all concerning Indic traditions. Yet, the term maintains its hold on scholars and readers alike. In part, that is because—despite its Christian and European heritage and despite Smith's claim—so many non-Christians and non-Europeans have appropriated, translated, and applied the notion to their own traditions. Indeed, Svāmī Vivekānanda demonstrated his firm embrace of the notion of religion as both a singular, general phenomenon as well as multiple, specific traditions when he described supreme knowledge, "This idea we find in every religion, and that is why religion always claimed to be supreme knowledge" (Paranjape 2015: 44). What perhaps began as a second-order term has become a first-order term, in no small part due to Western political and cultural hegemony. While it may appear only appropriate to expunge the term from scholarly usage in order to counter this hegemony, Western scholars face the troublesome possibility of replicating asymmetrical power dynamics by declaring the use of "religion" and "religions" inappropriate in the Indic context even as many Indians use the term. Meanwhile, many Hindus have eschewed the term "Hinduism" in favor of "Sanātana Dharma" or "Hindu Dharma," yet many others continue to identify with Hinduism. Having all passed through the historical looking glass of European imperialism that globalized the intellectual outcomes of the Protestant Reformation and the Enlightenment, almost everyone on the planet would have an impossible time pushing this implacable terminological genie back into the lamp.

In part, scholars are compelled to wrangle with "religion" and "religions" because without these categories they would have little basis to compare religious phenomena. Given the injustices enacted out of ill-informed and malicious comparisons, perhaps this would all be for the good. Indeed, some might suggest that comparing Sikh Dharam and Zoroastrian tradition is like comparing apples and oranges. However, when you think of it, we casually compare apples and oranges whenever we bring to mind fruit. "Fruit" provides a meta-category of comparison that asserts similarity (seed-holding structures grown by flowering plants) even as it allows for variety. This proves useful as we determine the different challenges of growing fruit instead of vegetables or the relative advantages of eating fruit rather than chocolates. While academic scholars have long wrangled over what commonality "religion" asserts, a comparison of the traditions described in this volume's chapters reflects how different historical communities have developed divergent and changing relationships with superhuman agents and/or transcendent realities. Describing communities, practices, ideas, or experiences as "religious" immediately signals a similarity with one another, even as we presume differences as well.

The problem, however, remains that most uses of the term "religion" invoke the notion of mutually exclusive systems. This may be more a problem in the interpretation of the term than in the term itself. We can do better by demonstrating greater nuance in our descriptions and uses of terminology. Historically and contemporarily, India proves particularly rich in case studies that help up reimagine and reclassify religious phenomena in ways that are less Eurocentric or Christocentric. However, in our approach to these, let's set aside the notion of "religion" in favor of "tradition," while using "religious" as an adjective. Additionally, we will also avoid the names of religions, except when mentioned by those who identify with them. This dual move allows us to avoid the reifications of abstractions like "Hinduism," "Christianity," and "Islam" while noting how some Indians identify their practices, beliefs, and objects with these terms, even as other phenomena associated with superhuman agents and/or transcendent realms fall outside or cut across what conventionally is identified with religions.

Traditions, religion scholar Michael L. Satlow (2012: 134–37) argues, represent a set of cultural resources defined by a community. However, unlike physical resources, such as food or fuel, these resources come with a built-in constraint concerning their use and limits as to the introduction of other resources. Communities may draw on a collection of sources for their traditions that change over time and yet—paradoxically—are often viewed as static and valued as such. For instance, I once observed a tense exchange between Muslims processing with a model of Ḥusayn's tomb at Karbalā' that was hung up in a pīpala tree limb overhanging their path and Hindus who objected to the idea of cutting the limb because of the special regard in which they hold pīpala trees. Both religious traditions—in this case Islamic and Hindu—provided resources for personal identification and communal expression. These included the constraints informed by claims to enduring performance of their rituals that the two groups considered to forbid them on the one hand from not marching and on the other from cutting down the bough. In so doing, their unwillingness to abandon their stand expresses stalwart belonging to their communities, yet their acceptance of a police effort to gently lift the branch out of the way also expressed a flexibility within these constraints. Religious traditions, then, are historical continuities (with discontinuities) of relationships between groups and superhuman agent(s) and/or transcendental realities.

One utility that the notion of "religious traditions" offers that "religions" does not is that it provides an escape from the world religion model. While "religious tradition" need not necessarily harken to the Protestant-defined template of religion, it does allow for Ṣūfī traditions, ascetic traditions, and amulet traditions that include many who identify as Hindus, Muslims, Christians, and so on. Sikhs who pray at Ṣūfī tombs no longer appear out of place as they do if "Ṣūfīsm" solely exists as a subcategory of Islam. Hindus who pray at a Catholic saint's tomb do not seem to defy their religion when they are understood as participating in the pan-South Asian tradition of engaging the animate dead. Despite significant variations among such examples as found among people claiming a variety of religious identities, we nevertheless find similarities that suggest continuities.

By adopting the pluralistic notion of traditions, we leave behind the sense of identity often ascribed (by insiders and outsiders) to those "belonging to a religion." Those participating in South Asian ascetic traditions by reverencing them need not share the ascetics' religious identity, if he or she has one. This is reflected in the commonly interchangeable terms many Indians use for such ascetics (*faqīr*, *sādhu*) without regard to the personal religious identity of either the speaker or the ascetic. The fifteenth-century *sant* Kabīr reflects that these dual uses long predate the current era as the poetry ascribed to him drew upon both of these terms in their effort to transgress what he describes as witless fixation on "Hindu" and "Turk" identities by those purportedly dedicated to Rāma/K͟hudā. This expansive and inclusive notion of tradition additionally enables us to recognize relationships and practices as definitive of traditions rather than mutually exclusive identities and beliefs. Just as those who watch a parade participate in it as much as those processing do (what would a parade be without onlookers defining the passageway of those who march?), so the housekeeper who gives a few rupees to a passing ascetic participates in the ascetic tradition.

Another example of religious tradition practiced among people from a variety of religious identities is *ḥāẓirī*, found throughout India. Mostly, although not entirely, associated with women, this practice involves a spirit's "presence" in an individual. Resulting from malignant *jādū* (magic), a human soul is trapped and manipulated by the *jādū* practitioner so that it inhabits the body of a victim and often causes him or her physical pain or aberrant behavior. As scholar of religion Carla Bellamy (2008) explains, *ḥāẓirī* provides the opportunity for imbalanced and destructive family matters to be resolved as young women, often with the least adult agency in homes, have their situation explained by the spirit, after physically drawing attention to the individual. *Ḥāẓirī* therefore represents a religious tradition involving superhuman agents with little regard to the religious identity of either the afflicted living or the animate dead.

While the notion of religious tradition helps avoid some of the most rigid understandings associated with the term "religion," we still need to consider theoretical models for describing the dynamics that give rise to the overlaps, mutual imbrications, and syntheses so evident throughout the subcontinent.

THEORIZING BRICOLAGE, HYBRIDITY, TRANSCULTURATION, CREOLIZATION, AND SYNCRETISM

Scholars have turned to a variety of terms in order to identify and describe the dynamics of interaction, interchange, interpenetration, and creative formation that can occur between two (or more) religion traditions. Part of the difficulty in describing and theorizing these dynamics arises from the scale of observation. Some discuss synthesis and merger on the macro level of "religion"—such as claims that Sikhism represents a merger of Hindu and Islamic traditions. Others focus on a more limited scale, such as the incorporation of caste into Catholic ritual in South India, which allowed for the mutual participation of Hindus and Catholics in local celebrations. Yet other scholars discuss microscale dynamics, in which individuals make personal choices of appropriation and incorporation of seemingly disparate religious elements. All of this reflects the categorical messiness of people, their behavior, and their thinking. At times categories of definitive belonging and mutual exclusion matter a great deal (as tragically evident during the Partition of India and Pakistan in 1947) and at other times not whatsoever (as suggested by broad participation at Ṣūfī tombs). In order to defy the cookie-cutter neatness of the misleading "world religions" model of religious life, we need to recognize all of these levels of interaction and the fact that many of those participating are not compelled to provide their own categorical justification or theoretical explanation for what they do as a matter of course. Instead, their choices represent only that—choices from a variety of religious traditions based on their needs and constrained by their particular commitments to specific traditions.

One dynamic of religious inter-relationship is bricolage, a term deriving from the French notion of jacks-of-all-trades making use of whatever is at hand. While the concept may suggest the creation of something new from what has been discarded, it may also reference how individuals and communities may literally cobble together diverse religious elements that sit adjoining—yet not opposite or antagonistic—to one another. The seminal anthropologist Claude Lévi-Strauss viewed cultural life in general to be a bricolage (Satlow 2012: 136), and certainly throughout India many people's religious lives manifest this dynamic. In the North Indian state of Bihar, I have seen families wander from a Ṣūfī tomb to a Viṣṇu temple to a dead Brāhmaṇa's shrine on the same day in the hope of bringing help to a family member suffering physical or mental pain. They do not seem to be as intent on synthesizing their understandings of these sites and the superhuman agents available there as they are on availing themselves of whatever aid they can access. Neither do they appear to attempt to create a lasting structure of practice or belief from this conglomerate, but only to engage whomever might help them, however that help may be acquired.

Another frequently used analytic term is hybridity. Originating from botany and animal husbandry to describe creating offspring from two different varieties or species (a mule is the hybrid of a horse and donkey), the word has been applied in regard to cultures and languages. Linguist and literary theorist Mikhail Bakhtin very helpfully delineated between intentional hybridity and everyday linguistic hybridizations that might emerge unconsciously (Johnson 2016: 756–57). Cultural theorist Homi K. Bhabha (2004) specifically addressed the notion in relation to Indian (as well as other) contexts by emphasizing the common condition of in-betweenness. He especially notes how in colonial situations hybridity is often viewed with suspicion or disdain as a mutation by state authorities yet represents a crucial response to it. For instance, Bhabha (2004: 159) describes the hybridity inherent in an Indian Christian evangelical who accepts the Gospels offered by the British yet rejects their self-imposed religious authority, sparking disapproval from British missionaries. Oddly, among those scholars who have most sharply disagreed with the use of the term "syncretism" because of its perceived assertion of blending two true types into an adulterated half measure, many prefer hybridity, despite the fact that this term derives from biological manipulations of exactly this dynamic.

Meanwhile, Clara A. B. Joseph (2004) describes the hybridity deliberately engaged by members of the Syro-Malabar Church, the second largest Asian Catholic church in North America. She notes the hybridity of the church in its South Indian roots where the community, tracing its origins to the first-century arrival on the Malabar coast of the apostle Thomas, mixed practices from Hindu, East Syrian, and, much later, Portuguese Catholic traditions. Roman Catholic officials, accompanying Portuguese imperial agents, sought to "de-hybridise" the St. Thomas Church through a Latinization process they described in terms of purity. In 1597, Archbishop Aleico de Menezes advised the pope, "I propose to purify all the Churches from the heresy and errors which they hold, giving them the pure doctrine of the Catholic faith, taking from them all heretical books that they possess." Drawing on Bhabha, Joseph identifies this claim to heresy as the marker of hybridity, because the "in-between" is inherently indeterminate and unrecognized by normative authorities as anything but an aberration. Four centuries later, immigrants to and their descendants in Canada and the United States face challenges of integration, acculturation, and nativist expectations. Joseph calls for an ideal of mutual acculturation or hybridity, in which Syro-Malabar Christians' neighbors culturally adapt to their presence in the manner in which many of them expect immigrants to do so.

Cuban scholar Fernando Ortiz in 1940 coined the term transculturation to describe exactly this process of mutual infiltration and adaptation between dominated or minority groups and the dominant or majority group (Johnson 2016: 768). Others refer to this as "interculturation" (Pinch 2011). Historian William R. Pinch describes the mutual infiltration of European and Indian traditions on both continents via devotions to the miraculous corpse of Saint Francis Xavier in Portuguese-colonized Goa. In a similar example, the "cautious integration" promoted by Jaina leaders allowed for any practices that did not obscure pure insight or violate the *vrata*s, thus opening a path to assimilation to dominant social norms encountered by minority Jaina communities. Hence, Jainas began to adopt *saṃskāra*s (Brāhmaṇic lifecycle practices) even as some of their practices influenced their Hindu neighbors. Sometime around the ninth century, *ācārya* Jinasena reformulated Jaina precepts so as to allow Jainas to adopt the caste system in order to appear less inconsistent with Brāhmaṇical expectations. Simultaneously, he redefined the superior status of Brāhman as resulting not from birth but from superior ethical conduct. Notably, Mohandas K. Gandhi describes in the opening chapter of his autobiography that—their family's Vaiṣṇava practices notwithstanding—his father frequently spoke with Jaina monks about religious and other matters and his family commonly helped feed them. Meanwhile, before the young Gandhi departed for studies in England, he accepted vows of abstinence from alcohol, sex, and meat as administered by a Jaina monk (who had previously been a Hindu svāmi). Meanwhile, despite his considerable criticism of Christian misapplication of Christianity, Gandhi drew from Christian resources in fashioning the public morality he sought to instill among Indians as well as the nonviolence at the heart of his Satyāgraha campaign. Conversely, many of what he identified as the Hindu and Jaina elements of Satyāgraha were absorbed, if even unwittingly, by those around the world who have appropriated components of his strategies. The black Christian leadership—such as Martin Luther King Jr.—so central to the American Civil Rights movement in the 1960s certainly demonstrated this dynamic.

In an apparently opposite move to Jaina-Hindu transculturation, three hundred thousand Hindu Dalits followed Bhimrao Ramji Ambedkar in 1956 when he embraced the Three Refuges and Five Precepts at a public ceremony in an attempt to achieve equality outside the caste system. For Ambedkar and his fellow "Neo-Buddhists," religious redefinition seemed a small yet necessary price to pay to escape caste. More recently, Neo-Buddhists seemingly have borrowed Hindutva tactics used to "recover" religious sites to which they allege original title. Like the Hindu nationalist endeavor to reclaim "temple sites" where Turks or Afghans built mosques atop temples they reputedly demolished, some Neo-Buddhists have asserted their right to control places associated with the Buddha's life. Despite their campaign to escape low ritual status among Hindus, these movements appear to recapitulate the strategies of those Hindus most antagonistic to Dalit Buddhists' broader cause. This leads us to reconsider the apparent completeness of "conversion," a term that seems to imply the total abrogation of one religious identity for another. Yet evidence from many self-identified Buddhists, Christians, and Muslims demonstrates how frequently such conversions seemed less like complete crossings than persistent bridgings.

Some Hindu nationalists depict India as endlessly absorptive of foreign intrusions and influences, including the (Muslim) Mughals and (Christian) British. They declare that Hinduism (or Sanātana Dharma) has the ability to accept religious truths and practices without threat to the continuation of its traditions. It has certainly been the case that innumerable Christian missionaries found only frustration when Hindus accepted the incarnate divinity of Jesus Christ and the significance of his ethical teachings yet dismissed the notion of an exclusively singular truth. Hindu nationalists differ among one another, however, regarding how to understand the impact on Hinduism in this interchange. Were the intruders absorbed, that is, acculturated? Or did they refashion India's religious landscape, less acculturating than transculturating, or interculturating? Some Hindutva proponents criticize Muslims and Christians for failing to embrace their inherently Hindu cultural identity, and thus refusing to acculturate adequately. They seldom celebrate contributions made to Indian cultures by these "foreigners." Among these actors—beyond doubting the acculturation of Muslims and Christians—transculturation does not seem to be a valued outcome. In contrast, the nationalist ideologue Martin Wickramasinghe portrayed Sri Lankan Buddhism as eternal and authentic because of its open and creative quality (Stewart and Shaw 1994: 7).

"Creole" initially was used to mark the racial purity of white Europeans born in the Americas but later meant those partly of African descent who grew up as American slaves, suggesting mixture. (A parallel change occurred to the term "Anglo-Indian," first intended to describe white Britons born in India and later used for those with a combined British and Indian heritage). "Creolization" became a recognized dynamic in the creation of new languages among those without a common language. Scholars of cultures and religions then adopted it for their own purposes (Johnson 2016: 758–59). Perhaps the formation of Sikh traditions represents an instance of a creole religion or a bricolage process, as reflected in the key text, the *Ādi Granth*. It combines the writing of most of the Sikh Gurūs with those from Ṣūfī, *sant*, and *bhakti* traditions like Shaikh Farīd and Kabīr. In mixing these various elements, a new religious tradition emerged that may have emphasized the monotheism associated with Islamic theologies yet makes the *Gurū Granth Sāhib* the focus point of devotional rituals in a manner somewhat reminiscent of the role of Hindu *mūrti*s (statues), though without the notion of superhuman indwelling. For more than a century at least, many Sikhs have resisted efforts of Hindu nationalists to characterize them as Hindus, demonstrating their commitment to viewing their traditions as distinctive and autonomous.

The most common—and most commonly contested—term for describing religious mixture is syncretism, a term with a long history of both positive and negative valences. In the study of religion, as opposed to anthropology, its use has been viewed suspiciously, because of assumptions that it implies the synthesis of two "original" or "pure" religions into something else, something less authentic. In early European Protestant discourse, syncretism suggested unwelcome change and compromise in a theological realm that demanded stasis and steadfastness (Rudolf 2004: 68–69). By the nineteenth century, comparative religion scholars viewed the ancient Roman endeavor to incorporate the religious cults of conquered people into the imperial cult as a syncretic (and degenerate) predecessor to uncompromised Christian monotheism (Stewart and Shaw 1994: 4). Cognizant of their discipline's Euro- and Christocentric history, most postcolonial scholars of religion have eschewed the term for fear of suggesting that they impugn the integrity and worth of any religious tradition by suggesting its origins lie elsewhere. They recognize that the term tends only to be employed by scholars outside of the traditions they describe, not by insiders (except for the negative historically Christian uses mentioned).

Despite these criticisms, the notion of syncretism has shown a stubborn staying power, undoubtedly due to the failure of any other term to describe what syncretism does and the enduring recognition that these dynamics require attention to reckon with religious changes in certain contexts. Since at least the twentieth century, many of the most prominent scholars of religion have declared that all religions are inherently syncretic. Yet the term's unfortunate politics appear to have interfered both with its broader acceptance and with this universal application. Part of the explanation for this may lay in the broadly accepted scholarly view that religious traditions tend not to be centripetal but centrifugal—inherently generating over time divergent practices, beliefs, and sentiment—hence making unnecessary the need for terminology that protects against essentialist descriptions. However, adequate models for describing and theorizing synthetic dynamics between traditions remain wanting, and the primacy of the "world religions paradigm" for imagining religions continues with little abatement, making the assumption of essentialism very much prevalent, at least among nonspecialists.

Unexpectedly yet significantly, anthropologist Peter van der Veer (2004: 209) draws our attention to the syncretism of the secular nation-state. While "secularism" is popularly viewed as the absence of religion (at least in the context of state polities), it alternatively often references the restriction and management of religion so as to ensure the stability of the state and the harmony of civil society. Each secular nation-state historically has developed its own forms of "managing" religion, and India is no different. Whereas "multiculturalism" and "pluralism" serve as catchphrases in many European contexts for the ideal integration of various religious traditions into an open civil society, "unity in diversity" serves similarly for the Indian central government. The Indian state's public recognition (if not celebration) of that diversity contrasts with the example of the United States and its polite governmental nod toward (but seldomly overt embrace) of religion. The list of "gazetted" holidays in India that close schools and government offices include six nominally Hindu celebrations, three Islamic, two Christian, one Sikh, one Buddhist, and one Jaina, as well as Republic Day, Independence Day, and Mahātmā Gandhi's Birthday. In contrast, of the ten federal holidays in the United States, only one has blatantly religious content (Christmas), while another (Thanksgiving) is arguably religious.

These contrasting calendars seem to suggest very different approaches to the amalgamation of religious traditions in civil society: the "quietist" American and the "actively" Indian. In the American example, the state noiselessly supports religious communities by partnering with them for social services through funding for their "faith-based initiatives" and by not taxing their places of worship. In India, the central government more stridently celebrates many of the nation's religious traditions. The difference can also be seen in government offices. In stark contrast with the neutrality of most American post offices and police stations devoid of religious symbols (especially after Supreme Court decisions such as in the 1984 *Lynch v. Donnelly*), India's counterparts frequently have images of Hindu deities or a calendar picturing Islamic sites on their walls. Despite these differences, both nations equally express majoritarianism as well, with the Christian and Hindu majorities enjoying more state-recognized holidays than minorities do, if the latter do at all.

Shifting the focus somewhat, scholar of religion Lindsey Harlan (2013) has investigated nationalist traditions of "cultural blending or fusion" in the context of Trinidad and Tobago. The state promotes Indian Arrival Day as a means of solidifying the blending of Indian heritage Hindus, Muslims, and Christians while simultaneously celebrating the cultural mixing of Indo-Trinidadians and Afro-Trinidadians. The national holiday emerged in 1995 following efforts to establish a celebration comparable to Emancipation Day, established in 1985 to commemorate the eventual liberation of slaves. It references an amorphously defined lost homeland from which Indians departed before settling throughout the Trinidadian territory, identifying themselves fully with the nation, while maintaining a dually shared yet distinct identity. In somewhat parallel ways, Harlan notes that Hosay—a traditionally Shīʿa commemoration of the death of the Prophet Muḥammad's grandson, Ḥusayn, at Karbalā'—has served to unite not only all Muslims but also all Indo-Trinidadians as an expression of ethnic unity. During British rule, it served as an anticolonial rallying point, especially after a British massacre in response to rioting during Hosay in 1884. Since then, Hosay acts as a metonym for Islam as an Indian religion, the Indo-Trinidadian community as sharing in national suffering, and the shared travails of all the nation's citizenry. In other words, it acts simultaneously as an Islamic, Indian, and Trinidadian holiday. In similar, yet very different ways, Dīvālī has been utilized to serve and solidify Hindu, Indian, and Trinidadian identities.

In another example of nationalist syncretic endeavor, the Census of India website, administered by the Government of India's Ministry of Home Affairs, currently reflects the ruling Bhāratīya Janatā Party's understanding of the theme of "unity in diversity" on the page "Religion":

> Religion returns in Indian census provide a wonderful kaleidoscope of the country s rich social composition, as many religions have originated in the country and few religions of foreign origin have also flourished here. India has the distinction of being the land from where important religions namely Hinduism, Buddhism, Sikhism and Jainism have originated at the same time the country is home to several indigenous faiths tribal religions which have survived the influence of major religions for centuries and are holding the ground firmly Regional con-existence of diverse religious groups in the country makes it really unique and the epithet unity in diversity is brought out clearly in the Indian Census. [sic][4]

Both of the unnamed sets of religions—"religions of foreign origin" and the "major religions" against which "tribal religions . . . are holding the ground firmly"—appear to reference Islam and Christianity, whose conversion successes the Hindutva members and allies of the BJP have long rued. A variety of state legislatures have attempted to pass bills requiring government permission for conversion or outlawing it entirely (as Nepal has done), with some construing "return" to one's ancestors' religion (read: Hinduism) as not conversion. Hindutva groups have viewed the latter as a key component of their *ghar wāpsī* ("returning home") campaign among Christians and Muslims.[5] Within this context, it becomes more apparent that the Ministry of Home Affairs strives not to celebrate equally all elements of the nation's religious diversity, but to gently characterize "important religions namely Hinduism, Buddhism, Sikhism and Jainism" along with "several indigenous faiths tribal religions" as original to India while calling out Islam and Christianity as "religions of foreign origin [that] have also flourished here" yet whose aggressiveness has impelled Indic-original religions into "holding the ground firmly." The essentialism inherent in such religious nationalism threatens to make Muslims and Christians aliens in their own homeland.

ANTI-SYNCRETISM

Conversely to a focus on syncretism, anthropologists Charles Stewart and Rosalind Shaw have emphasized anti-syncretism as a crucial force, especially in the discourse of many religious nationalists, such as some of those mentioned above. Anti-syncretism has been a prominent feature of various Islamic reform groups, such as the Deobandi and Tablīghī Jamāʿat movements. These have endeavored to shear from "Islam" accretions they judge to be outside of true Islam. Revivalist Salafī groups seek to declare as non-Islamic any Muslim practices or beliefs that cannot be found among the *al-salaf al-ṣāliḥ* (the first three generations of Muslims who are considered the most authentic). For Salafīs, Ṣūfī teachings and practices synthesized non-Islamic elements that must be eschewed. Asim Roy notes these dynamics in his seminal work *The Islamic Syncretistic Tradition in Bengal* (1983). He demonstrates how in 1926 one Muslim Bengali author noted, "we find people from both Hindu and Muslim communities come in tens of thousands to accept the spiritual discipleship of the so-called *faqīrs* and *shāhs*." Referencing a tradition of mendicant, religious folk singers, he addressed Salafī revivalists active in the province,

> I, therefore, urge the promoters of *sharia* (Islamic religious laws) to try to realize themselves the truth and beauty in the lives of Muslim *bāuls*.... It is no use issuing decrees providing for the destruction of *bāuls*. What we really need today is to adapt the ideals of *bāuls* and *faqirs*, as far as possible, to make them acceptable to our needs for both diversities and happiness in life.
>
> (cited in Roy 1983: xx)

At this time, some of these revivalists, in the effort to establish a strict hedge between Muslim and non-Muslim practices, went so far as to issue a *fatwā* (legal opinion) that Bangla was the "language of Hindus," and so neither could the Qur'ān or *ḥadīth* be translated into it nor any Islamic issue be discussed using it. Other Muslims pushed back on this linguistic chauvinism (see Roy 1983).

Perhaps an example of a simultaneous syncretic and anti-syncretic effort can be viewed among Bahā'ī communities in India that appear to adopt Sanskritic forms while dissociating from Islamic ones. On the one hand, their Sanskritization endeavors seem an example of intentional or strategic syncretism. Bahā'ī publications use Hindu idioms and tropes, as evidenced by the effort to identify the Prophet Bahā'ullāh with the Vaiṣṇava *avatāra* Kalkī. Devotional songs described as *bhajana*s draw on yet other Vaiṣṇava figures. On the other hand, Bahā'ī Hindi translations of seminal works pull so heavily on Sanskrit vocabulary as to nearly erase the original Arabic and Persian terminology as part of an effort to avoid identification with Islamic traditions. Deliberately demonstrating the notion that categories of religious belonging need not be mutually exclusive, Bahā'īs encourage new members to remain committed to their initial religious traditions, suggesting a complementary notion of identity.

Meanwhile, Asim Roy demonstrates how syncretic tactics could be employed, paradoxically, in anti-syncretic campaigns. He gives examples of early modern Muslim authors attempting to draw Bengali Muslims away from Hindu-themed *mangal-kāvya* literature by usurping that literary form and inserting Muslim heroes and heroines into narratives dominated by Hindu superhuman agents, some of which were already known and inhabited by Hindu figures. For example, the *Imām-churi* described an otherwise unknown story of the Prophet's grandsons—Ḥasan and Ḥusayn—being kidnapped and rescued using the components of the popular narratives regarding the Bengali Vaiṣṇava teacher Caitanya. In other cases, Muslim authors used Bengali literary forms to portray the upheaval Muslim heroes caused to Hindu deities. Hence, Hayat Mahmud's *Ambiyā* describes how Muḥammad's birth overthrew the god Indra's throne, broke his royal canopy, and blocked the gate to his heavenly realm, while throwing all the other gods into confusion (1983: 88–91). The incorporation of gods other than Allāh in a narrative seemingly intended to demonstrate the supremacy of the Prophet's mission reflects a tactic of appropriating and retasking them in order to diminish their stature without outright denying them. More generally, however, Roy emphasizes how the Perso-Arabic literary tradition failed to resonate on a popular level among most Bengalis, and so many Muslim authors adopted local language, literary forms, and symbolic resources in order to promote Islamic themes.

GOING BEYOND "THE INTRODUCTION TO THE RELIGIONS OF INDIA"

Which of these various notions of borrowing, mixture, and synthesis serve us best in describing religious dynamics in India? Clearly, no obvious answer emerges. However, what we do realize through this review are the diverse contexts in which Westerners have struggled with categorical messiness and how colonial and imperial settings played such a prominent role in provoking deliberations about them. We also note that many of these analytic notions rely on the idea of transgressing boundaries: "Hinduism" into "Buddhism," "Jaina" into "Hindu," "Islamic" into "Hindu." But to what degree are those performing these transgressions aware of or concerned about these supposed boundaries? Are scholars doing more to assert the significance of the borders than is warranted?

Meanwhile, we also need to realize that many of those involved in bricolage, syncretism, transculturation, creolization, and hybridity may not be drawing consciously on traditions so much as engaging in embodied practices, oral traditions, textual hermeneutics, and emotional sentiments instilled in them since childhood by family and/or evident to them from their immediate community. Our examples of conversion notwithstanding, most people do not adopt their religious identity as adults after a process of weighing alternative propositions and intellectual choices. "They, like all of us, are born into interpretative and performative worlds that shape and saturate their somatic, affective, and—perhaps last of all—intellectual reflexes until various premises and conclusions are simply and unreflexively 'common sense'" (see page 254). There is no contradiction here in "mixing" traditions, only living through traditions and gauging effectiveness.

A final example helps illustrate this point, while also demonstrating how—ultimately—the minutia of daily interactions often escapes theorization because of the incredible social and religious complexities involved. Scholar of religion Anna Bigelow (2010) describes the village of Malerkotla in Punjab where, for centuries, a Ṣūfī tomb has served as a narrative hub for Muslim, Hindu, and Sikh residents. Different people describe the significance of Haider Shaykh in different ways: for some he was a founder of the village, for others his death has not dampened his miracle-making abilities, and for yet others his person matters less than the pluralistic civic space created around his tomb. Hence, this one site serves as a commonly recognized touchstone for villagers despite their religious—or nonreligious—orientations and practices. For generations, this quality has generated a powerful social adhesive that has made Malerkotla a haven against communal violence even in the bloody upheavals of Partition in 1947 (Roy 1983: 88–91).

With this in mind, we need to differentiate between tactical synthesis and strategic synthesis. Tactical synthesis arises from the quotidian endeavors of people to engage one another and superhuman agents based on the everyday options available to manage life's challenges and opportunities. Strategic synthesis has broader and more long-term concerns in mind, such as when missionaries deliberately imbued Catholic ritual forms with Hindu elements or when Hindu Dalits become Buddhists. Conversely, we recognize that there are those among Hindus, Muslims, Sikhs, Christians, and others who decry such synthetic traditions because they consider them unacceptably transgressive of religious norms or because of political interests in policing strictly exclusive religious identities. Whichever the case, scholars must avoid accepting their essentialist, anti-syncretic claims of orthodoxy, orthopraxy, or identity at face value.

Ultimately, perhaps it would be best to assume syncretic dynamics and *note as unusual* anti-syncretic dynamics and endeavors. If we could reformulate common understandings of religion and religions in this manner, then we would inherently assume the inexorability of change and the ever-present possibilities of engagement and integration, even in light of resistance and reaction. Change is, after all, the one immutable rule of all cultures.

• DISCUSSION QUESTIONS

1. According to this chapter, in what ways is the term "religion" (a) useful and probably unavoidable, or (b) misleading and problematic if not used with awareness of its limitations as a descriptive and analytical tool?

2. Does the term "identity" add something potentially helpful to a discussion of religions (or traditions) of India, or is it necessary to think in the plural rather than the singular about "identities" and multiple dimensions or contexts in which identities develop and get expressed?
3. How could terms such as "transculturation" and "creolization" help you to describe and explain some of the effects migration and globalization have had on religious beliefs and practices in the contemporary world?

• NOTES

1 "Union Primary Census Abstract—2011." Census of India website. www.censusindia.gov.in/2011census/hlo/pca/pca_pdf/PCA-CRC-0000.pdf. Accessed November 5, 2016.

2 "C-1 Population by Religious Community." Census of India website. www.censusindia.gov.in/2011census/c-01.html. Accessed November 5, 2016.

3 Buchanan later took the name Francis Buchanan-Hamilton.

4 Census of India website. http://censusindia.gov.in/Census_And_You/religion.aspx. Accessed October 25, 2016.

5 "MHA Sends Back Anti-Conversion Bills." *The Hindu*. December 21, 2015. www.thehindu.com/news/national/mha-sends-back-anticonversion-bills/article8011172.ece. Accessed October 25, 2016.

• BIBLIOGRAPHY

Bellamy, Carla. 2008. "Person in Place: Possession and Power at an Indian Islamic Saint Shrine." *Journal of Feminist Studies in Religion* 24, 1: 31–44.

Bhabha, Homi K. 2004 [1994]. *The Location of Culture*. London: Routledge.

Bigelow, Anna. 2010. *Sharing the Sacred: Practicing Pluralism in Muslim North India*. New York: Oxford University Press.

Fazal, Tanweer. 2015. *"Nation-State" and Minority Rights in India: Comparative Perspectives on Muslim and Sikh Identities*. New York: Routledge.

Harlan, Lindsey. 2013. "Indian Arrival Day: Shifting Boundaries in the Celebration of a National Holiday in Trinidad." *In* Eliza F. Kent and Tazim R. Kassam, eds., *Lines in Water: Religious Boundaries in South Asia*, 356–87. Syracuse: Syracuse University Press.

Johnson, Paul Christopher. 2016. "Syncretism and Hybridization." *In* Michael Stausberg and Steven Engler, eds., *The Oxford Handbook for the Study of Religion*, 754–74. New York: Oxford University Press.

Joseph, Clara A. B. 2004. "Rethinking Hybridity: The Syro-Malabar Church in North America." *In* Knut A. Jacobsen and P. Pratap Kumar, eds., *South Asians in the Diaspora: Histories and Religious Traditions*, 220–30. Leiden: Brill.

Kamenetz, Rodger. 2007 [1994]. *The Jew in the Lotus: A Poet's Rediscovery of Jewish Identity in Buddhist India*. New York: HarperCollins.

Lipner, Julius J. 2005. "The Rise of 'Hinduism'; or, How to Invent a World Religion with Only Moderate Success." *International Journal of Hindu Studies* 10, 1: 91–104.

Masuzawa, Tomoko. 2005. *The Invention of World Religions: Or, How European Universalism Was Preserved in the Language of Pluralism*. Chicago: University of Chicago Press.

Mayaram, Shail. 2003 [2000]. *Against History, Against State: Counterperspectives From the Margins*. New York: Columbia University Press.

Meer, Nasar, Tariq Modood, and Ricard Zapata-Barrero, eds. 2016. *Multiculturalism and Interculturalism: Debating the Dividing Lines*. Edinburgh: Edinburgh University Press.

Nandy, Ashis. 1990. "The Politics of Secularism and the Recovery of Religious Tolerance." *In* Veena Das, ed., *Mirrors of Violence: Communities, Riots and Survivors in South Asia*, 69–93. New Delhi: Oxford University Press.

Owen, John. 1807. *An Address to the Chairman of the East India Company, Occasioned by Mr. Twining's Letter to That Gentleman, on the Danger of Interfering in the Religious Opinions of the Natives of India, and on the Views of the British and Foreign Bible Society, as Directed to India*. Second Edition. London: J. Hatchard.

Paranjape, Makarand R. 2015. *Swami Vivekananda: A Contemporary Reader*. New Delhi: Routledge.

Pinch, William R. 2011. "The Corpse and Cult of Francis Xavier, 1552–1623." *In* Mathew N. Schmalz and Peter Gottschalk, eds., *Engaging South Asian Religions: Boundaries, Appropriations, and Resistances*, 113–31. Albany: State University of New York Press.

Powlett, P. W. 1878. *Gazetteer of Ulwur*. London: Trübner & Co.

Roy, Asim. 1983. *The Islamic Syncretistic Tradition in Bengal*. Princeton: Princeton University Press.

Rudolf, Kurt. 2004. "Syncretism: From Theological Invective to a Concept in the Study of Religion." *In* Anita Maria Leopold and Jeppe Sinding Jensen, eds., *Syncretism in Religion: A Reader*, 68–85. New York: Routledge.

Satlow, Michael L. 2012. "Tradition: The Power of Constraint." *In* Robert A. Orsi, ed., *The Cambridge Companion to Religious Studies*, 130–50. Cambridge: Cambridge University Press.

Schmalz, Mathew N. 2011. "Boundaries and Appropriations in North Indian Charismatic Catholicism." *In* Mathew N. Schmalz and Peter Gottschalk, eds., *Engaging South Asian Religions: Boundaries, Appropriations, and Resistances*, 85–111. Albany: State University of New York Press.

Shaw, Rosalind and Charles Stewart. 1994. "Introduction: Problematizing Syncretism." *In* Charles Stewart and Rosalind Shaw, eds., *Syncretism/Anti-Syncretism: The Politics of Religious Synthesis*, 1–26. New York: Routledge.

Smith, Jonathan Z. 1998. "Religion, Religions, Religious." *In* Mark C. Taylor, ed., *Critical Terms for Religious Studies*, 269–84. Chicago: University of Chicago Press.

van der Veer, Peter. 1994. "Syncretism, Multiculturalism and the Discourse of Tolerance." *In* Charles Stewart and Rosalind Shaw, eds., *Syncretism/Anti-Syncretism: The Politics of Religious Synthesis*, 196–211. New York: Routledge.

Waterfield, Henry. 1875. *Memorandum on the Census of British India: 1871–72*. London: Eyre and Spottiswoode.

Glossary

- **Abhidhamma**—the third of three major collections (*piṭaka*) of Buddhist texts in Pali; systematic classification and exposition of constituents or categories of existence; Buddhist cosmology.
- **Ādi Granth**—primary Sikh scripture; literally "first book"; compiled by Gurū Arjan and expanded by later Sikh masters; after the death of the tenth master, it has the authority of a living master as *Gurū Granth Sāhib.*
- **Ahiṃsā**—nonviolence and nonattachment; more specifically avoidance of all harm or injury; put into practice most completely by Jaina mendicants, less radically by Buddhists and Hindus; a basic principle for social activists such as Mohandas K. Gandhi and Martin Luther King, Jr.
- **Ahriman**—the negative one of two powerfully opposed spirits created by Ahura Mazdā; Angra Mainyu, the destructive or evil twin counterpart to the holy Spenta Mainyu.
- **Akāl Purakh**—the Timeless One; Sikh designation for the immortal and ultimate divine being.
- **Allāh**—Arabic term for the sole creator and ultimate being worshiped by Muslims.
- **Ambedkar**—Bhimrao Ramji Ambedkar (1891–1956); highly accomplished low-caste law expert, social and religious leader who led mass conversions to Buddhism, helped draft Constitution of India.
- **Amrit**—drink of deathlessness; sweetened beverage prepared for initiates into Sikh Khālsā.
- **Artha**—one of four appropriate aims of Hindu life; material well-being; economic and political power.
- **Āryan**—Indo-Āryan language speakers; early migrating tribes or settled residents of India; "noble" people who transmitted the Veda; also, nineteenth-century Vedic revivalists in the Ārya Sāmaj; in short, a richly evocative, important, and controversial term.
- **Āśrama**—a series of four ideal stages of life for Hindus; also, a place of retreat or pilgrim rest-house (also called *dharamśālā*).

- **Ātman**—indestructible core self in every form of life; affirmed by many Hindu theologies, denied by Buddhists who instead acknowledge pervasive impermanence (*anattā*).
- **Avatāra**—"descent" and appearance of some form of the divine, typically at a time of crisis and in response to need; Viṣṇu is conventionally understood to have ten epochal or major ones.
- **Avesta**—collection of authoritative Zoroastrian religious texts; when together with commentaries, is referred to as Zend-Avesta.
- **Avidyā**—"Ignorance" is identified as a root cause of suffering and bondage in the Upaniṣads and in Buddhist tradition; Jaina tradition, however, identifies harmless action rather than knowledge or wisdom as the key to liberation from *saṃsāra*.
- **Bag͟hdādī**—West Asian Jewish traders who settled in urban areas in India and later migrated to Israel.
- **Baptism**—Christian initiation and ritual cleansing by sprinkling, pouring, or immersion in water.
- **Bene Israel**—Jews in India who were identified with the "lost tribes," became economically successful in the colonial era, reincorporated traditional Judaic practices and emigrated to Israel.
- **Bhagavad Gītā**—Hindu text in form of a dialogue between Kṛṣṇa and Arjuna at the commencement of the Mahābhārata War, reinterprets traditional concepts such as action, renunciation, sacrifice.
- **Bhakti**—devotion to a divine being, whether loving service of a human person to a divine person (*saguṇa bhakti*) or identification with the divine as beyond all names and forms (*nirguṇa bhakti*).
- **Bhikkhu**—Theravāda Buddhist male monk; follower of the precepts, guided by Saṅgha rules.
- **Bible**—in Judaic tradition the books of the Law (Torah, Pentateuch), Prophets, and Writings (Hagiographa); in Christian tradition those three (as Old Testament) and the New Testament.
- **Birādarī**—the kinship group in traditional communities that manages and enforces proper social relations and marriage alliances; see Caste, Lineage.
- **Bodhisatta**—Gotama in previous lives; someone who has advanced far enough along the path to embody wisdom and compassion that inspires service for the welfare of all living beings.
- **Brahman**—ultimate reality beyond description (*nirguṇa*) and immanent in all (*saguṇa*); a key topic in the classical Upaniṣads and in Hindu Vedānta philosophy.
- **Brāhmaṇa**—a set of commentaries on Veda; a human being with admirable qualities; a *varṇa* in which adult males have traditional priestly functions.

- **Bricolage**—disparate items at hand that are assembled or conjoined; improvisation and its results.
- **Buddha**—a title given Gotama following his transformation at Bodh Gayā; the status or nature of an "awakened" or "realized" being.
- **Canon**—a measure, standard, or criterion, thus an authoritative source or a scripture collection.
- **Caste**—a term introduced in India by Portuguese traders; division of human society into hereditary status or functional groups; Vedic and classical Hindu fourfold model of society (*varṇa*); social position and relationships (dining, marriage) as determined by birth (Jāti).
- **Caturvidhasaṅgha**—the "fourfold community" of Jainas that is comprised of monks, nuns, laymen, and laywomen.
- **Christian**—a person inspired by, devoted to, and attempting to follow the life and teachings of Jesus.
- **Christianity**—institutional authorities and forms of Christian life; for example, Eastern (Orthodox), Western (Roman Catholic, Protestant), and many other short-lived and long-term variants.
- **Christmas**—celebration of the birth of Jesus, annually observed on December 25th; along with Easter it is one of the two most widely observed Christian holidays.
- **Church**—a place where Christians worship; an institution with rules of procedure, designated leaders with special titles and distinctive functions that vary from one Christian organization to another.
- **Cochin Jews**—possibly the earliest Jewish arrivals on the subcontinent, they settled in Kerala (Malabar); after India's Independence, most of them emigrated to other countries.
- **Constantine**—Roman emperor (306–337 CE) who became a Christian, changed imperial policy to tolerance for Christians, and was a patron of early councils that established Christian doctrines.
- **Convert**—to change religious affiliation and identity; to engage in missionary activity; to proselytize; these terms tend to be associated (positively or negatively) with Buddhists, Christians, and Muslims.
- **Council**—a traditional Christian way of establishing institutional arrangements and settling doctrinal disagreements; an organizational structure for affiliating groups of churches with one another to share resources and activities, for example, National Council of Churches in India.
- **Creed**—a formal statement of belief or of theological doctrine; important in Christianity.
- **Creole**—a language (or, by extension, institution, tradition, culture) formed by mixing elements from separate and distinctive languages (institutions, traditions, cultures); see Bricolage, Transculturation.

- **Crucifixion**—a torturous ancient Roman method of capital punishment by binding or nailing a person to a wooden crossbeam; death came slowly, painfully, and usually by suffocation.
- **Dalit**—a term used by B.R. Ambedkar to refer to lowest caste groups that M.K. Gandhi called Harijan, and government institutions have referred to as depressed classes or scheduled castes; indigenous people beneath or beyond *varṇa* classifications.
- **Dāna**—the virtue of generous giving; a key ethical value in Dhārmic traditions.
- **Darśana**—the six classical schools of Hindu philosophy; the vision or sight of a holy or divine being, and the benefits or positive effects that can result from the experience of an auspicious sight.
- **Deva**—in Dhārmic traditions, a male divine being (the female counterpart is Devī); in early Vedic religion Asuras were regarded to be dangerous superhuman beings opposed to Devas; Zoroastrian religion reverses the functions of these opposing divine categories, hence Ahura Mazdā.
- **Dharma**—with its near equivalents *dhamma* and *dharam*, a central theme of the major indigenous traditions of India.
- **Digambara**—the "sky clad" tradition of Jainas in which male ascetics live naked and without property.
- **Dukkha**—life as unsatisfying and marked by suffering through experiences of birth, aging, illness, and death; the first noble truth of the Buddha.
- **Easter**—one of two major Christian holiday festivals; the other (Christmas) celebrates the birth of Jesus while this one celebrates his resurrection or return from death to life after his crucifixion.
- **Endogamy**—marriage limited to a restricted acceptable pool in which suitable prospective mates are determined by genetic, lineage, social, or cultural factors, for example, caste endogamy.
- **Eucharist**—also known as the Mass, the Lord's Supper, or Holy Communion is a Christian sacrament, ordinance, or at minimum a customary practice in which a small portion of bread and wine (or juice) are served during worship as a reminder of the last supper of Jesus before his arrest and, in some Christian churches, as a mystical form of participation in his death and resurrection.
- **Five Ks**—Pañj Kakār in Punjabi, five outward signs of being an initiated member of the Sikh K͟hālsā.
- **Five Pillars**—five observances undertaken by many Muslims: profession of faith, ritual prayers, almsgiving, daylight fasting during the month of Ramaḍān, pilgrimage to Makka.
- **Gandhi**—Mohandas Karamchand Gandhi (1869–1948) was trained as an attorney, became a leader of nonviolent civil disobedience movements in colonial South Africa

and India, and encouraged interreligious harmony and respect for the most marginalized people in society.

- **Gāthās**—seventeen hymns attributed to the authorship of Zarathustra that serve as the core of Zoroastrian liturgy.
- **Gender**—a key determinant in whether a religious or social role should be prescribed, permitted, or prevented because of a person's biological identity; gender is a salient defining factor in most traditional religious settings and, unlike modern contexts, is rarely open to challenge or change.
- **Gurdwārā**—a Sikh place of worship; a copy of the *Ādi Granth* is installed and honored there; a free kitchen (*laṅgar*) typically is located in close proximity, and *kaṛāh prasād* is distributed there.
- **Gurmat**—the teachings that are central to a Sikh way of life.
- **Gurmukh**—a faithful Sikh who internalizes and behaves in accord with Gurmat; contrasts with Manmukh, a self-centered person who is likely to fall prey to Haumai.
- **Guru**—a teacher, expert, or master in any field, but with more profound meaning in a religious context; Sikhs acknowledge ten (and only ten) human masters; Hindu tradition acknowledges many.
- **Ḥadīth**—traditional accounts of sayings and practices of the Prophet Muhammad; along with the Qur'ān, the various collections of them provide resources for Muslim law and guidance for right living.
- **Harappā**—a village in Pakistan from which the name was taken to designate the early urban-based culture of northwest India that also is known as the Indus Valley Civilization .
- **Hasidic**—an eighteenth century Eastern European Jewish spiritual movement that continues to be a vital influence in contemporary Judaism.
- **Haumai**—a Sikh term that refers to the source of self-centeredness and of five evil impulses.
- **Hijra**—the 622 CE migration of the Prophet Muḥammad and his followers from Makka to Yat͟hrib (Madīna) which serves as the starting point for the Muslim calendar.
- **Householder**—in traditional India, a person who is living in society, marries, and raises children; the householder life contrasts with that of the Śramaṇa or Bikkhu or some other type of renunciant who lives a solitarily wandering life or lives a life organized by rules of a monastic institution.
- **Hukam**—divine command; to enter into harmony with the divine Order of things; it can refer to the popular Sikh practice of opening the *Ādi Granth* at random and reading there to receive guidance.
- **Hybridity**—a term from postcolonial theory that evokes the plight or perspective of people "in between," for instance, in between indigenous and colonial spheres of power; the

notion of mixing diverse cultural or religious elements (see Bricolage, Creole) is further complicated by this term.

- **Incarnation**—a key doctrine in Christianity that identifies Jesus as the divine being who uniquely becomes a human being (with or without loss of divine powers or identity); in Dhārmic traditions, by contrast, repeating cycles rather than a singular or unique circumstance are evoked by the term; in short, every incarnation is a reincarnation or a rebirth; nothing takes place only once; repetition is the rule.
- **Islam**—the monotheistic ideal for human life that was transmitted through the final prophet, Muḥammad, and to which Muslims aspire with support from traditional experts and institutions.
- **Iṣṭadevatā**—a form of the divine that a Hindu devotee chooses for worship and life guidance.
- **Itihāsa**—the category of received history and cosmology that is preserved primarily in the two great Hindu epics, the *Mahābhārata* and the *Rāmāyaṇa.*
- **Jesus**—for Christians the unique savior of human souls; a Jew from Galilee who taught for a few years, healed people, challenged religious and political authorities, was arrested, tried, and put to death; some early followers believed he returned from the dead, ascended into heaven, and will come again to reward the righteous and judge the wicked.
- **Jina**—"victor"; one who has "crossed over" and "passed beyond" the world of time and change; a Tīrthaṅkara; the ideal state that Jaina ascetics and others hope eventually to reach.
- **Jīva**—in Jaina tradition, the formless nonmaterial soul that undergoes modifications by association or attachment (*karma*) through long cycles of time in *saṃsāra* but has potential for separation and release from all material entanglements and, like all Jinas, attain innate blissful freedom.
- **Kāla**—time, duration, the fourth and last in the cycle of major ages or epochs; is closely associated with *saṃsāra*, suffering, death, and the powers and beings that preside over them.
- **Kāma**—longing, desire, sensory pleasures; also aesthetic appreciation and enjoyment; one of four chief goals in a well-balanced human life.
- **Karma**—*kamma* in Pali language; activity, action, or work and the traces left and trajectory established by acts over multiple lifetimes; an important key concept in Dhārmic traditions.
- **K͟hālsā**—the Sikh initiate order founded by Gurū Gobind Siṅgh in 1699; the nineteenth-century Tat K͟hālsā movement revived emphasis on separate and distinctive Sikh values rooted in the K͟hālsā.
- **Kīrtan**—devotional singing, chanting, and recitation practices; see Bhakti.

- **Lama**—a Tibetan teacher of Buddha Dhamma; some are considered reincarnate "advanced" beings.
- **Laṅgar**—a free community kitchen that welcomes all people; typically attached to a Sikh *gurdwārā.*
- **Lineage**—continuity over generations by affiliation (*guru-śiṣya*) or genetic inheritance through male (patrilineal) or female (matrilineal) descent.
- **Mahābhārata**—the world's longest epic; a library of Hindu lore and values; see *Bhagavad Gītā.*
- **Mahāvīra**—the title given to the twenty-fourth Tīrthaṅkara who is honored by Jainas as the restorer, but not founder, of Jaina Dharma.
- **Mahāyāna**—a branch of Buddhist tradition designated as the big or great vehicle; predominant in Central and East Asia; contrasts with the somewhat demeaning term Hīnayāna (small vehicle).
- **Makka**—commercial town in the Arabian Peninsula where first Muslims lived before relocating to Madīna; see Hijra.
- **Mārga**—a way, path, or road; by extension, a method or program for spiritual development that may center in right action (*karma*), devotion (*bhakti*), or discriminating insight (*jñāna, bodhi*).
- **Martyrdom**—undeserved or extreme suffering and death are acknowledged in many religious traditions; martyrs feature prominently in Christian, Muslim, and Sikh religion; they exist but function rather differently due to enlarged assumptions about time and lives in Jaina, Buddhist, and Hindu traditions; modern Judaic tradition is exceptional due to recent horrors of the Holocaust.
- **Māyā**—a term with multiple meanings; among them is power to generate beguiling appearances.
- **Missionary**—a person sent to recruit new members of a religious community or the enterprise itself; conversion is closely identified with proselytizing religions such as Buddhist, Christian, and Muslim.
- **Mokṣa**—escape, liberation, realization; freedom from suffering, death, rebirth; see Saṃsāra.
- **Muḥammad**—for Muslims, the final prophet, messenger of Allāh who nevertheless remains human.
- **Mūrti**—image or icon; may be a conventional and consecrated representation of divine presence that conforms to traditional standards and is ritually "awakened" for worship in home or temple.
- **Muslim**—one who practices the religion of Islam; see Five Pillars, Muḥammad, Qur'ān.

- **Nām(a)**—the divine name; repeating, singing, chanting it is a form of devotion in Dhārmic traditions; Sikhs call it remembering the name (*nām simaraṇ*); see Kīrtan; some followers of *jñāna-mārga* and Buddha Dhamma engage in practices to surpass or transcend all distinctions of name and form.
- **Nānak**—the first Sikh master, considered by some to be the "founder" of Sikhism.
- **Ordination**—a ritual that "sets apart" or authorizes a religious vocation such as ministry, priesthood, monastic life, or other holy orders; there are Buddhist, Christian, Hindu, Jaina, Judaic, and Zoroastrian examples; there is no Muslim ordained clergy, but law experts have an analogous status.
- **Orthodox**—pure, true, straight, or correct belief; also, the so-called Eastern churches of Christianity.
- **Parsi**—Persian immigrants to the subcontinent who retained their Zoroastrian religious practices.
- **Passover**—Pesach; a major commemorative ritual in the Jewish religious year.
- **Pentateuch**—a Greek term that refers to the Torah, the Law or the five books of Moses.
- **Pentecost**—a Christian feast day observed fifty days after Easter that recalls the descent of the Holy Spirit into the early Christian community in Jerusalem during the Jewish Shavuoth; a type of Christian church (Pentecostal) that incorporates emotional expression and glossolalia into worship.
- **Pilgrimage**—an almost universal religious phenomenon in which people singly or in groups visit sites specially associated with formative figures and events in their religious tradition.
- **Pūjā**—reverence or honor offered to a divine being; typically formalized in a variety of liturgical patterns; may be called *mūrti pūjā* when directed to a consecrated image of a divine being; this is largely a post-Vedic Hindu practice that for the most part replaced Vedic *yajña* (sacrificial ritual), but the Ārya Samāj movement in the nineteenth century reinstituted a vegetarian version of *yajña*.
- **Purāṇas**—ancient or old; a large category of Sanskrit texts that preserve Jaina and Hindu traditional information about deities, rituals, and cosmology; there are eighteen major Hindu ones and are generally consistent with Veda, and are sometimes called a fifth Veda, but considerably expand the range of Vedic concerns.
- **Purity**—a nearly universal religious theme that is integral to rituals for passage through crisis and for development through the lifecycle; water, oil, and other scented materials may be used to ritually purify a person as part of an initiation, after a period or condition of bodily uncleanliness, or after close contact with a dangerous substance or the dead; techniques to retain one's purity and avoid pollution vary from tradition to tradition and from one spiritual discipline or path to another.

- **Qur'ān**—the Islamic book, written in poetic Arabic, said to have been transmitted in instalments by the angel Gabriel over twenty-two years to the Prophet Muḥammad who was commanded to recite it, later it was organized into a standard version in which sections are arranged by length from shortest to longest; memorizing and reciting it are regarded as admirable spiritual accomplishments.
- **Rahit**—rules or code of behavior to guide the life of a good Sikh; see Five Ks.
- **Rāmakṛṣṇa**—born Gadadhar Chattopadhyaya (1836–86), he became a world-renowned Hindu mystic who inspired the formation of several teaching and service institutions that continue to offer education and healthcare today; his most widely known devotee was Svāmī Vivekānanda.
- **Rāmāyaṇa**—the shorter but more beloved of the two great Hindu epics; provides inspiration to live an honorable Hindu life in which one respects and embodies one's traditionally prescribed roles—whatever one's age, gender, or current position in family or society, and whatever the temptations one may encounter.
- **Refuge**—a follower of Buddha Dhamma, at a minimum one takes refuge in the so-called "three gems," namely, the Buddha, the Dhamma, and the Saṅgha.
- **Resurrection**—in Christianity, the return of Jesus from the realm of the dead after crucifixion.
- **Rosh Hashana**—the festival of the Jewish new year in the traditional lunar calendar.
- **Sacred Thread**—the symbol of Vedic initiation given to males of the top three *varṇa* during a ceremony that begins the student stage of life; see Saṃskāra.
- **Saṃhitā**—the collection of *mantra*s, prayers, and ritual prescriptions in the oldest core of the Veda, later augmented by commentaries and elaborations in the Brāhmaṇas, Āraṇyakas, and Upaniṣads.
- **Sampradāya**—a Hindu school of thought and practice that maintains continuity across generations of descent from master to succeeding master along with their body of pupils, devotees, and general following; it may put emphasis on a particular set of texts, commentaries, and rules of behavior.
- **Saṃsāra**—wandering in the ocean of existence; the world as determined by *karma* and rebirths.
- **Saṃskāra**—a mental or psychological imprint or deflection; a ritual of the lifecycle that mitigates or overcomes the effects of the first meaning of the word, enabling one to continue the transition to a new phase in life safely and effectively.
- **Saṅgha**—an assembly or association of monks; the Buddhist monastic order; by extension the term can be used to refer to all Buddhists.
- **Sevā**—selfless service done without expectation of reward; Karma Yoga; a type of action that is integral to the values in Dhārmic religious traditions.

- **Shahāda**—the testimony or profession of faith that is basic to being a religious Muslim; it affirms the unity and singularity of Allāh and the status of the Prophet Muḥammad as his messenger.
- **Shīʿa**—the largest minority tradition in Islamic religion; distinguished from the majority by belief that the Prophet Muḥammad designated a successor; includes further subdivisions that differ from one another by their allegiance to different lineages of succession after the Prophet; see Lineage.
- **Śiva**—the multifaceted divine being who incorporates contrasting qualities and opposing energies; he is known by his Hindu devotees as Mahādeva (the great god); in some circumstances he displays the characteristics of an accomplished *yogī*, in others a householder or family man, and in yet others an epic hero who performs incredible feats.
- **Śramaṇa**—an ascetic; a mendicant; a spiritual seeker who lives an austere life; one who renounces the short-lived pleasures of the saṃsāric world in order to seek *mokṣa*; contrasts with Householder.
- **Śruti**—that which is heard; orally transmitted knowledge; the Veda and Vedic canon; contrasts with Smṛti (that which is remembered) as embodied in commentaries and other authored texts that complement and expand on Śruti.
- **Sunnī**—the majority tradition in Islamic religion; has generated schools of Islamic law that resolve questions about the behavior and activities that are permitted to Muslims based on the Qur'ān and examples from the life of the Prophet Muḥammad.
- **Śvetāmbara**—the "white clad" tradition of Jainas which split with the Digambaras in 80 CE and accord women the status of being capable of *mokṣa* or, as the Jinas, passing beyond *saṃsāra.*
- **Syncretism**—the aggregation, mixing, or blending of religious teachings or practices from different source traditions; see Bricolage, Creole, and Hybridity, Transculturation.
- **Talmud**—learning or instruction; a lengthy commentary on Torah in more than six thousand pages that contains Rabbinic discussions, arguments, commentaries; a crucial source for Rabbinic Judaism.
- **Tantra**—a set of Buddhist and Hindu texts that are non-Vedic, esoteric, and are most safely explored under direct guidance from a qualified living master; very important in Tibetan Buddhism.
- **Temple**—a fixed structure that functions as a place for ritual activities; Vedic rites were conducted at temporary sites rather than in temples; post-Vedic Hindu tradition as well as the other traditions introduced in this book have constructed permanent buildings with designs suited to their functions and purposes, whether fire temples, *gurdwārās*, synagogues, churches, or mosques.

- **Theosophy**—the generic meaning is study and wisdom concerning divine things; a Society founded in 1875 by Helena Petrovna Blavatsky that became a significant religious and cultural influence in colonial India in the late nineteenth and early twentieth centuries among Hindus, Parsis, and Buddhists.
- **Theravāda**—the early form of Buddhist monasticism based on the Pali Canon, particularly important in Southeast Asia, that was deeply involved in the nineteenth-century Buddhist revival in India.
- **Thomas, Saint**—identified by some with the "doubting" apostle, he is widely believed to have been the earliest Christian missionary to India.
- **Tīrtha**—a fording or crossing place; a sacred site for Jainas or Hindus; see Pilgrimage.
- **Tīrthaṅkara**—a Jina who has forded or crossed over the ocean of existence and has gone beyond the grip of *karma*, rebirth, suffering, and attachments that determine the world of Saṃsāra.
- **Torah**—the scroll of the Law; the five books of Moses; the key portion of scripture in Judaic religion.
- **Transculturation**—the meeting and convergence of previously separate cultures to produce a new mixture of cultural features, lifestyles, and values; a particularly important process in the formation of colonial, postcolonial, and globalized societies; see Bricolage, Creole, Hybridity.
- **Umma**—the worldwide community of Muslims as equals, an ideal reinforced by observance of the Five Pillars and acceptance of the authority of the Qur'ān, *ḥadīth*, and *sharīʿa*.
- **Varṇāśrama Dharma**—the Hindu traditional ideal of society as organized by four main orders (*varṇa*) of Brāhmaṇa, Kṣatriya, Vaśiya, and Śūdra as well as by four main phases of life: student, married householder, retired, and solitary world-renouncer. Veda wisdom or knowledge; for Hindus it refers to authorless, timeless, inspired teachings and prescriptions that serve as the basis for a ritually centered traditional society; Veda is preserved and transmitted in Sanskrit, recited by Brāhmaṇas, and is the main criterion of who is or is not Hindu.
- **Viṣṇu**—a major Hindu deity who appears in several forms, including his *avatāra* manifestations of which the most widely popular are Rāma and Kṛṣṇa; see Rāmāyaṇa, Bhagavad Gītā.
- **Vivekānanda, Svāmī**—a Hindu monk, born Narendranath Datta (1863–1902), represented Hindu tradition at the 1893 World's Parliament of Religions in Chicago and became popular worldwide; see Rāmakṛṣṇa.
- **Yajña**—Vedic sacrificial ritual, largely succeeded in classical and later Hindu ritual life by *pūjā* performed in homes and temples; see *pūjā*, Temple.

- **Yom Kippur**—a day of atonement; culmination of the "high holy days" following the traditional lunar new year during which repentance, prayer, and fasting replace worldly activities; see Rosh Hashana.
- **Zionist**—one who supports the establishment and maintenance of a Jewish national homeland.

Index